Advances in Mental Health and Addiction

Series Editor

Masood Zangeneh, Richmond Hill, Canada

Over the past several decades we have witnessed dramatic shifts in prevailing approaches to mental health and addiction. Significant scientific achievements have led to novel treatment options that impacted the experiences of individuals with mental disorders. In recent years, new perspectives have begun to influence the way we address mental health and substance dependencies, resulting in a greater emphasis on mental health promotion and prevention strategies. Despite these progressions, mental health care systems too often remain stagnant, fragmented, and peripheral.

Dionisio Nyaga • Masood Zangeneh
Editors

Critical Ethics on Mental Health and Madness

Springer

Editors
Dionisio Nyaga
School of Social Work
Algoma University
Sault Ste. Marie, ON, Canada

Masood Zangeneh
Humber College
Woodbridge, ON, Canada

ISSN 2570-3390 ISSN 2570-3404 (electronic)
Advances in Mental Health and Addiction
ISBN 978-3-032-10165-5 ISBN 978-3-032-10166-2 (eBook)
https://doi.org/10.1007/978-3-032-10166-2

This Springer imprint is published by the registered company Springer Nature Switzerland AG
The registered company address is: Gewerbestrasse 11, 6330 Cham, Switzerland

Acknowledgment

We extend our gratitude to all the authors who took the time to craft such a compelling and authoritative work, one that challenges and reshapes our perspectives on mental health, psychiatric practices, policies, and research.

Introduction

This book project explores theoretical, epistemological, methodological, and ontological definitions of mental health and addiction, aiming to pose "new" ethical questions that extend beyond the current discourse on these topics. The key plan in this book is to re-examine and rethink the discourse surrounding mental health and addiction in ways that pave the way for compounding perspectives that envision the worlds of mental health and addiction in various ways. This way, we may open multiple worlds that think of mental health and addiction from a place that is historical and that values people's realities and values. Imagining the world anew entails recognizing that the current world we inhabit is founded on the notion that individuals grappling with mental health issues and addiction are disposable and broken, requiring salvation from their emotions (Einboden et al., 2021). This form of understanding mental health and addiction is a colonizing one and is mostly supported by the psychiatric industry (Dyck, 2017). Emotions serve as the basis for labeling individuals living with mental health issues and addiction as unworthy and readily disposable (Power, 2015). This form of disposability is rooted in a colonial framework, asserting that individuals who experience emotions pose a threat to public life and therefore must be segregated from public spaces (Thornicroft, 2007). The public sphere becomes reserved for rational thinkers, relegating individuals grappling with mental health issues to the status of "private" entities deemed unintelligible. This gendered private/public divide must be questioned to explore how to utilize new intersecting accounts of individuals living with mental health issues and addiction. This dual perspective on mental health and addiction also helps to hide and conceal colonial oppression in its various operations within the mental health and addiction industry. It is equally important to look at emotions as a privileged point of understanding mental health and the ways in which some bodies are marked as unable to be emotional but rather as driven by instinct. Such bodies, the majority of whom are Black and African, are assumed to be no-body. African bodies that are marked as instinctual beings cannot fit within a world that is driven by metrics, emotions, and rationality, and are therefore marked as schizophrenic. This marker of the African body as a "schizo" body leaves no space to be accounted as a living body, and instead, they come to be imagined as bodies that cannot fit and are left to disappear between the heteronormative gap between private and public spheres. This book has several pieces that look at African bodies within such a world that attempts to rationalize them, yet such rationalization is met with equal resistance. This book therefore must be seen within the context of bodies that cannot be added up into the current psychiatric metric for measuring mental health and addiction.

The current singular and Western discourse within mental health and addiction continues to operate in reductive and quantitative ways (Root, 2009). Consequently, many individuals living with mental health issues and addiction are forgotten and deprived of their humanity (Maisel, & Ruby, 2022). This Western discourse is grounded in a sanist and heteronormative worldview that perceives the world as belonging to the sane while spacing out those who live with mental health issues. Such forms of spatial elimination are clearly mapped out in the operations of psychiatric institutions that work as organizing and training spaces for those who face mental health and addiction. These forms of managing those who face mental health and addiction are grounded in the belief that the only way to line up and straighten those who face mental health and addiction is through militaristic means (Agorastos et al., 2013). Consequently, those who grapple with emotional challenges are often stigmatized and viewed as requiring psychiatric protection and provision, therefore, making mental health issues as a gendered practice (Tichenor, 2024), and discounting other forms of life beyond the Western understanding of mental health.

This Western discourse on mental health and addiction is rooted in a neoliberal market framework that seeks to rationalize, package, and sell labels and commodities (interpreted here as individuals living with mental health issues and addiction) for profit in the marketplace (Timimi, 2010). To achieve this, individuals living with mental health issues and substance use disorders must be commodified and then sold to the highest bidder. This process becomes even more complex when other identity markers are considered, further increasing profit margins for the corporate world (Levine, 2017). Therefore, it is crucial to recognize colonial violence as the foundation upon which people living with mental health and addiction are dehumanized and reduced to products for sale. This implication will aid in understanding how individuals living with mental health issues and addiction are quantified as property that can be owned and sold for profit. The question of property and Black bodies is one that must be understood within the context of ownership and slavery. The operation of slavery and property-making is one that is inextricably connected to the operation of the psychiatric system. Black lives have over time been overdiagnosed with schizophrenia (Metzl, 2009, Olbert et al., 2018) and reduced to a tablet. Such forms of reduction of life into a substance must be seen within the context of the historical disappearance of Black life, which continue to be perpetrated by the current psychiatric system. In Canada, the psychiatric system has operated as marker of Black people as improper bodies that must be reduced to property. Labels such as drapetomania were employed to locate and return slaves who ran away from overbearing masters. This in essence points to the fact that we cannot imagine mental health and substance use without putting into context the historical perspective of colonial violence and the alterity of the human.

Being a rational thinker is synonymous with being appropriately positioned in the world of property and therefore sane. Such a Western view of life is made up of sanist practices of property ownership by making improper bodies into products that can be sold. In this context, Western discourse simplifies individuals living with mental health issues into products, labeled through everyday psychiatric branding, and ultimately sold to sustain major corporations and their profitability (Bradfield, 2002). Issues of labeling within the contemporary neoliberal mental health landscape are contextualized in a manner that promotes a particular, singular formula for understanding mental health and madness, while erasing other experiences as not mentally capable of any health. This numerical conceptualization contributes to the prevalence of sanism, as individuals with mental health issues and addiction are continually funneled into the neoliberal construct of the knowing subject—a process marked by the violent normalization (Bragatti, 2021). One of the ways through which individuals living with madness are reduced to property is through the codification of ethics that drive the neoliberal discourse of mental health and addiction, facilitating profit maximization and capital accumulation. Land and madness have a common cord that is facilitated by nature and that resists any form of commodification. Land and madness are two Siamese twins who exist with nature in uncodified way. They exist at the intersection of a radical review of how we think about the modern world. They question how we think of the world in a binary fashion. Land and madness are expressions of epistemological and ontological orientations that unmark the market rationality and the place of property-making. In this regard, land and madness are expressions of resistance to colonial control and must be considered in understanding the operation of the psychiatric systematization of those living with mental health issues. To put such an assertion forward is to argue for a "new" imagination of mental health from a place that is based on the land and the experiences of mad people in their various realities.

This book argues that while codes are important tools in mental health and addiction care, they rationalize, quantify, and simplify the marginalized experiences of those living with mental health and addiction, rendering their lives disposable and easily forgettable. By reducing them to numerical figures, these codes confine individuals living with mental health issues and addiction to a social prison designed to control their movement (Gupta et al., 2023). Such forms of control are oppressive in a sanist way and must be challenged and disrupted. The book argues that mental health is intertwined with issues of power and influence, used to regulate populations living with mental health issues in violent and traumatizing ways. It examines colonialism's impact while implicating social work practice in the collective trauma faced by Indigenous communities and other marginalized groups in Canada and globally. Operating within a colonial mental health and addiction framework, the book engages with mental health discourse, intersectionality, and reflexivity, highlighting how gender, race, sexual orientation, immigration, and imperialism intersect to oppress those living with mental health issues. The manuscript presents alternative approaches to mental health, envisioning it through new ethical lenses rooted in people's values, realities, and histories. Central to these conversations is the illumination of various manifestations of violence in people's lives.

This book has several chapters that employ a covid pandemic experience and methodologies to argue for a more nuanced understanding of mental health and addiction. This will help bring to bare the complexity of mental health and alterity of the human. Covid 19 has had an immense impact on Indigenous communities. In this special volume we attempt to look at how Covid 19 affected the mental health of Indigenous and Black communities, and many other marginalized groups. Available scholarship on mental health and addiction among Indigenous and Black peoples speaks to the disproportionate impact the pandemic had on Indigenous communities. While we speak of the post pandemic era, we equally need to pay attention to the ways in which the pandemic exacerbated historical colonial injustices that have been and continue to be traumatic to Indigenous and Black communities. Colonialism has clearly impacted Indigenous communities and their descendants in Canada. In Canada, the history of colonialism is tied to forms of social erasure that were state-sanctioned and meant to make Indigenous and Black people as expendable bodies. The question of the Indian Act is a testament to systemic forms of anti-Indigenous racism that continue to inform every aspect of society, including how Indigenous people in Canada face mental health and addictions (Gray & Cote, 2019). The policy has had and continues to have an immense material and symbolic impact on Indigenous communities. Among the most significant historical issues that Indigenous peoples have and continue to face are the effects of the residential school system in Canada. Many Indigenous children were apprehended by social workers and placed in residential schools. These colonial policies authorized the apprehension of Indigenous children and denied them the opportunity to learn or speak their languages. Most of these children were abused in various ways—all in the name of civilizing and improving them from what was considered their broken and dangerous habitats. The effect of these colonial schools and policies has been the traumatic impact that continues to affect the community to date. When Covid hit, these communities were further oppressed regarding their mental health and addiction. This volume seeks to bring to the fore the various ways in which Covid 19 affected Indigenous and various communities in compounded ways; therefore, the book seeks an ethical and holistic understanding of mental health beyond the current singular and neat model.

Suleyman M. Demi and Sonja Hettmann look at the ways in which the Covid 19 pandemic affected Black communities and the ways in which they navigated issues of mental health. Ebenezer Inkumsah looks at how the prison system is connected to the psychiatric system and the ways in which those colonial connections work against Black and African lives. Tanya Shute looks at epistemic erasure within the mental health sector, specifically within the consumer survivors. Tom McDowell and Mohammad Ferdosi look at income insecurity and its connections to mental health. McDowell and Ferdosi argue that basic income helps communities cope with various stressors. Johnson Nzau Mavole and Mary Syokoli Mutisya examine the question of gender and the role of climate change in shaping gender roles in a study undertaken in Kenya. Shazia Yusuf explores psychological distress and the question of social support, also examining the effect of media on psychological distress. Muskan Girhotra and Md. Zamilur Rahman look at the ways in which we can be proactive in dealing with mental health issues more so during pandemics. The two authors attempt to predict mental health issues such as anxiety while recognizing the compounding effects of such predictions. Tom and Mohammad Ferdosi further explore issues of poverty and their connections to mental health. Their study focuses on Ontario Basic Income Program and how it could help reduce issues of poverty and subsequently help in overcoming mental health issues among most marginalized communities. Moses Ndwiga Kavengi examines how mental health affects youth in Kenya and proposes an Indigenous African perspective as an antidote for healing mental health issues among Kenyan youth. Renée Lemoyne brings Indigenous ways of teaching into understanding ourselves and those around us. Maryam Motia discusses support systems that can be employed to cater for the mental health of immigrant women. Rose Torres looks at the power of forgiveness and how it works in care provision. Nuzha Allassad Alhuzail examines the ways in which Covid 19 affected Bedouin women in Israel. The focus of this paper is to bring up issues of income insecurity and the ways in which Covid 19 perpetuated income inequality, leading to mental health issues among women. Dr. Dawn Onishenko and Marco Giuliani look at issues of homelessness among marginalized youth and the ways in which Covid 19 amplified their mental health challenges. Dion LaFleur and Donna Richards examine the incarceration of Black bodies and the effects this has on Black mental health. Boakye-Yiadom, Noah, Akuamoah-Boateng, Mary, Amakye, and Ebba Gifty explore how Covid-19 exacerbated the already precarious position of Black and African communities. They discuss the question of colonialism and anti-Black racism and how these manifested in care provision. Claudia McNulty and Candice-Marie Sage provide anti-oppressive perspectives at the intersection of housing, mental health, and substance use. Julia Read, PhD, and Stewart J. Smith look at the expansion of social work skills and practice in understanding spirituality. Roghieh Nooripour, Ainaz Shateri, Sepideh Safarpoor Dehkordi address culturally informed mental health perspectives for Iranian youth. Nob'Doran examines the role of lived experiences in reimagining how we deal with mental health during pandemics. Rose Ann Torres employs the pedagogy of healing and forgiveness to bring forward issues of Indigenizing mental health discourse. Dionisio Nyaga reviews the literature on mental health to reimagine the notion of the "post" in a pandemic world and argues for an intersectional perspective toward resolving future pandemics. Walter Chan explores Indigenous perspectives and the question of disability movements. Dionisio Nyaga follows up with a literature review on Covid 19 and its various effects on marginalized communities. Dionisio Nyaga further examines the issue of pandemics and their effects on the mental health of African and Black communities. Moses Ndwiga looks at how we can employ Indigenous African perspectives to heal issues of mental health issues in Kenyan context.

Dionisio Nyaga
Masood Zangeneh

References

Agorastos, A., Nash, W. P., Nunnink, S., Yurgil, K. A., Goldsmith, A., Litz, B. T., Johnson, H., Lohr, J. B., & Baker, D. G. (2013). The Peritraumatic Behavior Questionnaire: development and initial validation of a new measure for combat-related peritraumatic reactions. *BMC Psychiatry*, *13*(1), Article 9. https://doi.org/10.1186/1471-244X-13-9

Bradfield, B. (2002). Mental Illness and the Conciousness of Freedom: The Phenomenology of Psychiatric Labelling. *Indo-Pacific Journal of Phenomenology*, *2*(1), 1–14. https://doi.org/10.1080/20797222.2002.11433871

Bragatti, J. A. (2021). Forced Normalization Revisited: New Concepts About a Paradoxical Phenomenon. *Frontiers in Integrative Neuroscience*, *15*, 736248–736248. https://doi.org/10.3389/fnint.2021.736248

Demi, S. M. (2024). Black People in Scarborough's Experiences with Mental Health During the COVID-19 Pandemic. In Nyaga, D. & Torres, R.A (eds). *Reimagining Mental Health and Addiction Under the COVID-19 Pandemic*. Springer Nature

Dyck, E. (2017). *Managing madness : Weyburn Mental Hospital and the transformation of psychiatric care in Canada* (1st ed.). University of Manitoba Press. https://doi.org/10.1515/9780887555374

Einboden, R., Choi, I., Ryan, R., Petrie, K., Johnston, D., Harvey, S. B., Glozier, N., Wray, A., & Deady, M. (2021). "Having a thick skin is essential": mental health challenges for young apprentices in Australia. *Journal of Youth Studies*, *24*(3), 355–371. https://doi.org/10.1080/13676261.2020.1728240

Gray, A. P., & Cote, W. (2019). Cultural connectedness protects mental health against the effect of historical trauma among Anishinabe young adults. *Public Health (London)*, *176*, 77–81. https://doi.org/10.1016/j.puhe.2018.12.003

Gupta, P., Muneshwar, K. N., Juganavar, A., & Shegekar, T. (2023). Beyond the Asylum Walls: Tracing the Tapestry of Mental Health Interventions Across Eras and Cultures. *Curēus (Palo Alto, CA)*, *15*(11), e48251–e48251. https://doi.org/10.7759/cureus.48251

Levine, A. D. (2017). *Mental Health, Inc.: how corruption, lax oversight and failed reforms endanger our most vulnerable citizens* (First edition.). The Overlook Press.

Maisel, E., & Ruby, C. (2022). *Critiquing the Psychiatric Model* (1st ed., Vol. 3). Ethics International Press Limited.

Metzl, J. (2009). *The protest psychosis : how schizophrenia became a Black disease*. Beacon Press.

Naragon, M. D. (1994). Communities in motion: Drapetomania, work and the development of African-American slave cultures. *Slavery & Abolition*, *15*(3), 63–87. https://doi.org/10.1080/01440399408575139

Olbert, C. M., Nagendra, A., & Buck, B. (2018). Meta-Analysis of Black vs. White Racial Disparity in Schizophrenia Diagnosis in the United States: Do Structured Assessments Attenuate Racial Disparities? *Journal of Abnormal Psychology (1965)*, *127*(1), 104–115. https://doi.org/10.1037/abn0000309

Power, M. J. (2015). *Madness cracked* (First edition.). Oxford University Press.

Root, E. E. (2009). *Kids caught in the psychiatric maelstrom : how pathological labels and "therapeutic" drugs hurt children and families*. Praeger.

Thornicroft, G. (2007). *Shunned : discrimination against people with mental illness* (Reprinted with corrections, 2007). Oxford University Press.

Tichenor, E. (2024). Reflections from "Revisioning Feminist Engagements with Madness": Borderline, Futurity, and Debility. *Atlantis*, *45*(2), 152–159. https://doi.org/10.7202/1114717ar

Timimi, S. (2010). The McDonaldization of Childhood: Children's Mental Health in Neo-liberal Market Cultures. *Transcultural Psychiatry*, *47*(5), 686–706. https://doi.org/10.1177/1363461510381158

Contents

Part I
Theme: Colonialism and the Mental Health Discourse

Chapter 1
Effects of the COVID-19 Pandemic on Well-Being and Mental Health of the Black Population in Scarborough

Suleyman Demi and Sonja Hettmann

Abstract The COVID-19 pandemic brought about a significant change in both global and local governance, leading to government-enforced lockdowns, quarantines, social isolation, and social distancing that aggravated Canadians' mental health and well-being. Although its effects were felt among the population generally, the pandemic disproportionately affected Black people. This study thus sought to address the following questions: How did the COVID-19 pandemic affect the overall well-being of the Black population in Scarborough, Ontario? What coping mechanisms did this community employ to manage the effects of the COVID-19 pandemic? The study recruited 20 Black people in Scarborough who access services from TAIBU Community Health Centre (TCHC) and 10 Black healthcare professionals in the Greater Toronto Area (GTA). The study employed in-depth interviews to collect data, and coding and thematization for data analysis. Findings revealed that the COVID-19 pandemic negatively impacted the Black population in Scarborough. Some of the effects included anxiety, depression, and increased unemployment caused by pandemic-related restrictions. Participants used strategies such as routine exercises, watching movies, driving around to unknown destinations, and resuming work on stalled projects to minimize the effect of the COVID-19 pandemic. The study recommends further investigation to ascertain the health, economic, and spiritual impact of the pandemic on Black communities.

Keywords COVID-19 pandemic · Black population · Mental health · Anxiety · Depression

---

S. Demi · S. Hettmann (✉)
School of Social Work, Algoma University, Sault Ste. Marie, ON, Canada
e-mail: suleyman.demi@algomau.ca; shettmann@algomau.ca

D. Nyaga, M. Zangeneh (eds.), *Critical Ethics on Mental Health and Madness*, Advances in Mental Health and Addiction,
https://doi.org/10.1007/978-3-032-10166-2_1

Introduction

Although the COVID-19 pandemic is now "well established and ongoing" and, since May 2023 "no longer fit[s] the definition of a public health emergency" (World Health Organization, 2024, para. 3), it represented a major crisis whose effects have been felt globally. The aggressiveness of the pandemic caused significant changes in both global and local governance, leading to government-enforced lockdowns, quarantines, social isolation, and social distancing. These changes affected Canadians' mental health and led to fears related to isolation and lockdowns (Dainton et al., 2021; Pongou et al., 2022). The government of Canada imposed social distancing safety measures to curb the spread of the coronavirus disease; however, the distancing from friends, family, and community resulted in increased psychological and emotional distress, depression, and levels of panic among the population as fears associated with the COVID-19 pandemic increased (Best et al., 2021).

While the mental health effects associated with the COVID-19 pandemic varied among different populations, depression, anxiety, and stress symptoms reached unprecedented levels among the general population (Saltzman et al., 2021). With depression and anxiety levels increasing, concerns about self-harm and suicide related to pandemic stressors also increased (Dainton et al., 2021; Pongou et al., 2022). Again, while the COVID-19 pandemic increased the mental health crisis amid the rise of health conditions experienced by the general population, the Black population in the Greater Toronto Area (GTA) experienced greater rates of COVID-19 infection when compared to the White population. Data gathered between 2020 and 2021 showed that Black people in the GTA (9% of the population) made up 14% of COVID-19 cases and 16% of hospitalizations (Ezezika et al., 2022). Data taken from September 30, 2020, showed that Black people at that time represented 24% of COVID-19 cases (again at 9.28% of the city's population) and White people made up 21.66% of COVID-19 cases, though representing 46.66% of the city's population (Mensah & Williams, 2022).

For the Black population in Canada, the COVID-19 pandemic reflects the social justice crisis of anti-Black racism metamorphosed into a health crisis. Mensah and Williams (2022) found that Black populations in the GTA were overrepresented in frontline occupations during the COVID-19 pandemic. The pandemic saw a rise in stigma towards visible minority groups and anti-Black racism due to the overrepresentation in frontline occupations, increasing attacks and harasment (Amoako & MacEachen, 2021).

The rise in anti-Black racism is not limited to frontline workers; Black healthcare patients were also affected. Beagan et al. (2024) contend that Black patients face racial stereotyping and a failure to take the health impacts of racism into account. Due to the continued history of racial discrimination within the Canadian healthcare system for Black healthcare providers and service users, there is an increased rate of vaccine hesitancy within Black populations and thus increased vulnerability to infection (Cénat et al., 2023). Mensah and Williams (2022) observed that the increased infection rates in Black communities are related to lower immunization rates.

Racial discrimination during the pandemic coincided with public racial-justice activism corresponding to public displays of police brutality towards unarmed Black people in America and the ensuing protests (Noble et al., 2022). For Black populations, isolation also meant dealing with the traumatic events of anti-Black racism away from the public eye (Fandino & Banerjee, 2022). Fandino and Banerjee (2022) highlight the minimal institutional support during the pandemic to combat the isolation faced by Black populations. In Canada, the ensuing systemic racism exacerbated health inequities among Black communities and undermined interventions by public health agencies to curb the spread of COVID-19 and its associated impacts on Black and other racialized communities (Kemei et al., 2023). Despite strategies adopted by community organizations and public health agencies, the experiences with racial discrimination limit the effectiveness of such approaches, placing Black communities in more vulnerable positions for infection (Cénat et al., 2023). Based on the above discussion, this study sought to address the following research questions: (a) How did the COVID-19 pandemic affect the overall well-being of the Black population in Scarborough, Ontario? (b) What coping mechanisms did this community employ to manage the effects of the COVID-19 pandemic?

Methodology

This article is a follow-up to Demi (2024). The study utilized Afrocentric and political economy theories to guide data collection, analysis, and discussion. The researcher recruited 20 Black people in Scarborough who access TAIBU Community Health Centre (TCHC) services. TCHC is the only community health centre in Toronto that provides healthcare focused on Afrocentric principles. The researcher selected TCHC because of the large number of Black populations in the GTA who patronize TCHC and because of its progressive approach to healthcare. Inclusion criteria for participant selection encompassed individuals 18 years of age and older who resided in Scarborough during the pandemic and who accessed services at TCHC. In addition, ten healthcare providers (two doctors and eight nurses) were also recruited to understand their perspectives on COVID-19 and the mental health and well-being of the Black population in Scarborough. The participants were labelled from 1 to 30 based on the first to last interviews conducted, respectively. The data collection began in April 2021 and ended in March 2022 to enable concurrent data collection and analysis and also to take into account changes in the COVID-19 situation and control measures.

The principal investigator (PI) who conducted all the interviews distributed a recruitment poster through the TCHC Listserv and social media handle with the help of senior TCHC staff. The poster informed participants to contact the researcher directly. Additionally, the PI contacted group leaders in charge of food distribution at TCHC who are knowledgeable about TCHC and the Black community in

Scarborough to understand their perspectives. Purposive sampling was used to select participants based on their experience and willingness to talk. The information was gathered through in-depth interviews, which involved the PI asking specific questions and allowing the participants to respond based on their unique experiences and expertise. Questions included: "What is your experience with the COVID-19 pandemic?" "How did COVID-19 affect you physically, mentally, and financially?" "How do you manage the effects of the COVID-19 pandemic?" Before the interview, the PI informed participants of their right to discontinue the interviews at any time, the right to refuse to answer uncomfortable questions without repercussion, and the right to anonymity. Furthermore, the PI read the informed consent to each participant and obtained verbal consent before the interview. The University of Toronto Ethics Board approved the study.

All the participants were interviewed in English, and interviews were audio recorded and transcribed manually. The PI began data analysis by reading through the transcripts several times to understand the information gathered. Furthermore, the PI manually coded the information and created subthemes based on the study's objectives. The subthemes were later regrouped into main themes. The patterns, consistencies, and agreements in information were noted and analysed, and inferences were drawn from the literature. The following section presents the study's findings.

Findings

Effects of the COVID-19 Pandemic

This study investigated how the COVID-19 pandemic affected the overall well-being of Black people living in Canada. Through discussions with the 30 participants, it was observed that the impacts of the pandemic are multifaceted. Much of the discussion relates to the toll on participants' mental health due to the changes throughout the pandemic. As shown in Table 1.1, results of the study indicate that

Table 1.1 Effects of the COVID-19 pandemic on the Black population in Scarborough

Effects of Covid-19 pandemic	Percentage (%)
Long queues at stores	14.6
Anxiety	31.6
Shortages of goods (e.g. food, sanitary products)	10.3
Health programs moved online	6.26
Did not affect me	10.3
No facility to store food	6.17
Developed depression	14.6
Increased unemployment	6.17
Total	100

anxiety (31.6%) and the development of depression (14.6%) were the most serious effects of the COVID-19 pandemic on the participants' mental health. The participants experienced overall negative impacts of the pandemic on their well-being. This finding agrees with earlier studies that also reported a negative impact of the pandemic on mental health (Gadermann et al., 2021; Gorfinkel et al., 2023).

However, social location (including race and gender) dictates access to care, quality of care, and effectiveness (Fandino & Banerjee, 2022). Access to care for mental health and well-being includes access to opportunities for physical activity. As identified by the participants (6.26%), one of the impacts of the COVID-19 pandemic was the moving of health programs to online formats. Due to the constraints of social distancing and stay-at-home orders, health services, including in-person exercise classes and the use of exercise facilities, were suspended (Callow et al., 2020). It has been found that both light and vigorous physical activity positively impacts symptoms of depression (Callow et al., 2020). Without access to in-person physical activity options, the mental health of those who rely on the service can suffer. The following participant describes how having limited mobility impacts the reliance on others to meet their daily needs and affects the mental health of those who lack the facility to exercise:

> I got depression, higher, a higher level because I have to be indoors. I only go out in summer because of my fractured ankle but this summer is out. If I can or am able to go out outside and walk is better because when it snows. ... I am not allowed to go there because of my foot.

The participant described how a fracture in her ankle limits her opportunities to go outside during the winter due to mobility issues and how her mental health has suffered as a result. The quote shows how the participant's mental health deteriorated due to the lack of ability to exercise or go out due to the COVID-19 restrictions. According to the participant, she fell and fractured her ankle before the onset of the pandemic. She was prevented from going out during winter to minimize the risk of falling again and worsening her condition. Hence, her hope to come out during the summer was dashed when COVID-19 occurred towards the end of spring. The COVID-19 restriction measures imposed by the government restricted her movement throughout the summer, with dire consequences. The constant stay at home, coupled with poverty due to the failure of the Ontario government to approve her Ontario Disability Support Program (ODSP) application, brought untold hardship to her, leading to poor mental health. Participants with a compromised immune system relied on their families or neighbours to assist them. The participant discussed their reliance on neighbours for those who are immobile: "Right. So, sometimes they sit at home, and they depend, they have to depend on people to help them, like their neighbours."

The participants contended that sometimes people in their neighbourhood or themselves volunteered to purchase groceries for immunocompromised elderly persons in their communities. According to the participants, sometimes they purchase the groceries out-of-pocket or sometimes the elders give them money for supplies when purchasing their groceries. This community support was vital to the survival of the elderly in the Black community, based on the disproportionate death rate of the elderly caused by the COVID-19 pandemic. One of the participants who doubles as a community leader in Scarborough noted:

> I know there's one lady who depends on her neighbours to help her, which they are doing, right? Or, you know, if they want to go and pick up something for themselves, like go to the pharmacy. They depend on neighbours to do that for them. So COVID, COVID has changed the situation over. Because, you see, number one, they're not getting to go out, they are stuck in their home. And it's not, it's not easy. A lot of stuff is done on Zoom, but not everyone has access to that. Though, it's not easy for the older, for seniors. Yeah, yes, it's not an easy thing.

The quote highlights how elderly people with compromised immune systems were badly affected by the COVID-19 pandemic. It further shows members of the Black community in Scarborough supported their neighbours, who, due to their poor health condition, had to isolate themselves further to prevent contracting COVID-19. The community members helped their neighbours to pick up their medical supplies and foodstuffs. However, participants recognized the toll of the pandemic in the community and how difficult it was to adjust their daily routines to accommodate their neighbours. Nevertheless, the goal of saving the lives of the members of their community motivated them to cater to each other. The participants revealed that a lot of health and wellness programs were moved online, but not everybody had the knowledge of or access to the Internet or technology to take part in the programs. Hence, moving programs online negatively affected some participants. This in part reflects how the effects of the COVID-19 pandemic have been enormous on the elderly population, which has affected their mental health.

The above quotes highlight the unique struggles of those who face mobility issues and the impact of COVID-19 restrictions on symptoms of depression. The pandemic similarly has unique impacts on anxiety levels, specific to intersections of Black populations in Canada. Kemei et al. (2023) noted that Black communities in Canada have high infection rates due to the socioeconomic impacts of higher representation of Black people in frontline work and shared housing with large families. Similarly, the study found that extended families of different generations who lived together had a higher chance of contracting COVID-19 due to a lack of space to practise social distancing (Ghosh et al., 2021). Many Black families believe in multigenerational-family shared living arrangements, in which the elderly pass on their knowledge to the young. The practice is to ensure that the grandmothers live at home to nurture the future generation; however, this practice was tested during the COVID-19 pandemic. Elderly people in nursing homes or long-term care facilities were also severely impacted by COVID-19 in Toronto. A nurse interviewed in the study who worked in a long-term care facility asserted that within the space of 2 weeks, COVID-19 killed more than one-third of the residents:

> Well, um, I worked at a long-term care. … We had 12 out of 32 of the residents who have died in the space of 2 weeks. So, it was really challenging and somehow heartbreaking to just see these families lose their loved ones and all that. So, it's not just the impact on those that have passed away, but the families and even the health workers, their mental health; it

won't be in terms of knowing that, well, these are people you've cared for, and suddenly an outbreak comes, and you start just losing them every day.

The participants recounted how the death toll affected the families of the deceased and the healthcare workers who catered to them. Some of the workers in long-term care have been with the patients for a long time and have developed a great fondness for them. Those with cordial relationships with the patients have become families of their patients. Therefore, losing 12 people within 2 weeks can be devastating even to the hardest hearts. The death toll in the nursing home brought heightened anxiety to the workers, management, and families of the residents who were deceased or those whose relatives were in the facilities but were not allowed to see them. Hence, the level of anxiety and depression came from different sources. Some nurses or front-line workers who could not handle the situation quit their jobs entirely. However, participants contended that those who quit their jobs were mostly White nurses who had other means of survival:

I will say, a lot of White [nurses], when COVID hit, they took off. A lot of them just decided to go on stress leave. A lot of them decided to go, to quit, some people just quit, quit working. And that's not an option for us. I managed to talk to a few of them and ask them, how do you quit work? How do they live? But you see … they have some backup, they know the system, they know how it works. Somehow, they had an idea of what to do, like when you're out of work, what do you do. We don't have those resources.

The participants revealed that some of their White colleagues could quit their jobs during the excesses of the COVID-19 pandemic because they had the means to do so. However, racialized and Black nurses lack the means to quit their jobs since most of them are breadwinners in their families. If they quit their job, returning to work would be a daunting task for most racialized people due to the colour-coded labour market that discriminates against racialized people (Block et al., 2019). Using the 2016 Census, Block et al. (2019) found that racialized people in Canada struggle to be absorbed in the labour market compared to non-racialized individuals. Consequently, they argued that Canadian "labour market discrimination continues to be gendered and racialized" (Block et al., 2019, p. 5). Therefore, quitting their job would not be prudent for most racialized people.

The COVID-19 pandemic created a multipronged burden on the healthcare workers—contemplating quitting their jobs or fear of losing their jobs, fear of contracting COVID-19, and fear of transmitting the COVID-19 virus to their loved ones—resulting in an unprecedented level of anxiety among Black healthcare workers. The position was succinctly opined by one of the participants:

So definitely there is a lot of anxiety around, you know, safety. Access to personal protective equipment was a problem as well. And just general uncertainty, knowing or not knowing patients that are coming to you may or may not have COVID-19. And then the anxiety of worrying that you are transmitting it to your loved ones and people around you.

For Black healthcare providers, the initial shortages of personal protective equipment (PPE) and the fact that they were disproportionately assigned COVID-19-infected patients, even when there were more experienced senior nurses, increased their level of anxiety. The finding confirms the observation made by Kemei et al.

(2023). Furthermore, anxiety about sharing spaces with family members and fears of infecting others are elevated in Black communities where large families sharing a home are more frequent (Kemei et al., 2023). Caretaking of family members can impact anxiety related to overarching existential fear of the risk or seriousness of infection or death, and fears of specific situations or susceptibilities, such as risks inherent in public spaces (West et al., 2021). Some of the healthcare users interviewed revealed their level of anxiety. One of the participants asserts, "Because of COVID and other situations, I came to develop anxiety. The doctor described it. Well, I know, I have depression. And I have high blood pressure."

These observations from the participants confirm that COVID-19 has increased the level of anxiety among Black frontline workers and healthcare users. Furthermore, the observations show the realities of anxiety related to the safety of frontline work, access to personal protective equipment, and transmitting the virus to others. There was considerable anxiety related to the safety of shopping for food, social distancing, and the availability of supplies (Pantano et al., 2020; West et al., 2021). Anxieties associated with the pandemic have changed shopping patterns, creating what Pantano et al. (2020) call the "scarcity effect." Pandemic-related anxiety related to access to goods impacts pricing, stockpiling habits, and queue lengths (Pantano et al., 2020). One of the participants described how he managed to reduce the risk of contracting COVID-19 by buying food in bulk that can last for a week or more. The following participant identifies his stockpiling habits during the COVID-19 pandemic and acknowledges the privilege of having access to facilities for stockpiled goods.

> I will go probably once a week, and I do most of my shopping at Costco. … So once or twice a week, I will go out and furnish it [grocery], but for the other stuff, I get it in bulk. And I have it for a couple of weeks and store it in the freezer. While other people may not be so inclined or don't have the facility to store.

The participant explained that he purchases foodstuffs early in the morning from Costco before the store is opened to the public. Costco initiated a special shopping hour for seniors to reduce the spread of COVID-19. So, he took advantage of the situation to store an adequate supply of food in his freezer. However, the participant recognizes the fact that some families, especially large households, lack enough space to store food and hence must resort to regular visits to shopping centres. Similarly, Lee et al. (2021) found that herding behaviours due to anxiety in shoppers increased according to their risk perception, positively influencing their willingness to wait in lines. Some participants revealed that long queues for purchasing food or essential products were a source of worry for them. The long queues associated with the COVID-19 pandemic were found to have a significant effect (14.6%), as explained by a participant in the following quote:

> Now there are long lines to check out. Even if they don't go stand up so much outside, now when you're checking out you have to be herded like cattle in these long lines. … You know what I mean? And they call you a number to this number go to that number. I find that a little annoying.

The participant in the above quote revealed how joining a long queue became discomforting, particularly when checking out. Furthermore, participants with health conditions that do not allow them to stand for a long time had to resort to other means to get their food or medical supplies. It highlights how the COVID-19 pandemic has changed the environment, impacting the mental health of Canadians.

COVID-19 Coping Mechanisms Employed by Participants

Certainly, the COVID-19 pandemic brought high levels of anxiety, uncertainty, and mental health challenges to people in Canada, especially the Black population. In addition to COVID-19, the stress of experiencing racial discrimination has been found to increase moderate to severe depressive symptoms in Canada and the United States (Thomas et al., 2022). Consequently, participants of this study adopted various strategies to minimize the impact of the COVID-19 pandemic on their mental health. Some of the strategies are outlined and discussed in this section. One way in which the participants cope with the effects of the pandemic involves routine "driving around" to no specific destination. The strategy became effective because even though people were not allowed to walk around, the enforcement of the COVID-19 restriction policy excludes people who drive around, provided they remain in their cars. One of the participants who employed this coping mechanism explained:

> My wife passed away. I don't want to stay home and get depressed. I try to be active so … I jumped in my car, and drove. There is a guide; I don't come out of the car. I just drive, go to, like, maybe go to Ajax, go to Bomerville or somewhere. I just turn around and come back home.

The participant above revealed that his wife died unexpectedly the year preceding the COVID-19 pandemic. The loss of his wife with no children around was hard on him. Hence, the stay-at-home order became unbearable to him, fearing that he would develop depression by continuing to stay at home. He therefore adopted a strategy of driving around every evening to an unknown destination and returning home to prepare to sleep. This coping mechanism helped him to improve his mental health by encouraging him to focus on driving and sightseeing rather than thinking about his wife and the excesses of COVID-19. Similarly, Kar et al. (2020) found that 26.7% of participants used "avoid thinking about it" as a coping mechanism to minimize the effects of the pandemic, which was found to have significant associations with anxiety and depression. The participants who said COVID-19 did not affect them also adopted a strategy of not thinking about it. Furthermore, the participant stated that he engages in regular exercise or works as a "handicapped" bus driver to remain active. This finding affirms the earlier study, which found that the majority (53.25%) of the participants "keep busy" as a means to avoid COVID-19 stressors (Kar et al., 2020). However, the study further emphasized that the strategy of "being active" can have a negative impact if inappropriately utilized to avoid thinking about stressors. Other participants agreed with the above observation by arguing that they also adopt routine exercise regimes to keep healthy. One of the participants elaborated on combining routine exercise with other strategies to improve their mental health:

> I exercise every day. Then I sleep well because of the exercise. And also, I've done quite a lot of work, my work. Even last evening, I got a movie and watched it, so I make sure I watch a movie every day. I tend to sleep well.

The participants listed several strategies employed to improve mental health. Apart from regular exercise, they get enough sleep to keep stay healthy. Furthermore, some participants used the extra time provided by the stay-at-home order to work on stalled projects. However, this strategy disproportionately favoured men compared to women (Krukowski et al., 2021; Peetz et al., 2023). Women who had reduced working hours maintained the extra burden of caring for children at home during the COVID-19 restrictions, due to school closures (Peetz et al., 2023). The presence of all the family members at home meant extra cooking time and other household burdens that affected female academics or career women. Due to the continued stay-at-home orders impacting depression and anxiety among people, some participants adopted watching various movies as a way of improving their mental health. Additionally, some participants reported sleeping and waking up late in the morning because they work at home.

Discussion

Humans by nature are social beings; therefore, anything that inhibits social interaction among people could present an imminent danger to human well-being. The COVID-19 pandemic caused unprecedented levels of stress both in terms of scope and scale (Best et al., 2021; Kindred & Bates, 2023). It is not surprising that participants overall experienced negative effects of COVID-19, and anxiety and depression represent the major effects the participants outlined. The Black populations already face multiple forms of oppression, including anti-Black racism, microaggression (Banaji et al., 2021), and economic challenges orchestrated by the Canadian colour-coded job market (Block et al., 2019). The COVID-19 pandemic exacerbated these challenges because of the immediate implementation of COVID-19 restriction measures before participants received relief packages. Furthermore, the application requirements of some of the relief packages, such as the Canada Emergency Response Benefit (CERB) program, eliminated a substantial number of people in need. These people either failed to meet the requirements or were afraid of the aftermath of the benefits. For instance, some CERB beneficiaries were forced to remit the money after COVID-19 subsided for periods when they were considered not qualified to access the benefits (Government of Canada, 2023).

Furthermore, international students could not qualify to apply for most of the relief packages. These people are the most vulnerable group due to a lack of social networks and social capital in Canada. These challenges created a heightened level of poor mental health among Black people. The mental health challenges were compounded by the closure of public parks and fitness clubs or spaces for people to exercise. Lack of exercise or physical activity is linked to poor mental health (Harris, 2018; Silva et al., 2020). Stay-at-home orders and the COVID-19 scare forced immunocompromised seniors to depend on their neighbours and families to get their medical supplies and groceries. The shift to online health programs limited the ability of people without Internet access to receive healthcare, including mental health support. Although this policy helped to provide healthcare at the doorsteps of the patients during the lockdown period, it also eliminated or denied access to healthcare to the poor and vulnerable populations who lack knowledge of or access to the Internet or technology.

The death toll of the pandemic further aggravated the mental health of the deceased persons' families and healthcare providers who cared for them (Galea & Ettman, 2021; Joaquim et al., 2021). The pain of losing loved ones is severe but even more devastating if people lack the opportunity to bid farewell to the deceased. Families were prevented from seeing their dead or dying relatives as a preventive measure to avoid spreading COVID-19. Although none of the participants reported losing their relatives during COVID-19, some knew families who lost loved ones and they sympathized with them. Nurses and personal support workers (PSWs) grieved the loss of people under their care and for whom they came to develop affection, much as their families. The death toll, therefore, impacted the mental health of the Black population in Scarborough; however, there was no provision of mental health care to the healthcare workers during the COVID-19 pandemic.

The COVID-19 pandemic widened social inequalities among health workers and the rich and the poor (Public Health Agency of Canada, 2022). For instance, participants reported that some of their White nurse colleagues quit their jobs due to the mental health toll of COVID-19. However, Black healthcare providers could not quit their jobs due to their financial responsibilities and difficulty in securing new jobs in a racialized job market. Lack of PPE at the onset of COVID-19 impacted the mental health of Black healthcare workers because of fear of transmitting the COVID-19 virus to their families. This caused increased levels of anxiety and depression reported among some participants.

Participants employed various measures to avoid catching the COVID-19 virus. Some participants resorted to buying food in bulk to reduce frequent visits to grocery stores. However, this applies to affluent people and those with bigger refrigerators to store the food. Those lacking financial means and storage facilities had to risk their lives by being exposed to the virus or experience food insecurity. To ease the situation, major grocery stores instituted a policy to open shops at certain times, usually early in the morning, to allow immunocompromised people (particularly the elderly) to shop before opening the store to the general public. This provided a window of hope for seniors to purchase groceries without fear of catching the COVID-19 virus.

As coping mechanisms, participants adopted several strategies to mitigate the impact of COVID-19 on their well-being. For instance, some participants adopted routine driving to assuage the boredom created by long stay-at-home orders. This strategy allowed car owners to circumvent the COVID-19 measures. However, those lacking cars could not take advantage of or adopt this measure, which further deepened social inequality (Public Health Agency of Canada, 2022). Some participants avoided talking about the COVID-19 pandemic to cope with the effects, as found in other studies (Kar et al., 2020). Some participants adopted routine exercise schedules due to the abundance of time spent at home. Others used the opportunity to watch movies to improve their mental health. However, studies found that children watching movies during the pandemic promoted a sedentary lifestyle, which is associated with chronic illnesses such as child obesity and cancer (Huston, 2022; Park et al., 2020). A sedentary lifestyle increases the incidence of hormone-related cancers, weight gain, adiposity, and elevated chronic inflammation (Park et al., 2020).

There is concern about an epidemic of chronic illnesses after COVID-19 because of the limited time dedicated to people suffering from chronic illnesses during the pandemic and the effects of the increased level of associated anxiety and depression. The findings of this study will help to evaluate pandemic preparedness policies related to the Black community due to their unique marginality and intersection of oppression. Furthermore, the findings will aid social workers in crisis management and those dealing with Black communities experiencing pandemic-related anxiety and depression.

Conclusion

This paper explored the effects of the COVID-19 pandemic on the well-being of the Black population in Scarborough in the GTA. This qualitative study used in-depth interviews to obtain the necessary information from the participants for analysis. The study's findings indicate that the COVID-19 pandemic negatively affected the well-being of the Black population in Scarborough. Some of the effects of the pandemic include anxiety, depression, and increased unemployment caused by COVID-19 restrictions. Furthermore, long queues at the grocery stores were a source of worry for most participants. Additionally, shortages of sanitary products and foodstuffs at the onset of the pandemic affected the well-being of the Black population and increased insecurity in the Black communities. The pandemic caused health programs to be moved online, and households without Internet and technology were negatively affected as they could not participate in the health programs. The participants used various COVID-19 coping mechanisms to minimize the impact of the COVID-19 pandemic. Some strategies included driving around without a destination to circumvent stay-at-home orders. Some participants adopted routine exercises to help them keep fit. This was made possible due to the abundant time during the lockdown period. Others used the opportunity to work on their stalled projects, but the odds favour men. Participants who were busy pre-pandemic used opportunities to take a long relaxation time, while others used the lockdowns to read books and other written materials. The study recommends further investigation to ascertain the health, economic, and spiritual impact of the pandemic on Black communities.

References

Amoako, J., & MacEachen, E. (2021). Understanding the blended impacts of COVID-19 and systemic inequalities on sub-Saharan African immigrants in Canada. *Canadian Journal of Public Health, 112*(5), 862–866. https://doi.org/10.17269/s41997-021-00558-9

Banaji, M. R., Fiske, S. T., & Massey, D. S. (2021). Systemic racism: Individuals and interactions, institutions and society. *Cognitive Research: Principles and Implications, 6*, Article 82. https://doi.org/10.1186/s41235-021-00349-3

Beagan, B. L., Bizzeth, S. R., Sibbald, K. R., & Etowa, J. (2024). Epistemic racism in the health professions: A qualitative study with Black women in Canada. *Health, 28*(2), 203–215. https://doi.org/10.1177/13634593221141605

Best, L. A., Law, M. A., Roach, S. P., & Wilbiks, J. M. P. (2021). The psychological impact of COVID-19 in Canada: Effects of social isolation during the initial response. *Canadian Psychology, 62*(1), 143–154. https://doi.org/10.1037/cap0000254

Block, S., Galabuzi, G. E., & Tranjan, R. (2019, December). *Canada's colour coded income inequality*. Canadian Centre for Policy Alternatives. https://policyalternatives.ca/publications/reports/canadas-colour-coded-income-inequality

Callow, D. D., Arnold-Nedimala, N. A., Jordan, L., Pena, G. S., Won, J., Woodard, J. L., & Smith, J. C. (2020). The mental health benefits of physical activity in older adults survive the COVID-19 pandemic. *American Journal of Geriatric Psychiatry, 28*(10), 1046–1057. https://doi.org/10.1016/j.jagp.2020.06.024

Cénat, J. M., Farahi, S. M. M. M., Bakombo, S., Dalexis, R. D., Pongou, R., Caulley, L., Yaya, S., Etowa, J., & Venkatesh, V. (2023). Vaccine mistrust among Black individuals in Canada: The major role of health literacy, conspiracy theories, and racial discrimination in the healthcare system. *Journal of Medical Virology, 95*(4), Article e28738. https://doi.org/10.1002/jmv.28738

Dainton, C., Donato-Woodger, S., & Chu, C. H. (2021). A multicenter study of short-term changes in mental health emergency services use during lockdown in Kitchener-Waterloo, Ontario during the COVID-19 pandemic. *BMC Public Health, 21*, Article 1840. https://doi.org/10.1186/s12889-021-11807-4

Demi, S. M. (2024). Black People in Scarborough's Experiences with Mental Health During the COVID-19 Pandemic. In Nyaga, D. & Torres, R.A (eds). *Reimagining Mental Health and Addiction Under the COVID-19 Pandemic*. Springer Nature.

Ezezika, O., Girmay, B., Mengistu, M., & Barrett, K. (2022). What is the health impact of COVID-19 among Black communities in Canada? A systematic review. *Canadian Journal of Public Health, 114*(1), 62–71. https://doi.org/10.17269/s41997-022-00725-6

Fandino, I., & Banerjee, P. (2022). Temporary residents, lasting issues: International graduate students and COVID-19. *Canadian Ethnic Studies, 54*(3), 33–62. https://doi.org/10.1353/ces.2022.0024

Gadermann, A. C., Thomson, K. C., Richardson, C. G., Gagné, M., McAuliffe, C., Hirani, S., & Jenkins, E. (2021). Examining the impacts of the COVID-19 pandemic on family mental health in Canada: Findings from a national cross-sectional study. *BMJ Open, 11*, Article e042871. https://doi.org/10.1136/bmjopen-2020-042871

Galea, S., & Ettman, C. K. (2021). Mental health and mortality in a time of COVID-19. *American Journal of Public Health, 111*(S2), S73–S74. https://doi.org/10.2105/AJPH.2021.306278

Ghosh, A. K., Venkatraman, S., Soroka, O., Reshetnyak, E., Rajan, M., An, A., Chae, J. K., Gonzalez, C., Prince, J., DiMaggio, C., Ibrahim, S., Safford, M. M., & Hupert, N. (2021).

Association between overcrowded households, multigenerational households, and COVID-19: A cohort study. *Public Health, 198*, 273–279. https://doi.org/10.1016/j.puhe.2021.07.039

Gorfinkel, L. R., Snell, G., Long, D., del Casal, M., Wu, J., Schonert-Reichl, K., Guhn, M., & Samji, H. (2023). Access to mental health support, unmet needs and preferences among adolescents during the first year of the COVID-19 pandemic. *HPCDP Journal, 43*(4), 182–190. https://doi.org/10.24095/hpcdp.43.4.03

Government of Canada. (2023, July 24). *Repay COVID-19 benefits: Why you may need to repay.* https://www.canada.ca/en/revenue-agency/services/payments-cra/individual-payments/repay-covid-benefits/why-may-need-repay.html

Harris, M. A. (2018). The relationship between physical inactivity and mental wellbeing: Findings from a gamification-based community-wide physical activity intervention. *Health Psychology Open, 5*(1), Article 2055102917753853. https://doi.org/10.1177/2055102917753853

Huston, P. (2022). A sedentary and unhealthy lifestyle fuels chronic disease progression by changing interstitial cell behaviour: A network analysis. *Frontiers in Physiology, 13*, Article 904107. https://doi.org/10.3389/fphys.2022.904107

Joaquim, R. M., Pinto, A. C. B., Guatimosim, R. F., de Paula, J. J., Souza Costa, D., Diaz, A. P., da Silva, A. G., Pinheiro, M. I. C., Serpa, A. L. O., Miranda, D. M., & Malloy-Diniz, L. F. (2021). Bereavement and psychological distress during COVID-19 pandemics: The impact of death experience on mental health. *Current Research in Behavioral Sciences, 2*, Article 100019. https://doi.org/10.1016/j.crbeha.2021.100019

Kar, N., Kar, B., & Kar, S. (2020). Stress and coping during COVID-19 pandemic: Result of an online survey. *Psychiatry Research, 295*, Article 113598. https://doi.org/10.1016/j.psychres.2020.113598

Kemei, J., Tulli, M., Olanlesi-Aliu, A., Tunde-Byass, M., & Salami, B. (2023). Impact of the COVID-19 pandemic on Black communities in Canada. *International Journal of Environmental Research and Public Health, 20*(2), Article 1580. https://doi.org/10.3390/ijerph20021580

Kindred, R., & Bates, G. W. (2023). The influence of the COVID-19 pandemic on social anxiety: A systematic review. *International Journal of Environmental Research and Public Health, 20*(3), Article 2362. https://doi.org/10.3390/ijerph20032362

Krukowski, R. A., Jagsi, R., & Cardel, M. I. (2021). Academic productivity differences by gender and child age in science, technology, engineering, mathematics, and medicine faculty during the COVID-19 pandemic. *Journal of Women's Health, 30*(3), 341–347. https://doi.org/10.1089/jwh.2020.8710

Lee, Y., Wu, W., & Lee, C. (2021). How COVID-19 triggers our herding behavior? Risk perception, state anxiety, and trust. *Frontiers in Public Health, 9*, Article 587439. https://doi.org/10.3389/fpubh.2021.587439

Mensah, J., & Williams, C. J. (2022). Socio-structural injustice, racism, and the COVID-19 pandemic: A precarious entanglement among Black immigrants in Canada. *Studies in Social Justice, 16*(1), 123–142. https://doi.org/10.26522/ssj.v16i1.2690

Noble, A., Owens, B., Thulien, N., & Suleiman, A. (2022). "I feel like I'm in a revolving door, and COVID has made it spin a lot faster": The impact of the COVID-19 pandemic on youth experiencing homelessness in Toronto, Canada. *PLoS One, 17*(8), Article e0273502. https://doi.org/10.1371/journal.pone.0273502

Pantano, E., Pizzi, G., Scarpi, D., & Dennis, C. (2020). Competing during a pandemic? Retailers' ups and downs during the COVID-19 outbreak. *Journal of Business Research, 116*, 209–213. https://doi.org/10.1016/j.jbusres.2020.05.036

Park, J. H., Moon, J. H., Kim, H. J., Kong, M. H., & Oh, Y. H. (2020). Sedentary lifestyle: Overview of updated evidence of potential health risks. *Korean Journal of Family Medicine, 41*(6), 365–373. https://doi.org/10.4082/kjfm.20.0165

Peetz, D., Preston, A., Walsworth, S., & Weststar, J. (2023). COVID-19 and the gender gap in research productivity: Understanding the effect of having primary responsibility for the care of children. *Studies in Higher Education, 48*(9), 1428–1439. https://doi.org/10.1080/03075079.2023.2201589

Pongou, R., Ahinkorah, B. O., Maltais, S., Mabeu, M. C., Agarwal, A., & Yaya, S. (2022). Psychological distress during the COVID-19 pandemic in Canada. *PLoS One, 17*(11), 1–14. https://doi.org/10.1371/journal.pone.0277238

Public Health Agency of Canada. (2022). *Social inequalities in COVID-19 mortality by area- and individual-level characteristics in Canada.* https://tinyurl.com/4sruantw

Saltzman, L. Y., Lesen, E. L., Henry, V., Hansel, T. C., & Bordnick, P. S. (2021). COVID-19 mental health disparities. *Health Security, 19*(S1), S5–S13. https://doi.org/10.1089/hs.2021.0017

Silva, L. R. B., Seguro, C. S., de Oliveira, C. G. A., Santos, P. O. S., de Oliveira, J. C. M., de Souza Filho, L. F. M., de Paula, C. A., Jr., Gentil, P., & Rebelo, A. C. S. (2020). Physical inactivity is associated with increased levels of anxiety, depression, and stress in Brazilians during the COVID-19 pandemic: A cross-sectional study. *Frontiers in Psychiatry, 11*, Article 565291. https://doi.org/10.3389/fpsyt.2020.565291

Thomas, J., Georges, M.-V., Ogoe, S., Hallberg, A., Veisman, N., Wilkinson, L., Holley, P., Shrestha, R., & Ladner, K. L. (2022). The role of financial insecurity, racial discrimination, and comorbid health conditions on mental health in Canada and the United States during the COVID-19 pandemic. *Canadian Ethnic Studies, 54*(3), 177–203. https://doi.org/10.1353/ces.2022.0019

West, E., Nair, P., Barrado-Martín, Y., Walters, K., Kupeli, N., Sampson, E. L., & Davies, N. (2021). Exploration of the impact of the COVID-19 pandemic on people with dementia and carers from Black and minority ethnic groups. *BMJ Open, 11*, Article e050066. https://doi.org/10.1136/bmjopen-2021-050066

World Health Organization. (2024). *Coronavirus disease (COVID-19) pandemic: Overview.* https://www.who.int/europe/emergencies/situations/covid-19

Chapter 2
From Jailer to Healer: Reimagining Justice, Addictions and Mental Health; Afrocentric Alternatives and Carceral Psychiatric Logics

Ebenezer Inkumsah

Abstract Prisons and psychiatric institutions, along with the criminal justice system, are remnants of colonial infrastructures that target racialized groups as a form of control; the overrepresentation of African Canadian individuals in these systems is not coincidental. They operate under carceral logics, which assert that criminality must be addressed through punitive confinement and persecutorial incarceration (Davis et al., 2022). Carceral logics further illustrate how racism criminalizes neurodivergence and mental illness, contributing to higher incarceration rates among those with psychiatric disabilities, disproportionately affecting African Canadian youth. Abolitionist theorists Angela Davis and Mariame Kaba critique punitive and carceral systems, advocating for their abolition through dismantlement and the reimagining of transformative and restorative justice. Therefore, African indigenous resurgence is required reimagining of carceral practices that moves away from existing repressive surveillance, control, and punishment towards fostering care through African Indigenous approaches. The poor outcomes of the carceral system for African Canadian youth have prompted an alternative approach in the form of Boot Camp for young offenders. However, the boot camp's results are also inadequate. This is likely because the boot camp for young offenders operates based on existing Eurocentric carceral logics, which are unsuitable for incarcerated African Canadian youth. This chapter compares the negative outcome of the boot camp with the positive outcomes of Adinkra Farm. This non-government-run program employs abolitionist strategies rooted in African Indigenous approaches, African ancestral healing practices, and social justice principles. It emphasizes restorative justice and culturally specific initiatives that serve young adults and homeless youth of African descent in Ontario. Adinkra Farm integrates African Indigenous methods that prioritize community and holistic healing methodologies, recognizing individuals as vital members of their families, communities, and cultures. These practices and tech-

E. Inkumsah (✉)
School of Social Work, York University, North York, Toronto, ON, Canada
e-mail: inkumsah@yorku.ca

D. Nyaga, M. Zangeneh (eds.), *Critical Ethics on Mental Health and Madness*, Advances in Mental Health and Addiction,
https://doi.org/10.1007/978-3-032-10166-2_2

niques are profoundly anchored in African traditions, underscoring ancestral ways of being and African spirituality while moving away from the school-to-prison pipeline (Davis, 2016). Moreover, Adinkra Farm supports African Canadian youth clients by facilitating the expungement of their criminal records upon successful completion of the program. Additionally, the African Indigenous program provides structured support for managing substance use disorder and has reportedly shown lower rates of reoffending compared to conventional youth correctional facilities in Ontario.

This comparison of the impacts of Eurocentric carceral approaches and African Indigenous approaches offers a powerful lesson for policymakers, the judiciary, and social workers. African Indigenous approaches highlight the urgent need for African Indigenous programs for incarcerated African Canadian youth management and further expose that the criminal justice system continues to fail African Canadian youth by criminalizing rather than supporting them.

Keywords Afrocentric · Criminal justice system · African Indigenous · Youth

Introduction

This chapter contrasts the carceral logics that inform Canada's justice system with African Indigenous approaches (AIA) to criminal justice and mental health. Carceral logics conceive of penitence as a principle of correction and rehabilitation (Ben-Moshe et al., 2014). These logics are evident even in alternatives to conventional prisons, including psychiatric institutions for the Not Criminally Responsible (NCR) and programs like the Bootcamp for Young Offenders (BYO). In contrast, African Indigenous Approaches' logics conceptualize responses to criminality primarily through a rehabilitation lens, emphasizing community implications for disruptive behaviours and community responsibility for rehabilitation. Therefore, African Indigenous resurgence is required a reimagining of prosecutorial incarceration through ancestral healing practices, equitable care, and justice.

African Indigenous Approaches has served as the basis for Adinkra Farm (AF), an experimental program in Ontario specifically designed for incarcerated African Canadian youth. When outcomes are compared, such as recidivism, mental health, and addictions for these African Canadian youth across these programs—Not Criminally Responsible, Boot Camp for Young Offenders, and Adinkra Farm—only Adinkra Farm's African Indigenous approaches help lift incarcerated African Canadian youth out of cycles of criminality and addictive behaviours (Walcott, 2021). In this paper, I explore the roles that carceral logics and African Indigenous approaches play in these outcomes, with implications for policy, intake practices, and sentencing for African Canadian youth.

The Youth Criminal Justice Act

More than 12 years after the enactment of the Youth Criminal Justice Act (YCJA), the overrepresentation of African Canadian youth in the criminal justice system poses one of the biggest challenges for African Canadian communities and, ultimately, for all Canadians (Khenti, 2021). The Youth Criminal Justice Act (YCJA), which applies to individuals under 18 years old, was enacted in April 2013 by the Canadian Parliament to replace the previous legislation, the Young Offenders Act (YOA). The YCJA accommodates Indigenous approaches to criminal justice, addiction, and mental health management, allowing Indigenous leaders to accompany defendants during non-violent court cases. This contributes to the court's understanding of the youth's context and supports a cultural community during their journey. The YCJA incorporated significant reforms to address concerns about how the youth justice system had evolved under the YOA. These concerns included the overuse of the courts and incarceration in less serious cases, and disparity and inequity in sentencing. The YCJA provided the legislative framework for a fairer and more effective youth justice system. But it has not removed the disparity in the incarceration rate of African Canadian Youth, despite having as one of its main provisions "custody as a last resort". One of the reasons for the disproportionate rate of incarceration of African Canadian youth may lie in the fact that the YCJA focuses on fair treatment of the crime itself, with limited focus on the causes or chronic factors that contribute to their criminality. For example, I have observed many African Canadian incarcerated youths who claim they are not criminals; they assert that their imprisonment arises from mental health issues, drug addiction, and racism. Similarly, I have witnessed society's response manifest as suppression through the imprisonment of African Canadian youth due to mental health challenges and drug addiction. Unless these underlying factors are addressed, Canadian society will not achieve social equity for such youth. Despite the parallel overrepresentation of Indigenous and African Canadian youth in Canadian prisons and jails, there are no similar African Indigenous approaches-centred cultural interventions for African Canadian youth under the YCJA. Anti Black racism, inequality in health care, and the lack of transformative healing practices that prioritize Afrocentric methods over punitive measures contribute to the disproportionate targeting of African Canadian youth in the justice system, serving as a precursor to their overrepresentation in prison (Lefrancios, 2013).

Incarceration and "Alternatives" Under Carceral Logics

Overrepresentation refers to how addiction and mental health issues stemming from colonial generational traumas result in high rates of Not Criminally Responsible and Bootcamp sentences among African Canadian youth (ACY). When ACY are classified as NCR and sent to psychiatric institutions, they encounter intake processes that resemble certain procedures and face various challenges. They are often overmedicated and then placed in isolation. They are not treated like patients, but as criminals. This treatment leads to the organization of thoughts and behaviours through punishment rather than healing. Under the guise of psychiatric treatment, the NCR system instils fear and enforces obedience to the law. These experiences are shaped by the carceral logics that are rooted in colonial institutional practices, which ultimately produce criminal outcomes for individuals deemed not criminally responsible. Drawing on my professional experience as a peace officer in Ontario's justice system and my volunteer work as a community elder at Adinkra Farm Centre in Angus, Ontario, an open space that operates outside of existing colonial psychiatric carceral logics. It employs an African Indigenous Approach centred on community rehabilitation and African spiritual healing practices and offers an Afrocentric culturally specific program for African Canadian youths in conflict with the Ontario justice system, young adults, and homeless youth of African descent in Ontario. By employing an African Indigenous Approach, this chapter builds on the work of Walcott et al. by arguing that the prison system is a continuation of the slavery-era plantation, and thus requires a radical, Afro-centric approach that can abolish the form of plantation ideologies.

I examine how these systems differ in their approaches to managing incarcerated youth. The Adinkra Farm Centre's approach prioritizes restoring human dignity, utilizing an Afrocentric value system that opposes Western carceral logics. They involve African Canadian elders and community members in creating a support system that helps the incarcerated youth's reintegration into the community as a man. Molefi Asante's African Indigenous Abolition perspective model, which emphasizes self-determination and holistic engagement, provides the theoretical foundation for reimagining abolition of Western carceral practices beyond punitive systems and reimaging new approaches that are based on African Indigenous approaches (Asante, 2020). Adinkra Farm not only supports African Canadian incarcerated youth through culturally grounded healing practices, but it also helps these youths in getting their criminal records expunged upon successful completion of the program. In addition to this, the program provides structured support for managing substance use disorder and has reportedly demonstrated lower rates of recidivism compared to regular youth jail facilities.

Community Space Under African Indigenous Logics

AF employs an African Indigenous Approach centred on community rehabilitation and spiritual healing. They involve elders and community members in creating a support system for African Canadian youth. Adinkra Farm is positive because it is a direct result of the programming informed by the African Indigenous approach. Adinkra Farm integrates African Indigenous perspectives that value community and spirituality, recognizing individuals as essential members of their families, communities, or cultures. These practices, techniques, and methodologies are deeply rooted in African Indigenous knowledge, which emphasizes healing, community, ancestral ways of being, and spirituality. A transformative alternative to the school-to-prison pipeline by catering care, connection, and cultural continuity rather than punitive incarceration and exclusion ((Davis et al., 2022). It employs an African Indigenous Approach centred on community, rehabilitation and spiritual healing. They involve elders and community members in creating a support system for African Canadian incarcerated youth. Drawing on Molefi Kete Asante's Afrocentric philosophy, this approach emphasizes spiritual healing, communal restoration, and the reintegration of individuals in a manner that is liberatory rather than conditional or punitive. Reintegration, in this context, is not a process of assimilating individuals back into systems that have already failed them. Instead, it is a radical return to culturally grounded belonging, one that restores dignity, affirms identity, and re-establish the individuals rightful place in their communities—a stark contrast to Western carceral philosophies, which often rely on surveillance, behaviour modification, exclusionary criteria that is shaped by criminogenic risk, mental health, stigma, addiction and pathologization (Asante, 2020).

Adinkra Farm Centre itself is not like a prison or a psychiatric facility. It is often referred to as an African community space that focuses on rebuilding trust and dignity, and programs are designed to educate. Adinkra Farm integrates mind, body, spirit, and community as part of the intake process. Healing is seen as the responsibility of the centre to return the client to their respective community. Cultural immersion, music, drumming, and dance are all part of the therapeutic approaches designed to reconnect individuals to their roots. Elders guide healing through cultural spiritual libations, and they lead generational trauma-informed group meetings under traditional African lava trees.

Meditation and African healing traditions are prioritized over pharmaceuticals. Although African Canadian youth are disproportionately affected by the criminal justice and involuntary mental health systems, Afrocentric alternatives remain absent in addressing the criminalization and overrepresentation of African Canadian youth in psychiatric wards and prisons. They reject Western psychiatric models that pathologize behaviours without understanding the roots of clients' trauma. This contrasts with Western psychiatric institutions, such as forensic psychiatric units, which criminalize mental health issues and rely on confinement, restraint, and control, punitive approaches that isolate individuals from their communities. Adinkra Farm views healing as a collective endeavour, whereas Western psychiatric and prison models seek to suppress the symptoms of behaviours or psychiatric illness. Adinkra Farm's approaches, on the other hand, prioritize holistic healing in ways that affirm African culture.

Boot Camp for Young Offenders

I will discuss the BYOs within the context of mainstream carceral logics, comparing them with an African Indigenous framework. Ontario's BYOs, implemented as an alternative to prisons, emphasize the pervasive nature of carceral logics. When African Canadian incarcerated youth are sentenced to BYO, they experience an intake process that involves a military-style structure, discipline, and drills—all under the guise of an alternative prison. However, this "alternative" to penal incarceration adheres strictly to carceral logics and borrows from parallel disciplinary norms that date back to the origins of disciplinary power (Foucault, 1978). This is evident with the BYO programs' focus on strict structure, discipline, surveillance, getting the inmate to do push-ups as a form of punishment, and behaviour control rather than rehabilitation. They do not constitute real alternatives in terms of the underlying values or the experiences of those subjected to the trauma of punitive incarceration. African Canadian incarcerated youth explain that what they experience "is worse than regular jail; in the joint, at least you get to watch TV from your cell at night and get to make phone calls when they turn the phones on." BYOs' focus on control and strict adherence, learning drills, and obedience perpetuate what Mbembe describes as Necropolitical governance, where marginalized youth are subjected to a system that manages their lives through punishment, incarceration, and discipline rather than holistic healing. These systems function as colonial processes of dehumanization and domination (Mbembe, 2016), and I argue that they reinforce trauma for African Canadian incarcerated youth.

The principles on which the BYO is based are rooted in strict, structured military-style programming, designed to disrupt criminogenic cycles; the intake process selectively excludes youth charged with murder or rape and provides limited opportunities for parole or probation (Doob, 1998). At the BYO, admission is typically conducted by the admissions and discharge officer who also serves as the drill sergeant and, in some cases, as the inmates' or cadets' primary worker. This officer will typically be responsible for overseeing the daily routine, discipline, and overall progression throughout the cadet's incarceration. The individual functions as a kind of mentor, guiding the young cadet through a series of workbook tasks that must be completed to earn privileges. The process mirrors the way a private advances through the military rank system. The welcome is abrupt and aggressive: the drill sergeant gets in your face, yelling and screaming in a style reminiscent of basic military training. From the moment the youth arrives at the institution, every effort is designed to break him down and rebuild him according to rigid military discipline. The cadet is constantly barked at in cadence, a technique designed to strip the cadet of individuality. This is the same as military recruit training methods. This approach is designed to break the cadet down from within and then rebuild them according to a rigid military structure. This reflects what Foucault describes in Discipline and Punishment as the production of docile bodies, where individuals are reshaped through surveillance, control, and discipline, rather than being healed or reintegrated as whole persons. During orientation, it is made clear that you will be told when to eat, sleep, and even when to use the washroom. Every activity is done, including marching, going to meals, and using the bathroom. Marching in cadence and unison suppresses whatever individuality is left within that individual. The process is not to rehabilitate but to achieve power, control, and obedience. It is about conformity. A dehumanizing reimagining of the self that suppresses agency and enforces obedience, aligning closely with a carceral mechanism of power and control (Foucault, 1978). It's a dehumanizing process that strips the individual's dignity and reduces them to a zombie-like existence.

The NCR Unit

The Intake process at the Not Criminally Responsible (NCR) unit often excludes families and communities, centring on the brief psychiatric assessment that fails to engage meaningfully with the clients, including many African Canadian youths (Khenti, 2021). In the inpatient unit of the NCR systems, the cadets are often placed on lockdown status, confined to their rooms for up to 23 h a day; they are permitted to leave only for meals, medications, psychological visits, and then return to isolation. They have access to commissary items and brief walks, which are strictly conditional, and are often used as tools to assess compliance and reinforce behaviours and control. NCR youth are made to believe that everything remains under control, but only if they are medicated and obedient. It is a form of psychiatric incarceration that Foucault describes in Discipline and Punishment, where surveillance, isolation, and compliance are normalized.

At the intake, the cadet is assessed and managed through a strictly clinical, *almost* military-like lens to formalize the treatment plan, not necessarily to rehabilitate, but to medicalize. Individuals are often heavily medicated, with no attention given to the root causes of the behaviours that got them into trouble or the social and psychological context of their environment. Not unlike the situation for military cadets, NCR inmates do not leave their rooms except for professional visits, meetings with judicial review committee members, and approved visits. The inmates are closely observed, monitored for medication adherence, and they are searched to and from smoke breaks and or from their daily walks or exercises in the courtyard. In many cases, patients are subjected to high doses of psychotropic medications. This process involves breaking down an individual so that they believe they are innately depleted in cognitive functionality. In its place, the institution extends beyond military-like control and pushes pharmacological control. Discharge typically occurs only after numerous evaluations and attempts to prove that the individual is better and that their criminal behaviour can be attributed to mental illness or addiction. The approaches described here employ carceral logics that regulate life through disciplinary mechanisms, surveillance, and control of the individual body, whether it is strip searches, military routine of the boot camp, or the NCR units with its heavily medicated regimentation. Inmates in both systems are subjected to behaviour management under the guise of alternative incarceration and carceral psychiatric healthcare. However, both situation takes away the individual's independence by breaking them down and rebuilding them all under the pretence of stabilization through medication.

Fela Kuti, a musician, saxophonist, and Pan Africanist, used his music to describe the violence of the colonial African regime of the 1970s. One of his famous songs, called "Zombie", describes how African soldiers and the military rule at the time became Instruments of repression. "They do not think for themselves", but are conditioned to obey commands, "go and kill, go and die". "They are told what to say, what they think when to march and when to salute". This "zombie-like" obedience Fela sings about reflects not just the militarism, but a deeper White colonial indoctrination. Fela Kuti's critique resonates with Mbembe's theory of necropolitics because it highlights how modern power decides who may live and who must die under conditions of colonial and postcolonial domination. The zombie condition described by Fela Kuti mirrors how incarcerated African youth are treated and dehumanized in both the NCR units and at the BYO (Kuti, 1970). The zombie-like states, the excessive medication, and the strict structure and military discipline of these two carceral approaches break the African incarcerated youth's sense of self so that they can be remade in the image of the White supremacist institution's disposable commodities.

In these institutions, zombie becomes both a military and medical strategy of domination under the guise of order, care, and so-called reform. These are all forms of colonial Eurocentric foundations of a carceral logic that pushes White norms onto the incarcerated African Youth, which has no respect for African Indigenous approaches to care and justice. These systems ignore the real reason behind the criminalization, which is often rooted in histories of poverty, racism, and trauma. By the time they are released, many incarcerated youths gain very few, if any, life skills that could help disrupt criminalization or support addictions and mental health recovery, even less with a focus on restorative or transformative justice. Instead, they are discharged or released into the community with just their medications. As Mbembe and Fabris describe in necropolitics, medication then becomes an extension and continuation of carceral control of the individual after release from the institution. In the context of NCR, responsibility, psychotropic drugs are not merely therapeutic but have a disciplinary function. Clients are often conditioned to believe that their freedom is tied to taking medication for the rest of their lives. This form of carceral logic suggests that they are safe from recrimination if they take their psychiatric medications; in this sense, medications become a tool of control instead of helping the youth to adjust to life after release from the inpatient unit.

This continues to shape and mold the individual for the rest of their lives, hoping that if they stay on top of their medication, they will not reoffend. This absolves the institutions from providing any meaningful support that can help them lead a transformative life after incarceration. These aftercare practices pathologize control and punishment rather than healing. Both the Boot Camp and the NCR unit operate under a system that reduces individuals to objects of discipline or diagnosis with minimal regard for their humanity, and they do not address the root causes of why an individual commits a crime.

Like the NCR unit, the BYO is also envisioned as an alternative to penal imprisonment, yet still operates within colonial and slave-era carceral logics. The strict disciplinary practices of the boot camp for young offenders promote control, subjugation, punishment, isolation, and dehumanization, reflecting the carceral logics of colonial slave-era offender management. The principles on which the BYO is based are rooted in strict, structured military-style programming, aimed at disrupting criminogenic cycles entrenched in punitive Western carceral ideologies. The intake process selectively excludes youth charged with murder or rape, providing limited opportunities for parole or probation (Doob, 1998). This system fails to foster holistic community integration and perpetuates cycles of isolation and control.

Disproportionality in the Criminal Justice System and Overdiagnosis of Schizophrenia

African Canadian youth are disproportionately diagnosed with "severe" (i.e. "dangerous") psychiatric disorders, leading to criminalization and overrepresentation in Ontario's criminal justice system. This situation can be attributed to mental health issues, drug addiction, and racism. The overrepresentation of African Canadian youth in prisons and psychiatric institutions is not coincidental, as both are linked to colonial ideologies aimed at oppressing Indigenous African peoples (Walcott, 2021). Prisons and psychiatric institutions, together with the criminal justice system, are remnants of colonial infrastructures that target racialized groups as a means of control.

Already Existing Practice to Learn from: Options for Indigenous Youth Who Are Likewise Disproportionately Incarcerated

Adinkra Farm represents an alternative stream in the existing criminal justice system, offering a precedent for what could be done to address the overcriminalization of African Canadian youth. According to Correctional Service Canada (2022), African Canadian youth in custodial care account for 27% of the incarcerated population despite constituting less than 2.7% of the entire Canadian population. Furthermore, 81% of African Canadian inmates have a mental health and substance use disorder. Although addiction and mental health illnesses can affect anyone, the consequences are disproportionately severe for African Canadian youth due to racism, poverty, and the criminalization of African Canadian youth's behaviours. For instance, drug addiction and mental health issues are more likely to be framed as a public health crisis in White communities. Opioid addiction in predominantly White communities across North America has sparked the debate on harm reduction policies, safe injection sites, and decriminalization measures.

Due to anti-Black racism, African Canadian communities facing addiction to crack cocaine have historically been criminalized instead of treated with comparable compassion. Such anti-Black racism, along with disparities in health care and the absence of transformative healing practices that prioritize Afrocentric methods over punitive measures, contributes to the disproportionate targeting of African Canadian youth within the justice system, serving as a precursor to their overrepresentation in prisons. I propose a decolonized vision of justice that dismantles punitive structures while emphasizing healing, accountability, and collective transformation. This framework could significantly advance abolitionist goals and address the overrepresentation of African Canadian youth in custodial care. Reimagining justice through the lens of Afrocentric Indigenous perspectives provides an alternative to punitive justice, presenting abolitionist strategies rooted in African Indigenous spiritual practices. These practices reflect Indigenous African beliefs and ancestral kinship systems, focusing on collective accountability and healing. They align with pre-colonial principles that fostered community and the restoration of cultural traditions grounded in care. Current North American Afrocentric abolition perspectives can be enriched by integrating authentic African Indigenous frameworks, offering a more comprehensive critique of existing systems by drawing on my experiences with gang-involved youth at Adinkra Farm, a boot camp for incarcerated youth, my work within Ontario youth justice institutions, and abolitionist discourse. Strategies that do not aim to colonize the minds of those incarcerated but instead concentrate on empowering individuals while reimagining alternative ways of being in the world, focus on community and individual fulfilment.

Boot Camp Blushes as Two Inmates Escape—Toronto Star 2002

Like the NCR unit, the Boot Camp for Young Offenders (BYO) is also imagined as an alternative to penal imprisonment but still operates within colonial and slave-era carceral logics. The strict disciplinary practices of the boot camp for young offenders promote control, subjugation, punishment, isolation, and dehumanization, reflecting the carceral logics of colonial slave-era offender management. BYO within the context of mainstream carceral logics, comparing it with an African Indigenous framework. The principles on which the BYO is based are rooted in strict, structured military-style programming, designed to disrupt criminogenic cycles entrenched in punitive Western carceral ideologies. The intake process selectively excludes youth charged with murder or rape, provides limited opportunities for parole or probation. This system fails to promote holistic community integration and perpetuates cycles of isolation and control. Premier Mike Harris and Solicitor General Bob Runciman's much-publicized alternative to youth justice was marred by a daring escape that shook the nation. The launch of Canada's First Boot Camp for incarcerated youth is in Hillsdale, Ontario. It was an embarrassment for the then-Ontario Premier Mike Harris. The reform was marketed as an alternative to youth imprisonment. However, inside the institution, a lot of the youth spoke about the grievances, not only in the programs, but the harsh conditions and how different it is from traditional jails.

The drill instructors typically wake them up at 5:30 and subject them to early morning runs, military drills, and discipline, disguised as rehabilitation. One racialized youth voiced, "what the fuck am I going to do with learning how to march and doing those fucking drills every fucking day when I get out?" Another question is the value of the carpentry program, which allows you to make only a toolbox. Youth were told when to eat, sleep, and shower, and there was a constant sense of "us" meaning Black versus "them," which amplified my anxieties and feelings of isolation. This made me feel unworthy, although they'd already broken us down with the military routine. The discipline, disguised as rehabilitation, made me realize, "what the fuck am I going to do with learning how to march and doing those fucking drills?" I also questioned the value of a carpentry vocational program that is disconnected from the realities of the day. "What am I going to do with the fucking toolbox because that's all I get to make up here?" The environment at the boot camp was more alienating, and participants began to rebel. One youth voiced some of these concerns and stated, "This is probably why those two idiots broke out; frankly, I'm proud of them, because they promised us an alternative and transformational programs, but what they're doing to us is humiliating and disempowerment and trying to instil fear into us to respect authority, but that's not going to fucking work with me." The boot camp reformation for incarcerated youth was marketed to us as a progressive, insightful alternative to youth management. In practice, it is the same, reinforcing the same carceral logics and claiming to want to reform. These programs are not true or real alternatives; they are an extension of sleep, error, and colonial control in a different guise. The participants themselves, the incarcerated youth at the facility, exposed the fraud and the fury that these models represent. These systems take away individual autonomy and further subject them to a regi men that ignores their identities and experiences. The drill instructors at the front line imposed a militarized, strict discipline in place of holistic healing. Youth spoke of their experiences and repeatedly felt marginalized at the boot camp, subjected to racialized authority figures who made them feel that, because of their crime, they were unworthy of the dignity of self-determination. Another youth remarked that in the regular jails, there was occasional recognition of race, language, and culture when they went to the yard, programs, or to the gym. These reflections confirm a long-held belief among Afrocentric scholars: the existing carceral logics rooted in Eurocentric Western epistemology fail to recognize African diasporic approaches. These so-called alternative institutions have no compromising sensitivities to community-based healing or any approach based on relationship, accountability, and ancestral knowledge, which Afrocentric philosophers refer to as Ubuntu. The carpentry classes and military drills are not necessarily neutral skills; they are designed to strip the youth of their cultural relevance or transformative potential and to assimilate the incarcerated youth into compliance. As one youth asks, "What am I going to do with a toolbox?" This question underscores the absurdity of imposing colonial models of labour training on a young person who has limited education and comes from a community facing a lack of employment opportunities, including structural barriers from racism and a criminal record.

Running for Terry
LIFE

Hollywood on Egoyan's mind
MOVIES

THE TORONTO STAR

Sunny to partly cloudy. High 25C | Friday, August 29, 1997 | www.thestar.com Metro Edition

Boot camp blushes as 2 inmates escape

OPENING DAY: It was a rough day at the Hillsdale boot camp yesterday after two inmates bolted hours before the official opening.

Teens recaptured after 'lightning' break-out wrecks official opening ceremony

By Moira Welsh and Catherine Dunphy
Staff Reporters

HILLSDALE — A bolt of lightning revealed a major security flaw in Ontario's first boot camp, allowing two teenage inmates to make a wild escape and destroying the government's high-profile plans for an opening ceremony yesterday.

Solicitor-General Bob Runciman's speeches were written and the invitations promised a parade of uniformed, marching young offenders, but the daring escape late Wednesday night from Project Turnaround dramatically altered the script.

"It was a little embarrassing, for the minister especially, on the day he had planned the opening," Premier Mike Harris admitted yesterday.

"We know we're not dealing with the easiest of young offenders … I would say that two of them outsmarted us, along with nature, on this occasion."

The jail, 20 kilometres north of Barrie, delivered on a key Tory promise in the 1995 election to get tough on young offenders. It puts repeat criminals through a rigid schedule of exercise, work and rehabilitation, with no time for watching TV or playing video games.

BOB RUNCIMAN: "Not the opening I had in mind," Solicitor-General says.

Indeed, it was a raucous night at the jail.

Two inmates had already been arrested earlier in the evening and removed from Ontario's first private jail for allegedly assaulting a jail guard.

Then lightning struck. The power went out.

The young offenders apparently discovered what Project Turnaround staff already knew — the electrical security system had no reliable backup, so all doors stayed unlocked when the power shut down.

One guard hurriedly parked a van in front of the dormitory door.

Inside, a lone guard watched helplessly as two 16-year-olds, serving time for property offences, kicked the door open. Fellow inmates held blankets over the windows so security guards on the outside couldn't

Please see Boot, A29

'Fed-up' Harris vows crusade on gas prices

He wants probe of oil companies

By Jane Armstrong and Frank Calleja
Staff Reporters

Oil companies are colluding to gouge consumers, Premier Mike Harris said yesterday, and he's prepared to lead the investigation into the latest round of summer price hikes.

He called on Ottawa to investigate. But if the federal government won't do so, Ontario will go it alone to get the answers, Harris vowed.

"We want a thorough investigation of whether there is something legal or illegal that the oil companies are doing, forcing up the price of gas."

There's hope for drivers, A28

Breaking a lengthy silence on an issue that has brought many a motorist's blood to the boil, Harris said, "I'm fed up.

"I'm on the side of the consumers," he said during a ground-breaking ceremony for a North York geriatric centre.

"My own opinion is that they're being gouged at the pumps."

He was backed up by angry motorists, fuming about oil company price fixing as they pumped some of the summer's most expensive gas.

"This is the last long weekend of the summer, so they're going to extract their pound of flesh," said Jack Lyons, who has spent

Please see Harris, A28

ANGRY DRIVER: Jack Lyons, filling up at a Mississauga gas station yesterday, says oil companies are going to "extract their pound of flesh" this weekend.

Creditors and Eaton's reach pact

Eaton's has found a way to satisfy those who said they could push the historic department store chain into bankruptcy and sell off what was left.

The deal, worked out over the past week, now gives creditors their money faster and at a higher interest rate than Eaton's had originally proposed.

"It's a very fair deal now," said Wilbur Ross, senior managing partner of Rothschild Inc. in New York.

He represents investment funds controlling $125 million owed to Eaton suppliers, and rejected a restructuring plan presented two weeks ago to get the chain out of creditor protection.

Eaton's president George Kosich said the chain, which will still go ahead with plans to close several stores, can now concentrate on attracting customers.

Full story, E1

Top court schedules Quebec case

But judge's retirement could affect Dec. dates

By William Walker
Ottawa Bureau Chief

OTTAWA — Canadians could know by next spring whether the Supreme Court of Canada believes it's legal for Quebec to unilaterally separate.

Chief Justice Antonio Lamer will hold a hearing Sept. 18 in Ottawa on the logistics of the Quebec case.

But the court has tentatively set aside three days, Dec. 8, 9 and 10, to hear the request from the federal government for a clarification on whether Quebec can unilaterally separate from Canada after a Yes vote in a future referendum.

The December Supreme Court schedule was drawn up before the announced retirement of Justice Gérard La Forest, who leaves at the end of September.

Sources at the court say it's unlikely that Lamer would agree to hear such a major case without a full complement of the court's nine judges.

If Prime Minister Jean Chrétien appoints La Forest's replacement within weeks, it's possible that Lamer could agree to hear the case in early December as scheduled, Supreme Court officials said.

In that case, it would be about six months, or early June, 1998, before the court would rule.

The federal government would like to have a ruling on the case before an election is called in Quebec.

The last Quebec election was in September, 1994, and Premier Lucien Bouchard could call another election for September of next year. A referendum on separation from Canada could come a year later if the separatist Parti Québécois government is re-elected.

Ottawa is asking the country's highest judicial body:

- If Canadian law allows Quebec to declare independence unilaterally.
- Could Quebec unilaterally de-

Please see Supreme, back page

C8

RATING TV: Symbol denotes shows suitable for kids aged 8 and older.

Parents to get TV rating guide for children

By Antonia Zerbisias
Media Reporter

On-screen ratings intended to help parents decide the viewing habits of their children will begin appearing on Canadian television screens next month.

Starting Sept. 29, viewers will see a graphic icon in the upper left of the screen for 15 seconds at the beginning of each show.

The icons will contain a letter — sometimes accompanied by a number — to denote the age group for which the program is most suited.

The ratings — determined by the broadcasters themselves — will not be seen on variety, sports, news, music, talk, documentary and other information programming.

But those that are rated — including U.S. shows telecast on Canadian networks — will carry a symbol meant to inform viewers how much violence, sex and profanity the shows contain.

What the graphics mean, A30

The ratings are an attempt by broadcasters to provide some method of telling caregivers about the content and suitability of a program for a specific age group.

Yesterday, the industry's Action Group on Violence on Television (AGVOT) unveiled the icons — a stylized square with a maple leaf edge — and their rating codes.

C denotes suitability for all ages, including very young children; C8 means the show is best for viewers over the age of 8; a G will go on programming aimed at general audiences; PG denotes a parental advisory; 14+ means the show should be watched by those over the age of 14, while an 18+ warns of adult content.

As well as the initial appearance at a show's beginning, the ratings symbol will be shown again at the beginning of the second hour of longer pro-

Please see New, A30

INSIDE

STAR SINGLE COPY PURCHASE PRICE
Monday to Friday 47¢ + 3¢ GST = 50¢
(higher outside Metro and surrounding suburbs)

Despite the chaos, Premier Harris and Mr. Runciman continue to discuss their ambitious conservative plans to build super jails and reform Ontario's YCJA as alternatives for managing incarcerated youth. They are committed to shaping the future of prosecutorial incarceration as a shift away from punitive approaches. However, the escape of the two inmates confirms a deeper entrenchment of carceral logics rather than any political talk of a meaningful shift towards treatment programs and rehabilitation. It further demonstrates that Ontario's first private alternative to jail and prison does not differ from existing carceral logics. The two inmates readily admitted to investigators that the boot camp was no different from any other jail they had experienced. They believe it is even worse than regular jails because they are sick and tired of getting up at 5:30 AM for morning runs and marching to and from the washroom, dining halls, and participating in daily military-style drills, which they must do as part of their routine while being yelled at by the drill sergeants. As one of the inmates puts it, "It is no different than being locked up, but in other jails, I get to watch TV from the cell, and I get to make phone calls when the phones get turned on."

African Alternatives to Western Carceral Logics

Adinkra Farm Centre itself is not a prison or a psychiatric facility. It is often described as an African community space that focuses on rebuilding trust and dignity, with programs designed to educate. Adinkra Farm integrates mind, body, spirit, and community as part of the intake process. Healing is viewed as the responsibility of the centre to return the client to their respective community. Cultural immersion, music, drumming, and dance are integral to the therapeutic approaches aimed at reconnecting individuals to their roots. Elders guide healing through cultural spiritual libations and lead generational trauma-informed group meetings under traditional African lava trees. Meditation and African healing traditions take precedence over pharmaceuticals. Although African Canadian youth are disproportionately impacted by the criminal justice and involuntary mental health systems, Afrocentric alternatives are still lacking in addressing the criminalization and overrepresentation of African Canadian youth in psychiatric wards and prisons. They reject Western psychiatric models that pathologize behaviours without comprehending the roots of clients' trauma. This stands in stark contrast to Western psychiatric institutions, such as forensic psychiatric units, which criminalize mental health issues and depend on confinement, restraint, and control—punitive approaches that isolate individuals from their communities. Adinkra Farm regards healing as a collective endeavour, whereas Western psychiatric and prison models aim to suppress the symptoms of behaviours or psychiatric illness. Adinkra Farm's methods, in contrast, prioritize holistic healing in ways that affirm African culture.

NCR Versus Adinkra Farm: Intake Process

African spiritualities and traditions form the main purpose of the Adinkra Farm intake process, which is to connect the individual with the ancestors for wisdom and the individual within a sense of collective history, community, and purpose. I will now contrast aspects of Adinkra Farm's approach with those of the NCR and the bootcamp to illustrate Adinkra Farm's Afrocentric alternatives in practice. At the Adinkra Centre, the intake process prioritizes community presence, native medicine practitioners, elders from the community, and dialect-specific communication, demonstrating a decolonization approach to criminal justice and mental health. By examining these practices, I critique the existing mainstream Canadian "alternative" to penal incarceration through which people are diverted to a psychiatric ward rather than a prison. Kimberly Crenshaw examines how overlapping systems of oppression create unique experiences of marginalization (i.e. Race, class and mental health) (Crenshaw, 1995). This theoretical framework is effective for analyzing how people with mental health issues, especially racialized and marginalized communities, are disproportionately affected and treated by both carceral and psychiatric systems. Disability and carceral logic further reveal how racism criminalizes neurodivergence and mental illness, leading to higher incarceration rates for those with psychiatric disabilities Ben-Moshe et al. (2014). Angela Davis and Mariame Kaba, abolitionist theorists, critique the punitive and carceral systems, advocating for their dismantlement and replacement with transformative and restorative justice. The overrepresentation of Black individuals in prison systems and psychiatric institutions is not coincidental, as both are linked to colonial ideologies aimed at oppressing Indigenous African peoples.

Conclusion

Prisons and psychiatric institutions, along with the criminal justice system, are remnants of colonial infrastructures that target racialized groups as a means of control; the overrepresentation of African Canadian individuals in these institutions is not coincidental. They operate using carceral logics, which state that criminality must be addressed through punitive confinement and persecutorial incarceration. These carceral logics further reveal how racism criminalizes neurodivergence and mental illness, leading to higher incarceration rates for those with psychiatric disabilities and African Canadian youth. Abolitionist theorists Angela Davis and Mariame Kaba critique punitive and carceral systems, advocating for their abolition through dismantlement, opening spaces for transformative and restorative justice.

The poor outcomes of a carceral system for African Canadian youth have given rise to an alternative in the form of BYOs. However, the boot camp's outcomes are also poor. This is also likely because the bootcamp runs based on carceral logics, which are not appropriate for incarcerated African Canadian youth. I compare the poor outcomes of the BYO with the good outcomes of Adinkra Farm, a non-government-run program that runs using abolitionist approaches rooted in African Indigenous approaches focus and emphasis on restorative justice and integrating African Indigenous Approaches and perspectives that value community and holistic healing, recognizing individuals as essential members of their families, communities, or Afrocentric cultures. These are promising examples of African Indigenous approaches that challenge prevailing carceral logics. Adinkra Farm exemplifies an African Canadian culturally specific program serving young adults and homeless youth of African descent in Ontario. This comparison of the impacts of carceral approaches and African Indigenous approaches will serve as a powerful lesson for policy, social workers, and justice officials seeking a genuine alternative to help address the social injustice, overrepresentation in the needs of African Canadian youth, and the ways the mainstream systems fail them and construct their criminality. The overrepresentation of African Canadian individuals in prison systems and psychiatric institutions is not coincidental, as both are linked to colonial ideologies aimed at oppressing Indigenous African peoples. This system fails to promote holistic community integration and instead perpetuates cycles of isolation and control.

In contrast, the Adinkra Farm Centre in Angus employs an African Indigenous approach centred on community rehabilitation and spiritual healing. It actively involves African Canadian elders and community members in creating support systems. Molefi Asante's African Indigenous abolition perspective model, which emphasizes self-determination and holistic engagement, provides the theoretical foundation for reimagining abolition beyond punitive systems. African Indigenous practices serve as the framework for care for African Canadian youth clients. This approach focuses on spiritual healing, reintegrating individuals into their communities and restoring them to the communities from which they came, rather than excluding them due to the stigma of incarceration. The Adinkra Farm Centre's theoretical framework centres on restoring human dignity, an Afrocentric value system that opposes Western carceral logic. Conversely, the BYOs represent a justice system deeply rooted in colonial and slave-era carceral logics. The strict disciplinary practices of the BYOs promote control, subjugation, punishment, isolation, and dehumanization, reflecting the carceral logics of the colonial era.

This book chapter argues that current North American Afrocentric abolition perspectives can be enriched by integrating authentic African Indigenous theoretical frameworks, offering a more comprehensive critique of systems by reflecting on my role as a community elder at Adinkra Farm, my work with Ontario youth Justice institutions and abolitionist discourses in the Western hemisphere, I propose a decolonized vision of Justice that dismantles punitive structures while emphasizing healing, accountability, and collective transformation. Reimagining Justice through the lens of African Indigenous perspectives offering an alternative to punitive Justice. It challenges carceral logics by offering abolitionist strategies rooted in African spiritual healing practices. These practices draw on Indigenous African beliefs and ancestral kinship systems and emphasize collective accountability and healing. They align with pre-colonial principles that fostered community and the restoration of cultural traditions rooted in care. This framework could play a transformative role in advancing abolitionist goals and addressing the overrepresentation of incarcerated African Canadian youth.

References

Asante, M. (2020). *Afrocentricity: The theory of social change*. African World Press.

Ben-Moshe, L., Chapman, C., and Carey, A. (2014). *Disability incarcerated: Imprisonment and disability in the United States and Canada*. Palgrave Macmillan.

Correctional Service Canada. (2022). gc.gov.ca. Correctional Service Canada Publications

Crenshaw, K. (1995). *Critical race theory the key: The key writings that formed the movement*. New Press.

Davis, A. Y. (2016). *Freedom is a constant struggle: Ferguson, Palestine, and the foundations of a movement*. Haymarket Books.

Davis, A. Y., Dent, G., Meiners, E. R., & Richie, B. E. (2022). *Abolition. Feminism. Now*. Haymarket Books.

Doob, A. (1998). *Responding to youth crime in Canada*. University of Toronto Press.

Foucault, M. (1978). *Discipline and punishment: The birth of the prison*. Pantheon Books.

Khentii, A. (2021). *Advancing justice: Human rights, poverty, racism, and Canada's criminal justice system*. Maytree Foundation Publishing.

Kuti, F. (1970). *Album title: Zombie.*

Lefrancios, B. (2013). The psychiatrization of our children, or, an autoethnographic narrative of perpetuating First Nations genocide through 'benevolent' institutions. *Decolonization: Indigeneity, Education & Society, 2*(1), 108–123.

Mbembe, A. (2016). *Necropolitics*. Duke University Press.

Walcott, R. (2021). *On property: Policing, prisons, and the call for abolition*. Biblioasis-Canadian trade paperback, Field Notes.

Chapter 3
The Ethics of Missed Epistemic Opportunities: The Erosion of Independent Peer-Run Organizations in Ontario's Mental Health System

Tanya Shute

Abstract Since their development in the 1990s, consumer/survivor-led organizations have provided crucial peer support and mutual aid alternatives within the mainstream mental health service delivery system. Over time, however, few have been able to sustain their organizational independence and autonomy originally encoded in the legislation that legitimized them as government-funded programs within Ontario's mental health system. Engaging Fricker's (Epistemic injustice: Power and the ethics of knowing. Oxford University Press, 2007) theory of epistemic justice/injustice, this chapter explores how the subjugation of consumer/survivor knowledge and peer-run practice perpetuates epistemological injustice, positioning the direct knowledge of mental health problems at the bottom of the epistemological hierarchy within the mainstream mental health system. It examines the challenges these organizations face in maintaining the values and principles rooted in the liberatory psychiatric/ex-patient movement that forms their foundation, raising ethical concerns about the role and relationship of peer-run organizations and peer support within the contemporary mental health system.

Keywords Epistemic · Justice · Injustice · Ethics

Summaries

This work explores the ethical and epistemological consequences of the erosion of independent consumer/survivor-led spaces within Ontario's mental health system. Drawing on Miranda Fricker's theory of epistemic injustice, it argues that the

T. Shute (✉)
Faculty of Education and Health, School of Social Work, Laurentian University, Sudbury, ON, Canada
e-mail: tg_shute@laurentian.ca

D. Nyaga, M. Zangeneh (eds.), *Critical Ethics on Mental Health and Madness*, Advances in Mental Health and Addiction,
https://doi.org/10.1007/978-3-032-10166-2_3

closure or custodial assimilation of these spaces represents a significant loss of not only choice in the mental health system, but of sites of critical consciousness, alternative knowledge production, and epistemic resistance. Consumer/survivor knowledge, grounded in direct experience, offers valid and necessary counter-narratives to psychiatry's continued dominance in the mainstream mental health system. Yet, these voices remain structurally marginalized or tokenized within mainstream systems that privilege the authority of the psy-disciplines and positivist knowledge claims.

Historically, peer-run spaces provided non-surveilled, low-barrier environments where individuals could explore distress and healing with their own agency. The erosion of these spaces in Ontario and elsewhere has narrowed the field of epistemic possibilities and silenced collective knowledge that could transform mental health care.

Ultimately, the loss of these spaces diminishes the system's ethical capacity for knowledge claims and care.

Introduction

First-person accounts from patients inside early iterations of asylums and hospitals document the dehumanizing and often experimental "treatments" imposed by the psy-disciplines on their brains and bodies. What we now recognize as egregious disregard for human rights were, for generations, the hidden realities of people who did not meet the standard set by psychiatry to be incapable of the highly individualistic ideal of independence and/or meet the hyper-capitalist value of "productive" living. Their confinements behind institutional walls cloaked systemic psychiatric violence—the imposition of psychiatry's dominance over establishing the meaning of the range of expression of mental distress, the rationalization for establishing the need for cure and correction of these experiences, and manifested through practices including, at any time in history, and in various forms: isolation/seclusion/exclusion, physical or chemical restraint, water "cures", shock/ECT, lobotomy, conversion "therapy". This violence was rationalized by the epistemic orientation of psychiatric dominance and the psy-disciplines (psychiatry-related disciplines, including nursing, social work, and occupational therapy, among others); disciplines that monopolized the authority to define, interpret, and "correct" mental distress. As part of this hegemonic project, was not only psychiatric violence but epistemic violence: the dismissal and devaluation of the meaning individuals made of their own experiences, replaced by biomedical and psychiatric interpretations presented as the one, only, and objective truth.

Many first-person accounts began to emerge when, not coincidentally, the people living in the asylums and institutions also began to emerge—as deinstitutionalization efforts coincided with broader intersecting civil rights movements—and helped to build a collective resistance. These testimonies became the foundation for alternate, counter-narrative epistemologies of mental distress, rooted in direct knowledge of what was wrong about the current psychiatric knowledge base and its interventions, and establishing the epistemological value of lived experience/testimony.

The epistemological violence of the psy-disciplines continues to subordinate direct knowledge of the mental health system and "treatment" despite gains made by the psychiatric consumer/survivor movement in North America (including critiquing the scientific foundation of a biochemical model of understanding mental disorders, exposing patient labour practices, ushering in the counter-biomedical paradigm of mental health recovery, what is referred to the recovery model of mental health; to expose the unethical influence of pharmaceutical dominance and profit; confronting the racism and colonialism embedded in psychiatric practices, and calling for non-coercive alternatives to the or to the mental health system.

This chapter employs Miranda Fricker's (2007) theory of epistemic in/justice to explore the epistemological ethical implications of the erosion of psychiatric consumer/survivor-led organizations and spaces in Ontario, It critiques mainstream organizations that appropriate x/s/c-run organizations and reduce their work to peer support services of mainstream organizations, where the radical work of x/c/s liberatory movement (exemplified in this chapter through the use of Judi Chamberlin's 1977 first-person account) and supporting each other in ways we find meaningful, including but was deeply about collective consciousness-raising, are often diluted or surveilled by psy-disciplinary norms. Alternatives, peer-led and controlled spaces and supports, such as those offered by Ontario's Consumer/Survivor Initiatives, offer some of the few genuinely non-judgmental, non-monitored spaces for many people, but especially those who reject the mainstream mental health system. In what ways does the erosion of psychiatric consumer/survivor-led spaces in Ontario constitute epistemic injustice, and what are the ethical implications for a mental health system without integrated autonomous sources of direct knowledge?

Inspired by a recent provincial webinar calling attention to the rise in Community Treatment Orders in Ontario—where one participant poignantly asked, "What the hell is going on in the system? Who is accountable for this? Where would we find out about these things? Where do we get to talk about this bull**it?"—this chapter calls for viewing the system afresh, exposing the erosion of consumer/survivor-run spaces as the loss of alternatives to the mental health system in Ontario, and reclaiming spaces were epistemological justice such as challenging sanism embedded in the system that devalues and subjugates x/c/s epistemological credibility, critical consciousness as spaces to be together, and resist.

Disclaimer: This chapter is written from a critical mental health/Mad perspective; however, the author wishes readers to understand that the psychiatric consumer/survivor(s) is/are an epistemologically inclusive community, making space for and respecting the voices and participation of those attribute their survival and wellbeing to the mental health system, those who continue to benefit from and enjoy their involvement in community mental health or hospital-based program, to those who are ambivalent, to those who have a more reformist view to those who oppose, resist, from Mad Pride to anti-psychiatry activists.

De/institutionalization and the Origins of Consumer/ Survivor Alternatives

In her seminal work, On Our Own: Patient Controlled Alternatives to the Mental Health System, Judi Chamberlin (1978) provides a first-person account of her involuntary psychiatric hospital experience in the US in the 1960s. She critiques the process of institutionalization as one of teaching individuals how to be "mental patients"—an identity that requires the denial of personal autonomy as a condition of institutional life and treatment. Part political commentary, her work also details radical alternatives to the mental health system established by ex-patients across the United States.

Chamberlin describes the institutional process of psychological brainwashing of patients to voluntarily surrender their personal autonomy as patients, accepting and internalizing psychiatry's definition of their experiences as pathological, as beyond their control, thus requiring protracted/invasive psychiatric intervention. "Successful" treatment produces a compliant mental patient who needs the psy-disciplines to manage their pathology. Patients' own meaning-making of what they experience and its causes, their beliefs or preferences about healing, and hopes for recovery displaced by scientific claims of psychiatric "knowledge", which predominantly framed their pathology to be lifelong, and manageable only through strict adherence to psy-discipline directives. Chamberlin's work and other critical first-person accounts of the mental health system are widely considered foundational works to the X/C/S movement.

Most scholars tend to trace the early beginnings of the X/C/S movements to the wave of mass asylum deinstitutionalization across North America and elsewhere. This process was propelled by several forces: the development and enthusiastic uptake of psychoactive medications amongst psy-professions; political concerns about the costs of maintaining so many people in such large institutions, whether by mental or mood deviance from the norm (for example, women who experienced long periods of sadness after losing a child, as in Chamberlin's case) or who were deemed unable to be independent due to neurodivergence from the norm (for example people deemed "idiots" or "mentally defective" depending on how symptoms were labelled at the time); combined with the accumulated pressures from civil rights movements as "interlocking communities" (Piepzna-Samarasinha, 2022) of liberatory work that extended to, for example, the psychiatrization and criminalization of being queer, or the existence of Jim Crow asylums or "Indian" asylums in the US.

Resistance to psychiatrization and the carceral project predates deinstitutionalization. There has always been resistance to the treatment and care of people in the crosshairs of the psy-disciplines' gaze at any socio-historical moment, such as the burning of women healers and midwives in the 1600s, the violence and incarceration sanctioned against 2SLGBTQ+ people as "sexually deviant"; the horrors of "modern psychiatric advancements" including lobotomy, ice baths, electroconvulsive shock, and myriad other abuses and violations that first-person accounts came to reveal. Political resistance was taken up by the intersecting concerns and interests of movements that touched the social identities of those being locked up and silenced behind the walls of the institutions—feminist, Black, and Indigenous resistance among them—for psychiatry's role in the heteropatriarchal colonial project.

The association of the origins of the X/C/S movement with deinstitutionalization may stem from the visibility and voice ex-patients claimed once they were visible and could be heard once they were released—their silenced knowledge no longer able to be contained. Their subjugated perspectives in the sanist project of institutionalization offered new insights into the failings of psychiatric knowledge.

Evicting patients from the custodial care, which had left many people completely dependent on the institution for all aspects of daily life, was done without much planning or investment for what would become of these ex-residents. Many were adrift, without family to return to, without access to independent finances, and without programs to support their reintegration into the community. First-person accounts of this time (such as Pat Capponi's Upstairs in the Crazy House: The Life of a Psychiatric Survivor, published in 1992) document the harsh realities of life post-institution due to the failure of governments and psy-disciplines to care about what would happen to patients after. Her first-person account documents how ex-patients turned to one another. Survivors not only came together for practical and collective survival but also to politicize.

Collective consciousness-raising is a hallmark of the x/c/s movement and part of the process of psychological deinstitutionalization (Chamberlin, 1978). Ex-patients began to organize, publish newspapers, and take other forms of direct and creative action that demanded recognition of their rights and voices. They began to agitate for mental health system and policy reform, to be openly critical of the powers of psychiatry and the ethics of a for-profit pharmaceutical industry. They called into question the scientific legitimacy of the psy/biomedical model and the insistence that their experiences were abnormal pathology. They organized and established empowering, non-coercive, and community-based alternatives run by and for psychiatric survivors based on self-help and mutual aid. They claimed a new language as psychiatric consumers or survivors, which offered an empowering alternative to the psy-discipline's reliance on "mental patient" identity. They reclaimed their collective knowledge and used it to challenge psychiatry and its dominance in defining and constraining their lives, challenging it as faulty, limited, or having unchecked power.

Mutual aid and peer support remain the cornerstone of the consumer/survivor movement as genuine alternatives to the mental health system, even more critical in the hyper-individualistic neoliberal welfare states in Canada and elsewhere, where everyone is expected to be "independent" (gainfully employed and not relying on government for supports) or "productive" (gainfully employed and not in need of social assistance) or "high functioning" if one does have a disability (employed, if not gainfully, and not requiring supports).

Consumer/Survivor/Peer-Run Alternatives in Ontario

Alternative approaches to the mainstream mental health system—particularly mutual aid, peer support, and consumer/survivor (x/c/s) activism grounded in lived experience and direct knowledge—led to the development of peer-run programs and organizations. Early peer-run organizations post-deinstitutionalization were typically unfunded and grassroots organizations and voluntary in nature. Some of these alternatives are advocated to be fully recognized and supported options in the mental health system. Recognizing their potential value in enhancing the formal mental health system, the Ontario Ministry of Health launched the Consumer/Survivor Development Initiative in 1991, committing $3.1 million to support such initiatives. By 1993, consumer/survivor mutual aid and self-help was formally recognized as a key pillar of Ontario's mental health reform agenda (Trainor et al., 1999).

Initial funding supported both independent consumer/survivor initiatives (CSIs) and peer-run projects hosted by mainstream community mental health organizations, with the stated goal of eventual independence. CSIs were recognized as distinct kinds of mental health organizations as they were meant to be fully governed and run by consumer/survivors for consumer/survivors. In fact, funding restrictions did not allow for CSIs to provide services in the traditional sense of expert providers administering services to clients in the formal mental health system and community organizations. The funding initiative was intended to support consumer/survivor-controlled organizations and strengthen alternative methods of support than the traditional service paradigm that dominated mental health services (Trainor et al., 1997).

In the early 1990s, approximately 36–42 initiatives received funding from the Ontario Ministry of Health and Long-Term Care. These included drop-in centres, alternative businesses, and peer-run programs offering social support and mutual aid. Advocacy was initially recognized as a legitimate part of their mandate—until political shifts in the mid-1990s, such as the closure of the Ontario Advocacy Centre and new restrictions on charitable organizations, began to limit these activities. As organizations developed and more were funded, alternative supports such as warm lines and peer-run crisis programs were developed, as were important rights-based bodies such as hospital patients' councils.

However, these founding principles have increasingly been eroded. In the early 2000s, the legislation that created CSIs was amended to allow for non-peer control over these organizations, largely in response to funder concerns for organizational performance or financial management of some CSIs. Since then, many CSIs have closed or been amalgamated—often due to being forced into fiscal or governance management by a mainstream mental health organization partner, thus losing their independence and autonomy as a peer-run organization, or because their budgets were so small, the provincial health authority required amalgamation with a mainstream organization. These closures reflect a broader pattern of epistemic injustice: the systemic devaluation of lived experience and peer-run knowledge within the mental health field. Despite their demonstrated contributions to healing, leadership development, and community solidarity, CSIs were consistently underfunded compared to their mainstream counterparts. Their staff were not hired for their organizational skills, but rather their direct knowledge and experience as people who identified as consumer/survivors. Operating on modest five-figure annual budgets, they were expected to provide community programming, maintain infrastructure, pay staff (often at minimum wage), and meet administrative requirements typically faced by larger organizations. Debate persists within the peer support community about whether government funding—with its inherent restrictions and demands—was ever a viable strategy. What is widely agreed, however, is that the conditions of funding often created a structural setup for failure. One CSI, emblematic of this tension, chose to return its funding and close rather than compromise its values.

The loss of these spaces, whether by closed doors or by relocating to mainstream professionally led organizations and their spaces, is of grave concern for the community. Individual x/c/s have fewer and fewer epistemic risk-free and genuinely nonjudgmental space to peacefully engage in their healing work. Their closures mean fewer spaces to be together unmonitored for critical consciousness-raising and organizing. For those who work/worked in these spaces, these closures and amalgamations mean fewer opportunities to develop/control their own working conditions, and the loss of leadership opportunities. Autonomous and independent peer-run organizations offer a tangible alternative vision of help and support. For psychiatric consumer/survivors no longer welcome in mainstream services or who distrust them, there are fewer and fewer options Their closures and amalgamations with non-x/c/s-run organizations (often organized around the very psy-disciplines the movement sought to provide alternatives to, including hospitals in some cases) can also be understood as an act of epistemic injustice and as lost epistemic opportunity for the mental health system.

Epistemic In/justice

British philosopher Miranda Fricker's concept of epistemic in/justice guides us to better understand the ethical as well as practical consequences for the mainstream mental health system with the closure/loss of psychiatric consumer/survivor-led spaces and programs in Ontario. From her 2007 work *Epistemic Injustice: Power and the Ethics of Knowing*, this chapter employs the concepts of "testimonial injustice", "hermeneutical injustice", and the concept that makes both possible, "hermeneutical marginalization". It is asserted here is twofold. First, the intentional (overt sanism in the mental health system) and unintentional (due to tenacious sanism bias within the system) marginalization of psychiatric consumers/survivors' voices, structurally inserted into the mental health system by way of consumer/survivor/peer-run organizations, prevents epistemic alternatives to the biomedically dominant understanding of "mental illness" in the mainstream mental health system. Second, their work within the system (whether it be autonomous organizations and programs or volunteering at mainstream mental health organizations that conceive of peer support as merely one of several "services" they offer), is what facilitates the structural and personal dismissal of knowledge held by these communities and movements, and therefore leads to an insufficient and distorted body of knowledge in the mainstream mental health system. Both pose a serious ethical concern: how can the people who require the mental health system be expected to tolerate one based on such limited knowledge of the experience of mental health distress, the myriad alternative ways to explain causality, and the myriad alternative ways people know they can heal?

That the voices of people with direct experience of mental/emotional distress, or what could be diagnosed by the epistemic authority of psychiatry and the Diagnostic and Statistical Manual of Mental Disorders (DSM), or the mental health system (voluntarily or involuntarily) are marginalized, subordinated, or silenced in the system (and in the world in general) is not a revelation. Despite decades of struggle for human rights and social justice, the credibility of the psychiatric consumer/survivor voice and knowledge authority, one could argue, remains yet to be fully and sustainably recognized. Although more recently we have seen some legitimization of the voice and value of greater direct experience involvement in participatory mental health research and policy development, in application, this greater participation often appears tokenistic, lacking even the substance of genuine consultation, let alone the recognition that without their knowledge contributions, the work is partial, if not flawed. The epistemic authority within the consumer/survivor community is still subordinated to other knowledge (professional knowledge of the psy-disciplines and researchers) because direct knowledge holders do not have control over any aspect of the system, stubbornly held and protected by psy-discipline practitioners and researchers.

Evidence-based/informed practice is the mantra of the health system. Interventions employed by the health system must meet the imperative that there is robust evidence for the effectiveness of the intervention. It is hard to argue that this is not an important priority, preventing practitioners from wielding tools based on whims, preferences, or curiosities on vulnerable patients. Critical debates though centre on larger questions, such as who determines what constitutes "evidence" and from what epistemological perspectives? Widely accepted among psy-disciplines and researchers is the heuristic of the *hierarchy of evidence*, basing the (positivist) rigour of the research employed to determine the effectiveness of interventions. At the top of the hierarchy are systematic reviews/meta-analyses of experimental research designs, midway, individual studies that employ randomized control trial designs with large samples, and at the bottom of the hierarchy, typically expert opinion and anecdotal evidence. The direct experience of patients/clients though is not considered to meet the standard of anecdotal evidence on its own, and evidence-based practice is often accused of prioritizing research-produced knowledge over direct knowledge.

Although for the past several decades we have seen a greater acceptance of the importance to integrating people with direct experience of problems related to mental health or the mental health system into research, this is primarily through small-scale, participatory research approaches (using direct experience knowledge holders as "peer researchers" with limited and subordinated research roles, or qualitative approaches which prioritize the voices of experience, but such research design is found at the lower levels of the hierarchy, because the epistemological appraisal is stubbornly positivist, valuing objectivity in design and the generalizability of findings. The epistemic authority of direct knowledge is more transformative in paradigm, recognizing that there is no objectivity possible in research and that "bias" is required and valued ("the personal is political," after all) and that generalizability is not favoured over trustworthiness as individual experiences translate to the collective experience. Survivor research (cite), would appear at the absolute lowest level of the hierarchy if it were to be recognized at all. An exercise in epistemic gaslighting, one could argue all people with direct experience of violence, coercion, systemic oppression and marginalization, such as sexual abuse survivors, formerly incarcerated people, and substance users, hold this same relegated space on the hierarchy of knowledge—as people whose epistemic testimony (and other forms of testimony) lack credibility and reliability.

Hermeneutical Marginalization

For Fricker (2007), *hermeneutical marginalization*—as described earlier—is the historically persistent phenomenon wherein individuals or communities are unable to have their knowledge contribute meaningfully to the broader social discourse, or what Fricker calls the "collective hermeneutical resource". This means such knowledge remains constrained within, and local to, its originating community and does not transcend its marginal boundaries to inform the understanding of others outside it.

To explain how this form of epistemic injustice becomes possible, Fricker draws attention to two causal concepts: *persistent testimonial injustice* and *hermeneutical injustice* (Fricker & Jenkins, 2017, p. 270). Testimonial injustice is relatively straightforward: one's testimony (i.e., lived knowledge) fails to be afforded the same credibility as other, more socially sanctioned forms of knowledge (such as that of psy-professionals), due to prejudice. In this context, that prejudice includes sanism, ableism, and intersecting biases held by the audience—even when this direct knowledge is shared by many, or potentially by a population that outnumbers the audience. For example, the psychiatric consumer/survivor community, as a collective hermeneutical resource, may numerically exceed the practitioners of the psy-disciplines, yet their testimony is often devalued compared to that of professionals, who retain control over both the medium and the message.

The prejudice fuelling this injustice is sanism, deeply rooted in the enduring dominance of the biomedical model, which confers a presumed lack of credibility or capacity onto those who speak from direct experience. This is reinforced by the culturally pervasive and violent "mental patient" myth—that individuals with mental illness are inherently unstable, unpredictable, or prone to violence unless monitored, restrained, or medicated.

Hermeneutical injustice emerges from this testimonial injustice. It refers to the systemic and historical obstruction of individuals' or communities' attempts to have socially significant experiences—such as mental or emotional distress—recognized and understood. It is also the frustration of seeing one's knowledge dismissed or denied legitimacy as a valid epistemic contribution. Such injustice is not only about being misunderstood; it is about being structurally prevented from contributing meaningfully to collective understanding, from having one's knowledge recognized as knowledge.

This is precisely what first-person narratives like Chamberlin's seek to address: they endeavour to push collective experiential knowledge beyond the local, while also strengthening the internal epistemic fabric of the community by validating others' direct experiences. Chamberlin (1978) writes, "The 'mental health industry' is an entrenched bureaucracy, resistant to change from within [epistemic privilege] and almost totally unresponsive to outside pressures [epistemic justice]" (block quotes are the author's).

Psychiatrists, at the top of the mental health knowledge hierarchy, practice a limited epistemic tolerance by allowing some space for related professional disciplines (e.g., nursing, social work, occupational therapy), so long as knowledge remains "firmly under professional control" (p. 68). What might be considered epistemic violence occurs when individuals internalize the roles assigned to them—when they "become mental patients" (Chamberlin)—and their meaning-making is supplanted by diagnostic labels such as "sick" or "disordered". This silencing occurs under the assumption that they are inherently untrustworthy, disorganized, or irrational—a manifestation of the epistemic ignorance required to sustain epistemic injustice.

In this way, dynamic knowledge about legitimate alternative ways of understanding mental and emotional distress—its nature, causes, and paths toward healing—is systematically devalued. These include collective approaches to care, community-based interventions (as opposed to individualized treatments), non-hierarchical ways of relating, and evidence of recovery outside the biomedical frame. These represent the living, breathing epistemic contributions of the psychiatric consumer/survivor community—a vast, underutilized collective hermeneutical resource. These are what Fricker and Jenkins (2017, p. 270) refer to as "missed epistemic opportunities"—with significant consequences for public and population health.

Despite the extensive expertise that has developed within the community mental health sector over decades, we are not successful by population health standards. Individuals labelled with "serious mental illness/disorders" continue to die prematurely, face disproportionate poverty, unemployment, social isolation, and violence—all at significantly higher rates than the general population. These already alarming trends are only exacerbated for those who are women or femmes, Black, Indigenous, or 2SLGBTQ+.

And still, certain voices—particularly those of 2SLGBTQ+, Black, and Indigenous people with direct knowledge and experience—have never been fully included, even in these alternative spaces. While the consumer/survivor movement has made vital contributions to resisting psychiatric dominance, it has historically centred White voices and perspectives. As a result, the knowledge, histories, and epistemic authority of racialized, Indigenous, 2SLGBTQ+, and other marginalized knowledge and voices have too often been excluded or undervalued in consumer/survivor organizations. These communities have experienced their own forms of epistemic violence, not only in the mainstream mental health system but also within the movement itself. While the consumer/survivor movement has challenged dominant psychiatric narratives, it has historically centred White, settler, and cisnormative perspectives. This has resulted in the marginalization of racialized, Indigenous, 2SLGBTQ+, and other historically oppressed communities—even within spaces meant to resist epistemic injustice. These communities have not only experienced *testimonial injustice*—where their lived experiences are deemed less credible—but also *hermeneutical injustice*, in which the frameworks necessary to make sense of their distinct forms of mental distress and resistance are absent or dismissed within both the mainstream system and the movement itself. Their exclusion reflects a broader *hermeneutical marginalization*, where their knowledge remains localized and constrained rather than recognized as integral to the collective hermeneutical resource.

Consumer/Survivor/Peer-Run Organizations and the Space for Epistemic Justice

Peer-run alternatives to the mental health system have existed for as long as the mental health system anywhere there has been a mental health system, however often informal, grassroots, underground, and unfunded by government or charities. They were increasingly necessary for a community of people for whom community mental health supports had not been developed post-deinstitutionalization or for whom the mental health system was not effective or not trusted. Over time, some of these supports began to develop organizations and to seek out sustainable funding. Some did not, noting that alternatives would not be genuinely possible in a government-dependent relationship. The recognition of the effectiveness of these community-driven, peer-run alternatives by funders, and their subsequent popularity and the political will that drove system reform to include these alternatives, could be attributed to that they were very cost-effective ways of introducing choice into the mental health system, owing largely to a voluntary approach to mutual aid or the poverty-level wages the system expected people to work for (and did) when funded. However, it needs to be recognized as one of the successes of the x/c/s movement, as many pushed for system reform to include the choice for alternative peer-run supports based on self-help and mutual aid.

In Ontario, as noted earlier, mental health policy reform in the 1990s included funding for Consumer/Survivor initiatives, and in accordance with policy, they were to operate as independent, autonomous organizations that provided programming that did not replicate what was already provided in the community mental health system. Beyond their value in alternative programming was their value in terms of providing places and spaces that were peer-only; a place where someone could go and be surrounded by their shared epistemic and experiential community. Places they would not be surveilled or monitored in their conversations, their mood, or their behaviour. Places that did not impose a code of conduct on the door perform intake assessments or expect their personal history in exchange for support. These were places where people could talk about their experiences with doctors and psychiatrists, and have genuine conversations about their experiences with medications or ECT, where they could talk about thoughts of living and dying without the fear of a premature call to 911. Where conversations could be held, feelings expressed, frustrations understood, where their beliefs or behaviours would not be monitored, surveilled, problematized, or psychiatrized. They were low-barrier, immediate access, and where people took care of one another because peer support is a relationship, not a service. Places where resources were offered that were demonized elsewhere, like MindFreedom's pamphlets on how to safely wean one's self from psychiatric drugs, or where Hearing Voices groups were held, and where no one in the space was not part of the shared experience and had no agenda to deny the experience, reality, or knowledge of any other as legitimate insight. This kind of space, where someone could experience validation and unconditional high regard, physical and emotional safety without the risk of being psychiatrized (further) or hospitalized, and where people could talk critically about the mental health system—these spaces are/were important sites of collective critical consciousness-raising as alternatives to the mental health system. As funded organizations of the mental health system, CSIs also represented the collective voice and concerns of their community with other parts of the mental health system at service coordination and policy tables and advocated for change across the entire system.

When these organizations are closed down, the system loses them as epistemic opportunities. But the x/c/s community loses not only the programs they provide, but the space they created. If not for peer-run organizations, where do x/c/s have to go to access support in such a freeing and safe environment? For our organizations that were once independent and autonomous but have accepted or been forced into custodial relationships with mainstream mental health organizations, their capacity to provide this space and its alternative potential is diminished to the degree that their mainstream community provider/custodial arrangements elect to support. For some of these organizations, they only provide the minimum of "back office" support, providing administrative support to the peer-run organization. For others, the parent organization may control all administrative functions such as budgets, reporting, and hiring, and for some peer-run organizations, this trade-off to independence is welcome, as these functions were entirely too burdensome and took the focus away from peer support, and they still get to keep their space and programming autonomy. For too many though, their organizations (and operating budgets) were completely absorbed into the mainstream organization, most of their staff let go, and they are turned into 2–3 peer supporters providing a peer support program within the mainstream organization and in their spaces, and often being required to engage in para-clinical practices dictated by employment in the mainstream organizations, such as providing case management or contributing to client case records—because they are working with the mainstream non-peer organizations' definitions (and faulty knowledge) of peer support outside of their epistemic expertise and environment. There are two reasons for these closures/amalgamations: (1) the appearance of operational mismanagement of these independent CSIs, thus requiring external correction and oversight from the mainstream mental health system, and/or, (2) the budgets of these organizations remain so small that to keep them as independent organizations did not align with austerity priorities of the provincial government funder.

However voluntary or involuntary these shifts to the original mandate of the development of CSIs, what occurred to justify it all needs to be understood as the epistemic injustice it was and is. The people who worked in these organizations were hired for one primary expertise: their lived knowledge and willingness to work from the identity of a peer. They were not hired because they had business degrees or human resources backgrounds. When they were accused of a lack of management or operational competence, they were custodialized or closed. Also, as most organizations operated with very little funding compared to their mainstream counterparts, there was no operational funding to allow for administrative positions. Often, the executive director was tasked with them all: human resources, finances, fundraising, Board relations, and all with no administrative support. Their failure to remain independent was structurally an inevitability. Consumer/survivor-controlled spaces and places, funded or otherwise, provide a counter to the prevailing narrative. In the case where our workers are now in mainstream mental health organizations, surveilled, even unintentionally, surrounded by mainstream discourse and practice, how free are they to dream and implement alternatives? With the loss of autonomy, whose knowledge, definitions, and approaches are valued or dominant? When these organizations are forced to close (voluntarily or involuntarily) or diminish their work to a narrowed version as service provision inside the mainstream mental health system's walls, much is lost in terms of the epistemic resistance these spaces provided to x/c/s and to the system itself.

Conclusion

That there has been movement and progress is largely due to the consciousness-raising within the consumer/survivor movement and the voices directed at the mental health system in calls for reform, revolution, or resistance—depending on how each person orients themselves to the system or the movement. These were voices exchanged over coffee in rooming houses and church basements, often spontaneous or clandestine, as the mental health system operated with little regard for, or in spite of, direct experience knowledge. Over time, the movement became organized, wrote, marched, and presented alternative ways of understanding experiences—such as interpreting extreme beliefs rather than "hallucinations"—and proposed new explanations for their origins, like framing them through neurodiversity instead of brain dysfunction or mood pathology. It also established alternatives to what the mainstream mental health system offered: spaces imagined and run by those with shared lived experience, where healing could be discussed and experiences—both of neurodivergence and of the system itself—could be meaningfully explored.

Without access to peer-run and peer-controlled spaces in every community in Ontario, perhaps the movement is returning to this grassroots form—street-level, genuinely consumer/survivor-led alternatives. These may once again take the shape of small, informal gatherings: the coffeehouse conversations, the clandestine peer support and mutual aid that originally arose in the absence of liberatory, empowering options. This vision offers a hopeful future—one that resists the co-optation risks associated with sustainable operational funding and the professional credibility demanded by a seat at the mental health system's table.

Yet the social change and advocacy role of CSIs was never just about service provision. It was about being a voice at that table, and about disseminating collective knowledge that challenges and expands dominant understandings of mental distress. That is what is at stake when we lose the epistemic autonomy made possible—and protected—within these spaces.

Is it epistemically ethical that consumer/survivor-led alternatives are no longer supported by the mental health system—or, when they do exist, are no longer independent or autonomous? These spaces have historically served as crucial, non-judgemental environments where consumer/survivors and service users could exercise epistemic authority, share knowledge, and experience community without surveillance or intervention by non-consumer/survivor or clinical professionals. Their loss represents not only a structural shift but a profound form of epistemic injustice. These were sites of consciousness-raising, where alternative understandings of mental and emotional distress—such as more dynamic, socially grounded, or culturally specific explanations—could be generated, shared, and legitimized.

The injustice is further compounded by the assumption that consumer/survivor knowledge stands in simple opposition to professional psychiatric knowledge. In fact, the movement has always encompassed a broad and diverse range of experiences and orientations—from those who oppose psychiatry entirely to those who attribute their healing in part to psychiatric interventions. The erasure of these autonomous spaces harms this diversity and erodes epistemic pluralism.

Opportunities to engage with new or alternative ways of understanding and responding to mental distress—and to the mental health system itself, including the harms it may inadvertently produce—are increasingly rare. While the pandemic has created valuable online spaces for dialogue, peer-led and autonomous spaces in Ontario continue to decline. We need not only a strong and visible presence as alternatives within the mental health system but also an active influence on its guiding principles. Our epistemological ethics—rooted in lived experience, collective values, and mutual care—must shape how the mainstream system understands support. This means promoting alternatives grounded in reciprocity, mutuality, and autonomy, and recognizing lived knowledge as a legitimate and essential epistemological resource.

Terms

For a less cumbersome reading experience, the ex-patient/psychiatric consumer/survivor/Mad community and movement will be referred to as the initialism X/C/S.

Also, the mental health industry typically uses the expression "mental health and addictions"; however, the concept of mental health/mental health problems includes the problematic experience of using substances (criminalized or industry-legitimized substances). The author will not refer to "addiction" nor will it be considered separate from the concept of mental health, as the experience is implied.

Consumer/Survivor Initiatives: This term refers very specifically to consumer/survivor-led organizations in Ontario that were funded as part of Ontario's community mental health system, and included consumer/survivor-run alternative businesses. This term may not be employed outside of Ontario for similar organizations. For those who do not hold this official status, these are referred to as consumer/survivor-run or peer-run organizations.

Discussion Questions

What are the ethical implications of mainstream mental health organizations amalgamating peer-run consumer/survivor organizations into arrangements without knowledge of the x/c/s movement's history, values, and principles?

In what ways does epistemic injustice manifest differently for racialized, Indigenous, and 2SLGBTQ+ people with lived experience in mainstream mental health? What would it take to meaningfully centre this knowledge in the current mental health system?

How can we reimagine mental health system care to re-value sustainable peer-run alternatives, given our current neoliberal priorities and austerity approaches to funding?

References

Capponi, P. (1992). *Upstairs in the crazy house: The life of a psychiatric survivor*. Viking.

Chamberlin, J. (1978). *On our own: Patient-controlled alternatives to the mental health system*. Hawthorn Books.

Fricker, M. (2007). *Epistemic injustice: Power and the ethics of knowing*. Oxford University Press.

Fricker, M., & Jenkins, K. (2017). Epistemic injustice: A role for recognition? In T. Routledge (Ed.), *Recognition theory as social research: Investigating the dynamics of social conflict* (pp. 251–272). Palgrave Macmillan.

Piepzna-Samarasinha, L. L. (2022). *Care work: Dreaming disability justice*. Arsenal Pulp Press.

Trainor, J., Pomeroy, E., & Pape, B. (1999). *A framework for support* (3rd ed.). Canadian Mental Health Association.

Trainor, J., Shepherd, M., Boydell, K., Leff, A., & Crawford, E. (1997). *Beyond the service paradigm: The impact and implications of consumer/survivor initiatives*. Canadian Mental Health Association.

Chapter 4
From Precarity to Stability: The Role of the Ontario Basic Income Pilot as a Structural Intervention in Mental Health and Substance Use

Tom McDowell and Mohammad Ferdosi

Abstract This article provides a mixed-methods analysis of mental health and substance use outcomes among participants in the Ontario Basic Income Pilot's (OBIP) Hamilton region, alongside a critique of the pilot's research design. While previous research has established a relationship between basic income and improved mental health, the mechanisms through which this occurs, particularly the role of chronic stress, remain underexplored. This article addresses this gap by examining how financial security can interrupt the feedback loop between poverty, stress, and diminished well-being. In doing so, it challenges neoliberal frameworks that present addiction as an individual deficit and obscure the social structures that encourage it as a coping mechanism. Quantitative results (N = 217) indicate that higher benefit levels and longer participation were strongly associated with improvements in depression, anxiety, stress, and confidence. Long-form qualitative interviews with 48 former participants affirmed that income stability helped alleviate poverty-related stressors, contributing to improved overall well-being. Reduced reliance on alcohol and tobacco emerged as a downstream effect of reduced stress and enhanced emotional well-being. Although basic income's unconditional nature could benefit Indigenous and other racialized communities, these benefits were not fully realized in OBIP due to its failure to include these communities in meaningful numbers or to account for structural inequality in its research design. Employing a Marxist framework, we critique OBIP's individualist methodological approach, which, by relying on randomized control trials, overlooks the structural nature of poverty and the ways these conditions shape agency.

T. McDowell · M. Ferdosi (✉)
Department of Politics and Public Administration, Toronto Metropolitan University, Toronto, ON, Canada
e-mail: thomas.mcdowell@torontomu.ca; mohammad.ferdosi@torontomu.ca

D. Nyaga, M. Zangeneh (eds.), *Critical Ethics on Mental Health and Madness*, Advances in Mental Health and Addiction,
https://doi.org/10.1007/978-3-032-10166-2_4

Keywords Basic income · Pilot · Mental health · Substance abuse

Introduction

The relationship between poverty and mental health is well established, with research highlighting its complex and multidimensional character (Murali & Oyebode, 2004, p. 216). Economic precarity contributes to heightened depression, anxiety, and chronic stress while limiting access to coping resources (Haushofer & Fehr, 2014, p. 862). These effects are often more pronounced among Indigenous and other racialized communities, who are disproportionately exposed to economic hardship and systemic barriers to care (Pulkingham et al., 2010, p. 267).

In the neoliberal era, traditional social assistance programs have become increasingly restrictive and difficult to access, often compounding rather than alleviating mental health and substance use challenges (Chouinard & Crooks, 2005, p. 19). This cycle is often misattributed to individual pathology. Conventional welfare frameworks individualize poverty and substance use, treating them as personal failings and obscuring the role of colonial legacies in shaping access to resources, disproportionately affecting racialized communities (Wacquant, 2009).

We adopt a Marxist perspective to the study of ethics, claiming that poverty is not an accident or the consequence of individual failings. Rather, it is a structural outcome of a capitalist system that privileges the class interests of the owning class at the expense of workers, who are forced to sell their labour on the market in exchange for a wage (Marx, 1973, p. 101). Meaningful change, then, requires confronting and dismantling the dominant systems that produce and sustain poverty.

The state under capitalism takes on a dual role: to both supervise capitalist relations and secure the conditions necessary for capital accumulation, as well as to legitimate the system by regulating the market and providing social support to workers unable to acquire a living wage through wage labour (O'Connor, 1973). Given the active role played by the state in producing and extending market relations, we claim that the modern state bears an ethical obligation to provide meaningful redress to victims of capitalism (Wacquant, 2009, p. 41).

One policy instrument gaining attention with potential to improve the lives of recipients along each of these dimensions is a basic or guaranteed income, which provides unconditional financial support to eligible individuals. Basic income conceives of poverty as a policy issue that can be addressed through the provision of a guaranteed income supplement to recipients, regardless of their health or employment circumstances (Widerquist, 2006).

Recent pilot projects have shown significant improvements in mental health outcomes associated with basic income (Kangas et al., 2019; Ruckert et al., 2018; Thoits & Hannan, 1979). By reducing financial stress, enhancing autonomy, and removing the stigma and conditionality of traditional welfare programs, basic income could support individuals in managing substance use and improving overall well-being.

However, although pilots have demonstrated the ability to insulate recipients from market failure and neoliberalized welfare systems, their reliance upon randomized control trials (RCTs) has often failed to address the structural and racialized nature of poverty, focusing instead on individuals as fragmented and atomized. Thus, while basic income's unconditionality could be particularly beneficial for Indigenous and racialized persons who have been disproportionately subjected to punitive, paternalistic welfare models, most of the pilot projects conducted to date remain limited in scope (Galabuzi, 2006).

Despite strong evidence linking poverty to chronic stress, relatively little research has examined how income support, such as basic income, might reduce stress-related outcomes, or how this stress reduction contributes to broader improvements in mental health and quality of life. Much of the existing literature on basic income focuses on employment or general well-being, with far less attention paid to how basic income might disrupt substance use trajectories rooted in structural poverty and chronic stress.

Our study addresses this gap by integrating quantitative and qualitative data to test the hypothesis that income security improves mental health and reduces the likelihood of addiction. We present a mixed-methods analysis focused on the relationship between income security and quality-of-life metrics associated with mental health and substance use. By combining quantitative data with qualitative insights, we show a clear relationship between mental health and income security, highlighting the wide-ranging impact of a guaranteed, unconditional income on daily life. Quantitative outcomes are assessed using two key indicators: (i) the sum of monthly benefits received and (ii) the length of each participant's enrolment in the pilot.

These categories are analyzed according to four themes: general mental health, depression, stress and anxiety, and confidence. These themes represent common psychological stressors exacerbated by poverty and income instability, offering a framework for evaluating the impact of financial security (Haushofer & Fehr, 2014, p. 862). Although substance use was not the primary focus of the pilot, our analysis highlights its relevance as an important behavioural outcome shaped by mental health and financial stability.

Quantitative findings are contextualized through qualitative interviews with recipients. Participants reported significant mental health benefits from financial security, including reduced depression and anxiety, along with improvements in confidence and outlook. In general, we found that basic income enabled participants to take control of their lives and regain a sense of agency. Higher income levels and longer durations on the pilot were positively correlated with improved mental health and reduced substance use.

Qualitative interviews revealed that improvements in mental health typically arose from multiple overlapping aspects of participants' lives (Haushofer & Fehr, 2014; Pearlin, 1989). OBIP alleviated the "scarcity mindset" associated with life in poverty, enabling participants to shift from survival-focused behaviour toward long-term personal objectives (Mullainathan & Shafir, 2013, p. 123). The integral benefits of basic income on multiple aspects of participants' lives contributed to the profile of a happier, healthier, and more confident individual, leading to improvements in other aspects of their lives.

While our data on substance use were not as conclusive as findings related to mental health, the evidence points to a clear bidirectional relationship: participants who experienced improved mental health were also more likely to reduce their alcohol and/or tobacco use (Boden & Fergusson, 2011, p. 908). The reduction in substance use operates as a secondary outcome resulting from the alleviation of chronic stress and overall improvements in mental health. Financial stability and improved mental health, in turn, reduced reliance on addictive substances used to manage poverty-related stress.

While OBIP improved the lives of those who received it, the pilot may have underrepresented Indigenous and racialized participants relative to regional demographics (Statistics Canada, 2017a, 2017b). This is particularly concerning given the "colour-coded" nature of poverty in Ontario, which disproportionately impacts Indigenous and other racialized communities (Block et al., 2019, p. 1).

We engage critically with this finding, using a Marxist framework to argue that this oversight was the consequence of a research design rooted in methodological individualism. This approach detaches behavioural analysis from structural inequity and the historically contingent conditions that shape agency and choice. A participatory model in which Indigenous and other racialized groups co-design enrolment processes could oppose bureaucratic exclusion and help move beyond the neocolonial logic that continues to shape many social assistance programs in Canada (Chouinard & Crooks, 2005, p. 19).

Structural Poverty, Mental Health, and Substance Use: A Marxist and Sociological Perspective

We conceive of ethics, not in terms of individual morality or personal virtue, but rather as a structural issue maintained and reproduced by the actions of the state. Although the state appears as a neutral arbiter in liberal theory, its activities are deeply embedded in the social relations of production, structured to serve the reproduction of the capitalist social order (Miliband, 1969, p. 3). Under capitalism, the state plays a dual role. First, it must regulate social affairs to secure the operation of the market. Second, it performs a legitimation function, working to contain the social dislocation capitalism generates by redistributing income to ensure workers can survive without having to earn an adequate income in the market (O'Connor, 1973, p. 8). Given this, we conceive of the state's ethical responsibility as generating the conditions necessary for human flourishing and addressing systemic harm produced by the market (Wacquant, 2009, p. 6).

Drawing on a Marxist theory of the state, we view poverty and precarity not as natural conditions, but as the result of political and economic policy decisions designed to benefit the accumulation of capital (O'Connor, 1973; Miliband, 1969). Capitalism estranges individuals from themselves, severing the connection between the worker and the products of their labour, and between labour and human flourishing. Rather than living in free and spontaneous ways, individuals are compelled to sell their labour under conditions that deny their essential capacities for creativity, sociability, and self-determination (Marx, 1964, pp. 70–72).

From this perspective, ethics cannot be separated from political economy. Ethical responsibilities arise not from abstract principles but from the concrete, historical role the state plays in producing and managing inequality. In settler colonial contexts like Canada, this includes a further role in maintaining racial and colonial hierarchies that compound the effects of class rule (Coulthard, 2014; Robinson, 1983).

This understanding of poverty as a structurally imposed condition is consistent with sociological research that traces the effects of inequality on health. As Pearlin (1989) has shown, poverty is not simply a correlate of poor health but a fundamental cause of stress exposure, operating through a range of mechanisms that disrupt daily life and restrict coping resources. Structural inequality generates chronic strain, undermining both physical and mental health by depriving individuals of the autonomy and stability necessary to manage life's demands. Seen in this way, poverty is not only a social determinant of health but a form of structural marginalization legitimated, managed, and reproduced by and through state institutions.

Stress serves as a key indicator of mental health outcomes, arising from a complex network of ongoing strains shaped by social status and access to financial resources (Haushofer & Fehr, 2014, p. 862; Murali & Oyebode, 2004, p. 217; Pearlin, 1989, p. 242). According to Pearlin (1989, p. 242), stress is attributable to "constellations of stressors," which accumulate over time. Chronic stress, triggered by financial insecurity, exacerbates both physical and mental health outcomes, creating a cycle of negative impacts on well-being (McEwen, 1998, p. 33).

Yet dominant policy responses rarely address these structural roots. Neoliberal welfare regimes reduce substance use to an individual deficit, divorcing it from the political-economic conditions that make coping strategies rational from the perspective of the user (Boyd, 2015, p. 87). This mirrors neocolonial logics that blame Indigenous and racialized communities for their marginalization (Coulthard, 2014). A structuralist analysis, by contrast, interrogates how poverty's overlapping effects are caused by those institutions that perpetuate labour precarity.

This cyclical relationship is reinforced by stress's influence on decision-making, which often leads to self-defeating behaviours such as time discounting. Time discounting describes a tendency to prioritize immediate short-term rewards over larger long-term benefits, thus deepening poverty's effects (Haushofer & Fehr, 2014, p. 865). Ridley et al. (2020, p. 2) further highlight how stress related to income volatility contributes to "stress proliferation", where interconnected strains amplify one another, generating new sources of distress.

Critically, ongoing exposure to poverty is associated with a diminished sense of control over one's environment, perpetuating stress and impairing cognitive function (Mani et al., 2013, p. 977). Stress in one domain often has a "carry-over effect", spilling into other areas of life and contributing to an increase in coping behaviours, such as substance use (Pearlin, 1999, p. 401). Societies with greater income inequality experience typically worse mental health outcomes, as social stress and status anxiety stemming from relative deprivation erodes resilience and encourages self-defeating behaviours (Mani et al., 2013, p. 977).

Mullainathan and Shafir's (2013, p. 123) concept of a "scarcity mindset" illustrates how financial strain monopolizes cognitive resources, impairing decision-making and increasing reliance on maladaptive coping mechanisms, such as substance use. They argue that poverty generates this state of mind by forcing individuals to become so preoccupied with immediate financial concerns that they struggle to focus on long-term planning or self-improvement, often turning to coping mechanisms like cigarettes and alcohol (Mullainathan & Shafir, 2013, pp. 13, 18).

These stressors are intensified by social hierarchies, where disparities in power, privilege, and prestige intersect with class, gender, race, and ethnicity (Pearlin, 1999, p. 401). Low-status and racialized individuals often face compounded disadvantages, wherein status inconsistency generates a "feedback loop" linking poverty, psychological distress, and economic decision-making (Haushofer & Fehr, 2014, p. 865). Moreover, relative poverty fosters anomie, a sense of isolation and dissatisfaction that, alongside stigmatization and exclusion, exacerbates mental illness (Ridley et al., 2020, p. 2).

The interplay between poverty, mental health, and substance use is well documented. Chronic stress and financial insecurity drive maladaptive coping strategies, with substance use serving as an immediate but detrimental way of coping with psychological burdens (Dawson et al., 2005, p. 454; Lasser et al., 2000, p. 2607). While these patterns are well-established, no major basic income pilot has systematically examined whether income security disrupts this cycle. This omission persists despite evidence that behaviours like chronic substance use, often misattributed to poor willpower, fundamentally reflect constrained agency under poverty (Gifford & Humphreys, 2007, p. 354). Our study directly addresses this gap by analyzing substance use as a secondary outcome of financial stability.

This bidirectional relationship creates a self-perpetuating cycle: stress and anxiety drive substance use, which in turn exacerbates mental health conditions (Boden & Fergusson, 2011, p. 908). Although substance use often emerges as a direct coping strategy for stress, our analysis indicates that the observed reductions in substance use occur as a secondary benefit following improvements in mental health. Research, including clinical reviews, suggests that alleviating depressive symptoms can be associated with declines in substance abuse, an idea that complements epidemiological findings on the co-occurrence of these conditions (Nunes & Levin, 2004).

The impacts of poverty are particularly acute for racialized and Indigenous communities, who experience a disproportionate burden of poverty-related stressors that exacerbate both psychological distress and behavioural coping responses. In Canada, Indigenous and other racialized groups face significantly higher rates of poverty, unemployment, and housing insecurity (Galabuzi, 2006, p. 37). Research consistently shows that Indigenous and other racialized groups in Canada are over-represented in low-income brackets and are more likely to experience cumulative disadvantages across the life course (Block et al., 2019, p. 13).

In summary, the literature overwhelmingly shows that mental illness, substance use, and poverty form a mutually reinforcing cycle, shaped by structural inequalities and intensified by chronic stress. We explore whether an unconditional income guarantee could disrupt these cumulative effects by alleviating financial strain, improving mental health, and reducing substance use.

Basic Income's "Unconditionality" as an Alternative to the Surveillance Model of Welfare Provision

Critiquing capitalist structures is essential in the age of precarity, where gig work and employment instability have become the norm, generating power dynamics that favour employers. This situation forces workers to accept low wages, endure long periods without work, and take on multiple jobs, often outside their vocational field, to make ends meet (Moncrieff, 2022; Lewchuk, 2016, p. 112). Many individuals today face insecurity due to underemployment or prolonged unemployment, highlighting the need for alternatives to punitive welfare models that attempt to coerce people back into the labour market as quickly as possible (Kalleberg, 2009, p. 1).

In Ontario, the two primary welfare support programs, Ontario Works (OW) and the Ontario Disability Support Program (ODSP), have come under considerable criticism from across the political spectrum for being ill-suited to the challenges that confront workers in the twenty-first century. In a society characterized by rising income inequality and labour market insecurity shaped by several decades of neoliberal policies, the traditional employment-based model of welfare service delivery has proven inadequate to meet many of the challenges welfare recipients face.

A key critique of the geared-to-employment model, central to both OW and ODSP, is its tendency to individualize the problem of poverty. Rather than addressing structural conditions such as precarious labour, racial discrimination, or systemic barriers to education and housing, this model frames poverty as the result of an individual's failure to integrate into the labour market. Wacquant (2009, p. 41) contends that modern welfare regimes operate as instruments of social discipline whose function is to regulate and stigmatize the poor, particularly racialized populations, through moralizing language and institutional surveillance. Welfare systems demand performative compliance from Black and Indigenous recipients while exempting the state from accountability for historic harms (Virdee, 2019; Simpson, 2017).

In an analysis of ODSP recipients, Chouinard and Crooks (2005, p. 19) contend that welfare support programs entrench notions of "ableness" as a necessary condition for access to social and economic justice. By requiring recipients to prove whether they are deserving or undeserving poor, often demanding a demonstration of willingness to find paid employment, existing models dehumanize service-users. Maki (2011, p. 47) argued that the state has cultivated a culture in which social assistance recipients are viewed as "deviants" who fail to be "good market citizens". Lightman et al. (2009, p. 1) claim that people often fall through the cracks of an ODSP system that is designed only to accommodate a rigid, legislatively constructed definition of disability, with episodic disabilities often deemed "not disabled enough". That is, they were considered too unwell to earn a sufficient living, but well enough to be employable.

This problem of rising precarity in the context of geared-to-employment welfare programs disproportionately affects Indigenous and other racialized individuals, particularly given the history of colonialism in Canada (Coulthard, 2014, p. 12). Colonial welfare policies in Canada have historically imposed paternalistic conditions on Indigenous communities, reinforcing dependency rather than autonomy (Chouinard & Crooks, 2005, p. 5). By framing poverty as an individual deficit, contemporary welfare programs tend to absolve the state and the market of responsibility to redress systemic inequities (Lightman et al., 2009, p. 1).

Basic income has gained popularity as a policy tool in the age of precarity, offering a guaranteed, non-conditional income to address issues like unreliable employment and inadequate social assistance (Laenen, 2023, p. 1). Most basic income programs begin from the standpoint that financial precarity and the mental health problems that emerge from it, are *policy* choices (Widerquist, 2006, p. 1). The state's obligation to intervene is not merely necessary for practical reasons, but also an ethical imperative grounded in Canada's responsibility for reparative justice for historic and ongoing harm (Truth and Reconciliation Commission, 2015, p. 182).

It directly addresses the shortcomings of traditional welfare systems by providing unconditional financial security to workers. Proponents argue that basic income provides financial security and autonomy, freeing individuals from the compulsion to sell their labour, thereby granting them greater economic independence (Standing, 2011, p. 34). Wright's concept of basic income as an "unconditional strike fund" underscores its transformative potential. Wright (2006, p. 5) argues that basic income could empower workers by providing them with financial security independent of employment, thereby reducing their dependence on wage labour and strengthening their bargaining power.

For Indigenous and other racialized communities, basic income could offer a means of financial support without the paternalistic requirements of existing social assistance programs. Unlike means-tested welfare, which often imposes surveillance and behavioural conditions, basic income avoids reinforcing colonial stereotypes of dependency (Pulkingham et al., 2010, p. 267). In Canada, Indigenous peoples have long been subjected to paternalistic policies, from the Residential School System, to the Indian Act, to restrictive social assistance programs (Chouinard & Crooks, 2005, p. 19). These systems pathologize poverty and reinforce narratives of personal failure, which in turn contribute to psychological distress and coping behaviours such as substance use (Boyd, 2015, p. 85).

Basic income, by contrast, holds the potential to reduce this cycle of institutional distrust and mental distress by providing support without judgement or oversight, thereby removing a key structural variable contributing to substance use. An adequately funded basic income aimed at addressing racial inequities could help dismantle these structures by providing financial security without oversight by welfare case workers who require recipients to seek paid employment. The following section explores mental health and addiction findings from previous basic income pilots.

Impact of Basic Income on Mental Well-being and Substance Use: Findings from Basic Income Experiments

The assumption underlying guaranteed income programs is that the largest impediment to well-being is a lack of income. By providing an unconditional income guarantee, basic income empowers individuals to assume control over their own time and choices, which has been shown to contribute to improvements in a variety of health problems, including mental illness and substance use (Birnbaum & De Wispelaere, 2021, p. 912).

The positive impact of guaranteed income on mental health and related outcomes has been observed across multiple experiments, spanning several decades and diverse locations, demonstrating consistent improvements in mental health and reductions in the use of intoxicants (McDowell & Ferdosi, 2021, p. 220). Historical studies provide strong evidence of these benefits. In the late 1970s, a series of North American longitudinal studies on forms of guaranteed income demonstrated improvements in various mental health measures. Notably, these studies, including the Negative Income Tax (NIT) experiments and recent pilots, focused primarily on labour supply and mental health metrics, while overlooking substance use outcomes. This omission persists despite robust evidence that poverty-related stress drives substance dependence and represents a critical gap our study seeks to address (Lasser et al., 2000).

Furthermore, most of these studies are grounded in a theory of methodological individualism, which conceives of individuals as autonomous decision-makers operating independently of the social structures around them. This perspective tends to downplay or obscure the ways in which systemic forces such as racism, colonialism, and economic inequality shape the lived experiences of poverty and marginalization. By focusing on individual behaviour rather than structural context, these studies often fail to account for how social determinants of health constrain choice and reproduce harm, ultimately limiting the explanatory power and policy relevance of their findings.

The reliance of past pilots, including OBIP, on RCTs, while valuable in isolating causal impacts, reinforces this individualist bias by abstracting participants from their structural location, treating social variables like race and class as control variables rather than as constitutive elements of lived experience. This methodological approach results in many basic income studies being poorly equipped to assess how structural oppression shapes both the existing contours of poverty as well as quality-of-life outcomes.

Among the first and largest pilots of basic income were the NIT experiments, including the New Jersey Income Maintenance Experiment, the Seattle-Denver Income Maintenance Experiment (SIME/DIME), and Mincome in Manitoba. These studies were primarily designed to assess individual behavioural responses to income support, such as changes in labour supply, family stability, and educational attainment.

Results from the NIT studies in Seattle and Denver showed positive outcomes for mental health, though Thoits and Hannan (1979, p. 123) noted a statistically significant increase in psychological distress among certain demographic groups, highlighting the nuanced effects of such programs. Similarly, the Mincome study conducted in Manitoba in the mid-1970s revealed significant reductions in health service use for accidents and mental health issues in the saturation site of Dauphin, where all adults were eligible to receive basic income benefits (Forget, 2011, p. 288). This reduction was attributed to the indirect effects of overall decreases in poverty-related stress, alcohol abuse, and violence.

Forget (2011, p. 290) found that hospital visits in Dauphin were 8.5% lower than in the control group, primarily due to fewer workplace accidents and mental health conditions. A qualitative analysis of participant experiences suggested that basic income allowed recipients to feel greater autonomy and self-respect compared to conventional social assistance programs, as they could remain employed while receiving support (Calnitsky, 2016, p. 35).

More recent pilots have reinforced these findings but have continued with the use of a positivist methodological framework. A basic income experiment in Finland in the mid-2010s revealed that 55% of the test group reported not feeling stress at all, or only to a small extent, representing a significant increase compared to the control group (Kangas et al., 2019, p. 42).

Similarly, a guaranteed income pilot in Barcelona, Spain, saw a 10% decrease in the probability of mental illness development, likely due to reduced stress levels associated with living in poverty (City of Barcelona, 2019, p. 15). A study of guaranteed income for schoolgirls in Malawi found that recipients were nearly 40% less likely to experience psychological distress than the control group, underscoring the broader social and psychological benefits of financial security (Ruckert et al., 2018, p. 5).

These findings align with evidence from a study of guaranteed income derived from casino revenues distributed by the Eastern Band of Cherokee Indians, which showed that recipients were less likely to experience psychiatric disorders, consume alcohol or cannabis, or participate in drug trafficking as they reached adulthood. Unlike externally imposed interventions, this initiative was governed and distributed by the Cherokee community itself, reflecting an approach rooted in self-determination rather than external imposition in a neo-colonial fashion (Costello et al., 2010, p. 1954; Marinescu, 2018, p. 15). However, this study was limited to young men aged 16 and under, limiting the generalizability of these findings (Marinescu, 2018, p. 15).

In summary, although existing research provides substantial evidence of basic income's mental health impacts, there remains a relative paucity of empirical work examining how basic income may reduce chronic stress and how such stress reduction mediates broader outcomes, particularly related to addiction. Our study offers insight into both, demonstrating how reductions in the utilization of substances are related to the wide-ranging improvements in mental health and stress associated with a basic income experiment held in a North American context (McDowell & Ferdosi, 2021).

The Ontario Basic Income Pilot

One of the largest and most generous basic income pilots in the world since the 1970s was conducted in the Canadian Province of Ontario between 2017 and 2019 (McDowell & Ferdosi, 2021). Prior to its premature cancellation by a new Progressive Conservative government in July 2018, the Ontario Basic Income Pilot sought to determine whether a basic income could improve life conditions for low-income citizens on a variety of different quality-of-life measurements.

OBIP's methodological structure was designed closely to the recommendations of a 2016 report led by former Canadian Senator Hugh Segal. He recommended that the pilot test whether it would be beneficial to replace the ineffective, inefficient, and cumbersome "policing, control, and monitoring now present in Ontario Works and the Ontario Disability Support Program", the two pillars of Ontario's social assistance programs, with a more humane approach that enables individuals to use their money and time as they desire (Segal, 2016).

The province adopted Segal's recommendation that payments be based upon 75 percent of the Low-Income Measure to provide a sufficient income to meet basic subsistence needs such as food, health, and housing (Government of Ontario, 2018). Single recipients received $16,989, while couples received $24,027 per year for a period of up to three years. An additional $500 each month was provided to persons with disabilities (Segal, 2016). When basic income recipients enrolled, OW provided $721 to singles and ODSP provided $1151 per month. On OBIP, singles received up to $1415.75 per month, which therefore represented a 96.25% increase over the previous OW benefit. Individuals with disabilities received up to $1915.75, which accordingly represented a 66.44% increase over the previous ODSP benefit (Ferdosi & McDowell, 2020, p. 8).

Recipients were permitted to go to school and/or work while receiving basic income. The pilot clawed back 50 cents for every dollar an individual earned through employment, meaning married basic income recipients could earn more than $64,000 per year while still receiving some monetary benefit from the pilot.

Four thousand recipients between the ages of 18 and 64 were chosen for the pilot from three communities across Ontario. The communities of Hamilton, Brantford and Brant County, Thunder Bay and surrounding communities, and Lindsay were chosen as the three sample sites. In both Hamilton/Brantford and Thunder Bay, 1000 recipients were selected to receive benefits, in addition to an unreported number of members who belonged to the comparison group.

The pilot employed RCTs, primarily in urban areas, where participants were randomly assigned to different treatment groups receiving varying levels of basic income or existing welfare benefits. It prioritized quantitative metrics, focusing on individual-level outcomes such as labour market participation, health and well-being, life and career choices, work behaviour, and education (Segal, 2016, p. 7).

Although the program was initially planned to last three years, a newly elected Progressive Conservative government prematurely terminated it in 2019, cutting off payments to recipients and ending the evaluation component before any meaningful data could be collected. Consequently, many recipients received only up to two years of basic income support, and the pilot's full potential and long-term effects were not fully assessed (Ferdosi et al., 2020, p. 14).

The early termination of the pilot led to vigorous community initiatives to rescue the experiment, including attempts to collect existing data to preserve any knowledge gained from the experiment. Our research team, hailing from one of the pilot locations (Hamilton), offers a characteristic example of these efforts.

Limitations of OBIP's Research Design: A "Race-Evasive" Framework

Although OBIP provided comparatively generous benefits and a low take-back rate that had a meaningful impact on poverty reduction for recipients, its research design also reflected a substantial methodological oversight that limited its capacity to examine poverty as a structurally embedded phenomenon (McDowell & Ferdosi, 2021, p. 16). Our evidence suggests that the pilot may have underrepresented Indigenous and other racialized communities.

In Hamilton, for example, racialized participants made up only 10.34% of our sample, despite comprising 19% of the population according to the 2016 Census, while Indigenous peoples accounted for just 5.21%, despite their well-documented and disproportionately high poverty rates (Statistics Canada, 2017b; Galabuzi, 2006, p. 72). Similarly, in Brantford, visible minorities represent 9.8% of the population (Statistics Canada, 2017a).

Although our findings indicate a lack of racialized representation, we cannot confirm whether this was the case for the pilot as a whole, as we did not have access to the complete participant list due to its premature cancellation. Instead, we relied on self-selected participation, which may have skewed demographic representation. We suggest that a methodological approach that conceives of individuals as isolated and abstracted from their social and historical context built these structural inequities into OBIP's research framework.

The report that provided the methodological framework for the pilot, *Finding a Better Way: A Basic Income Pilot Project for Ontario* (2016), was predisposed to a selection bias that underrepresented Indigenous and other racialized groups. Despite its focus on examining individual-level variables such as employment, health, and education, which are commonly regarded as indicators of poverty, the report does not critically engage with the structural conditions that give rise to poverty. Rather, the report frames poverty as a generalized condition that can be alleviated through individual interventions like basic income. In doing so, it overlooks how intersecting structural inequalities contribute to the persistence of poverty.Karl Marx's critique of abstraction helps to illuminate the theoretical limitations of OBIP's approach. In the *Grundrisse*, Marx warns against the tendency of political economy to abstract from the historical and social relations that constitute economic categories:

> This method of rising from the abstract to the concrete is the only one which corresponds to the nature of scientific abstraction, the construction of the concrete as a result of many determinations (Marx, 1973, p. 101).

That is, any scientific understanding of society must begin from real, historically grounded relations rather than isolated, idealized categories.

A critical methodology from a Marxist perspective, then, should move from concrete relations to abstract ideas and then reconstruct the concrete totality from multiple determinations, establishing a conceptual framework grounded in actual, rather than imagined, categories. By isolating the issue of poverty from its broader social and historical context, OBIP bracketed out the interlocking effects of race, class, and colonialism from its analysis. A Marxist approach to poverty views it not as the result of individual failings but as the product of exploitative economic relations and colonial histories that limit opportunities for marginalized communities.

This concern is particularly evident in the selection of pilot sites. The pilot did not collect data on participants' race or Indigenous identity, making it impossible to assess whether Indigenous or other racialized groups were adequately represented. Only one of the three communities selected for OBIP, Thunder Bay in Northern Ontario, has a significant Indigenous population.

Furthermore, Brantford borders Six Nations, the most heavily populated Reservation in Canada, but for unknown reasons its residents were excluded from participation in the pilot. The selection criteria offered by Premier Wynne (as cited by Global News, 2017), who explained the sites represented "a mix" of population and demographic variables, provided little evidence of attention to structural inequalities or to racialized poverty as a primary criterion.

A structurally transformative basic income initiative would reject the colonial logics embedded in conventional welfare systems by centring participatory governance and community sovereignty in its design. An inclusive model of basic income implementation would involve the co-design of enrolment protocols in partnership with Indigenous and other racialized communities. These criteria would allow for the inclusion of individuals often excluded by formal means-testing frameworks (Beresford & Degerickx, 2021, p. 170). The result would be a policy mechanism capable not only of alleviating poverty but also of transcending the structures that produce Indigenous and racialized precarity.

Methodology

Hamilton and its surrounding areas, including Brantford, were selected as test sites for the Ontario Basic Income Pilot. Hamilton, with a population of approximately 536,000 and a poverty rate of nearly 15%, and Brantford, with around 97,000 residents and a poverty rate of 15.5 % (Statistics Canada, 2017a; Statistics Canada,

2017b), provided a critical backdrop for our mixed-methods study, which combined quantitative and qualitative analyses to evaluate the effects of OBIP on well-being.

Our quantitative component consisted of a 70-question online survey administered through McMaster University's Lime Survey service from January to August 2019. The survey, completed by 217 former recipients from Hamilton, Brantford, and Brant County, aimed to capture indicators of well-being, including mental health, depression, and confidence. Participants responded using a three-point Likert scale to indicate the frequency or quality of their experiences. Survey responses were analyzed using Stata software, providing structured insights into how basic income affected well-being.

For each well-being indicator, we presented two descriptive tables: one evaluating its relationship with the income amount and the other with enrolment duration. This allowed us to determine whether higher income or longer enrolment correlated with improved well-being. By examining both benefit levels and duration, we explored how basic income alleviates stress in absolute and temporal terms. Higher benefit levels provided immediate financial relief, while longer enrolment reduced chronic stress from ongoing income instability.

The qualitative aspect of our study involved in-depth interviews with 48 OBIP recipients from Hamilton and Brantford, conducted between June and August 2019. Interviewees were selected from nearly 80 individuals who expressed interest and participated in semi-structured, open-ended interviews lasting about 90 minutes. These interviews provided detailed personal insights into the social and psychological transformations experienced during OBIP. Interviewees provided proof of their enrolment (in the form of government documentation in most cases) and were compensated with C$100 for their participation. Nearly all interviewees informed us that they had completed the survey as well.

Our team utilized NVivo, a qualitative data analysis software, to systematically analyze and identify recurring themes. The coding process involved an iterative and inductive approach, where initial codes were generated, reviewed, and refined to develop broader themes. NVivo's features allowed us to maintain an audit trail of the coding process, enhancing the transparency and credibility of our findings. Initially, the transcripts were imported into the NVivo environment, where they were organized and prepared for coding.

After familiarizing ourselves with the content of each transcript, we began the coding process by identifying salient phrases, keywords, and concepts that appeared repeatedly across the interviews. Thematic analysis was employed to transcribe and analyze the interviews, identifying key themes such as improved overall health, financial security and independence, and reduced poverty stigma (Braun & Clarke, 2019, p. 5).

We report upon the following qualitative themes: (1) improved financial security and independence; (2) improved overall health; (3) reduced stigmatization; 4) reduced utilization of addictive substances. To facilitate the coding process within NVivo, we created a set of thematic nodes representing the emergent themes. As we reviewed the transcripts, relevant text segments were assigned to the appropriate thematic nodes. This iterative process involved ongoing revisions based on continuous analysis.

The mixed-methods approach allowed us to combine broad, measurable patterns from the quantitative data with the depth and context offered by the qualitative interviews. This integration provided a more comprehensive understanding of OBIP's effects on well-being, particularly in terms of financial and psychological impacts. As Creswell (2014, p. 16) notes, mixed-methods research is particularly beneficial in addressing complex social issues because it allows for the examination of both quantitative trends and personal narratives. This approach enables us to draw stronger, more nuanced relationships to our quantitative evidence, enhancing the validity of our findings.

Given that our study was conducted in the wake of OBIP's controversial cancellation, the study is limited by several factors. First, we accessed responses from only 217 recipients for the quantitative portion, a number far lower than the approximately 4000 recipients involved in the pilot and in most other guaranteed income experiments.

Second, we cannot guarantee that participant responses are representative of the experiences of the 1000 former recipients in the Hamilton-Brantford site. Since we did not have access to a list of recipients in our region for a random sample, our recruitment methods relied on individuals who were willing to learn about our study to complete the survey and reach out for an interview.

Third, there are potential issues of reliability due to our reliance on self-reported data. We attempted to address this issue by including three verification questions: one question asked participants for a government-issued Ontario 12-digit number in a comment box, while two less intrusive multiple-choice questions requested the total number of characters in the respondent's reference number and the colour of the stripe appearing at the bottom of the correspondence letters.

Fourth, the generalizability of our study was limited by its focus on only one of the three test sites. Consequently, we can only draw conclusions about the effects of OBIP in the Hamilton region. We also lacked access to administrative data available to pilot evaluators, such as hospital or prison records, which would have allowed us to analyze broader social trends.

Fifth, given the pilot's early cancellation, most recipients received basic income for less than 17 months, making the longer-term impacts of a guaranteed income impossible to assess. Consequently, we cannot determine what the benefits of OBIP could have been if it had been carried out for its full duration.

Sixth, we lacked access to a control or comparison group with which to compare our results, relying instead on recipients' self-assessments of their experiences receiving basic income relative to those before the pilot.

Seventh, everyone who completed our survey did so months after the cancellation was announced, complicating the interpretation of their responses. Before payments to recipients ended on March 29, 2019, 139 survey respondents had completed the survey, while 78 completed it on or after March 30, 2019. Interviews were conducted by the end of August 2019, raising the possibility that some participants may have had difficulty recalling their experiences while receiving basic income.

Impacts of Basic Income Amounts and Enrolment Periods on Mental Health and Substance Use

In this section, we examine the effects of basic income security on various quality-of-life measurements, beginning with an overview of participant demographics and moving to an analysis of mental health outcomes and substance use patterns. The following tables provide a detailed breakdown of our findings, starting with the age, gender, racial minority, and Indigenous identification of participants, and concluding with changes in alcohol and tobacco consumption. By focusing on monthly benefit levels and duration of time spent on the pilot program, we assess how these factors influence well-being and some of the social determinants of mental health.

We hypothesized that higher monthly basic income levels and longer enrolment in the pilot would positively correlate with mental health outcomes, including reduced stress, improved access to healthcare, an enhanced outlook on life, as well as a reduction in the utilization of substances. This suggests that greater financial stability and long-term support can contribute to overall well-being and better mental health and lower rates of addiction. Approximately 1000 low-income individuals from Hamilton and Brantford were enrolled in OBIP, with nearly 84% of the 217 survey respondents coming from Hamilton. Participants joined at different times, with enrolment durations varying from mid-2017 to mid-2018.

The demographic data reveal that the majority of participants were between the ages of 25 and 44 (58.87%), with smaller proportions in the 18-24 (7.01%) and over-55 (11.21%) age groups. In terms of gender, 56.02% of respondents identified as female, 42.59% as male, and 1.39% as other genders, including gender non-conforming, two-spirit, and transgender individuals.

Among the respondents, over 60% received basic income for less than 17 months, while nearly 40% received it for 17 months or longer. Specifically, enrolment breakdowns were as follows: 29.03% for 5–12 months, 33.18% for 13–16 months, 23.04% for 17–20 months, and 14.75% for 21–26 months. The pilot targeted low-income individuals aged 18 to 64, with almost 60% of respondents aged between 25 and 44.

In addition to mental health outcomes, this section also explores changes in addictive substance use, including alcohol and tobacco consumption, among participants. These findings provide further insight into how basic income may influence health behaviours and coping mechanisms. By examining these interrelated factors, we aim to offer a comprehensive understanding of the broader impacts of basic income on quality of life (Table 4.1).

Table 4.1 Personal identification (racialized minority)

Racialized	Freq.	Percent	Cum.
No	182	89.66	89.66
Yes	21	10.34	100.00
Total	203	100.00	

Table 4.2 Personal identification (Indigenous)

Indigenous	Freq.	Percent	Cum.
No	200	94.79	94.79
Yes	11	5.21	100.00
Total	211	100.00	

Table 4.3 OBIP benefit levels (general)

Monthly basic income	Freq.	Percent	
<$699	16	7.44	
$700–$1399	96	44.65	
$1400–$1999	92	42.79	
>$2000	11	5.12	
Total	215 (n)	100.00	

Table 4.4 OBIP duration (general)

Enrolment duration	Freq.	Percent	
<13 months	63	29.03	
13–17 months	72	33.18	
17–21 months	50	23.04	
21–27 months	32	14.75	
Total	217 (n)	100.00	

The table presents participants' responses regarding whether they identify as a member of a racialized minority group. The vast majority of respondents (89.66%) indicated "No", while a smaller proportion (10.34%) identified themselves as members of a racialized minority group. The cumulative percentage shows that most participants (89.66%) do not identify as racialized minorities, reflecting the demographic composition of the sample. This distribution highlights the predominance of non-racialized individuals in the study population (Table 4.2).

The table presents participants' responses regarding whether they identify as Indigenous. The vast majority of respondents (94.79%) indicated "No", while a smaller proportion (5.21%) identified as Indigenous. The cumulative percentage shows that most participants (94.79%) do not identify as Indigenous. This distribution highlights the limited representation of Indigenous individuals in the study population (Table 4.3).

Table 4.4 displays subgroups within our survey sample, showing different monthly basic income amounts received. The majority (87.44%) received between $700 and $1999, while the remainder either received below $699 or exceeded $2000 per month.

These data present the mental health and substance use outcomes of OBIP survey respondents categorized by enrolment duration. It shows the percentage of respondents reporting somewhat or much worse, about the same, or somewhat or much better mental health and substance use across four duration categories. In the

Table 4.5 Benefit levels and overall mental health

Mental health during OBIP	Clusters of survey participants categorized by the level of monthly basic income received				
	<$699	$700–$1399	$1400–$1999	>$2000	
Somewhat or much worse	14.29	4.26	12.50	9.09	
About the same	28.57	3.19	11.36	9.09	
Somewhat or much better	57.14	92.55	76.14	81.82	
Total (n)	14	94	88	11	207

Table 4.6 Duration of pilot and overall mental health

Mental health during OBIP	Clusters of survey participants categorized by duration of enrolment in the pilot				
	<13 months	13–17 months	17–21 months	>21 months	
Somewhat or much worse	13.33	13.04	0.00	3.13	
About the same	13.33	7.25	6.25	6.25	
Somewhat or much better	73.33	79.71	93.75	90.63	
Total	60	69	48	32	209

"Somewhat or much better" category, a higher proportion of respondents experiencing improved mental health is found in the longer enrolment groups (13–17 months, 17–21 months, and >21 months), suggesting that longer enrolment in OBIP is associated with improved mental health outcomes. Comparing the two datasets indicates that positive outcomes generally increase with higher basic income levels and longer enrolment durations (Table 4.5).

These data present the mental health outcomes of survey respondents during the pilot, categorized by the level of monthly basic income received. It shows the percentage of respondents across four basic income clusters who experienced somewhat or much worse, about the same, or somewhat or much better mental health. Notably, in the "Somewhat or much better" category, a higher proportion of respondents reporting improved well-being is found in the three higher basic income clusters: (1) $700–$1399: 92.55%; (2) $1400–$1999: 76.14%; and (3) >$2000: 81.82%. In contrast, only 57.14% of respondents in the lowest income cluster (<$699) reported somewhat or much better mental well-being. This suggests that higher levels of basic income correlate with improved mental well-being among respondents (Table 4.6).

This table presents the mental health outcomes of survey respondents during OBIP, categorized by the duration of enrolment in the pilot. It shows the percentage of participants in four different duration clusters (<13 months, 13–17 months, 17–21 months, >21 months) who reported their mental health as "somewhat or much worse", "about the same", or "somewhat or much better" during their participation. Notably, in the "Somewhat or much better" category, the proportion of respondents reporting improved mental well-being increases with longer enrolment in the pilot. For instance, 93.75% of respondents enrolled for 17–21 months and 90.63% of

Table 4.7 Depression

Depressed during OBIP	Clusters of survey participants categorized by the level of monthly basic income received				
	<$699	$700–$1399	$1400–$1999	>$2000	
Somewhat or much less often	41.67	94.44	77.65	90.00	
About the same	25.00	1.11	10.59	0.00	
Somewhat or much more often	33.33	4.44	11.76	10.00	
Total	12	90	85	10	197

Table 4.8 Depression

Depressed during OBIP	Clusters of survey participants categorized by duration of enrolment in the pilot				
	<13 months	13–16 months	17–21 months	>21 months	
Somewhat or much less often	78.18	75.38	93.75	93.55	
About the same	5.45	10.77	6.25	3.23	
Somewhat or much more often	16.36	13.85	0.00	3.23	
Total	55	65	48	31	199

those enrolled for over 21 months reported better mental health, compared to 73.33% of those enrolled for less than 13 months. Meanwhile, those reporting "somewhat or much worse" mental health outcomes are concentrated in the shorter duration groups, with 13.33% in the <13 months category and only 3.13% in the >21 months group. These findings suggest that longer participation in the basic income pilot is associated with better mental health outcomes, potentially highlighting the importance of sustained income security over time in improving well-being (Table 4.7).

The data indicate the frequency of depression among survey participants during the pilot, categorized by their monthly basic income levels. In the "Somewhat or much less often" category, respondents receiving higher basic income levels ($700–$1399, $1400–$1900, and >$2000) more frequently report experiencing fewer episodes of depression. In contrast, fewer than half of those in the lowest income group (<$699) report similar experiences. This suggests a correlation between higher basic income levels and a decrease in depression frequency among respondents (Table 4.8).

The data reveal a relationship in the "Somewhat or much less often" category, showing that a higher proportion of respondents experiencing fewer episodes of depression are among those enrolled for 17–21 months and over 21 months, with these proportions exceeding 90%. In contrast, shorter enrolment durations (over 13 months and 13–16 months) yield lower proportions. This indicates that longer enrolment in OBIP is associated with decreased depression frequency among respondents. A comparison of the datasets infers that a lower frequency of

Table 4.9 Stress and anxiety

Stress/anxiety during OBIP	Clusters of survey participants categorized by the level of monthly basic income received				
	<$699	$700–$1399	$1400–$1999	>$2000	
Somewhat or much less often	58.33	93.41	82.56	90.91	
About the same	16.67	2.20	2.33	0.00	
Somewhat or much more often	25.00	4.40	15.12	9.09	
Total	12	91	86	11	200

Table 4.10 Stress and anxiety

Stress/anxiety during OBIP	Clusters of survey participants categorized by duration of enrolment in the pilot				
	<13 months	13–16 months	17–21 months	>21 months	
Somewhat or much less often	77.19	81.82	97.96	93.33	
About the same	7.02	1.52	2.04	0.00	
Somewhat or much more often	15.79	16.67	0.00	6.67	
Total	57	66	49	30	202

depression correlates with higher basic income levels and longer enrolment durations (Table 4.9).

A relationship is evident in the "Somewhat or much less often" category, where a greater percentage of participants reported experiencing stress and anxiety less frequently, particularly among the latter three groups who received higher levels of basic income support. Once again, the data indicate that higher levels of basic income are connected with more significant improvements (Table 4.10).

The data show a relationship in the "Somewhat or much less often" category, with a higher proportion of respondents experiencing less stress and anxiety among those enrolled for 17–21 months and over 21 months. Conversely, the shortest enrolment duration group reported the lowest proportion of reduced stress and anxiety. This suggests that the longer individuals receive basic income support, the less likely they are to experience stress and anxiety. Comparing the datasets, participants receiving higher basic income levels and those with longer enrolment durations generally report lower stress and anxiety levels. Stress and anxiety decrease with higher basic income levels and longer durations of enrolment, but this decrease does not follow a consistent pattern with increasing basic income levels (Table 4.11).

The data suggest a positive correlation between the level of monthly basic income received and participants' confidence during the pilot. As the amount of basic income received increases, the percentage of participants reporting an improvement in confidence also increases (Table 4.12).

The data indicate a correlation between enrolment duration and participants' confidence levels. As enrolment duration increases, the percentage of participants

Table 4.11 Confidence

Confidence during OBIP	Clusters of survey participants categorized by the level of monthly basic income received				
	<$699	$700–$1399	$1400–$1999	>$2000	
Somewhat or much worse	16.67	2.20	10.34	9.09	
About the same	50.00	10.99	9.20	0.00	
Somewhat or much better	33.33	86.81	80.46	90.91	
Total	12	91	87	11	201

Table 4.12 Confidence

Confidence during OBIP	Clusters of survey participants categorized by duration of enrolment in the pilot				
	<13 months	13–16 months	17–21 months	>21 months	
Somewhat or much worse	13.79	7.69	0.00	3.23	
About the same	8.62	16.92	12.24	9.68	
Somewhat or much better	77.59	75.38	87.76	87.10	
Total	58	65	49	31	203

reporting improved confidence also rises. Specifically, those enrolled for 17 months or longer show over 87% reporting increased confidence, compared to shorter enrolment periods. Both the level of basic income and duration of enrolment influence confidence.

Reductions in Substance Use as a Downstream Effect of Financial Security

Quantitative and qualitative data reveal that reductions in alcohol and tobacco use were strongly associated with improved mental health, supporting our hypothesis that substance use declines as a secondary effect of lowered stress levels. Participants receiving higher benefit levels or longer durations of support were 20–30% more likely to report reduced substance use (Tables 4.13, 4.14, 4.15 and 4.16), with qualitative interviews attributing these changes to diminished financial anxiety. Notably, these effects were not uniform: those with the lowest incomes (<$699/month) saw smaller reductions, suggesting that benefit adequacy mediates substance use outcomes.

Our findings indicate that a higher proportion of respondents reported reduced tobacco consumption among those enrolled for 17–21 months and over 21 months, compared to those who received OBIP for a shorter period. Conversely, the group with the shortest enrolment duration reported the lowest proportion of decreased tobacco use. This suggests that the longer individuals receive basic income support, the more likely they are to reduce their consumption of tobacco products. Comparing the datasets, participants receiving higher basic income levels and those with longer

Table 4.13 Tobacco consumption

Tobacco	Months_new				
	<13 months	13–17 months	17–21 months	>21 months	Total
Somewhat or much less often	10	17	12	10	49
	16.67	25.00	25.00	31.25	23.56
Quit tobacco use during pilot	3	7	8	3	21
	5.00	10.29	16.67	9.38	10.10
About the same	17	16	7	7	47
	28.33	23.53	14.58	21.88	22.60
Somewhat or much more often	4	3	0	0	7
	6.67	4.41	0.00	0.00	3.37
Never used tobacco	26	25	21	12	84
	43.33	36.76	43.75	37.50	40.38
Total	60	68	48	32	208
	100.00	100.00	100.00	100.00	100.00

Table 4.14 Tobacco consumption

Tobacco	Income				
	<699	700–1399	1400–1999	>2000	Total
Somewhat or much less often	0	26	18	5	49
	0.00	27.96	20.45	45.45	23.79
Quit tobacco use during pilot	2	9	7	3	21
	14.29	9.68	7.95	27.27	10.19
About the same	4	20	21	2	47
	28.57	21.51	23.86	18.18	22.82
Somewhat or much more often	1	0	6	0	7
	7.14	0.00	6.82	0.00	3.40
Never used tobacco	7	38	36	1	82
	50.00	40.86	40.91	9.09	39.81
Total	14	93	88	11	206
	100.00	100.00	100.00	100.00	100.00

enrolment durations generally reported lower levels of tobacco use. Tobacco consumption decreases with higher basic income levels and longer durations of enrolment, though this decrease does not follow a consistent pattern as basic income levels increase.

Nearly one-quarter of respondents who received at least $700 per month in basic income support reported reduced tobacco consumption. This evidence suggests that higher levels of basic income are associated with a greater likelihood of decreased tobacco use. Participants receiving higher basic income levels generally reported lower levels of tobacco consumption, though this decrease does not follow a consistent pattern across all income brackets.

Table 4.15 Alcohol consumption

Alcohol	Income				
	<699	700–1399	1400–1999	>2000	Total
Somewhat or much less often	2	30	30	2	64
	14.29	31.91	34.09	18.18	30.92
Quit drinking alcohol during pilot	0	3	3	1	7
	0.00	3.19	3.41	9.09	3.38
About the same	4	33	28	3	68
	28.57	35.11	31.82	27.27	32.85
Somewhat or much more often	0	5	2	3	10
	0.00	5.32	2.27	27.27	4.83
Never drank alcohol	8	23	25	2	58
	57.14	24.47	28.41	18.18	28.02
Total	14	94	88	11	207
	100.00	100.00	100.00	100.00	100.00

Table 4.16 Alcohol consumption

Alcohol	Months_new				
	<13 months	13–17 months	17–21 months	>21 months	Total
Somewhat or much less often	11	21	21	11	64
	18.33	30.88	42.86	34.38	30.62
Quit drinking alcohol during pilot	3	2	1	1	7
	5.00	2.94	2.04	3.13	3.35
About the same	22	18	17	11	68
	36.67	26.47	34.69	34.38	32.54
Somewhat or much more often	2	3	4	1	10
	3.33	4.41	8.16	3.13	4.78
Never drank alcohol	22	24	6	8	60
	36.67	35.29	12.24	25.00	28.71
Total	60	68	49	32	209
	100.00	100.00	100.00	100.00	100.00

About one-fifth of respondents who received more than $700 per month in basic income support reported reduced alcohol consumption compared to before joining the program. This suggests that higher levels of basic income are associated with a greater likelihood of decreased alcohol use. Comparing the datasets, participants receiving higher basic income levels generally reported lower levels of alcohol consumption, though this decrease does not follow a consistent pattern across all income brackets. The findings indicate that financial support, particularly at higher levels, may contribute to reductions in alcohol use, potentially by alleviating stress or providing resources for healthier lifestyle choices.

Nearly one-third of respondents who received OBIP for longer than 13 months reported reduced alcohol consumption compared to before joining the program. This suggests that longer durations of basic income support are associated with a greater likelihood of decreased alcohol use. When combined with findings from the previous table, which showed that about one-fifth of those receiving more than $700 per month also reported reduced alcohol consumption, the data indicate that both higher income levels and longer enrolment durations contribute to lower levels of alcohol use.

Summary of Quantitative Findings

The findings from the OBIP reveal a strong connection between mental health improvements and enhanced well-being. Participants reported significant improvements in mental health outcomes, including reduced stress, anxiety, and depression, along with increased confidence. One of the most notable findings was a reduction in stress and anxiety, especially among those who received higher income levels and longer durations of support. By alleviating financial insecurity and providing a stable income, basic income helped to reduce the psychological burden of poverty. Participants enrolled for 17 months or longer reported significantly lower levels of stress and anxiety.

In addition to reductions in stress and anxiety, the data reveal consistent improvements across a broader range of mental health indicators, particularly among those receiving higher monthly payments and longer durations of support. Participants receiving more than $700 per month or enrolled for over 17 months were significantly more likely to report experiencing fewer episodes of depression, greater emotional stability, and a more optimistic outlook on life. These improvements were not merely marginal. As seen in Tables 4.5 through 4.10, more than 90% of participants in the highest duration groups reported somewhat or much better mental health, and similar trends appear in measures of reduced depression and anxiety. These findings suggest that mental health gains were not incidental but integral to the OBIP's impact, emerging as a direct consequence of sustained income security. For many, basic income alleviated the chronic psychological effects of financial instability, such as the persistent worry of meeting basic needs or the mental strain of long-term unemployment.

While use of addictive substances was not the primary focus of this analysis, reductions in alcohol and tobacco consumption were observed as a likely downstream impact of the mental health improvements. Participants who reported better mental health were more likely to reduce alcohol or tobacco use (Tables 4.13, 4.14, 4.15 and 4.16). This connection was later affirmed by our qualitative research, where participants frequently linked their reduced use of alcohol or tobacco to lower stress levels and improved financial independence, rather than the income itself. For instance, those who smoked less often cited decreased stress and greater financial freedom as key factors.

Participants who reported mental health improvements were more likely to reduce their alcohol and tobacco consumption. Nearly one-third of those enrolled for longer than 13 months reported drinking less, and one-fifth of those receiving more than $700 per month reported similar outcomes. Additionally, a higher proportion of participants enrolled for 17–21 months and over 21 months reported reduced tobacco use. By targeting the root causes of stress, basic income may have indirectly supported participants in developing healthier coping mechanisms.

However, these findings should be interpreted within the context of a sample that was predominantly non-racialized. Only 10.34% of participants identified as members of racialized minority groups, and just 5.21% identified as Indigenous. This limited representation raises questions about the extent to which these mental health and addictive substance use outcomes can be generalized to populations that face compounded structural barriers.

Given the well-documented links between race, poverty, and health disparities, the underrepresentation of Indigenous and other racialized communities in the sample constrains the study's ability to fully capture how systemic racism intersects with economic insecurity in shaping mental health and substance use outcomes. These limitations point to the need for more inclusive research approaches in future basic income experiments, ensuring that racialized and Indigenous populations are adequately represented and that their experiences with structural disadvantage are considered.

Qualitative Impacts of the Ontario Basic Income Pilot

Our interviews with participants confirmed the findings from our quantitative survey, providing critical context for understanding the observed improvements in overall health, confidence, and reductions in stress, anxiety, and depression. The income security provided by basic income played a central role in reducing various psychological stressors that, when combined, often lead to heightened stress and worsened mental health outcomes. Participants shared their experiences, highlighting how this financial stability alleviated the burdens associated with poverty, enabling them to focus on their well-being and fostering a sense of control over their lives.

"Your Whole Self Feels Better": Mental Health Effects of OBIP

The results from the Hamilton region depict a program with wide-ranging mental health benefits. Most participants reported that their overall mental health was somewhat or much better than before they began the pilot, improving several measures commonly associated with the psychological impacts of poverty. In addition to the general benefits of increased material security, recipients also reported improvements in some of the relative impacts of poverty that can contribute to mental illness.

During interviews, recipients described the broad range of benefits associated with a stable income. Three main patterns emerged:

First, improved financial security and independence provided by OBIP enabled recipients to pay off debts, cover essential expenses, and avoid financial stress. This is consistent with the literature demonstrating that financial stability contributes to improvements in mental health and well-being (Golberstein, 2015, p. 30). The support provided by OBIP enabled recipients to resolve financial crises and engage in long-term planning, allowing them to take steps to improve their overall health and well-being.

This income security also led to improved confidence and self-esteem as the stress associated with being unable to afford necessities was reduced.

For instance, a 34-year-old woman with Post-Traumatic Stress Disorder from severe abuse who received $1800 per month for 14 months was "physically and mentally healthier" because she no longer worried about having enough money to pay the rent or afford to eat. "I had more confidence," she said. "I wasn't constantly living in survival mode on basic income, at least financially." This increased confidence led to her getting a paid job for the first time in her life. "Just to be working was kind of a big deal," she said.

The ability to assert control over one's own time and life circumstances was a common theme noted by participants. This is consistent with literature showing that real- or perceived-time pressures correlate negatively with mental health (Zuzanek, 1998, p. 30). One young woman who received $1400 per month for one year, for instance, recalled being in "a really bad place before the pilot", feeling "underpaid, stressed out, and hopeless". However, the reliability of OBIP support enabled her to take time off from work to "fix myself, my debts, and take a little better care of myself".

Second, participants also reported significant improvements in overall health, which played a crucial role in enhancing their mental well-being. Our findings align with other research that shows time spent in good physical health is essential to overall mental health (Ohrnberger et al., 2017, p. 45). As physical health problems could be more readily addressed, recipients experienced reduced stress and anxiety.

A 47-year-old woman who received basic income for 17 months recalled that while "stress and anxiety over money" previously caused debilitating "stomach issues", these health problems largely vanished while she was receiving OBIP. "I felt better because I was getting the proper food and able to socialize," she said. "When you are feeling better, your whole self feels better."

One 39-year-old woman who received $1800 per month for 12 months and had not been able to access "good counselling" while on OW was able to see "doctors who charged" for psychological support. With the ability to afford professional assistance, she improved her overall mental health and well-being, noting that many of these changes carried over into other areas of her life. "Basic income provided me with the opportunity to take care of myself," she said.

One family that received OBIP for 18 months was able to use the money they received from basic income to purchase a lift to help their disabled daughter. "There have been times when she has broken multiple bones at once, so she could have casts everywhere on her body. She would have a very hard time going up the stairs. The movement upstairs could cause her to break a bone. We would also have to watch her cry because she's in pain, bumping around," her mother said. "The lift in the home was really great. She had a broken hip once, and she couldn't go up the stairs at all. With the lift, she could use it on her own as well."

Thirdly, our findings suggest that basic income effectively mitigates the effects of relative poverty, leading to substantial destigmatizing impacts. By reducing the feelings of shame and humiliation commonly associated with low income, basic income enabled recipients to feel more valued and respected by their peers (Foster, 2021, p. 490). Our findings, which align with previous studies demonstrating a relationship between basic income and a reduction in stigma, show that it provided recipients with the financial means to improve living conditions and manage finances, leading to an enhanced self-image, increased confidence, and improved social relationships (Calnitsky, 2016, p. 35). Recipients reported feeling more empowered and able to engage fully in social life, contributing to a greater sense of respect and inclusion within their communities.

One 24-year-old man, who previously worked in the retail sector before receiving $1900 of income support per month for 12 months while receiving OBIP, claimed the "humiliation" of life in poverty caused him to attempt suicide three times in the five years leading up to his enrolment in OBIP. However, basic income enabled him to attend university, which gave him the kind of "upward social mobility" that reduced the stigma of poverty and caused him to feel more self-confident. "In a way, you could say basic income saved my life," he said. "I could very well have seen myself doing myself in."

Others recalled the mental health impacts of being able to purchase a new wardrobe. One man who received $1900 in support each month said basic income allowed him to purchase a new wardrobe for the first time in years, helping to improve his self-image. "Every moment I'm wearing these clothes I feel more dignity. It's like, look what I'm worthy of, look what my society says I'm worthy of, even though I'm unable to work because our system isn't set up for people like me to work," he said. "It's like, look what society says I'm worthy of."

From Stress to Stability: Reductions in the Use of Alcohol and Tobacco under OBIP

For many participants, reductions in stress and anxiety contributed to a general decrease in alcohol and cigarette consumption, as they felt empowered to make healthier choices. This aligns with research by Dawson et al. (2005, p. 454), which found that financial stress is a key predictor of alcohol misuse, and Lasser et al. (2000, p. 2607), who highlight the high prevalence of smoking among individuals with mental health conditions. By alleviating financial stress and providing a sense of stability, basic income created the conditions under which participants could focus on their well-being and gradually move away from substance use as a coping mechanism. These improvements in substance use are best understood as secondary effects of improved mental health brought about by income security.

This pattern is vividly illustrated by the experience of a 57-year-old woman who received about $1150 per month for 18 months through OBIP. The income security enabled her to enter a smoking cessation program because she felt she "had some hope". She reported that she "wasn't drinking as much and wasn't taking as many pills" while receiving basic income, because she "didn't have as much worry and stress". However, after the pilot was cancelled, she "just quit and took up smoking again". Her experience underscores the importance of sustained income support in maintaining these positive changes. The loss of financial stability reversed the mental health improvements she had made, resulting in resumed substance use.

Similarly, another participant reduced her smoking while receiving basic income, attributing this change to a reduction in stress. A 30-year-old woman, who received about $1500 per month in support for 16 months, exemplified this pattern. Prior to the pilot, she smoked frequently to cope with anxiety. However, she recalled that she was "smoking much less on basic income", because she was no longer "as stressed out". "I was coughing up blood before," she said. "I felt less need to smoke, and so I began to give up smoking." She explained that she had previously used smoking as a way to cope with stress, but with her mental health improving, the compulsion to use addictive substances lessened.

Basic income disrupted this cycle by providing her with financial stability and the flexibility to take control of her life. With the stress of financial insecurity alleviated, she was able to focus on improving her health and well-being. The reduction in stress and anxiety was a key factor in her decreased intake of alcohol and pills, as she no longer relied on these substances to cope.

Another important factor was the ability to take time off work to attend recovery programs. A 52-year-old woman who participated in the pilot for 16 months was able to take two months off from her job to enrol in an alcohol recovery treatment program. She highlighted the profound effects of income security on her ability to address her substance use. "I was drinking at the time before the pilot. I went to a treatment centre just maybe two months after I started, and then I've been in AA ever since," she said. "Basic income gave me comfort knowing I can go away, the mortgage will be paid, the bills will be paid, I don't have to worry about anything. … And then I can go look after myself and then come back."

The qualitative findings from OBIP reveal significant improvements in mental health among participants, largely attributed to the financial stability provided by basic income. Participants reported experiencing reduced anxiety and stress levels, as the assurance of a reliable income alleviated the pervasive concerns associated with financial insecurity (Ridley et al., 2020, p. 2). Many described a sense of liberation from the daily struggle to make ends meet, which allowed them to redirect their focus toward personal development and well-being. For some, this mental health improvement created the conditions that made them less dependent on addictive substances, reinforcing the hypothesis that reduced substance use is a downstream effect of improved mental health under conditions of income security.

In summary, our findings from OBIP demonstrate that income security leads to holistic benefits that alleviate some of poverty's cumulative effects. By reducing the psychological burden of chronic financial instability, OBIP created the conditions for improved mental health and, as a result, reduced reliance on substances as coping mechanisms.

Summary of Qualitative Findings

The qualitative findings from OBIP highlight the wide-ranging benefits of financial stability on participants' mental and physical health, as well as overall well-being. The income security provided by OBIP alleviated both psychological and material stressors associated with poverty, enabling individuals to focus on their health, build stronger relationships, and regain a sense of control over their lives. These improvements in mental health and reduced stress also had a carry-over effect, contributing to a reduction in substance use (Pearlin, 1999, p. 401). That is, participants noted that once stress was alleviated and their mental health improved, they became less reliant on alcohol and tobacco as coping mechanisms.

A central theme was the reduction in stress and anxiety, which participants consistently attributed to the financial stability provided by OBIP. With the immediate pressures of poverty eased, individuals reported feeling less overwhelmed and more capable of addressing their mental and physical needs. This enabled them to adopt healthier coping mechanisms and prioritize long-term well-being over short-term survival.

Improved confidence and self-esteem were also significant outcomes of the pilot. Participants described feeling more empowered and in control of their lives, which reduced the helplessness and worthlessness often associated with poverty. This change in self-perception not only enhanced their mental health but also encouraged healthier behaviours and decision-making. Participants also reported a sense of dignity and respect stemming from receiving income without the surveillance, conditionality, or punitive oversight typical of traditional welfare systems.

This absence of scrutiny was experienced as a reduction in stigmatization, thereby reducing participants' exposure to the constant moral judgment and bureaucratic monitoring that often accompany means-tested assistance (Wacquant, 2009, p. 72). Such destigmatizing effects could be especially impactful for Indigenous and other racialized groups, who are disproportionately subjected to both systemic poverty and institutional surveillance (Pulkingham et al., 2010, p. 267).

Reductions in substance use for some participants emerged as a carry-over effect of these overlapping benefits (Pearlin, 1999, p. 401). Participants consistently reported that improved mental health and reduced stress led directly to better life choices and a noticeable decrease in alcohol and tobacco consumption. They were also given the time and opportunity to step away from wage labour to attend recovery programs.

In sum, OBIP provided substantial, integral benefits across overlapping and intersecting areas of participants' lives, contributing to the profile of a happier, healthier, and more confident person. The unconditionality basic income provided relieved the pressures of life in poverty, enabling recipients to assert control over their circumstances and engage in long-term planning in ways consistent with their goals and aspirations.

Conclusion

Our study reinforces the finding that basic income substantially improves mental health. Participants reported significant reductions in stress, anxiety, and depression, coupled with increased confidence, stronger social relationships, and overall health. Our evidence suggests that reductions in the use of alcohol and tobacco emerged as a carry-over effect of the income security provided by OBIP (Pearlin, 1999, p. 401).

Three key findings emerge. First, participants experienced notable mental health benefits across various well-being measurements. In our quantitative survey and interviews, participants reported reductions in depression, anxiety, and anger, along with improvements in confidence and outlook on life. These findings align with Pearlin's (1989, p. 242) claim that poverty creates overlapping challenges that compound over time. OBIP provided participants with a stable financial foundation that reduced these cumulative stressors, enabling them to escape the burdens of poverty (Haushofer & Fehr, 2014, p. 862).

Second, we observed a strong correlation between general well-being and higher benefit amounts. While both benefit level and program duration were critical, higher benefit levels over longer periods played a significant role in improving mental health and overall well-being. Higher income enabled recipients to address financial crises and plan for the future, further enhancing their mental health, confidence, and self-esteem. These findings reinforce the notion that a sustained, adequate income over a longer duration is essential for alleviating the compounded stressors of poverty.

Longer participation in the program also led to more reliable, predictable lives and deeper, sustained improvements in mental health, although not to the same degree as benefit level. Those receiving basic income over extended periods showed better psychological resilience and more lasting benefits, reinforcing evidence that prolonged support addresses long-standing mental health and well-being issues that short-term relief cannot resolve (Haushofer & Fehr, 2014, p. 862).

Third, improvements in mental health resulted in a secondary, or carry-over, effect on alcohol and tobacco consumption (Pearlin, 1999, p. 401). The reductions in substance use observed in our study emerged primarily through the alleviation of the chronic stress associated with poverty, reducing participants' reliance on alcohol and tobacco as coping mechanisms rather than through direct behavioural conditioning. This bidirectional relationship, in which alleviating stress indirectly reduces substance use, aligns with existing research on the interconnected nature of mental health and substance use (Boden & Fergusson, 2011, p. 908; Mojtabai & Crum, 2013, p. 1658). Participants indicated that once their chronic stress and anxiety diminished, they were better able to make healthier choices, breaking the cycle in which stress drives addictive substance use and that same use further exacerbates mental health problems.

Stable financial support enabled participants to shift their focus from survival to pursuits such as self-care, education, and community work. This shift disrupted the "scarcity mindset" that often traps individuals in cycles of addictive substance use, as they were no longer preoccupied with immediate financial crises (Mullainathan & Shafir, 2013, p. 123). By alleviating this cognitive burden, basic income empowered participants to make healthier choices, breaking the bidirectional cycle in which stress drives addiction.

From a Marxist perspective, OBIP's findings suggest that basic income can begin to resolve some of the contradictions of market society by partially decommodifying the means of subsistence (Wright, 2006, p. 5). By providing unconditional income, the program disrupted the wage relation and temporarily loosened the grip of market dependence. Participants gained time, stability, and autonomy.

However, these gains were limited by the pilot's failure to engage with the racialized and colonial foundations of poverty in Canada. A structurally transformative basic income ought to do more than redistribute income; it must confront the systemic causes behind the historical production of inequality. Although our findings suggest that basic income can help disrupt the stress-substance use cycle, the pilot's underrepresentation of racialized communities (10.34% of our sample) limits our ability to assess its impact on those most exposed to intersecting forms of structural violence.

OBIP's reliance on methodological individualism overlooked critical structural factors such as race and class, which are essential to understanding both poverty and recovery. By failing to recognize how knowledge is shaped through colonial frameworks, and by excluding those most affected by systemic harm, OBIP reinforced dominant ways of knowing that marginalize alternative epistemologies and lived experience (Beresford & Degerickx, 2021).

Future pilots must therefore prioritize participatory co-design with racialized and Indigenous communities to ensure that redistributive efforts serve broader goals of social equity and justice (Gee & Ford, 2011; Boyd, 2015). A more holistic and structurally grounded approach would attend to the co-constitutive relationship between racism and capitalism and better address the structural foundations of poverty.

Beyond mere inclusion, a transformative basic income must dismantle the colonial and capitalist logics that individualize poverty and legitimize inequality. This entails rejecting means-testing, embedding restorative justice for Indigenous participants, and placing the voices of marginalized communities at the centre of program design (Simpson, 2017). Without this shift, even progressive policies such as basic income risk reproducing the very inequalities they seek to resolve by framing poverty as a behavioural issue rather than the outcome of structural injustice.

In sum, OBIP offered a glimpse into what partial decommodification can achieve in terms of improving mental health and reducing addiction, but it also revealed the limits of technocratic redistribution when severed from struggles for structural transformation. A genuinely ethical basic income must begin not with individual behaviour, but with a critique of the social relations that produce poverty.

References

Beresford, P., & Degerickx, H. (2021). Participatory pathways in social policymaking: Between rhetoric and reality. In K. Driessens & V. Lyssens-Danneboom (Eds.), *Involving service users in social work education, research and policy* (pp. 170–182). Bristol University Press.

Birnbaum, S., & De Wispelaere, J. (2021). Exit strategy or exit trap? Basic income and the "power to say no" in the age of precarious employment. *Socio-Economic Review, 19*(3), 909–927.

Block, S., Galabuzi, G. E., & Tranjan, R. (2019). *Canada's colour coded income inequality*. Canadian Centre for Policy Alternatives.

Boden, J. M., & Fergusson, D. M. (2011). Alcohol and depression. *Addiction, 106*(5), 906–914.

Boyd, S. (2015). *From Witches to Crack Moms: Women, Drug Law, and Policy* (2nd ed.). Carolina Academic Press.
Braun, V., & Clarke, V. (2019). Reflecting on reflexive thematic analysis. *Qualitative Research in Sport, Exercise and Health, 11*(4), 589–597.
Calnitsky, D. (2016). More normal than welfare: The Mincome experiment, stigma, and community experience. *Canadian Review of Sociology, 53*(1), 26–71.
Chouinard, V., & Crooks, V. A. (2005). Because they have all the power and I have none: State restructuring of income and employment supports and disabled women's lives in Ontario, Canada. *Disability & Society, 20*(1), 19–32.
Costello, E. J., Erkanli, A., Copeland, W., & Angold, A. (2010). Association of family income supplements in adolescence with development of psychiatric and substance use disorders in adulthood among an American Indian population. *JAMA, 303*(19), 1954–1960.
Coulthard, G. (2014). *Red skin, white masks: Rejecting the colonial politics of recognition.* Minneapolis: University of Minnesota Press.
Creswell, J. W. (2014). *Research design: Qualitative, quantitative, and mixed methods approaches* (4th ed.). SAGE Publications.
Dawson, D. A., Grant, B. F., & Ruan, W. J. (2005). The association between stress and drinking: Modifying effects of gender and vulnerability. *Alcohol and Alcoholism, 40*(5), 453–460.
Ferdosi, M., & McDowell, T. (2020). More than welfare: The experiences of employed and unemployed Ontario basic income recipients. *Basic Income Studies, 15*(2), 1–35.
Ferdosi, M., McDowell, T., Lewchuk, W., & Ross, S. (2020). *Southern Ontario's basic income experience.* McMaster University, Department of Labour Studies.
Forget, E. L. (2011). The town with no poverty: The health effects of a Canadian guaranteed annual income field experiment. *Canadian Public Policy, 37*(3), 283–305.
Foster, S. (2021). Socioeconomic status and mental illness stigma: How income level and social dominance orientation may help to perpetuate stigma. *Stigma and Health, 6*(4), 487–498.
Galabuzi, G. E. (2006). *Canada's economic apartheid: The social exclusion of racialized groups in the new century.* Canadian Scholars' Press.
Gee, G. C., & Ford, C. L. (2011). Structural racism and health inequities: Old issues, new directions. *DuBois Review: Social Science Research on Race, 8*(1), 115–132.
Gifford, E., & Humphreys, K. (2007). The psychological science of addiction. *Addiction, 102*(3), 352–361.
Global News. (2017, April 24). Ontario launches basic income pilot project in three cities. *Global News.* https://globalnews.ca/news/3399143/ontario-basic-income-pilot-project/
Golberstein, E. (2015). The effects of income on mental health: Evidence from the social security notch. *The Journal of Mental Health Policy and Economics, 18*(1), 27–35.
Haushofer, J., & Fehr, E. (2014). On the psychology of poverty. *Science, 344*(6186), 862–867.
Kalleberg, A. L. (2009). Precarious work, insecure workers: Employment relations in transition. *American Sociological Review, 74*(1), 1–22.
Kangas, O., Jauhiainen, S., Simanainen, M., & Ylikännö, M. (Eds.). (2019). *The basic income experiment 2017-2018 in Finland: Preliminary results.* Ministry of Social Affairs and Health.
Laenen, T. (2023). The popularity of basic income: A public opinion perspective. *Basic Income Studies, 18*(1), 1–20.
Lasser, K., Boyd, J. W., Woolhandler, S., Himmelstein, D. U., McCormick, D., & Bor, D. H. (2000). Smoking and mental illness: A population-based prevalence study. *JAMA, 284*(20), 2606–2610.
Lewchuk, W. (2016). The precarity penalty: How insecure employment disadvantages workers and their families. *Alternate Routes: A Journal of Critical Social Research, 27.*
Lightman, E., Vick, A., Herd, D., & Mitchell, A. (2009). 'Not disabled enough': Episodic disabilities and the Ontario disability support program. *Disability Studies Quarterly, 29*(3).
Maki, K. (2011). Neoliberal deviants and surveillance: Welfare recipients under the watchful eye of Ontario Works. *Canadian Review of Social Policy, 65*(66), 38–53.
Mani, A., Mullainathan, S., Shafir, E., & Zhao, J. (2013). Poverty impedes cognitive function. *Science, 341*(6149), 976–980.

Marinescu, I. (2018). *No strings attached: The behavioral effects of U.S. unconditional cash transfer programs*. NBER Working Paper No. 24337.
Marx, K.. (1964). *Economic and Philosophic Manuscripts of 1844*. Translated by M. Milligan. International Publishers. (Originally written, 1844; first published, 1932).
Marx, K. (1973). *Grundrisse: Foundations of the Critique of Political Economy*. Translated by M. Nicolaus. Vintage Books. (Originally written, 1857–1858).
McDowell, T., & Ferdosi, M. (2021). The impacts of the Ontario Basic Income Pilot: A comparative analysis of the findings from the Hamilton region. *Basic Income Studies, 16*(2), 209–256.
McEwen, B. S. (1998). Stress, adaptation, and disease: Allostasis and allostatic load. *Annals of the New York Academy of Sciences, 840*(1), 33–44.
Miliband, R. (1969). *The state in capitalist society*. Basic Books.
Mojtabai, R., & Crum, R. M. (2013). Cigarette smoking and onset of mood and anxiety disorders. *American Journal of Public Health, 103*(9), 1656–1665.
Moncrieff, J. (2022). The political economy of the mental health system. *Frontiers in Sociology,* 17 (6): 771-875.
Mullainathan, S., & Shafir, E. (2013). *Scarcity: Why having too little means so much*. Picador.
Murali, V., & Oyebode, F. (2004). Poverty, social inequality, and mental health. *Advances in Psychiatric Treatment, 10*(3), 216–224.
Nunes, E. V., & Levin, F. R. (2004). Treatment of depression in patients with alcohol or other substance use disorders: A critical review of the evidence. *Journal of Substance Abuse Treatment, 27*(2), 105–119.
O'Connor, J. (1973). *The fiscal crisis of the state*. St. Martin's Press.
Ohrnberger, J., Fichera, E., & Sutton, M. (2017). The relationship between physical and mental health: A mediation analysis. *Social Science & Medicine, 195*, 42–49.
Pearlin, L. (1989). The sociological study of stress. *Journal of Health and Social Behaviour, 30*(3), 241–256.
Pearlin, L. I. (1999). The stress process revisited. In C. S. Aneshensel & J. C. Phelan (Eds.), *Handbook of the sociology of mental health* (pp. 395–415). Springer.
Pulkingham, J., Fuller, S., & Kershaw, P. (2010). Lone motherhood, welfare reform, and active citizen subjectivity. *Critical Social Policy, 30*(2), 267–291.
Ridley, M., Rao, G., Schilbach, F., & Patel, V. (2020). Poverty, depression, and anxiety: Causal evidence and mechanisms. *Science, 370*(6522).
Robinson, C. (1983). *Black Marxism: The making of the Black radical tradition*. University of North Carolina Press.
Ruckert, A., Huynh, C., & Labonté, R. (2018). Reducing health inequities: Is universal basic income the way forward? *Journal of Public Health, 40*(1), 3–7.
Segal, H. (2016). *Finding a better way: A basic income pilot project for Ontario* (pp. 1–101). Government of Ontario. https://www.ontario.ca/page/finding-better-way-basic-income-pilot-project-ontario
Simpson, L. B. (2017). *As we have always done: Indigenous freedom through radical resistance*. University of Minnesota Press.
Standing, G. (2011). *The precariat: The new dangerous class*. Bloomsbury Academic.
Statistics Canada. (2017a). Census profile, 2016 census: Brantford [Population centre], Ontario and Ontario [Province]. *Statistics Canada*. Catalogue no. 98-316-X2016001.
Statistics Canada. (2017b). Focus on geography series, 2016 census: Hamilton, Ontario. *Statistics Canada*. Catalogue no. 98-404-X2016001.
Thoits, P., & Hannan, M. (1979). Income and psychological distress: The impact of an income-maintenance experiment. *Journal of Health and Social Behaviour, 20*, 120–138.
Truth and Reconciliation Commission of Canada. (2015). *Honouring the truth, reconciling for the future: Summary of the final report of the Truth and Reconciliation Commission of Canada*. McGill-Queen's University Press.
Virdee, S. (2019). Racialized capitalism: An account of its contested origins and consolidation. *The Sociological Review, 67*(1), 3–27.

Wacquant, L. (2009). *Punishing the poor: The neoliberal government of social insecurity*. Duke University Press.
Widerquist, K. (2006). The bottom line in a basic income experiment. *Basic Income Studies, 1*(2), 1–5.
Wright, E. O. (2006). Basic income as a socialist project. *Basic Income Studies, 1*(1), 1–10.
Zuzanek, J. (1998). Time use, time pressure, personal stress, mental health, and life satisfaction from a life cycle perspective. *Journal of Occupational Science, 5*(1), 26–39.

Chapter 5
Implications of Climate Change on Gender Roles: The Effects of Climate Change on the Socio-economic Development of Women, Children, and Young People in Magarini Sub-County, Kilifi County, Kenya

Johnson Nzau Mavole and Mary Syokoli Mutisya

Abstract In Magarini Sub-County, where natural resources serve as the primary livelihood source for most residents, the sustainability of these resources heavily depends on favorable weather conditions. However, the effects of climate change exacerbate vulnerabilities, impacting women, men, children, and young people differently. Particularly, women, children, and young individuals face distinct challenges due to their socioeconomic status and cultural norms, as they are direct beneficiaries of resources like water, forests, and farmland. Climate change has significantly reduced the productivity of these resources, leading to heightened suffering, especially among women, young people, and children. This desktop study aims to demonstrate the correlation between climate change variables and the deteriorating gender-related development indicators in Magarini Sub-County, Kilifi County, Kenya. Specifically, it will examine variations in temperatures, precipitation, relative humidity, and water sources, among other variables, in relation to prevalent issues such as under-age marriage, adolescent birth rates, gender-based violence, access to basic water sources, food security, school attendance and completion rates, access to livestock foliage, and the general state of health among women, young people, and children. The study recognizes that the impacts of climate change can have long-lasting effects on the physical, psychological, and social well-being

J. N. Mavole
Faculty of Humanities and Social Sciences, Sociology Department, St. Augustine University of Tanzania (SAUT), Mwanza City, Tanzania
e-mail: jmavole@saut.ac.tz; https://www.saut.ac.tz

M. S. Mutisya (✉)
Faculty of Arts and Social Sciences, Department of Social Sciences and Development Studies, The Catholic University of Eastern Africa (CUEA), Nairobi, Kenya
e-mail: msyokoli@cuea.edu; https://www.cuea.edu

D. Nyaga, M. Zangeneh (eds.), *Critical Ethics on Mental Health and Madness*, Advances in Mental Health and Addiction,
https://doi.org/10.1007/978-3-032-10166-2_5

of individuals and communities. Guided by theories and frameworks for gender analysis, attitudes, and adaptation mechanisms, this desktop review will lay the groundwork for future empirical research and potential interventions, depending on resource availability. Specifically, the study will explore sustainable strategies for water provision in Magarini Sub-County. By integrating mental health considerations into the analysis, the study aims to highlight the interconnectedness between climate change impacts and mental well-being, providing insights for more holistic and effective adaptation and mitigation efforts in the region.

Keywords Climate change · Mental health · Gender roles · Water sources · Vulnerability

Background of the Study

Climate change is one of the most pressing challenges of our time, with far-reaching implications for human health, well-being, and livelihoods. As global temperatures rise and extreme weather events become more frequent and severe, the mental health impacts of climate change are increasingly recognized as a critical concern. Experiences of COVID-19, combined with the effects of climate change, have had profound implications on Kenya's vulnerable populations, particularly on their mental health ranging from mild emotional distress to severe psychiatric conditions such as anxiety, depression, trauma-related disorders, and substance abuse. In Magarini Sub-County, Kilifi County, Kenya, where natural resources serve as the primary source of livelihoods for residents, climate change poses significant threats to the well-being of women, children, and young people. Kilifi County is characterized by high poverty, estimated at 71.7% and widespread food insecurity affecting approximately 67% of the households. Low-input and rain-fed agriculture is the main source of livelihood in the County, contributing about 52.7% to the average household income and directly employing more than half of the total County population (IPCC, 2023). This study sought to understand the differential impacts of climate change on gender roles and socio-economic indicators in this region, with a focus on identifying key mental health vulnerabilities and proposing sustainable interventions.

Study Objective

This study investigated the implications of climate change on the socio-economic development and mental health of women, children, and young people in Magarini Sub-County, Kilifi County, Kenya.

Theoretical Approach

Social Ecological Systems Framework (SES) Proposed first by Berkes and Forker (1998), this framework emphasizes the interconnectedness between social and ecological systems. It recognizes the influence of gender roles and relations on individuals' access to resources and adaptive capacities. The SES framework can help explain why individuals from certain social groups or communities may experience higher rates of mental health problems, as these groups may face unique stressors or lack access to resources.

Adaptive Governance Theory Some of the well-known proponents of this theory are Ostrom (2005) and Gunderson and Holling (2002). This theory highlights the importance of flexible and inclusive decision-making processes in managing complex social-ecological systems. The theory emphasizes flexibility and learning in complex systems, which can be applied to mental health by promoting decentralized, participatory approaches that adapt to evolving needs and contexts, potentially improving outcomes and resource allocation. There are different dimensions through which adaptive governance theory is relevant in mental health: Decentralized and Participatory Service Delivery; Context-Specific Interventions; Learning from Experience: Promoting Mental Health Literacy; Integrating Mental Health into Other Systems.

The above discussed frameworks provide valuable perspectives for understanding and addressing the gender dimensions of climate change challenges and adaptations.

Literature Review

Climate change disproportionately affects women, children, and young people due to their socio-economic status and cultural roles (Chant, 2019; UN Women, 2020; Plan International, 2021). Women often bear the brunt of climate-related disasters, experiencing increased workloads, food insecurity, and gender-based violence (FAO, 2021a, 2021b; CARE, 2019). Children and young people face risks of malnutrition, interrupted education, and compromised health (UNICEF, 2021; Save the Children, 2020). Cultural norms and gender inequalities magnify vulnerabilities, limiting access to resources, decision-making power, and opportunities for socio-economic development (Kabeer, 2019; ILO, 2021). As a result, climate change magnifies existing inequalities and hinders the ability of women, children, and young people to realize their full potential and participate meaningfully in society.

Climate change affects natural resources in Magarini Sub-County by affecting food production, which is a significant value chain in the region. Farmers in Magarini face challenges that limit the full exploitation of their potential due to climate change (James et al., 2024), such as unpredictable rainfall patterns and increased pest infestations. These challenges result in lower crop yields and unstable income for the farmers. Despite these obstacles, the farmers in Magarini continue to work hard to find innovative solutions and adapt to the changing environment. They are resilient and determined to secure their livelihoods and provide for their families (James et al., 2024). Climate change alters precipitation patterns, leading to increased variability in rainfall (IPCC, 2021a, 2021b). As a result, Magarini Sub-County is experiencing more frequent and severe droughts, followed by periods of heavy rainfall (UNEP, 2019a, 2019b). These fluctuations disrupt traditional water sources, such as rivers, streams, and shallow wells, making water availability unreliable (O'Brien et al., 2020). This has resulted in increased competition and conflicts over access to water resources. During prolonged dry spells, surface water levels decrease, concentrating pollutants and contaminants. Subsequent heavy rainfall events then wash these pollutants into water bodies, further compromising water quality (Mekonnen & Hoekstra, 2019). This degradation of water quality poses significant health risks to communities reliant on these sources for drinking, cooking, and sanitation (UNICEF, 2020a, 2020b).

With changing climate conditions, the demand for water escalates, particularly for agricultural irrigation and domestic use (World Bank, 2020). However, dwindling water supplies coupled with rising temperatures can lead to increased water stress (Wada et al., 2018). Competing demands for water resources exacerbate tensions among different user groups, including farmers, pastoralists, and urban residents, further increasing vulnerabilities (Kuria et al., 2021). Climate change alters the timing and duration of growing seasons, disrupting traditional agricultural practices (FAO, 2020). In Magarini Sub-County, farmers rely heavily on rain-fed agriculture, with specific planting and harvesting schedules aligned with historical rainfall patterns. However, irregular rainfall and prolonged dry spells have led to crop failures, reduced yields, and decreased agricultural productivity (Rosenzweig et al., 2019). Climate change is associated with an increased frequency and intensity of extreme weather events, such as droughts, floods, and storms (Ebi et al., 2018). These events pose significant risks to agricultural production, causing soil erosion, crop damage, and livestock losses (Smith et al., 2020). In Magarini Sub-County, where subsistence farming is prevalent, such disruptions have devastating consequences for food security and livelihoods (IFPRI, 2021). Warmer temperatures and altered precipitation patterns create favorable conditions for the proliferation of pests and diseases that affect crops and livestock (Altizer et al., 2019). In Magarini Sub-County, invasive species and plant pathogens may thrive in the changing climate, posing new challenges to agricultural sustainability (Ziska et al., 2020). Farmers may face increased pressure to adopt pest management strategies and disease-resistant crop varieties to mitigate losses (Chakraborty et al., 2019).

Methodology

This study adopted a desktop review-based approach, drawing on existing literature and data sources to analyze the impacts of climate change on mental health and gender-related development indicators in Magarini Sub-County. Climate variables such as temperature, precipitation, relative humidity, and water sources were examined in relation to key socio-economic indicators, including underage marriage, adolescent birth rates, gender-based violence, access to water and food security, school attendance and completion rates, access to livestock foliage, and mental health. In Magarini Sub-County, Kilifi, a range of climate variables influences the local environment and mental health. These variables include Climate change and Socio-economic gender interplays against the prevalence of underage marriage, adolescent birth rates, gender-based violence rates, access to basic water sources, access to food security, school attendance rates and completion rates (basic education), and the general state of health of women, young people, and children.

Discussion

Climate Variables and Socio-economic Effects

Climate change aspects such as temperature variation, precipitation patterns, and relative humidity affect water availability, agricultural production, and food security (Muthoni et al., 2022). Reduced agricultural harvests and water scarcity may cause food insecurity, income loss, and increased poverty within communities (Wambua & Mwazighe, 2021). Vulnerable populations such as women, children, and young individuals are disproportionately affected, encountering risks of malnutrition, disrupted education, and compromised health (Nyamai & Mutie, 2021). Climate change significantly impacts children's and women's socio-economic status, contributing to heightened vulnerability and mental distress (Scholastica & Lawal, 2022). The elderly are at increased risk of mental health issues due to climate change because of existing health conditions, social isolation, and reduced mobility.

Gender-Specific Impacts

Underage Marriages The impact of climate change such as crop failures, prolonged droughts, and economic instability puts young girls at significant risk of early marriage, exposing them to domestic violence, sexual abuse, and other harmful practices that heighten their mental health vulnerabilities, according to Amollo et al. (2021a, 2021b). Research by Ong'wen et al. (2020) highlights how economic vulnerability resulting from climate-related disasters, such as crop failures and loss of livelihoods, increases the likelihood of families resorting to underage marriages as a coping mechanism. Economic hardships push families to prioritize immediate survival needs over the long-term well-being of their children, leading to early marriages. A study done by Giatu et al. (2029) showed that 19.4% were married when they were below 14 years, 43.9% were married between 15 and 18 years and 36.7% between 19 and 24 years. Of the 310 respondents who had ever been married, 96% were female. The child marriage rate among female respondents aged 18–24 years was 22% in Magarini Sub-County. Significantly, more females than males had experienced child marriage. Early and forced marriages, often driven by economic vulnerability exacerbated by climate change, can have profound mental health implications for young girls. Forced marriage may lead to feelings of powerlessness, depression, and anxiety, as well as increased risk of domestic violence and abuse (Ong'wen et al., 2020; Nyamai & Mutie, 2021).

Adolescent Birth Rates Climate-related shocks and challenges could disrupt access to healthcare services, leading to poor reproductive health services and information access for adolescents, potentially contributing to increased birth rates (UNICEF, 2020a, 2020b). Disruptions in education due to climate-related disasters also play a significant role in driving adolescent birth rates. Research by Mwangi et al. (2022) and Chepkoech et al. (2017) demonstrates how school closures, reduced access to sexual and reproductive health education, and increased economic pressures on families during climate emergencies contribute to higher incidences of early pregnancies among adolescents. Kilifi County was one of the counties with the highest adolescent pregnancy rates in Kenya at 22%. Moreover, 18% of young women ages 15–49 had begun childbearing and married, 15% had already had a live birth, and 3% were pregnant with their first child (Wanyeki, 2020). High rates of adolescent pregnancies, influenced by climate-related factors such as economic insecurity and disruptions in access to reproductive health services, can result in heightened stress, stigma, and mental health challenges for young mothers and their families (Mwangi et al., 2022).

Gender-Based Violence Climate-related disasters such as floods and droughts can intensify tensions within households and communities, resulting in instances of gender-based violence (GBV) due to heightened stress levels and diminishing resources (FAO, 2021a, 2021b). Climate-induced displacement and environmental degradation contribute to increased rates of GBV in Magarini Sub-County. Studies by Mutiso et al. and Muthoni et al. demonstrate how displacement from rural areas to urban centers or informal settlements, coupled with overcrowding and inadequate infrastructure, creates conditions conducive to GBV, including intimate partner violence, sexual assault, and exploitation. According to statistics from Magarini Sub-County in Kilifi County, in every 84 households, there is a case of sexual assault. Research by Ouma et al. (2021) and Nyawira et al. (2017) highlights the challenges faced by survivors in accessing legal recourse, healthcare, and psychosocial support, particularly in remote and underserved areas where services are scarce or inaccessible.

Access to Essential Resources

Access to Clean Water Climate change exacerbates water scarcity and contamination, disproportionately affecting women and girls responsible for water collection. Research by Musyoka et al. (2021) and Mwenda et al. highlights how climate change exacerbates water scarcity and contamination in Magarini Sub-County. Erratic rainfall patterns, prolonged droughts, and rising temperatures lead to decreased water availability in rivers, streams, and shallow wells, while increased runoff and flooding can contaminate water sources with pollutants, pathogens, and sedimentation. Although the Sabaki River passes near some villages, most households still travel between 1 and 15 km to reach piped water, and overall sanitation coverage in the sub-county remains very low (FAO, 2020). Being their gender-related role, the issue of water insecurity in Magarini falls squarely under women and girls, which may increase their levels of anxiety, depression, and psychosocial distress.

Access to Food Security Climate-related disruptions in agriculture lead to food shortages and decreased access to nutritious food, particularly for vulnerable populations. Climate change and extreme weather events can disrupt agricultural productivity, leading to food shortages and decreased access to nutritious food, particularly for vulnerable populations such as women, children, and young people (FAO, 2021a, 2021b). Increased food insecurity resulting from climate change may exacerbate malnutrition and health disparities, particularly among children and pregnant women, leading to long-term health consequences (Save the Children, 2020). Based on the findings of the SMART survey, it was noticed that child-feeding behaviors among young children were found to be unsatisfactory, as shown by the Minimum Dietary Diversity (MDD) rate of 33.6%, Minimum Meal Frequency (MMF) rate of 68.7%, and Minimum Acceptable Diet rate of 24.1%. The majority of diets provided to young children consisted primarily of cereals/grains and vegetables, with eggs, meat, and fruits being the least common. 35.6% of young children were provided with solid, semi-solid, or soft foods. According to the SMART report, it was found that 48% of families in the Sub-County consume food categories ranging from cereals/grains (92%) and vegetables (83%). Conversely, the least consumed food groups include fish, tubers, meats, and offal, which account for 3%, 7%, and 14%, respectively. There is a high rate of undernourishment, which is evidenced by the high prevalence of stunting in children of 39.1% (KNBS, 2020).

Attendance and Completion Rates in Basic Education Severe weather events linked to climate change have the potential to interrupt school activities, resulting in rates of absenteeism and school dropouts in rural regions where schools are susceptible to flooding and other dangers (Plan International, 2019). Research by Chepkwony et al. (2021) and Odhiambo et al. (2019) highlights how climate change effects, such as floods, droughts, and extreme weather events, disrupt education systems in Magarini Sub-County. Infrastructure damage, school closures, and displacement of students and teachers during climate-related disasters can lead to interruptions in learning, absenteeism, and decreased school attendance and completion rates, particularly among vulnerable populations. The sub-county has a low primary school enrolment rate at 59.4%, ranking at 48th nationally, and a secondary school enrolment rate at 43.5%, ranking at 63rd in the country. Disruptions in education due to climate-related disasters and economic challenges may result in stress, frustration, and feelings of hopelessness among students, parents, and educators striving to maintain educational continuity and opportunities for children and youth in Magarini (Chepkwony et al., 2021; UNESCO, 2019).

Mental Health Impact

Research by Clayton et al. (2018) highlights the psychological impacts of climate change, including increased anxiety, depression, and trauma among affected populations. Similarly, studies by Berry et al. (2019) and Fisher et al. (2020) emphasize the psychological toll of extreme weather events and environmental disasters on mental well-being. Vulnerable populations, such as children, the elderly, and marginalized communities, are disproportionately affected by the mental health impacts of climate change. Research by Smith et al. (2020) and Wang et al. underscores the heightened vulnerability of these groups to climate-related stressors and the need for targeted interventions to address their mental health needs. Climate anxiety and eco-despair are emerging phenomena characterized by feelings of hopelessness, powerlessness, and existential distress in response to the perceived threat of climate change. Studies by Reser et al. (2019) and Cunsolo and Ellis (2020) explore the psychological dimensions of climate anxiety and its implications for mental health.

Climate-related disasters, such as hurricanes, floods, and wildfires, can lead to widespread trauma and post-traumatic stress disorder (PTSD) among affected populations. Research by Lowe et al. (2018) and Norris et al. (2020) examines the long-term psychological impacts of climate-related trauma and the importance of trauma-informed care in post-disaster recovery efforts. Climate change intensifies existing social and environmental injustices, leading to disparities in mental health outcomes. Studies by Leung et al. (2019) and Bullard et al. (2021) explore the intersectionality of climate change, race, and socioeconomic status, highlighting the disproportionate burden of climate-related mental health impacts on marginalized communities. Recognizing and addressing the mental health impacts of climate change is crucial for promoting resilience and well-being in affected communities.

Conclusion

In summary, the studies reviewed offer insights into how climate change intersects with gender dynamics in arid areas of Kenya, specifically focusing on Magarini Sub-County in Kilifi County. The research emphasizes the effects of climate variability and change on groups, especially women, children, and youth. It underscores the importance of incorporating gender approaches in climate adaptation and resilience-building efforts. The impact of climate change worsens with existing socio vulnerabilities in these regions, affecting agriculture, water resources, and livelihoods. Women, children, and young people bear the highest burden due to gender disparities and societal norms that limit their access to resources, decision-making authority, and adaptive strategies.

Recommendations

Decision makers, government bodies, and the community should prioritize gender equality, equity, and the empowerment of women in efforts related to climate adaptation and resilience building. This involves integrating gender considerations into climate policies, allocating resources for initiatives led by women, and encouraging the participation and leadership of women in decision-making processes. Advocating for policy reforms and raising public awareness about the importance of mental health in the context of climate change resilience is crucial for garnering political support and mobilizing resources for mental health initiatives in Magarini Sub-County. Policymakers, advocacy groups, and community leaders should collaborate on advocacy campaigns that highlight the human rights dimensions of mental health, promote destigmatization efforts, and advocate for increased funding and support for mental health services and programs.

Investing in and Strengthening Community Resilience

Boosting community resilience to climate change requires collaboration among stakeholders, including government bodies, non-governmental organizations, and local communities. Investing in infrastructure such as water collection systems and irrigation projects can enhance water security and agricultural productivity. Additionally, promoting climate mitigation methods and diversifying livelihood options can enhance the community's resistance to climate-related challenges. Empowering communities to address their mental health needs and build resilience requires fostering a sense of agency, self-efficacy, and social cohesion. Community-based organizations, local leaders, and grassroots initiatives can play a pivotal role in mobilizing resources, facilitating peer support networks, and providing psycho-social interventions that promote mental health awareness, coping skills, and social support systems.

To effectively tackle the gender aspects of climate change, we need inclusive approaches that acknowledge the obstacles and possibilities experienced by women, children, and young individuals. Empowering women, advocating for gender equality, and fostering women's involvement and leadership in decision-making processes are crucial for creating resilient communities. The integration of mental health considerations into research and future directions is paramount for addressing the multifaceted challenges posed by climate change and promoting resilience in Magarini Sub-County. By recognizing the interconnectedness of environmental, social, and psychological factors, we can develop more holistic approaches to understanding and addressing the impacts of climate change on mental well-being. By engaging local communities as partners in the research process and advocating for policies that prioritize mental health, we can promote equity, justice, and resilience in Magarini Sub-County.

Research and Future Directions

Although existing research sheds light on how climate change affects gender dynamics, there are still gaps in knowledge in Magarini Sub-County that need attention. In the future, researchers should focus on carrying out localized studies and engaging in initiatives to gain an understanding of the specific vulnerabilities and adaptation approaches of communities in the area. Conducting longitudinal studies that track changes in mental health outcomes over time can provide valuable insights into the cumulative impacts of climate change and environmental stressors on community resilience and mental well-being in Magarini Sub-County. Long-term data collection efforts can help identify trends, patterns, and trajectories of mental health challenges, as well as factors that contribute to resilience and adaptation over time. It is also possible to model Magarini for sustainable livelihoods in Arid/Semiarid zones in Kenya.

References

Altizer, S., Ostfeld, R. S., Johnson, P. T., Kutz, S., & Harvell, C. D. (2019). Climate change and infectious diseases: From evidence to a predictive framework. *Science, 341*(6145), 514–519.

Amollo, I., et al. (2021a). Gender dynamics in climate change adaptation: A case study of Magarini Sub County, Kilifi County, Kenya. *Gender, Technology and Development, 25*(1), 23–42.

Amollo, I., Suleiman, A., & Maranga, E. K. (2021b). The nexus between climate change and women's reproductive health: A case study of Kilifi County, Kenya. *Journal of Sustainable Development, 14*(3), *55–68.*

Berry, H. L., Waite, T. D., Dear, K. B. G., et al. (2019). The case for systems thinking about climate change and mental health. *Nature Climate Change, 8*, 282–290. https://doi.org/10.1038/s41558-018-0102-4

Berkes, F., & Folker, C. (1998). *Linking social and ecological systems: Management practices and social mechanisms for building resilience*. Cambridge University Press.

Bullard, R. D., Wright, B., & Johnson, G. S. (2021). Environmental justice and climate change: Assessing the unequal impacts. *Journal of Environmental Justice, 13*(1), 40–56.

CARE. (2019). *Gender implications of climate change*. CARE International.

Chakraborty, S., Tiedemann, A. V., & Teng, P. S. (2019). Climate change: Potential impact on plant diseases. *Environmental Pollution, 146*(2), 323–333.

Chant, S. (2019). Women, gender and the informal economy in urban sub-Saharan Africa: A review of literature. *The European Journal of Development Research, 31*(2), 176–196.

Chepkoech, A., Mutisya, J., & Kiprop, M. (2017). Determinants of adolescent pregnancy in pastoral communities of Kenya. *Journal of Reproductive Health, 4*(2), 19–29.
Chepkwony, A. B., Maina, J. G., & Kiplimo, J. K. (2021). Climate variability and its impacts on food security in arid and semi-arid lands of Kenya: A case of Turkana County. *International Journal of Environmental Science and Technology, 18*(7), 1577–1592.
Clayton, S., Manning, C., Krygsman, K., & Speiser, M. (2018). *Mental health and our changing climate: Impacts, implications, and guidance*. American Psychological Association.
Cunsolo, A., & Ellis, N. R. (2020). Ecological grief and climate anxiety: Emerging psychological responses to climate change. *Current Opinion in Environmental Sustainability, 45*, 12–18.
Ebi, K. L., Ogden, N. H., Semenza, J. C., & Woodward, A. (2018). Detecting and attributing health burdens to climate change. *Environmental Health Perspectives, 126*(4), 043508.
FAO. (2020). *The State of Food Security and Nutrition in the World 2020*. Food and Agriculture Organization of the United Nations.
FAO. (2021a). *The State of Food Security and Nutrition in the World 2021*. Food and Agriculture Organization of the United Nations.
FAO. (2021b). *Women, food security, and agriculture: A global perspective*. Food and Agriculture Organization of the United Nations.
Fisher, S., Bristow, L., & King, N. (2020). Climate-related distress: Psychological responses to extreme events. *Journal of Environmental Psychology, 70*, 101435.
Giatu, T., Muriuki, E., & Kenga, J. (2029). Child marriage prevalence and socio-economic drivers in coastal Kenya. *Journal of Gender and Development Studies, 8*(3), 44–59.
Gunderson, L. H., & Holling, C. S. (2002). *Panarchy: Understanding transformations in human and natural systems*. Island Press.
IFPRI. (2021). *Global Food Policy Report 2021*. International Food Policy Research Institute.
ILO. (2021). *World Employment and Social Outlook: Trends 2021*. International Labour Organization.
IPCC. (2021a). *Climate Change 2021: The Physical Science Basis*. Cambridge University Press.
IPCC. (2021b). *Climate Change 2021: The Physical Science Basis*. Contribution of Working Group I to the Sixth Assessment Report of the Intergovernmental Panel on Climate Change.
IPCC. (2023). *Climate Change 2023: Impacts, Adaptation and Vulnerability*. IPCC Secretariat.
James, Bahati, Eunice, Serah, Doreen, Rebecca. (2024). *Status and challenges facing pineapple (Ananas comosus) production in Magarini Sub-County of Kilifi County in Coastal Kenya*. http://science.sdpublishers.org/id/eprint/2491/
Kabeer, N. (2019). Gender, poverty, and inequality: A brief history of feminist contributions in the field of international development. *Gender & Development, 27*(2), 231–245.
KNBS. (2020). *Kenya Demographic and Health Survey 2020*. Kenya National Bureau of Statistics.
Kuria, D. N., Mwangi, M. W., & Muthee, D. M. (2021). Gendered vulnerability and adaptation strategies to climate change among rural households in Gatundu North Sub-County, Kenya. *Gender, Place & Culture, 28*(2), 171–191.
Leung, C. W., Adamkiewicz, G., et al. (2019). Environmental justice and climate vulnerability. *American Journal of Public Health, 109*(S2), S207–S213.
Lowe, S. R., Rhodes, J. E., & Waters, M. C. (2018). Psychological distress following climate-related disasters. *American Journal of Community Psychology, 61*(1–2), 1–17.
Mekonnen, M. M., & Hoekstra, A. Y. (2019). Global grey water footprint and water pollution levels related to anthropogenic nitrogen loads to fresh water. *Environmental Science & Technology, 53*(21), 12170–12178.
Musyoka, S. M., et al. (2021). Water scarcity and contamination patterns in Kilifi County. *Journal of Water and Sanitation, 19*(3), 77–94.
Muthoni, P. N., et al. (2022). Impacts of climate change on water resources and agriculture in Magarini Sub County, Kilifi County, Kenya. *Journal of Environmental Management, 299*, 113642.
Mwangi, R., Kiprono, J., & Waweru, L. (2022). Adolescent pregnancy and socio-economic shocks in coastal Kenya. *African Journal of Reproductive Health, 26*(4), 112–127.

Norris, F. H., Tracy, M., & Galea, S. (2020). Post-disaster mental health trajectories. *Journal of Traumatic Stress, 33*(3), 321–331.

Nyamai, C., & Mutie, J. (2021). Gender disparities in climate change impacts: A case study of Magarini Sub County, Kilifi County, Kenya. *Gender & Behaviour, 19*(2), 16512–16532.

Nyawira, E., Ochieng, P., & Mutiso, R. (2017). Barriers to reporting gender-based violence in rural Kenya. *Journal of Gender Studies, 6*(1), 55–66.

O'Brien, K., Eriksen, S., Nygaard, L. P., & Schjolden, A. (2020). Why different interpretations of vulnerability matter in climate change discourses. *Climate Policy, 20*(1), 29–45.

Odhiambo, M. O., Kanyago, A. N., & Njoroge, P. M. (2019). Climate variability and its impact on food security among smallholder farmers in Kenya: The case of Kakamega County. *Sustainable Agriculture Research, 8*(2), 52–68.

Ong'wen, K., Mutune, J., & Wekesa, A. (2020). Economic vulnerability and early marriage in climate-affected communities. *African Journal of Social Sciences, 15*(1), 41–56.

Ostrom, E. (2005). *Understanding institutional diversity*. Princeton University Press.

Ouma, L., Wanjiku, M., & Ruto, J. (2021). Sexual violence trends in rural Kenya. *Journal of Gender-Based Violence, 5*(2), 201–219.

Plan International. (2019). Girls in crisis: *The hidden impact of climate emergencies*. Plan International.

Plan International. (2021). *Adolescent girls in crisis: Voices from Beirut*. Plan International.

Reser, J. P., Bradley, G. L., & Ellul, M. (2019). Climate change anxiety: Psychological dimensions. *Journal of Environmental Psychology, 65*, 101338.

Rosenzweig, C., Elliott, J., Deryng, D., Ruane, A. C., Müller, C., Arneth, A., & Folberth, C. (2019). Assessing agricultural risks of climate change in the 21st century in a global gridded crop model intercomparison. *Proceedings of the National Academy of Sciences, 111*(9), 3268–3273.

Save the Children. (2020). *The hidden impacts of climate emergencies on children*. Save the Children International.

Scholastica, U., & Lawal, O. (2022). Women and girls' vulnerability to climate change: Gender-based policy strategies for sustainable development. *Asian Research Journal of Arts & Social Sciences*, 54–64. https://doi.org/10.9734/arjass/2022/v16i230283

Smith, M., Goldenberg, R., Taheripour, F., & Wittwer, S. (2020). Economic impacts of climate change on agriculture: A comparison of process-based and statistical yield models. *Climate Risk Management, 28*(3), 100222.

UN Women. (2020). *Progress of the world's women 2019-2020: Families in a changing world*. United Nations Entity for Gender Equality and the Empowerment of Women.

UNEP. (2019a). *Emissions Gap Report 2019*. United Nations Environment Programme.

UNEP. (2019b). *Global Environment Outlook-6: Healthy planet, healthy people*. United Nations Environment Programme.

UNESCO. (2019). *Education under attack: Climate-related disruptions in learning*.

UNICEF. (2020a). *Climate change and children: A human security challenge*. United Nations Children's Fund.

UNICEF. (2020b). *Water under threat*. United Nations Children's Fund.

UNICEF. (2021). *The State of the World's Children 2021*. United Nations Children's Education Fund.

Wada, Y., van Beek, L. P., Bierkens, M. F., & Bierkens, M. F. (2018). Non-sustainable groundwater sustaining irrigation: A global assessment. *Water Resources Research, 50*(9), 7182–7190.

Wambua, M., & Mwazighe, E. (2021). Climate variability and change impacts on agriculture in Magarini Sub County, Kilifi County, Kenya. *International Journal of Climate Change Strategies and Management, 13*(3), 269–288.

Wanyeki, J. W. (2020). *Community empowerment and child marriage in Kilifi County, Kenya*.

World Bank. (2020). *World Development Report 2020: Trading for development in the age of global value chains*. World Bank.

Ziska, L. H., Crimmins, A., Auclair, A., DeGrasse, S., Garofalo, J. F., Khan, A. S., & Showler, A. (2020). Climate change and agricultural diseases of importance to the US: Current knowledge, trends, and gaps. *Climate Change, 52*(2), 171–189.

Part II
Theme: Neoliberalism and Mentalism

Chapter 6
Prediction on the Severity of Anxiety Using Machine Learning During the COVID-19 Pandemic

Muskan Girhotra and Md Zamilur Rahman

Abstract The COVID-19 pandemic has introduced unprecedented challenges to global mental health, with anxiety disorders emerging as a prevalent concern. This research study aims to predict the severity of anxiety using advanced machine learning techniques by analyzing the dataset collected from Statistics Canada that include behavioral and demographic variables, indigenous identity, labor market variables, mental health variables, and sociodemographic characteristics. This study attempts to expand on our knowledge of the pandemic's effects on mental health by identifying important predictors of anxiety severity. The outcomes of this research are anticipated to help advance proactive approaches, providing tailored psychological assistance and focused treatments to efficiently reduce anxiety during and after the pandemic. This work not only bridges the gaps left by the COVID-19 pandemic but also uses machine learning to improve the predictive power of mental health assessments, which could lead to advancement in more flexible mental health service frameworks.

Keywords COVID-19 · Mental health · Anxiety disorders · Machine learning · Statistics Canada

---

M. Girhotra
Department of Computer Science and Mathematics, Algoma University, Sault Ste. Marie, ON, Canada
e-mail: mgirhotra@algomau.ca

M. Z. Rahman (✉)
Department of Computer Science and Mathematics, Algoma University, Sault Ste. Marie, ON, Canada

School of Computer Science, University of Windsor, Windsor, ON, Canada

NORDIK Institute, Sault Ste. Marie, ON, Canada
e-mail: zamilur.rahman@algomau.ca

D. Nyaga, M. Zangeneh (eds.), *Critical Ethics on Mental Health and Madness*, Advances in Mental Health and Addiction,
https://doi.org/10.1007/978-3-032-10166-2_6

Introduction

A global mental health crisis, leading to anxiety disorders, has been brought on by the COVID-19 pandemic, in addition to disrupting daily life (World Health Organization, 2022). The quick spread of the virus and the newfound use of social distancing and lockdowns as public health measures have had a profound effect on people's psychological health all over the world. The pandemic, its underlying mental health issues, and the intervention are all consistent with the marked increase in the incidence of anxiety disorders that have been observed (Pongou et al., 2022). The earlier methods such as the Hamilton Anxiety Scale (HAM-A) and the Beck Anxiety Inventory (BAI) were more focused on the reactive than the proactive approach, making the identification and prediction of these disorders difficult and understudied (Hamilton, 1959; Beck et al., 1988).

The limitations of traditional mechanisms for mental health support, usually unavailable or insufficient to handle the spike in demand for psychological services, emphasize the urgency of the need to address this growing mental health crisis (Wainberg et al., 2017). Furthermore, heterogeneity in anxiety symptoms and their interactions with social, cultural, and economic factors make it even more difficult to develop effective, targeted interventions (Hofmann et al., 2010). A static approach would not be adequate because of the complexity involved, since the pandemic was dynamic and ever-evolving. For instance, the Canadian government launched *Wellness Together Canada*, a digital platform that provided free and confidential mental health and substance use support, which included self-assessments, counselling sessions, and peer support. This was introduced to help address the increase in anxiety, stress, and depression during the COVID-19 pandemic (Department of National Defence, 2021).

In response to these difficulties, our study uses machine learning's predictive powers to predict the severity of anxiety disorders during the COVID-19 pandemic. This will aid in closing the gap between the increasing demand for mental health services and the capacity of the current healthcare system to deliver individualized, efficient, and timely interventions. To address the structural inequities, we have used a dataset from Statistics Canada, which includes a wide range of sociodemographic factors. This guarantees that our models are sensitive to structural injustices and encourages fair mental health care for various communities. The methodology utilized in this research can be adapted and extended to similar datasets from other regions to gain better insights and introduce broader applicability.

This section presents a general domain overview of mental health and machine learning. The background and related work relevant to the concepts and technologies used in this research are first introduced. This is followed by an overview of the materials involved, including the methodology and performance metrics. The subsequent part outlines the experimental results and their analysis. Finally, the work concludes with a summary of the key findings of the study.

Mental Health

Mental health includes emotional, psychological, and social well-being (Substance Abuse and Mental Health Services Administration, 2024). The World Health Organization (WHO) defines mental health as a state where people are aware of their abilities, can manage everyday stressors, work effectively, and contribute to their community. It is more than just being free from mental illnesses or impairments; it also involves the capacity to overcome challenges, build resilience, and maintain emotional well-being (World Health Organization, 2023). All aspects of life, from interpersonal relationships to social engagement, are affected by mental health.

Anxiety

Anxiety is a normal stress response, and it acts as a danger warning system. Occasional worry is a normal part of life, whereas when it goes beyond temporary worry it turns into anxiety disorders. This could interfere with daily activities, professional performance, and relationships if they worsen over time. These can affect anyone regardless of their age (National Institute of Mental Health, 2024). According to the American Psychiatric Association (APA), these disorders affect nearly 30% of adults at some point in their lives. (American Psychiatric Association, 2023).

Generalized Anxiety Disorder 7-Item (GAD-7)

The GAD-7 (Spitzer et al., 2006) represents a widely used manual questionnaire (Fig. 6.1) for GAD screening and measurement of its severity within both clinical and research contexts. It consists of seven items that ask respondents how often they have experienced key symptoms of GAD, such as feeling nervous, anxious, or on edge; worrying too much about different things. (Anxiety and Depression Association of America, 2023).

Anxiety, according to the GAD-7 score, ranges from 0 to 21 and is categorized into four levels: minimal (0–4), mild (5–9), moderate (10–14), and severe levels of anxiety fall in the range of 15–21, as shown in Fig. 6.2. The scale provides an appropriate tool in finding cases with anxiety disorder, evaluating the severity of symptoms, and monitoring treatment responses over time.

GAD-7 Anxiety

Over the <u>last two weeks</u>, how often have you been bothered by the following problems?	Not at all	Several days	More than half the days	Nearly every day
1. Feeling nervous, anxious, or on edge	0	1	2	3
2. Not being able to stop or control worrying	0	1	2	3
3. Worrying too much about different things	0	1	2	3
4. Trouble relaxing	0	1	2	3
5. Being so restless that it is hard to sit still	0	1	2	3
6. Becoming easily annoyed or irritable	0	1	2	3
7. Feeling afraid, as if something awful might happen	0	1	2	3

Column totals ____ + ____ + ____ + ____ =

Total score ______

Fig. 6.1 GAD-7 questionnaire

Scoring GAD-7 Anxiety Severity

This is calculated by assigning scores of 0, 1, 2, and 3 to the response categories, respectively, of "not at all," "several days," "more than half the days," and "nearly every day."
GAD-7 total score for the seven items ranges from 0 to 21.

0–4: minimal anxiety

5–9: mild anxiety

10–14: moderate anxiety

15–21: severe anxiety

Fig. 6.2 GAD-7 scores

Machine Learning

Machine learning (ML) is a revolutionary approach that allows computers to extract meaningful information from data without explicit task programming (Samuel, 1959). A computer program "learns" from experience *E*, concerning a task *T*, and a performance measure *P*, if its performance on *T*, as measured by *P*, improves with *E* (Mitchell, 1997).

In this research, we use machine learning algorithms to forecast anxiety severity, a critical mental health concern made worse by the COVID-19 pandemic. The dataset comprises various variables related to behavior, mental health, and demographics. We utilize pattern recognition techniques and machine learning models to predict and classify an individual's anxiety levels by analyzing the features from our dataset, without relying on traditional questionnaires like the GAD-7. This approach is efficient, specifically in times like COVID-19, when the existing methods are less accessible.

Related Work

In this section, we present a thorough review of the relevant prior research that provides the foundation for our study (Table 6.1).

Materials

Our research uses machine learning (ML) to predict the severity of anxiety disorders during the COVID-19 pandemic. Since our dataset is labeled and includes a range of variables, including mental health assessments and demographic data, we employ supervised learning models. We selected this approach as the supervised learning models can process labeled data, allowing precise anxiety severity predictions based on patterns found in the dataset.

Methodology

The methodology is divided into multiple steps (Fig. 6.3), the first of which is preprocessing the data to make sure it is ready for analysis. To preserve consistency throughout the dataset, this step involves bucketing, normalizing features, and encoding categorical variables. The data are then split into two sets: a test set for model evaluation and a training set for learning. Then, we train the machine learning algorithms and evaluate their performance using various performance metrics.

Dataset

A large dataset from Statistics Canada 2020 (Statistics Canada, 2023) forms the basis of our machine learning model and is essential for training our algorithms to forecast anxiety levels during the COVID-19 pandemic. This dataset is in CSV file format and consists of 45,989 records. It encloses a wide range of attributes, including behavioral patterns, demographic factors, labor market impacts, mental health status, and sociodemographic characteristics, with 43 features, out of which 40 are categorical and the remaining three are numerical. The target variable is the severity of anxiety disorders as determined by the GAD-7 scale, and it is represented by the

Table 6.1 A synopsis of research papers that address mental health disorders and use machine learning

Reference	Year	Mental health target	Purpose	Description and data domain
Combating mental disorders (Ganguly et al., 2022)	2022	COVID-19 Impact	To evaluate the COVID-19 pandemic's effects on mental health and investigate the use of artificial intelligence (AI) and machine learning (ML) to remotely identify and treat mental diseases in situations where access to traditional therapy options is restricted	A systematic review of remote access data types, such as audio/video, social media, and smart wearables data is done to understand and address mental health issues worsened by the COVID-19 pandemic
Data analytics (Haq et al., 2020)	2020	General mental health disorders	To investigate the use of big data and ML techniques in understanding and the prediction of different mental health conditions, emphasizing the contribution of intelligent healthcare systems to the improvement of mental health services	Examines psychological behavior by applying sentiment analysis to social media data, particularly Twitter. Based on user-generated content, the study uses ML algorithms like k-means clustering, random forest, and Naive Bayes to predict mental health conditions
Mental health early signs (Srivastava et al., 2024)	2024	Mental health among young adults	To explore machine learning's potential in identifying early signs of occupational stress, anxiety, and depression for timely intervention	With an emphasis on occupational stressors and their psychological effects, the study compiles case studies and research articles about machine learning applications in mental health to guide early detection and prevention techniques
Big data and ML (Shatte et al., 2019)	2019	Management and diagnosis	To map and summarize the body of research on big data and machine learning applications in mental health care, from public health to diagnosis	Review of 300 papers across four main domains of mental health applications using ML, with a focus on conditions like depression and schizophrenia, utilizing techniques such as SVMs, decision trees, and neural networks

(continued)

Table 6.1 (continued)

Reference	Year	Mental health target	Purpose	Description and data domain
ML and NLP (Glaz et al., 2021)	2021	Mental health research	Analysis of the methodological and technical applications of ML and natural language processing (NLP) in mental health research, to assess their potential for use in clinical settings	Examined 327 papers from 4 significant medical databases, focusing on NLP and machine learning usage to classify the severity of illnesses, extract symptoms, and assess the efficacy of treatments. The main data sources were social media and medical records and Python was used for analysis

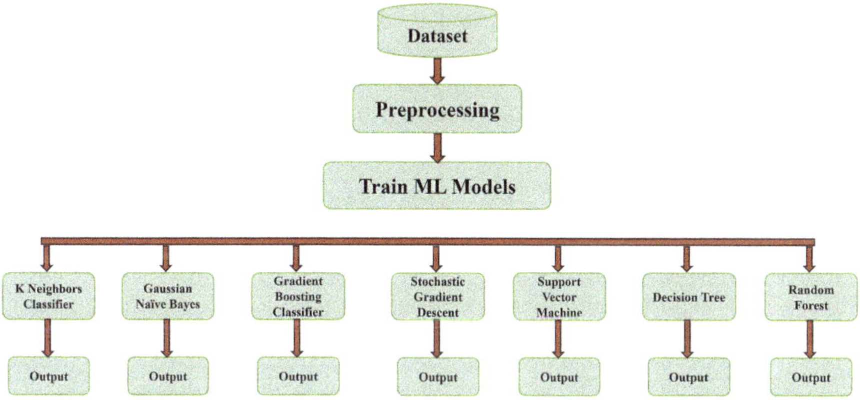

Fig. 6.3 Methodology

label column, "Category." Four columns—*VERDATE*, *ANXDVGAC*, *ANXDVSEV*, and *ANXDVGAD* were excluded from the dataset as they were unrelated to the prediction task and redundant since they were based on the predicted column.

Pre-processing

Our machine learning methodology's preprocessing stage entails several crucial actions to get the data ready for analysis.

PRURURB
2
1
9

→

PRURURB_Rural	PRURURB_Urban	PRURURB_ Not Stated
0	1	0
1	0	0
0	0	1

Fig. 6.4 One-hot encoding

Converting Categorical Attributes

A technique, one-hot encoding, that converts categorical attributes into numerical vectors has been utilized in our study. Each category within a feature is represented by a binary value, either as 1 (hot) if it corresponds to the category or 0 (cold) for all the other categories (Géron, 2019). This conversion improves the handling and interpretation of categorical data by machine learning algorithms.

For example, the *PRURURB* attribute in our dataset, which denotes whether an area is rural or urban, is one-hot encoded (see Fig. 6.4), so that each category is represented as a distinct binary feature.

There are 196 columns in the final dataset after the one-hot encoding process, which includes the original and newly created dummy variables.

Data Splitting

We separated the training (80% of the data) and testing (which is the remaining 20%) data from our dataset to accurately assess the performance of our models. This division is essential to machine learning techniques because it allows us to watch out for possible overfitting since evaluation is based on the models' efficacy and capacity to generalize to fresh, untested data.

Feature Scaling

This is used to normalize the range of independent variables or data features. To ensure that all numerical input variables contribute equally to the analysis, we scaled the variables in our study so that the performance of the model is not disproportionately affected by variables with larger ranges, as discussed previously.

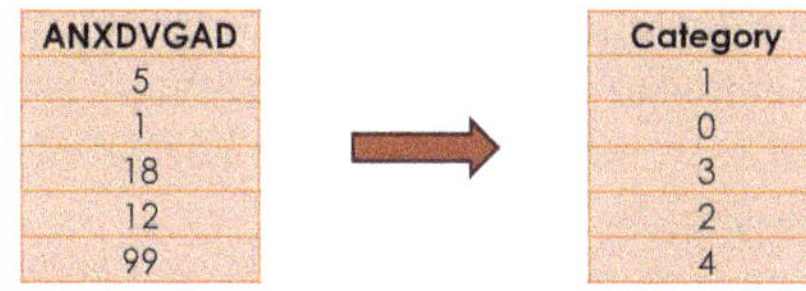

Fig. 6.5 Bucketing process

Binning/Bucketing

This involves converting numerical features into categorical bins, or buckets, by setting up a sequence of thresholds that divide these numerical features into discrete groups, each of which stands for a particular range of values (Google Developers, 2024). This helps establish a stronger correlation with the target variable, reduces the model's complexity, and enhances interpretability.

For instance, in our dataset, the *ANXDVGAD* column, which indicates the GAD-7 scale anxiety scores, has been binned into categorical buckets as shown in Fig. 6.5. These buckets are defined as per the GAD-7 score ranges: 0–4 for minimal anxiety, 5–9 for mild anxiety, 10–14 for moderate anxiety, and 15–21 for severe anxiety. Consequently, the continuous *ANXDVGAD* scores are categorized into a new "Category" column with discrete, ordinal values representing varying anxiety levels.

Train ML Models

Following our pre-processing, we train different classification models to classify anxiety severity levels. These models include K-neighbors (Duda et al., 2001), Gaussian Naive Bayes (Murphy, 2012), Gradient Boosting (Friedman, 2001), Stochastic Gradient Descent (Bottou, 2010), Support Vector Classifier (Vapnik, 2000), Decision Trees (Hastie et al., 2009) and Random Forest (Breiman, 2001). These models were chosen due to their various capacities in pattern identification and representation of the said complexities in our dataset.

The categorical "Category" column that emerges from the binning of the *ANXDVGAD* scores is interpreted by each of these classification models through training. This method aids healthcare professionals in making decisions by enabling the clinical interpretation of anticipated anxiety levels.

Performance Metrics

Finally, we use a set of performance metrics to assess our machine learning model's performance in predicting and classifying the severity of anxiety. These include accuracy, precision, recall, F1 score, ROC AUC score, and cross-validation. These metrics collectively provide a multidimensional picture of the model's effectiveness and the reliability of the classification performance. Our model incorporates diverse features to include some sensitivity around cultural and societal factors for a more inclusive model evaluation. The details of all key performance metrics used in this research are as follows:

- **Accuracy:** one of the most intuitive performance measures. It is the ratio of correctly predicted observations to the total observations.

$$\text{Accuracy} = \frac{TP + TN}{TP + TN + FP + FN} \tag{6.1}$$

- **Precision:** measures the accuracy of positive predictions. It is the ratio of correctly predicted positive observations to the total predicted positive observations.

$$\text{Precision} = \frac{TP}{TP + FP} \tag{6.2}$$

- **Recall:** measures the ability of a model to find all the relevant cases within a dataset. It is the ratio of correctly predicted positive observations to all observations in the actual true class.

$$\text{Recall} = \frac{TP}{TP + FN} \tag{6.3}$$

- **F1 Score:** harmonic mean of precision and recall. This score takes both false positives and false negatives into account.

$$\text{F1Score} = 2 \times \frac{\text{Precision} \times \text{Recall}}{\text{Precision} + \text{Recall}} \tag{6.4}$$

- **ROC AUC score:** analyzes a binary classification model's effectiveness. It shows the likelihood that a positive instance selected at random will be ranked higher by the classifier than a negative instance selected at random.

$$\text{AUC} = \int_{1}^{0} \text{TPR}(\text{FPR})\, d(\text{FPR}) \tag{6.5}$$

where TPR = recall and $\text{FPR} = \frac{FP}{FP + TN}$

- **Cross-validation score:** divides the dataset into k consecutive folds, with the remaining $k - 1$ folds acting as the training set and each fold acting as a test set methodically.

$$\text{Cross-validation}(\text{k}) = \frac{1}{k} \sum_{k}^{i=1} \text{scores}_i \tag{6.6}$$

where TP: # of true positives, TN: # of true negatives, FP: # of false positives, FN: # of false negatives, scores = [accuracy, precision, recall, F1 score, and ROC AUC score].

Experiments

Gradient boosting, decision tree, and random forest models, as shown in Table 6.2, outperform other models in our analysis with the highest accuracy, precision, recall, F1 score, and ROC AUC score, demonstrating their capability to differentiate between anxiety severity levels effectively.

We can easily visualize the performance and grasp our models' efficacy across a range of metrics by using bar graphs, as given in Fig. 6.6. The machine learning algorithms' accuracy, precision, recall, F1 score, and ROC AUC score are represented by the height of each bar in these graphs, which displays the model's performance.

Conclusion

The research successfully predicted the severity of anxiety disorders on a large dataset from Statistics Canada by utilizing cutting-edge machine learning models. Our approach eliminates the need for traditional analysis methods like GAD-7 surveys and facilitates efficient and scalable assessments by analyzing various mental health-related features. The ML model's superior performance implies that these classifiers are useful instruments for accurate mental health evaluations in pandemic situations and other real-world scenarios.

The future areas of development have been identified from the limitations of this study. Some of these include accounting for the dynamic nature of psychological conditions and pandemics in machine learning techniques to enhance adaptability. Others include data diversification to reduce overfitting, addressing sociocultural discrimination related to mental illnesses, incorporating more relevant features for model robustness, and incorporating cross-cultural validation for global applicability.

Table 6.2 Performance metrics

Classification models	Training set results (%)					Test set results (%)				
	Accuracy	Precision	Recall	F1 score	ROC AUC score	Accuracy	Precision	Recall	F1 score	ROC AUC score
K neighbors	81.06	81.24	81.06	80.87	94.81	80.70	80.90	80.70	80.45	94.55
Gaussian Naive Bayes	92.55	92.92	92.55	92.61	99.04	92.40	92.77	92.40	92.46	98.11
Gradient boosting	*100*	*100*	*100*	*100*	*100*	*100*	*100*	*100*	*100*	*100*
Stochastic gradient boosting	92.80	93.04	92.80	92.43	98.95	89.53	90.00	89.53	88.51	98.11
Support vector classifier	92.80	93.04	92.80	92.43	99.99	99.10	99.10	99.10	99.10	99.99
Decision tree	*100*	*100*	*100*	*100*	*100*	*100*	*100*	*100*	*100*	*100*
Random forest	*100*	*100*	*100*	*100*	*100*	*100*	*100*	*100*	*100*	*100*

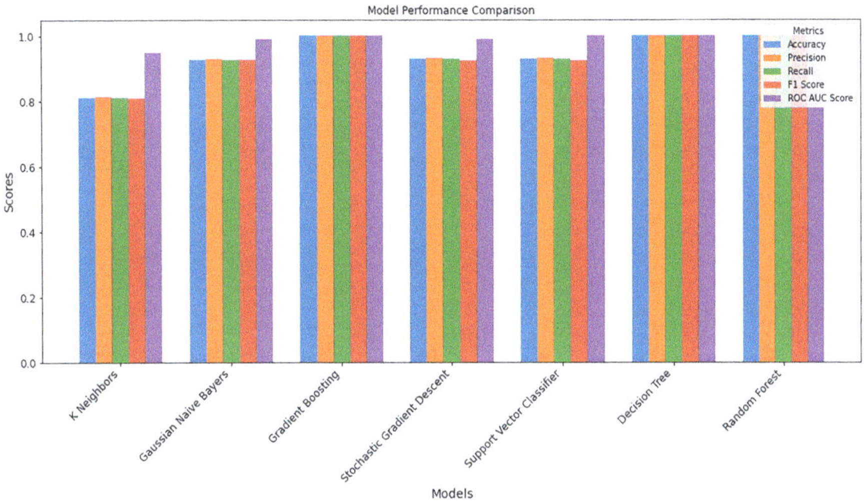

Fig. 6.6 Classification report

References

American Psychiatric Association. (2023). *Anxiety disorders*. Retrieved April 01, 2024, from https://www.psychiatry.org/patients-families/anxiety-disorders

Anxiety and Depression Association of America. (2023). *Gad-7 anxiety scale*. Retrieved April 01, 2024, from https://adaa.org/sites/default/files/GAD-7 Anxiety-updated 0.pdf

Beck, A. T., Epstein, N., Brown, G., & Steer, R. A. (1988, December). An inventory for measuring clinical anxiety: Psychometric properties. *Journal of Consulting and Clinical Psychology, 56*(6), 893–897. https://doi.org/10.1037/0022-006x.56.6.893

Bottou, L. (2010). Large-scale machine learning with stochastic gradient descent. In Y. Lechevallier & G. Saporta (Eds.), *Proceedings of compstat'2010* (pp. 177–186). Physica-Verlag HD. doi: 10.1007/978-3-7908-2604-316

Breiman, L. (2001). Random forests. *Machine Learning, 45*(1), 5–32. https://doi.org/10.1023/A:1010933404324

Department of National Defence. (2021, June). *Wellness together canada – support is just a click or call away*. Retrieved April 29, 2025, from https://www.canada.ca/en/department-national-defence/maple-leaf/defence/2021/06/wellness-together-canada-support-is-just-click-call - away.html

Duda, R. O., Hart, P. E., & Stork, D. G. (2001). *Pattern classification*. John Wiley & Sons.

Friedman, J. H. (2001). Greedy function approximation: A gradient boosting machine. *Annals of Statistics, 29*(5), 1189–1232. https://doi.org/10.1214/aos/1013203451

Ganguly, C., Nayak, S., & Gupta, A. K. (2022). Mental health impact of covid-19 and machine learning applications in combating mental disorders: a review. In S. Jain, K. Pandey, P. Jain, & K. P. Seng (Eds.), *Artificial intelligence, machine learning, and mental health in pandemics* (pp. 1–51). Academic Press. https://doi.org/10.1016/B978-0-323-91196-2.00016-8

Géron, A. (2019). *Hands-on machine learning with scikit-learn, keras, and tensorflow: Concepts, tools, and techniques to build intelligent systems*. O'Reilly Media, Inc.

Glaz, A. L., Haralambous, Y., Kim-Dufor, D., Lenca, P., Billot, R., Ryan, T., et al. (2021). Machine learning and natural language processing in mental health: Systematic review. *Journal of Medical Internet Research, 23*(5), e15708. https://doi.org/10.2196/15708

Google Developers. (2024, October). *Binning*. Retrieved April 30, 2025, from https://developers.google.com/machine-learning/crash-course/numerical-data/binning

Hamilton, M. (1959). The assessment of anxiety states by rating. *The British Journal of Medical Psychology, 32*(1), 50–55. https://doi.org/10.1111/j.2044-8341.1959.tb00467.x

Haq, A. K. U., Khattak, A., Jamil, N., Naeem, M. A., Mirza, F., & Ali, S. (2020). Data analytics in mental healthcare. *Scientific Programming, 2020*, 2024160. https://doi.org/10.1155/2020/2024160

Hastie, T., Tibshirani, R., & Friedman, J. (2009). *The elements of statistical learning: : Data mining, inference, and prediction*. Springer.

Hofmann, S. G., Anu Asnaani, M. A., & Hinton, D. E. (2010). Cultural aspects in social anxiety and social anxiety disorder. *Depression and Anxiety, 27*(12), 1117–1127. PMCID: PMC3075954. https://doi.org/10.1002/da.20759

Mitchell, T. M. (1997). *Machine learning*. McGraw-Hill.

Murphy, K. P. (2012). *Machine learning: A probabilistic perspective*. The MIT Press.

National Institute of Mental Health. (2024, December). *Anxiety disorders*. U.S. Department of Health and Human Services, National Institutes of Health. Retrieved April 29, 2025, from https://www.nimh

Pongou, R., Ahinkorah, B. O., Maltais, S., Mabeu, M. C., Agarwal, A., & Yaya, S. (2022). Psychological distress during the COVID-19 pandemic in Canada. *PLoS One, 17*(11), e0277238. https://doi.org/10.1371/journal.pone.0277238

Samuel, A. L. (1959). Some studies in machine learning using the game of checkers. *IBM Journal of Research and Development, 3*(3), 210–229. https://doi.org/10.1147/rd.33.0210

Shatte, A. B. R., Hutchinson, D. M., & Teague, S. J. (2019). Machine learning in mental health: a scoping review of methods and applications. *Psychological Medicine, 49*(9), 1426–1448. https://doi.org/10.1017/S0033291719000151

Spitzer, R. L., Kroenke, K., Williams, J. B., & Löwe, B. (2006). A brief measure for assessing generalized anxiety disorder: the GAD -7. *Archives of internal medicine, 166*(10), 1092–1097. https://doi.org/10.1001/archinte.166.10.1092

Srivastava, A., Rawat, S., & Singh, A. (2024). Mental health analysis among adults using artificial intelligence. *International Research Journal of Modernization in Engineering, Technology and Science, 06*(01), 381.

Statistics Canada. (2023). *Canadian internet use survey*. Retrieved April 01, 2024, from https://www23.statcan.gc.ca/imdb/p2SV.pl?Function=getSurvey&SDDS=5323#a2

Substance Abuse and Mental Health Services Administration. (2024). *Mental health*. Retrieved April 01, 2024, from https://www.samhsa.gov/mental-health

Vapnik, V. (2000). *Support vector machines for pattern classification*. Springer.

Wainberg, M. L., Scorza, P., Shultz, J. M., Helpman, L., Mootz, J. J., Johnson, K. A., et al. (2017). Challenges and opportunities in global mental health: a research-to-practice perspective. *Current Psychiatry Reports, 19*(5), 28. https://doi.org/10.1007/s11920-017-0780-z

World Health Organization. (2022). *COVID-19 pandemic triggers 25% increase in prevalence of anxiety and depression worldwide*. Retrieved April 01, 2024, from https://www.who.int/news/item/02-03-2022-covid-19-pandemic-triggers-25-increase-in-prevalence-of-anxiety-and-depression-worldwide

World Health Organization. (2023). *Mental health: strengthening our response*. Retrieved April 01, 2024, from https://www.who.int/news-room/fact-sheets/detail/mental-health-strengthening-our-response

Chapter 7
Mental Health and Income Security: Insights from the Ontario Basic Income Pilot

Tom McDowell and Mohammad Ferdosi

Abstract This study investigates the mental health impacts of the Ontario Basic Income Pilot (OBIP) in the Hamilton region. Launched in 2017, OBIP was designed to test the effectiveness of a basic income model as an alternative to traditional social assistance programs, with the goal of reducing poverty and improving overall well-being. We found that basic income led recipients to experience greater income security than before, resulting in various benefits that address the constellation of stressors contributing to worsened mental health outcomes. Our study suggests that an adequately funded basic income scheme could improve mental health by addressing the cyclical interaction of conditions associated with poverty. An adequately funded basic income scheme, then, holds the potential to surpass traditional social assistance models in addressing poverty and its adverse effects on mental health. Its unconditional nature shields individuals from market failures and punitive welfare models while providing financial relief during economic shocks such as the COVID-19 pandemic.

Keywords Ontario Basic Income · Income security · Poverty · Mental health

Introduction

The connection between poverty and mental health has been extensively researched, revealing a complex web of causal relationships (Murali & Oyebode, 2004, p. 216). Examining these connections has become increasingly critical in the neoliberal era, as the welfare state apparatus has been weakened by decades of austerity and market-oriented reforms. Social assistance programs have increasingly adopted a

T. McDowell · M. Ferdosi (✉)
Department of Politics and Public Administration, Toronto Metropolitan University, Toronto, ON, Canada
e-mail: thomas.mcdowell@torontomu.ca; mohammad.ferdosi@torontomu.ca

D. Nyaga, M. Zangeneh (eds.), *Critical Ethics on Mental Health and Madness*, Advances in Mental Health and Addiction,
https://doi.org/10.1007/978-3-032-10166-2_7

punitive approach, prioritizing employment outcomes over well-being, which has diminished their ability to support those in need compared to previous decades (Maki, 2011, p. 47).

This shift is further complicated by the evolving nature of work and the rise of precarious employment, which amplify financial instability and stress (Lewchuk, 2016, p. 87). As a result, there is a growing call for alternative policy approaches that move beyond the limitations of the neoliberal consensus and address the broader impacts of poverty on mental health (Van Parijs, 2004, p. 7).

The Ontario Basic Income Pilot (OBIP), conducted from 2017 to 2019, represented one such effort to address these challenges by offering an unconditional income guarantee as an alternative to traditional social assistance. This article reports the findings of qualitative interviews with more than 40 former OBIP recipients, examining whether basic income could improve mental health outcomes compared to existing social support programs like the Ontario Disability Support Program (ODSP) and Ontario Works (OW) by providing reliable, unconditional, and long-term income security. Advocates of basic income claim that the financial security it offers holds the potential to empower workers, enabling them to "say no" to exploitative work and take increased control over their lives (Widerquist, 2013, p. 8).

Our results revealed considerable mental health benefits from the provision of an income guarantee, including reduced feelings of depression, anxiety, and anger, as well as improvements in confidence and outlook. Positive mental health typically did not result from benefits in just one area of participants' lives but in multiple aspects, as the financial security OBIP provided led to overlapping benefits associated with greater personal freedom and social recognition.

By offering a stable, reliable source of income, basic income is a policy instrument that empowers individuals to take ownership over their circumstances, leading to a self-reinforcing cycle of positive behaviours that, when taken together, hold the potential for significant improvements in overall mental health.

This stability and security extended beyond the pilot period. A study of OBIP recipients three years after the pilot found that the financial security provided helped them navigate the COVID-19 crisis, demonstrating the long-term benefits of income support even after the pilot was cancelled (Ferdosi et al., 2024). COVID-19 relief programs, such as the Canadian Emergency Response Benefit (CERB), further demonstrated the effectiveness of this unconditional model on a larger scale, providing temporary stability during a time of widespread economic hardship (Béland et al., 2021).

The Relationship Between Mental Health and Poverty

The interplay between mental health and socioeconomic factors such as income and social conditions has long been documented. Cumulative stress arises from "constellations of stressors" over time, blending primary and secondary sources of strain

(Pearlin, 1989, p. 241). Pearlin (1989, p. 247) argues that anticipated income volatility contributes to "stress proliferation," where stressors exacerbate each other, leading to additional strain.

Pearlin (1989) describes poverty as a form of economic strain that results from the lack of financial resources to meet basic needs, contributing to psychological stress. Social and economic circumstances, which shape stress experiences, are commonly amplified by disparities in power and social class (Pearlin, 1989, p. 241). Low-status individuals often face a cycle of disadvantages and status inconsistency, which further contributes to worsened mental health. Those occupying one low status are predisposed to occupy another, reinforcing a cycle of disadvantage (Pearlin, 1989, p. 242).

Pearlin (1989, p. 247) argues that anticipated income volatility contributes to "stress proliferation," where stressors amplify each other, leading to additional strain. For instance, individuals who grow up in low-income households may have limited access to quality education, reducing their chances of securing higher-paying jobs. These challenges are particularly pronounced for those facing racial discrimination, as racialized Canadians earn significantly less than their non-racialized counterparts, even when education and experience are accounted for (Block & Galabuzi, 2011, p. 19).

According to Pearlin (1989, p. 242), individuals occupying one low status are predisposed to occupy another, contributing to a cycle of disadvantage. Perceived powerlessness in impoverished communities creates a "feedback loop" where poverty affects mental well-being and economic choices, perpetuating the cycle of poverty (Haushofer & Fehr, 2014, p. 862). Relative poverty, characterized by feelings of isolation and dissatisfaction compared to others, can lead to stigmatization and social exclusion, contributing to mental illness (Ridley et al., 2020, p. 10).

In short, there is a well-documented causal relationship between poverty and mental health, showing that income insecurity intensifies various stressors that contribute to worsening psychological well-being. By addressing income volatility, it is possible to break this cycle, leading to improved mental well-being by alleviating the compounded effects of economic and social strain (Pearlin, 1989, p. 241).

The Ontario Basic Income Pilot

Basic income has been proposed as one such potential policy solution to the problem of rising poverty. Van Parijs (2004, p. 10) defines a guaranteed or basic income as "an income paid by a political community to all its members on an individual basis, without a means test or work requirement," aiming to redistribute cash universally to all adults regardless of income (Widerquist, 2006, p. 2).

The underlying assumption of guaranteed income programs is that inadequate and unreliable income significantly impedes positive mental health and well-being. By offering an unconditional income, basic income aims to empower individuals, potentially improving various health issues, including mental illness (Birnbaum & De Wispelaere, 2021, p. 909).

The Ontario Basic Income Pilot was designed as an alternative to the province's traditional social assistance system, which is marked by high conditionality, minimal benefits, constant surveillance, and stigmatizing entry requirements (Maki, 2011, p. 47). It aimed to assess whether an unconditional income guarantee could improve upon the punitive, conditional nature of OW and ODSP by enhancing recipients' well-being across a variety of quality-of-life indicators, such as health, education, employment, and financial security (Segal, 2016, p. 6).

OBIP targeted approximately 4000 participants from three regions—Hamilton-Brantford (urban), Thunder Bay (semi-urban), and Lindsay (rural)—who were between 18 and 64 years old and earned less than $34,000 CAD as individuals or $48,000 CAD as couples. OBIP represented a substantial increase over the benefits of the province's traditional social assistance program, which ranged from $721 to $1151 a month. However, on the pilot, singles received up to $1415 per month and those with health conditions received up to $1915. Benefits were reduced by 50 cents for every dollar earned through employment.

Although the program was designed to last three years for each recipient, it was prematurely cancelled in 2019 by a newly elected Progressive Conservative government, which cut off payments and ended the evaluation component, leaving it to the academic research community to fill the research void.

Methodology

Qualitative data were collected through interviews with basic income recipients from Hamilton and Brantford between June and August 2019. Forty participants were selected to ensure diverse perspectives. Each semi-structured, open-ended interview lasted about 90 minutes, allowing participants to discuss various topics related to their experiences. Interviewees, who provided proof of enrolment through government documentation, were compensated with $100 CAD.

The study employed a codebook thematic analysis approach to interpret narratives and explore the impacts of basic income on quality-of-life measurements (Braun & Clarke, 2023, p. 696). Ethics approval for this study was provided through the McMaster University Research Ethics Board in 2018. The codebook was developed and refined through iterative reviews of interview transcripts, ensuring alignment and comprehensive analysis. Rigour and credibility were maintained through data engagement, information triangulation, an audit trail, and reflexivity discussions.

Our analysis is limited by the fact that we had to rely on self-reporting, since the pilot's early cancellation meant no participant data were available. Our focus on one of three pilot sites also reduces the generalizability of our conclusions.

The Ontario Basic Income Pilot and Mental Health

Our findings showed that basic income significantly impacted several, often overlapping quality-of-life indicators associated with positive mental health. Participant interviews revealed three main patterns. First, OBIP notably improved participants' **overall health** by enabling access to medical care, technology, medicines, and healthy food. For instance, a 39-year-old single mother reported improved mental health due to affordable doctor visits. "It felt wonderful. It felt stress-free," she said, highlighting the benefits of being capable of meeting basic needs. Similarly, a 63-year-old woman was able to afford taxis to her chemotherapy sessions, reducing the stress she faced in getting to and from her appointments. Many others recounted the mental and physical health benefits of being able to eat nutritious foods for the first time in years.

Second, recipients saw improved **social and community relations**, including reduced stigma. A 57-year-old man, for example, bought a new wardrobe, enhancing his self-image. "Every moment I'm wearing these clothes I feel more dignity. It's like, look what I'm worthy of," he said. A 50-year-old grandmother of six felt less "embarrassed" at Christmas, noting, "Last year was the best Christmas ever. I got the turkey, made the dinner, and bought decent gifts… It makes you feel good." Several former ODSP and OW recipients also reported feeling less surveilled and stigmatized while receiving OBIP, given its unconditionality, as they were not required to provide regular employment and health updates to government caseworkers.

Third, the increased **financial stability** provided by OBIP allowed recipients to better control their time and circumstances, providing "psychological security" that facilitated personal growth and well-being. A 22-year-old woman, previously "underpaid, stressed out, and hopeless", for instance, used the stability to "fix myself, my debts, and take better care of myself". Many participants recalled how, for the first time in years, the ability to pay off debts and make essential purchases led to a reduction in cumulative stress as well as improved self-esteem and self-confidence. This financial stability also enabled some recipients to leave employment in which they experienced harassment and abuse, to find work more consistent with their personal interests, skills, and life circumstances.

Our findings from OBIP's Hamilton region demonstrated that income security leads to a "constellation" of benefits that can alleviate some of poverty's cumulative effects (Pearlin, 1989, p. 241). By allowing individuals to focus on well-being, access to medical care, the ability to pay off debts and purchase essential items, as well as strengthened community connections, OBIP provided a variety of integral benefits that intervene with the negative feedback loop of circumstances that can contribute to cumulative stress and worsened mental health outcomes (Haushofer & Fehr, 2014, p. 862).

Conclusion

In sum, the results from OBIP's Hamilton region revealed that basic income supports led to substantial, multifaceted benefits for recipients. Unlike traditional social assistance programs, which often impose rigid conditions and perpetuate financial insecurity, basic income provides a reliable and sufficient source of income, enabling it to intervene in the cycle of stressors that exacerbate poverty and mental health challenges.

The benefits of basic income extend beyond mere financial relief. By reducing financial precarity, OBIP enabled recipients to access medical care, secure stable housing, and afford essential goods, mitigating cumulative stress and fostering a sense of psychological security. As recipients experienced improvements in areas such as health or social relations, these changes often triggered a positive feedback loop, enhancing other aspects of their well-being. The ability to leave exploitative work, reduce stigma, and regain control over one's time and circumstances underscores how income stability can shape long-term personal and economic outcomes (Pearlin, 1989).

Given these integral benefits, our study suggests that an unconditional, adequately funded basic income scheme could effectively enhance mental health, breaking the cyclical interaction between poverty and psychological distress. Such a program would represent a substantial improvement over traditional, neoliberalized social assistance models, offering a more effective and dignified approach to alleviating poverty and its adverse effects on mental health.

References

Béland, D., Cantillon, B., Hick, R., & Moreira, A. (2021). "Social policy in the face of a global pandemic: Policy responses to the COVID-19 crisis." *Social Policy & Administration, 55*(2), 249–260.

Birnbaum, S., & De Wispelaere, J. (2021). Exit strategy or exit trap? Basic income and the 'power to say no' in the age of precarious employment. *Socio-Economic Review, 19*(3), 909–927.

Block, S., & Galabuzi, G. E. (2011). *Canada's colour-coded labour market: The gap for racialized workers*. Canadian Centre for Policy Alternatives.

Braun, V., & Clarke, V. (2023). Is thematic analysis used well in health psychology? *Health Psychology Review, 17*(4), 695–718.

Ferdosi, M., Graefe, P., & McDowell, T. (2024). *Redefining futures: The role of basic income in career and educational development in Ontario*. Toronto Metropolitan University.

Haushofer, J., & Fehr, E. (2014). On the psychology of poverty. *Science, 344*(6186), 862–867.

Lewchuk, W. (2016). The precarity penalty: How insecure employment disadvantages workers and their families. *Alternate Routes: A Journal of Critical Social Research, 27*, 87–108.

Maki, K. (2011). Neoliberal deviants and surveillance: Welfare recipients under the watchful eye of Ontario Works. *Surveillance & Society, 9*(1/2), 47–63.

Murali, V., & Oyebode, F. (2004). Poverty, social inequality and mental health. *Advances in Psychiatric Treatment, 10*(3), 216–224.

Pearlin, L. I. (1989). The sociological study of stress. *Journal of Health and Social Behavior*, 241–256.

Ridley, M., Rao, G., Schilbach, F., & Patel, V. (2020). Poverty, depression, and anxiety: Causal evidence and mechanisms. *Science*, 370(6522).

Segal, H. (2016). *Finding a better way: A basic income pilot project for Ontario*. The Government of Ontario.

Van Parijs, P. (2004). Basic income: A simple and powerful idea for the twenty-first century. *Politics & Society, 32*(1), 7–39.

Widerquist, K. (2006). The bottom line in a basic income experiment. *Basic Income Studies, 1*(2), 1–5.

Widerquist, K. (2013). *Independence, propertylessness, and basic income: A theory of freedom as the power to say no*. Springer.

Chapter 8
Harnessing African Indigenous Psychosocial Approaches to Address Mental Health Challenges and Substance Addiction Among Youths in Kenya: An Integrative Framework for Culturally Responsive Interventions

Moses Ndwiga Kavengi

Abstract The intersection of mental health disorders and substance addiction among Kenyan youths is a growing public health crisis. A 2024 ACCTI survey found that 45.6% of youths aged 15–24 have used substances, with over 60% of them experiencing co-occurring mental health issues such as depression, anxiety, and suicidal ideation. This study uses a mixed-methods approach to assess prevalence, evaluate policy effectiveness, and explore culturally informed interventions. Despite Kenya's progressive mental health policies, including the Mental Health Policy (2015–2030) and Action Plan (2021–2025), implementation is weakened by severe underfunding only 0.01% of the national health budget and a critical shortage of mental health professionals. Western treatment models often fail to resonate with local cultural beliefs, which view psychological distress through spiritual and Indigenous lenses. Indigenous African healing practices such as storytelling, rituals, and spiritual counseling offer accessible, trusted alternatives. The study recommends integrating these Indigenous knowledge systems with Western care modalities, scaling up youth-targeted programs, and fostering culturally grounded, community-based interventions. Bridging this cultural gap is essential for effective, sustainable mental health and addiction care in Kenya.

Keywords African Indigenous · Integrative framework · Culturally responsive interventions

M. N. Kavengi (✉)
Mental Health & Psychosocial Support Services, Amani Counselling Centre & Training Institute, Kenya, Nairobi
e-mail: moseskavengi@amanicentre.org

D. Nyaga, M. Zangeneh (eds.), *Critical Ethics on Mental Health and Madness*, Advances in Mental Health and Addiction,
https://doi.org/10.1007/978-3-032-10166-2_8

Background of the Study

The prevalence of mental health challenges and substance abuse among African youths, especially Kenyan youths, is on the rise, exacerbated by factors such as unemployment, urbanization, and socio-political instability. Youths aged 15–24 in Kenya face a heightened vulnerability to substance use, with recent studies showing that 45.6% have used at least one substance in their lifetime, and 26.6% are currently using substances such as alcohol, tobacco, cannabis, and synthetic drugs like methamphetamine and betapine (ACCTI, 2024). Additionally, conventional Western-based mental health services often fail to resonate with Kenya's culturally diverse populations. The dominant biomedical model tends to overlook local explanatory models of illness, many of which are embedded in Indigenous African epistemologies that view psychological distress through spiritual, communal, and ecological lenses (Ojalade, 2009; Sodi & Bojuwoye, 2011). The mismatch between these paradigms contributes to the underutilization of mental health services and the perpetuation of stigma.

Statement of the Problem

Mental health disorders and substance addiction among youths in Kenya are on the rise, posing a dual burden that existing mental health frameworks are ill-equipped to address. Despite the presence of national policies and guidelines, such as the Mental Health Policy (2015–2030) and the Mental Health Action Plan (2021–2025), implementation remains fragmented due to systemic issues including weak inter-sectoral coordination, shortage of professionals with only 140 psychiatrists nationally and minimal integration of culturally grounded approaches (Ministry of Health, 2024; Kenya National Bureau of Statistics, 2024). Their implementation remains weak due to structural limitations, including inadequate funding, lack of trained professionals, and limited community outreach.

Aggravating this crisis is the cultural dissonance between Western treatment paradigms and the lived realities of Kenyan youths. Many existing mental health interventions fail to acknowledge the cultural, spiritual, and social dimensions that influence how mental illness and substance use are experienced and addressed in local contexts. Indigenous African psychosocial approaches, which offer culturally resonant and community-embedded solutions, are largely marginalized or excluded from formal mental health systems (Ojalade, 2009; Sodi & Bojuwoye, 2011).

The absence of a culturally integrative framework exacerbates the crisis. While policies exist, their top-down implementation neglects grassroots realities, leaving youths without accessible or relatable support. Meanwhile, substance use driven by idleness, peer pressure, and economic despair becomes a coping mechanism, further entrenching the cycle of addiction and mental illness. This study seeks to address the gaps by asking: How can African Indigenous psychosocial approaches be harnessed to create effective, culturally reverberant interventions for Kenyan youths? By centrering community based Knowledge and decolonizing mental health care, this study seeks to evaluate the effectiveness of current policy interventions and propose integrative frameworks grounded in African Indigenous psychosocial knowledge systems that amplify marginalized voices.

Objectives

i. To establish the prevalence of mental health conditions associated with substance addiction among youths in Kenya.
ii. To evaluate the effectiveness of existing policies in addressing the dual burden of mental illness and substance addiction.
iii. To explore African psychosocial Indigenous approaches that can be adapted to address mental health challenges and substance addiction among Youths in Kenya.

Literature Review

The nexus between mental health and substance addiction among African youths has become a thorny issue, with recent data highlighting alarming trends that necessitate a holistic approach to care and intervention. In Nigeria, a 2018 national survey found that 14.4% of people aged 15–64 had used a drug (excluding alcohol and tobacco) in the past year, with youths accounting for over 70% of this group (UNODC, 2018). According to a study by National Authority for the Campaign Against Alcohol and Drug Abuse (NACADA, 2024), it was revealed that 1 in every 11 young people in this age group is currently abusing drugs or other substances. The most commonly abused substances include alcohol, khat (miraa), tobacco, cannabis, and prescription drugs Amani Counselling Centre & Training Institute (ACCTI, 2024) clinical survey underscores this concern, revealing that 45.6% of youths aged 15–35 years have used at least one drug or substance in their lifetime, with 26.6% currently using substances such as alcohol, tobacco, cannabis, and emerging drugs like methamphetamine and betapine. It is also established that substance abuse can exacerbate existing mental health issues, while mental health challenges can increase vulnerability to substance use as a coping mechanism (Bravo et al., 2018; Conway et al., 2018). Alarmingly, over 60% of these young individuals also exhibit mental health disorders such as depression, anxiety, suicidal ideation, and stress, including unemployment, broken families, unhealthy relationships, and undiagonised or untreated mental illnesses. This intersected aspect of social life must be taken into consideration to help understand and imagine the differentiated treatment modalities. The intersectional approach represents a critical policy gap.

This study aims to address this gap by developing a framework that is culturally grounded, socially informed, and reflective of youths values and realities.

In response to this growing crisis, Kenya introduced several policies and guidelines aimed at reforming mental health care and integrating it with substance use treatment. The Mental Health Policy 2015–2030 provides a long-term framework for mental health reform and emphasizes the integration of services into primary health care. This is further supported by the Kenya Mental Health Action Plan (2021–2025), which outlines practical steps to improve access to mental health and Substance Use Disorders (SUD) services, train healthcare workers, and establish mental health units in county hospitals (Ministry of Health, 2021). The gap between policy and community-level intervention has prompted organizations like ACCTI to step in, not only with evidence-based clinical models but also by championing culturally grounded approaches that resonate with local realities (Moodley et al., 2013). However, this call is yet to be materialized based on the cultural stigma associated with local healing practices in Kenya and other African countries (Khan et al., 2013). It is noteworthy that Indigenous perspectives orient mental health and substance use practice towards land based techniques, which situate an individuals struggle within the broader context of their spiritual and psychic being. Such a focus seeks to heal the co-existence of mental health and addiction in ways that are beyond the modern forms of rationalized treatments (Ojalade, 2009).

Notably, Indigenous African psychosocial and healing practices offer untapped potential in addressing these compounded challenges. We argue that within the Indigenous perspective that is holistic, issues of co-existence of mental health and addiction are not just dual occurrences but are unique and confounding. Such a way of thinking about mental health and addiction seeks to be intersectional and avoid any dual perspective. This duality, rooted in colonial and heteronormative worldviews, hides and conceals the spiritual aspect of social existence. This spirituality is the bedrock of the Indigenous perspective on mental health and addiction. In so doing, mental health becomes a process of living with nature rather than outside nature (Ojalade, 2009). These Indigenous methodologies to healing must be taken into consideration when engaging people of face mental health and addiction. Indigenous perspectives on healing are community based and grounded in people's lives, realities, values, and ways of being. According to Bujuwoye

The African Indigenous knowledge systems developed for healing are integral parts of the African cultures. The African Indigenous knowledge systems represent the whole of the beliefs, attitudes, customs, methods, and established practices indicative of the worldviews of the African people (Sodi & Bojuwoye, 2011). Traditional African Indigenous knowledge systems have existed since time immemorial. The roots of the African Indigenous knowledge systems are traceable to the time when the foundations of the African cultures were being laid. These African Indigenous knowledge systems reflect how African people perceive reality within their environments. Consequently, they shape African worldviews, which in turn inform cultural meanings and practices related to human nature, ideal functioning, quality of life, and conceptions of health, illness, and healthcare delivery (Bujuwoye, 2020). African people have drawn on these knowledge systems to solve specific developmental and environmental problems for hundreds of years (Mohamedbhai, 2013).

Therefore, mental health and substance use are not merely individual issues but are fundamentally connected to the legacies of colonialism and imperialism (Rege, 2009). This framework conceptualizes the person experiencing mental health and substance use challenges not as an isolated case, but as a manifestation of an ongoing colonial violence that is perpetuated through their very being. Key to mental health healing is overcoming such colonial violence with indigenizing methodologies of healing rather than just treatment (Marangu et al., 2021).

Across various Kenyan communities, elders, spiritual leaders, and traditional healers (waganga) continue to serve as frontline providers of emotional and psychological support. These figures leverage Indigenous techniques such as storytelling, rituals, communal dialogue, and proverbs to facilitate healing, foster resilience, and restore social harmony (ACCTI, 2024). According to Wangari et al. (2018), these practitioners are often the first point of contact for mental health concerns in rural and peri-urban regions. They provide counselling, rituals, and herbal remedies within a culturally accepted framework, often addressing spiritual and social dimensions of addiction and mental illness. These culturally embedded systems often provide a more accessible and trusted alternative to formal mental health services, particularly in rural and marginalized settings. These culturally embedded systems often provide a more accessible and trusted alternative to formal mental health services, particularly in rural and marginalized settings. As noted by Abbo (2011), traditional healers in East Africa play a crucial role in managing mental illness by offering culturally acceptable explanations and treatment options that align with community beliefs. Similarly, Sorsdahl et al. (2010) emphasize that traditional and faith-based practitioners are often the first point of contact for individuals with mental health issues in sub-Saharan Africa due to high levels of stigma and lack of access to formal care.

However, the enduring legacy of colonialism continues to shape mental health paradigms across Africa, perpetuating a systemic epistemological bias that privileges Western therapeutic models while marginalizing African psychosocial approaches and practitioners. This legacy, often referred to locally as *ukoloni wa mambo leo* (neocolonialism), manifests through the global mental health discourse's persistent undervaluation of Indigenous knowledge systems and the skepticism directed toward African-trained therapists.

Nwoye (2015) argues, African therapists and culturally grounded healing practices are not only overlooked but are frequently subjected to structural prejudice—both within African countries and in international professional circles. This epistemological hierarchy reinforces a monocultural approach to mental health care that dismisses the value of community-based, spiritual, and relational healing traditions deeply embedded in African societies.

The consequences of this bias are profound: it delegitimizes contextually relevant interventions, restricts the development of locally adapted mental health systems, and alienates communities who might otherwise engage with culturally familiar forms of care. Such marginalization is not merely professionally discriminatory; it actively hinders the effectiveness and sustainability of mental health interventions by disregarding the cultural fabric and lived realities of African populations.

Integrating Indigenous and clinical approaches has been supported by several scholars. Mburugu and Mbugua (2018) highlighted the resilience of local support systems and their relevance to mental health programming. Gichuru and Muriithi (2021) proposed a hybrid framework that combines African spiritual traditions and communal ethics with evidence-based counseling.

Further developments include Kenya's 2024 release of national clinical guidelines for common mental disorders, aligned with the World Health Organization's Mental Health Gap Action Programme (mhGAP) to strengthen primary care response (Ministry of Health, 2024). In addition, Kenya established standardized protocols for substance use disorder treatment in 2022 and, in 2025, the High Court decriminalized attempted suicide, underscoring a shift toward human rights–based mental healthcare.

Despite these advances, quite a number of challenges remain in existence. Mental health remains critically underfunded, receiving just 0.01% of the national health budget, far below the level recommended by the World Health Organization (WHO). According to WHO (2021) notes that over 75% of people with mental, neurological, and substance use disorders in Sub-Saharan Africa receive no treatment. There is also a severe shortage of qualified mental health professionals. Kenya has only about 140 psychiatrists, and only 22 of its 47 counties have at least one psychiatrist. The ratio of psychologists to clients is one to every 4.6 million people, significantly short of the recommended ratio of one per 15,000, Kenya National Bureau of Statistics (KNBS, 2024). Moreover, stigma surrounding mental illness continues to limit access to care and often results in human rights abuses.

Methodology

This study employed a mixed-methods approach, integrating both qualitative and quantitative methods to gain a comprehensive understanding of the mental health challenges and substance addiction among Kenyan Youths. Data were analyzed using Statistical Package for the Social Sciences (SPSS) version 28.

Case Studies

Four detailed case studies from Amani Counselling Centre & Training Institute (ACCTI) were used to explore real-life interactions between substance use and mental health. These illustrated both systemic gaps and successful intervention models.

Findings of the Study

The findings of the study are presented in line with the research objectives. First, regarding the prevalence of mental health conditions associated with substance addiction among youths in Kenya, recent findings by ACCTI (2024) indicate a troubling rise in substance use among Kenyan youths aged 15–24 years, with 1 in every 11 currently using drugs and approximately 45.6% having experimented with at least one substance in their lifetime. These figures reflect a growing public health crisis and signal a deepening vulnerability among adolescents and young adults in the country. The substances most commonly abused include widely accessible legal substances such as alcohol, khat (miraa), and tobacco, as well as illicit drugs like cannabis and a range of prescription opioids. Alarmingly, there has been a notable increase in the use of emerging synthetic drugs, including methamphetamine and codeine syrup, especially in informal urban settlements and among high school and university students.

These synthetic substances are often cheap, easily available, and extremely addictive, exacerbating the psychological and physical risks for users. Several factors contribute to this escalating trend. Peer pressure, social media influence, unemployment, family dysfunction, and poverty are major social determinants driving youths toward substance use as a form of escape or coping mechanism. Additionally, the normalization of drug use in music, online platforms, and youth culture further glamorizes harmful behaviors. In many communities, access to addictive substances is easier than access to counseling or rehabilitation services. Moreover, the lack of structured engagement opportunities, such as youth centers, sports programs, and creative arts initiatives, leaves many young people idle and susceptible to risky behavior. The situation is worsened by the limited mental health literacy among families and educators, who may misinterpret early signs of distress or substance dependence as mere defiance or delinquency. Among those using substances, over 60% are concurrently battling mental health challenges such as depression, anxiety, PTSD, bipolar disorder, and suicidal ideation. This co-occurrence points to a strong link between psychological distress and substance dependency. Male youths are more likely to engage in risky substance use, while female youths are often underdiagnosed due to cultural taboos and gender-based violence related trauma that goes unaddressed. Qualitative feedback from focus group discussions and key informant interviews confirmed these trends. One youth participant remarked: You can buy shash (cannabis) from a backstreet kiosk. It's cheaper than food and easier to get than help. This underscores the widespread availability and normalization of harmful substances within youth spaces. A community health promoter noted: The youth tell us they just want to forget. They are stressed, jobless, and many feel ignored by society. Drugs are their way of coping.

A case study from ACCTI featured a 19-year-old male recovering from cannabis and meth addiction who said, I dropped out because I had no fees. I just hung out in the estate, smoking with friends to kill time. It became a routine until I lost myself.

Second, concerning the evaluation of the effectiveness of existing policies in addressing the dual burden of mental illness and substance addiction, it was found that while Kenya has developed robust mental health frameworks such as the Mental Health Policy 2015–2030 and the Mental Health Action Plan 2021–2025, their implementation has been hampered by chronic underfunding, bureaucratic inefficiencies, and weak inter-ministerial coordination.

These gaps have limited the realization of policy goals at the community level. As a response, organizations like ACCTI have taken on a critical advocacy and implementation role, bridging policy and practice by piloting community-based models, engaging traditional and faith-based actors, and advocating for increased domestic resource allocation and accountability in mental health programming. Furthermore, ACCTI has played a key role in national policy development, contributing to the formulation of critical legal and institutional frameworks, including the Kenya Counselling Psychology Act (2014), the Mental Health Act (2022), and various state departments' mental wellness policies. These contributions underscore ACCTI's longstanding commitment to systemic change, positioning it as both a technical resource and an advocacy leader in Kenya's mental health landscape. Mental health continues to receive only 0.01% of the total health budget, far below the WHO-recommended 5%. This has resulted in under-resourced facilities, a lack of medication, and burnout among the few trained professionals. Kenya has only about 140 psychiatrists and very few clinical psychologists, social workers, and addiction counselors. The ratio of mental health practitioners to the population remains critically low, especially in rural areas.

There is no centralized mental health information management system, and data on prevalence, treatment outcomes, and relapse rates remain fragmented and unreliable. A large segment of the population remains unaware of the mental health policies, available services, or their rights, which limits service uptake. Service providers affirmed that dual diagnosis (substance use co-occurring with mental health disorders) is prevalent yet poorly understood or addressed at the community level. A clinical psychologist observed, most of the youths we see have unprocessed trauma. Substance use is the visible part, but beneath it are deep mental scars.

Third, in exploring African psychosocial indigenous approaches that can be adapted to address mental health challenges and substance addiction among youths in Kenya, the study found that in many Kenyan communities, traditional support systems remain deeply embedded in the social fabric and continue to play a significant role in the emotional and psychological well-being of individuals, particularly among rural and marginalized populations. These systems often revolve around the guidance and presence of elders, traditional healers, and spiritual leaders, who are respected custodians of communal wisdom, cultural values, and conflict resolution mechanisms. For generations, such figures have been the first point of contact for individuals experiencing psychological distress, trauma, or spiritual crises. Elders often serve as informal counselors and mediators, using culturally grounded approaches such as storytelling, rituals, proverbs, and communal dialogue to promote healing, resilience, and restoration of social harmony. Traditional healers may offer herbal remedies and spiritual cleansing practices believed to remove curses or malevolent forces that communities often associate with mental illness or addiction. Spiritual leaders, including pastors, imams, and indigenous religious figures, also provide critical psychosocial support through prayer, faith-based counseling, and community support networks. In many cases, youths and their families may feel more comfortable seeking help from these familiar, trusted figures than from formal medical or psychological services, particularly where stigma and misconceptions about mental illness persist.

Training programs implemented by the Amani Counselling Centre & Training Institute (ACCTI) have taken a pioneering approach in bridging the gap between formal mental health systems and traditional community structures. Recognizing the critical role that traditional leaders such as elders and spiritual leaders play in shaping community attitudes and practices, ACCTI has strategically involved them in its psychosocial outreach initiatives. These programs begin by capacity building, equipping traditional leaders with foundational counseling skills, basic mental health literacy, and crisis response techniques. Through tailored training modules, they are empowered to identify signs of psychological distress, provide empathetic support, and refer individuals to appropriate care pathways when needed. Importantly, these leaders are not treated as peripheral actors but are actively integrated into the delivery of psychosocial support services.

This inclusive approach not only enhances trust and cultural alignment but also amplifies the reach and acceptance of mental health interventions in communities where formal mental health services are limited or stigmatized. By leveraging the deep-rooted respect these leaders command, ACCTI's model helps destigmatize mental illness and substance use, challenging harmful myths and encouraging help-seeking behavior. It also fosters a sense of shared responsibility and ownership over community mental well-being. This innovative integration of traditional and modern practices exemplifies how culturally responsive strategies can strengthen mental health systems and make psychosocial support more accessible, acceptable, and sustainable within Kenyan communities. Conventional mental health approaches may not resonate with local beliefs or values, especially where psychological distress is interpreted through spiritual or social lenses. In many African societies, mental illness is viewed not simply as a clinical issue, but as a manifestation of disrupted social harmony, spiritual imbalance, or ancestral displeasure. Consequently, treatment models that fail to incorporate these culturally embedded dimensions risk being perceived as irrelevant, ineffective, or even alienating, especially at the grassroots level. The dominance of Western models also overlooks the potential of integrative, community-based practices rooted in African traditions.

For instance, traditional healing practices through storytelling, music, rituals, and communal dialogue offer culturally resonant pathways to healing that are often more accessible and trusted in local settings. These approaches are not only therapeutic but also restore a sense of belonging and collective identity, which are essential for long-term recovery from both mental illness and substance use disorders. ACCTI has challenged this disconnect by promoting hybrid models that blend evidence-based counseling with indigenous healing practices. ACCTI's programs have successfully engaged community elders, faith leaders, and traditional healers as frontline psychosocial support agents, equipping them with basic mental health literacy and counseling skills. This strategy has proven instrumental in destigmatizing mental illness, encouraging help-seeking behavior, and expanding the reach of mental health services into culturally conservative and resource-limited areas. Programs implemented by ACCTI have successfully integrated traditional wisdom with modern counseling techniques. For example, community forums using storytelling, music, and rituals have proven effective in breaking the silence around substance use and trauma. A youth participant said, it felt safe. We sang, we danced, and then we talked about depression. I realized I wasn't alone.

Indigenous artistic expressions such as dance, drumming, poetry, storytelling, and community theater have long served as therapeutic tools in African societies to address emotional and psychological distress. These expressive forms allow individuals, especially young people, to process trauma, grief, addiction, and mental health challenges in culturally resonant ways. At ACCTI, such approaches are not only recognized but actively integrated into psychosocial support programs. Through structured art-based sessions, ACCTI engages both children and youths in safe, creative spaces where they can express complex emotions, build resilience, and foster social connection. These initiatives also serve as entry points for further mental health intervention, allowing counselors to assess emotional states and provide targeted support in a non-threatening, empowering manner. By blending traditional artistic practices with therapeutic intent, ACCTI effectively bridges the gap between culture and mental health, making healing more accessible and meaningful to the communities it serves.

Conclusion

To holistically decolonize mental health, there must be a conscious effort to elevate and integrate Indigenous African frameworks, validate the expertise of African practitioners, and foster epistemological pluralism that respects the diversity of healing traditions. Only then can mental health services in Africa become truly inclusive, effective, and equitable.

Recommendations

The Ministry of Health, in collaboration with local organizations such as ACCTI, should formalize the inclusion of traditional healing practices and community-based psychosocial support systems into the national mental health framework. This can include: Developing culturally appropriate training modules to equip them with basic counselling skills and mental health literacy; Creating regulatory and referral mechanisms to ensure ethical and effective collaboration between traditional and formal health systems.

To address the chronic underfunding of mental health, the Kenyan government should allocate specific resources to youth-focused mental health and substance use programs, especially in underserved rural and informal urban settlements, and integrate mental health and substance use education into school curricula and life skills programs.

In order to curb the shortage of mental health professionals, there is an urgent need to promote locally contextualized curricula in universities and colleges that incorporate African psychosocial knowledge systems and establish incentives such as scholarships, salary parity, and rural service allowances to attract and retain professionals.

Promote youth empowerment by institutionalizing and scaling up initiatives in sports, creative arts, vocational training, and entrepreneurship through the development and equipping of infrastructure across all devolved units, ensuring equitable access and long-term sustainability.

Strengthen inter-ministerial collaboration for mental health and substance abuse programs across the Ministries of Health, Education, Youth, and Interior.

References

Abbo, C. (2011). Profiles and outcome of traditional healing practices for severe mental illnesses in two districts of Eastern Uganda. *Global Health Action, 4*(1), 7117. https://doi.org/10.3402/gha.v4i0.7117

Amani Counselling Centre & Training Institute. (2024). *Clinical survey on youth mental health and substance use in Kenya*. ACCTI Internal Report.

Bravo, A. J., Hurlocker, M. C., & Pearson, M. R. (2018). A longitudinal examination of mental health, substance use, and intimate partner violence among a community sample of young adults. *Journal of American College Health*, 66(8), 803–811. https://doi.org/10.1080/07448481.2018.1454929

Bujuwoye, O. (2020). Indigenous African Healing. In R. Moodley & E. Lee (Eds.), *The Routledge international handbook of race, culture and mental health*. Taylor & Francis Group.

Conway, K. P., Green, V. R., Kasza, K. A., Silveira, M. L., Borek, N., Kimmel, H. L., Sargent, J. D., Stanton, C. A., Lambert, E., Hilmi, N., Reissig, C. J., Jackson, K. J., Tanski, S. E., Maklan, D., Hyland, A. J., & Compton, W. M. (2018). Co-occurrence of tobacco product use, substance use, and mental health problems among youth: Findings from wave 1 (2013–2014) of the population assessment of tobacco and health (PATH) study. *Addictive Behaviors, 76*, 208–217. https://doi.org/10.1016/j.addbeh.2017.08.009

Gichuru, W., & Muriithi, P. (2021). Hybrid counseling models: Integrating African communal values into substance abuse recovery programs. *African Journal of Psychology and Mental Health, 8*(1), 12–24.

Kenya Ministry of Health. (2021). Kenya Mental Health Action Plan 2021–2025

Kenya National Bureau of Statistics. (2024). *Kenya demographic and health statistics report*. KNBS. https://www.knbs.or.ke/

Khan, S., Odek-Ogunde, M., & Pate, K. (2013). Exploring barriers to the utilization of formal mental health servicesin Kenya: A perspective from traditional healers. *Journal of Community Psychology*, 41(6), 745–762

Marangu, E. M., Moodley, R., & Lee, E. (2021). Culture and mental health in Kenya. In *The Routledge international handbook of race, culture and mental health* (Vol. 1, 1st ed., pp. 411–421). Routledge. https://doi.org/10.4324/9781315276168-41

Mburugu, E., & Mbugua, M. (2018). Indigenous support systems and mental health: Opportunities for integration. *Journal of Indigenous Knowledge and Development, 6*(2), 25–39.

Ministry of Health. (2024). *National clinical guidelines for the management of common mental disorders*. Government of Kenya. https://www.health.go.ke/

Mohamedbhai, G. (2013). The contribution of higher education to the international dimension of sustainable development. In D. Teferra & M. L. Savage (Eds.), *African higher education: The international dimension* (pp. 78–95). UNESCO.

Moodley, R., Gielen, U. P., Wu, R., & Gielen, U. P. (2013). *Handbook of counseling and psychotherapy in an international context* (1st ed.). Routledge. https://doi.org/10.4324/9780203864906

National Authority for the Campaign Against Alcohol and Drug Abuse. (2024). *Status report on drug and substance abuse among the youth in Kenya*. https://nacada.go.ke/

Nwoye, A. (2015). What is African psychology the psychology of? *Theory & Psychology, 25*(1), 96–116. https://doi.org/10.1177/0959354314565116

Ojalade, I. I. (2009). *Use of indigenous African healing practices as a mental health intervention* (Order No. 3401611). Available from ProQuest Dissertations & Theses Global. (304893272). https://login.ezproxy.algomau.ca/login?url=https://www.proquest.com/dissertations-theses/use-indigenous-african-healing-practices-as/docview/304893272/se-2

Rege, S. (2009). State of indigenous mental health in Australia - A colonial legacy? *International Psychiatry: Bulletin of the Board of International Affairs of the Royal College of Psychiatrists, 6*(4), 98–100. https://doi.org/10.1192/S1749367600000801

Sodi, T. & Bojuwoye, N. (2011) Cultural embeddedness of health, illness and healing: Challenges for integrating traditional healing and western oriented health care systems. *Journal of Psychology in Africa*, 21, 349–356. https://doi.org/10.1080/14330237.2011.10820467

Sorsdahl, K., Stein, D. J., & Flisher, A. J. (2010). Traditional healers in the treatment of common mental disorders in South Africa. *The Journal of Nervous and Mental Disease, 198*(6), 434–439. https://doi.org/10.1097/NMD.0b013e3181e6a6b2

United Nations Office on Drugs and Crime (UNODC). (2018). *World Drug Report*. https://www.unodc.org/

Wangari, M., Odhiambo, L., & Wambua, J. (2018). The role of traditional healers in community mental health: A Kenyan perspective. *East African Medical Journal, 95*(4), 223–230.

World Health Organization. (2021). *Mental health atlas 2021*. https://www.who.int/publications/i/item/9789240036703

Chapter 9
Selecting a Fishing Spot

Renee Lemoyne

Abstract This research examines the wholistic health impacts of an 8-day Anishinaabemowin (Ojibwe language) land-based immersion course. Grounded in Indigenous pedagogies, the program was developed and taught by an Elder and Knowledge Holders who integrate language learning with ceremony, song, and reciprocal relationships with the land. The study posits that the disconnection from language and community caused by colonization and the COVID-19 pandemic has contributed to poor health outcomes. Through a mixed-methods approach utilizing surveys and interviews, the research analyzes changes in participants' mental, physical, emotional, and spiritual well-being. Findings indicate that the immersive experience of learning on the land within a supportive community acts as a healing process, fostering clarity, strength, and a profound understanding of foundational concepts like reciprocity (Miigwetch).

Keywords Holistic health impacts · Anishinaabemowin · Land-based immersion course · Miigwetch

Introduction

My community (hello), to introduce myself in a culturally appropriate manner, I will explain who I am, my clan and where I am from. Renée Lemoyne ndowe, Bimijiwan ndowe, Migizy ndodem, Kebaowek ndonjibaa. I am Renée Lemoyne, my spirit's identity is Running Water, and I am Eagle clan from Kebaowek First Nation, in Kipawa QC.

There are three teachers involved in the Anishinaabemowin land-based immersion course at Laurentian University, including Elder Lorney Bob and Knowledge

R. Lemoyne (✉)
Laurentian University, School of Indigenous Relations, Sudbury, ON, Canada
e-mail: Rlemoyne@nosm.ca

D. Nyaga, M. Zangeneh (eds.), *Critical Ethics on Mental Health and Madness*, Advances in Mental Health and Addiction,
https://doi.org/10.1007/978-3-032-10166-2_9

Holder Paula Potts who have been working together for over 20 years, along with Maajiijiwan, Charles Petahtegoose. Elder Lorney Bob was taught Anishinaabemowin by his grandmother who knew the language and culture very well as they were descendants of Inherited/Hereditary Chiefs. Knowledge Holder Paula Potts is a spiritually connected Kwe who was born and raised on Bear Island. The third Knowledge Holder is Maajiijiwan, Charles Petahtegoose, who is an Anishinaabemowin learner that was taught by Elder Lorney Bob. As a student himself, Maajiijiwan uses his perspective to aid the students in their language learning. The ideas and pedagogies involved in this course were primarily constructed by these three.

Through the Master of Indigenous Relations program at Laurentian University, I conducted research on the effects of Anishinaabemowin learning in a land-based immersion course. The 8-day Anishinaabemowin course was held at the N'Swakamok Friendship Centre Grounds in August 2023. The course teaches students the philosophy of the Anishinaabe language, the vowel sounds and begins to pave the way toward fluency.

Through my time working with this language learning community, I witnessed and experienced firsthand how healing this process can be. Spending time outdoors with this community allowed people to find clarity and direction in their life while living and learning in a supportive space. The inclusion of songs and ceremony into the language learning program allows the students and instructors alike to open up, be honest and grow stronger together. Being largely disconnected from our language and community throughout colonization has taken a huge toll on the health and well-being of all Anishinaabe in some form (Petahtegoose, 2024). Further, the isolation felt from our communities during the COVID-19 pandemic was immense (Petahtegoose, 2024). Being unable to access ceremony due to the effects of the Indian Act paired with COVID-19 has led to poor health outcomes (Warbrick et al., 2023). According to the professors, being together on the land, learning the language and partaking in ceremony is thought to counteract these health issues that have arisen (Bob, 2023; Petahtegoose, 2024). This is why Elder Lorney Bob, Knowledge Holder Paula Potts, and Knowledge Holder Maajiijiwan work together to offer this programming through Laurentian University; they care about the well-being of these students.

Gathering of Supplies: Miigwetch

The professors stress the important role of the land in this course. They believe that the land takes care of us (Bob, 2023; Petahtegoose, 2024). Elder Lorney Bob (2023) explains that "the land transfers its good energy to the people who walk on it" which in turn supports the students through the healing process of learning the language. One part of the learning that is done through this program is to see how Shkagamik-Kwe (Mother Earth) is taking care of us and in return we must take care of her (Bob, 2023). Reciprocal relationships such as the one that we have with Shkagamik-Kwe are of the utmost importance to creating and leading a healthy life. This idea is exemplified in the translation of the word Miigwetch that is given by Elder Lorney Bob (2023) which states that it does not simply mean "thank you," it is much deeper and represents the idea where "He (Creator/God) gives and we receive [good things]." Not only is this a major lesson in the course, it is essentially the foundation of life itself, including being a major part of the fishing metaphor used as the theoretical framework for this research. Ensuring that Miigwetch is a part of our lives and research methods decreases the chances of harming others and increases the opportunity to do the most good by having reciprocity as the basis.

Miigwetch may be an easy phrase to remember and say at community events; however, fully understanding and embodying the idea of both giving and receiving in life can be difficult. Particularly for those in our communities that are constantly doing things to help others, it can be uncomfortable to suddenly be receiving and having others take care of you (Bob, 2023). Throughout the course, the students practice receiving and doing good things for others, especially through the kitchen where a group of 2–4 students per day cook the meals for everyone. Further, when a student is fire keeping, they have their meals brought to them as they are not able to leave the fire alone (Petahtegoose, 2024). At the beginning of the course this makes those that are used to giving (in their regular life) feel great when they are delivering food but uneasy when they are being served and cared for in return (Bob, 2023). The idea is that this not only helps them to understand Miigwetch on a practical level, but also helps their mental and emotional well-being as they are getting accustomed to the idea that they are important and worthy of help (Bob, 2023). It shows them that needing and asking for help is not weak, but a strength (Potts, 2023). This idea rests upon the traditional ways of working together as a community and that independence is essentially a lie as nothing is truly done alone and even if it was, it is stronger when done as a community (Potts, 2023). It is these teachings and understandings that are found in the language that contribute to the healing that the language brings and adds to the importance of protecting this language to ensure that this is not forgotten (Bob, 2023).

Research Methods: Filleting the Fish

In this research, the changes in the wholistic health of students during the Anishinaabemowin land-based immersion course were studied. Four aspects of wholistic health were analyzed: mental, physical, emotional, and spiritual. This was done through surveys that were answered before and after, along with interviews which provided a voice for the statistics that were derived from the surveys, producing eight graphs found below.

Results: Feasting and Community Growth

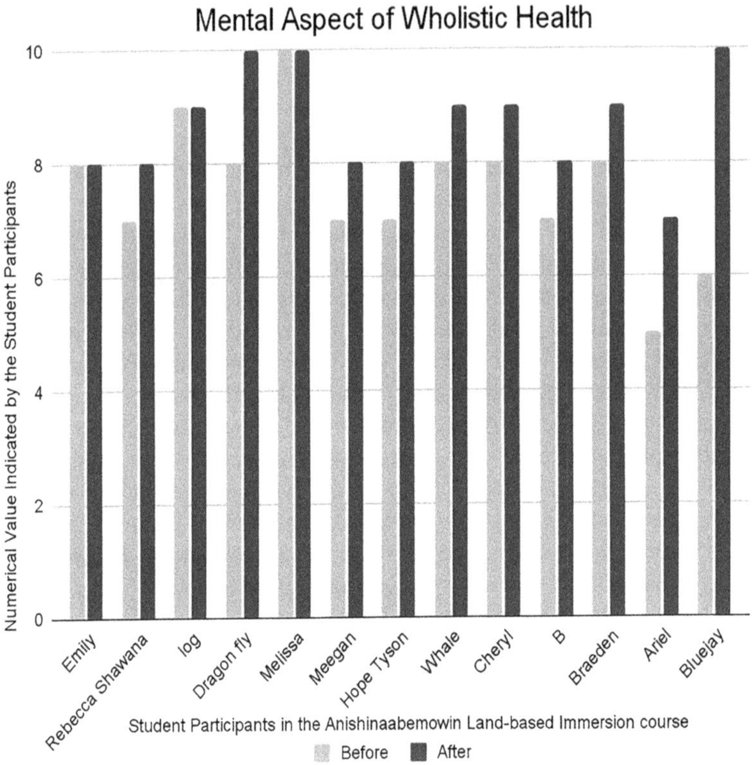

Before the course, I would never reflect alone. I would not care about my emotions. Now I know that it is okay to take time and care for myself and my mind. (Melissa).

Mentally I felt broken down at the beginning of the course. Through the course I realized that my ego takes over too often, and I need to learn to speak from my heart. (Anonymous).

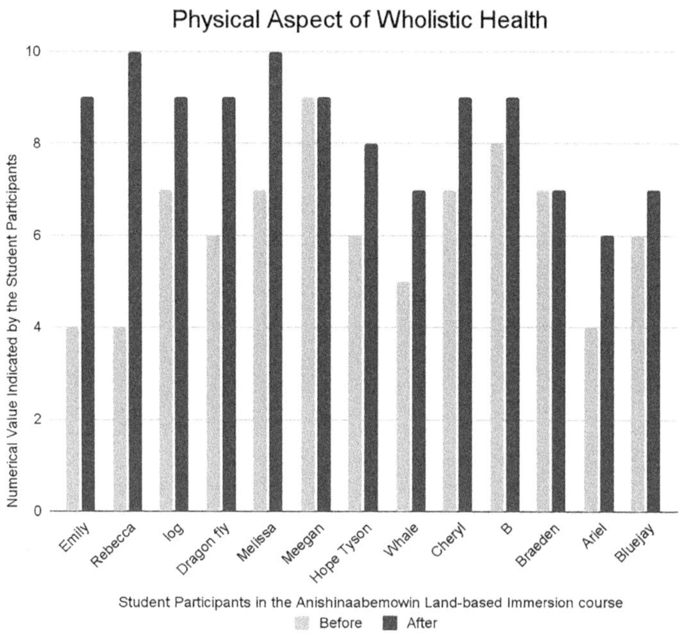

I felt like the teachings were physically transmitted into my body. (Anonymous). One participant was struggling with an eating disorder and benefitted from letting go of body-shame thoughts while eating nutritious food and learning Anishinaabe perspectives on bodies, food, and health found in the language.

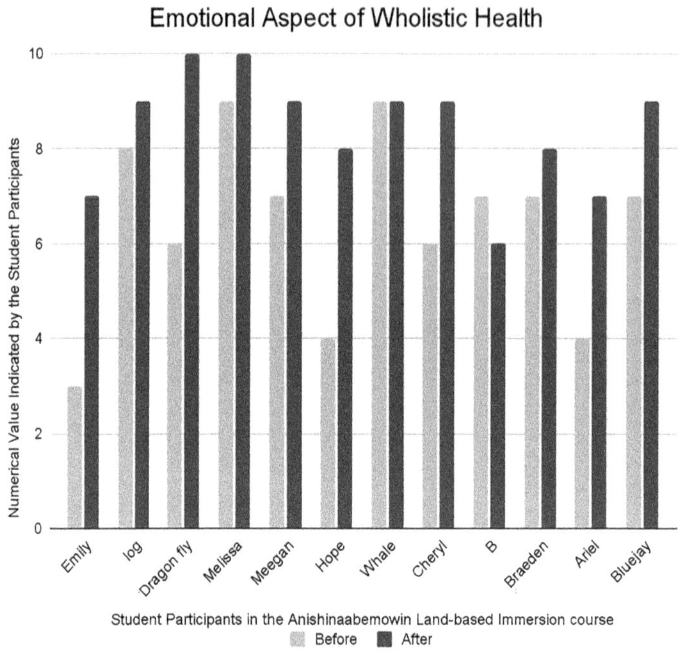

I learned so much about how to take care of my emotional health through this course. I learned about the importance of having balance. I also got clarity on what was happening to me so that I could figure out the next steps to healing. (Ariel).

I went from complete exhaustion, to finally being able to relax. (Emily).

I felt very low from grief going into the course. I felt very unbalanced. It felt good to be on the land and find balance again. Medicine picking mixed with the alone time was super helpful. Teaching others how to do things that I knew how to do in the bush felt nice. Overall, I left the course feeling much better. (Bluejay).

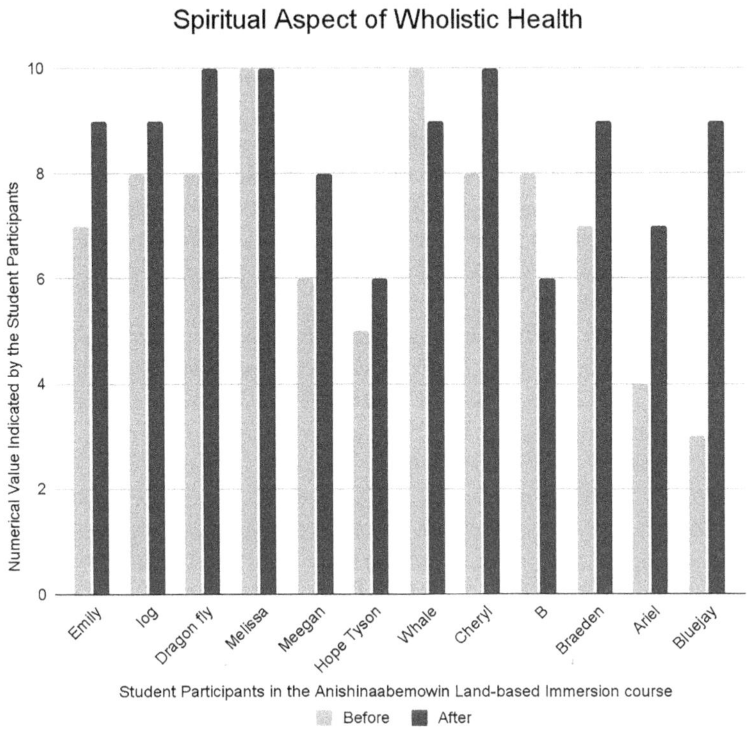

Spiritually I felt a strong connection to spirit on the land. (Anonymous).

I learned awareness, developed clarity, and created new life goals through the course. (Meegan).

I learned that the spirits of every living being can be seen. For me, the camp was a spiritual awakening. (Anonymous).

Discussion: Feasting on, Salting, and Freezing the Fish

Anishinaabemowin, according to Elder Lorney Bob (2023), creates a direct connection between our words, thoughts, and actions to our heart (Meshake, 2019). Freeland (2015) has indicated that Anishinaabemowin is a language that does not speak from logical mind to mind, but instead allows for a dialogue between two hearts. In this context, speaking from the mind is understood as filtered speech from our brain's ego which uses our lived experiences, anxieties, and fears to change how we express ourselves, however, speaking from the heart is raw, pure and fueled by true emotion. Having a direct line of communication coming from the heart, is thought to avoid the ego and allow true feelings to be spoken (Bob, 2023). Cutting off the ego essentially fosters a relationship where the heart and spirit can be louder and help guide the person to where they need to be in this life and ultimately toward better wholistic health outcomes (Potts, 2023). One anonymous participant noted that this course helped them "realize that ego takes over often" and used their time in the course as "an evolution of self" where they built confidence. This participant credits this growth with improving their wholistic health. Another participant (Melissa) credits the course with showing her how to reflect and care for her emotions and ultimately herself. Melissa noted that the wholistic nature of the program provided her with a lot of closure in her life. The personal growth that the participants went through allowed them to learn to speak from their heart and express their feelings in a fulsome manner, which ultimately led them toward better wholistic health outcomes (Potts, 2023).

Building off of the idea that this language speaks from heart to heart, it can also be understood that thinking and speaking in this language would help foster the connection between our mind, heart, and spirit (Potts, 2023). When these three parts of us are working together, it can help us to create an understanding that every part of you loves you and wants you to not only survive but to thrive (Potts, 2023). Having this be the core of your being can lead you to take charge to give your body the nutrients and support it needs to take care of you in return. This goes back to the reciprocal relationships of Miigwetch while also tying in the need for body integrity or lack of body shame (Bob, 2023; De Vries et al., 2018; Monks et al., 2021). Paula Potts (2023) believes that our spirit or soul is kept alive by our body which consists of cells that work tirelessly to keep our body functioning. Elder Lorney Bob (2023) believes that since our body loves and protects our spirit unconditionally, there should be no reason to feel shame in regards to a physical being with such a pure love. These body shame ideas are hard to break out of, but with the teachings found in this course, many students were able to begin to let go of the negative ideas, such as those found in the media, that were told to them since they were young (De Vries et al., 2018; Monks et al., 2021).

Conclusions: Feasting and Community Growth

The language contains many ideas, teachings, and responsibilities that we cannot forget. Within this, are words like Miigwetch which remind us to take care of Shkagamik-Kwe (Mother Earth) as she takes care of us. When we take care of ourselves by learning to receive good things in life while working with others to create a beautiful life, we inherently improve our mental and environmental health.

References

Bob, E. (Elder). (2023). Atikameksheng Anishinaabek First Nation. Anishinaabemowin Classes, Indigenous Sharing and Learning Centre, 2023, January–November. Shared on Robinson-Huron treaty territory of 1850.

De Vries, D. A., Möller, A. M., Wieringa, M. S., Eigenraam, A. W., & Hamelink, K. (2018). Social comparison as the thief of joy: Emotional consequences of viewing strangers' Instagram posts. *Media Psychology, 21*(2), 222–245.

Freeland, M. (2015). Anishinaabe ways of knowing and being. *Studies in American Indian Literatures, 27*(3), 120–124.

Meshake, R. (2019). *Injichaag: My soul in story: Anishinaabe poetics in art and words*. University of Manitoba Press.

Monks, H., Costello, L., Dare, J., & Reid Boyd, E. (2021). "We're continually comparing ourselves to something": Navigating body image, media, and social media ideals at the nexus of appearance, health, and wellness. *Sex Roles, 84*(3), 221–237.

Petahtegoose, M. (Knowledge Holder). (2024) Atikameksheng Anishinaabek First Nation. Discussions during the May and July courses, Atikameksheng Sacred Grounds, 2024, May–August. Shared on Robinson-Huron treaty territory of 1850.

Potts, P. (Knowledge Holder). (2023). Temagami First Nation. Discussions during the May, July and August courses, N'Swakamok Friendship Centre Sacred Grounds, 2023, May–August. Shared on Robinson-Huron treaty territory of 1850.

Warbrick, I., Heke, D., & Breed, M. (2023). Indigenous knowledge and the microbiome—Bridging the disconnect between colonized places, peoples, and the unseen influences that shape our health and well-being. *Msystems, 8*(1), e00875–e00822.

Part III
Theme: Gender Based Mental Violence

Chapter 10
Culture and Mental Health Among Immigrant Women in Canada

Maryam Motia

Abstract Canada has remained one of the most popular destinations for immigrants. Most specifically, the number of immigrant women is growing so that by 2031, more than 52% of immigrants in Canada will be women. Immigration may be a challenging process with potentially detrimental consequences, especially for marginalized immigrant women, resulting from the intersectionality of gender and other factors, such as immigration status, race, religiosity/spirituality, and socioeconomic status.

Studies suggest the protective effects of social support for the mental health of immigrant women. Social support from family, friends, ethnic community, and Canadian-based institutions may help these women fulfil their diverse demands. Additionally, creativity and artmaking may provide individuals with a tool, other than words, to express themselves. Artmaking can also be an avenue toward financial empowerment and a medium by which immigrant women can deepen their understanding of factors contributing to their mental health.

Exchanging social support and creating artworks may simultaneously occur in community arts programs with promising influence on mental health. In my doctoral research project, I use a Constructivist Grounded Theory and a combination of arts-based methodologies and in-depth interviews to explore mental health-related stories of immigrant women in Canada. In this paper, I discuss the impact of culture on the mental health of this population through affecting their agency and resiliency during and after COVID-19. Findings have implications for researchers, practitioners, and policymakers.

Keywords Culture · Immigrant Women · Mental Health

M. Motia (✉)
Wilfrid Laurier University, Faculty of Social Work, Kitchener, ON, Canada
e-mail: mmotia@wlu.ca

D. Nyaga, M. Zangeneh (eds.), *Critical Ethics on Mental Health and Madness*, Advances in Mental Health and Addiction,
https://doi.org/10.1007/978-3-032-10166-2_10

Introduction

The number of immigrant women in Canada is growing so that by 2031, women constitute 52% of the immigrant population (Hudon, 2015). Starting life in a different country from one's birth country may be challenging for mental health (Islam et al., 2018; Veenstra et al., 2020). However, such a transition may be more stressful for women (Dela Cruz et al., 2023; Koh, 2018), given the intersectionality of gender and other factors, such as immigration status, race, religion or spirituality, and socioeconomic status.

Research with immigrant women shows that social support may preserve their mental health (Turin et al., 2020; Zou et al., 2021). Similarly, artmaking may protect their mental health (Clini et al., 2019; Hanania, 2018). Community art programs may be a venue for socializing and exchanging support while creating artwork (Jo et al., 2018; Rose et al., 2018). Despite the existence of abundant community art programs for immigrant women across Canada, few scholarly studies in this country have examined the impact of participation in such projects on the mental health of immigrant women. My doctoral dissertation aims to address this gap. In this project, using Constructivist Grounded Theory (Charmaz, 2006; Charmaz, 2014), I will develop a theory that explains factors contributing to the mental health of immigrant women in Canada. Additionally, I use art-based methods to explore the role of art as a research method in assisting these women in expressing themselves.

The Scrapbooking Project

In this arts-based project, immigrant women of diverse demographic backgrounds were recruited from across Canada. Participants attended a brief introduction session. They then participated in 3 weekly group scrapbooking sessions. Each scrapbooking session had a particular theme, and participants illustrated their conceptualization and experiences related to the theme. The theme for the first session was "Trust & Mental Health and Well-being". In the second session, participants created artwork in accordance with the theme, "Social Relationships and Social Support". In the third session, titled "Wrap-up and Collective Sharing", participants completed their scrapbooks and shared pertinent stories. After the completion of all sessions, participants attended an exit individual interview. The project was entirely completed via Zoom. Participants were compensated for their contribution to this study.

In the following, I share findings related to my data collection in 2022 with one of the research participants, whom I refer to as the Participant hereafter:

The Participant is a 29-year-old immigrant woman who was born in Syria. When she was 2 years old, her family immigrated to the Emirates, and she grew up in Abu Dhabi. In 2016, at the age of 24, she immigrated to Waterloo, Canada, as an international student. She then received her master's degree and started working as a freelance Arabic teacher.

I developed various themes with data I collected from the Participant. I discuss three of the most relevant themes associated with mental health, consistent with my presentation at the conference: Complexity of Mental Health, Belonging, and Nature of Support.

Complexity of Mental Health

This theme was developed based on the Participant's scrapbook and explanations during the scrapbooking sessions. She has divided her scrapbook (Picture 10.1) into three time slots: the roots of the tree show the past (i.e., Syria), the trunk of the tree represents the present (Canada), and the branches illustrate the future.

Picture 10.1 Complexity of mental health

Regarding her understanding and experience of mental health, she said: "When I started to think of mental health as something separate to physical health, and this realization that I've been always an immigrant, and I've struggled with belonging, and how belonging has always connected to my vague sense of identity, and this, in parts, connected to my turbulent mental health, let's say, mainly feelings of sadness or not knowing who I really am."

The roots of the tree (i.e., the past) are very colourful, as colours are associated with beautiful memories. She also loves flowers; thus, she has used flowers in this section. She explains that apricots are very nostalgic as they grow a lot in Syria, and the taste of apricots reminds her of Syria. Likewise, the golden button belongs to her grandmother, who played a significant role in her upbringing. Specifically, the Participant could not talk about mental health with her parents and her siblings because it was stigmatized. However, her grandmother was aware of the importance of this topic, and she could discuss her mental health-related experiences with her. Safety, self-love, and hope are emotions that have been woven into the roots of the tree.

Flowers on the golden line represent that those flowers, roses, tulips, and hydrangea grow in both countries. The golden line shows the move (i.e., immigration). The building shows her current residence in 2022. She is wondering if she belongs to this building. The tree in front of her building reflects heritage, memories, and traditions. Sequins on the trunk of the tree remind the Participant of her grandmother, link her with traditions, and contribute to her strength and resilience. Connection, hope, and resiliency reflect her mental health-related experiences during and immediately after the pandemic.

The branches of the tree illustrate her viewpoint toward the future. She is hesitant about keeping her hope for the future. Concerning her academic and career future, she is unsure whether she should become a researcher or an artist. She also emphasizes the importance of self-discipline.

Some elements (i.e., the button, sequins) associated with the Participant's cultural background are vivid in the picture. These symbols represent the Participant's social relationships and social support as dynamics deeply rooted in her cultural background. As such, even remembering those connections impacts her mental health.

Belonging

This theme was developed based on the Participant's scrapbook, explanations in the scrapbooking sessions, and the final interview. It reflects the exploration of the importance of belonging to her as well as diverse meanings and aspects of belonging. Similar to the previous picture, there are flowers and sequins in this scrapbook (Picture 10.2) as well.

Grounded in her illustration and statements, questions, and investigation of her experience of belonging (Picture 10.2) can be divided into two main categories:

Picture 10.2 Belonging

Belonging to tangible matters and belonging to intangible matters. Concerning tangible matters, she explores belonging to people (e.g., family or grandmother) or places (e.g., Syria, Emirates, Canada, more specifically Waterloo, or Grandmother's house in Syria). However, eventually, she indicates that she never felt belonging to a place or country. Intangible matters encompass questioning her belonging to her memories, ideas, fantasies, past, religion, and traditions.

Finally, she illustrates belonging as a spiral reflecting her uncertainty about where she belongs. Sometimes people help her to get out of this spiral and feel belonging; however, such an experience is temporary. She sees herself as a sunflower; a sunflower can grow in different soils, reflecting that she does not have to feel belonging to a particular place.

A quote from her final interview reflects her viewpoint of belonging: "I had this opportunity to explore my ability to create social relationships, create friendships, create meaning, and in those relationships, and what I do, so, this contributed positively at the beginning, when I first arrived in Canada, but then, later, with the very negative experience at work, cultural differences, those feelings of uprootedness and belonging started to come again, and I started to, until today, I feel like: where do I belong? I don't think I'm very happy here; I don't think I can relate to people here, and people cannot relate to me; I don't think my soul is settled in here, and there are lots of opportunities, and support on a materialistic level, on a financial level … but at the same time, when you don't feel that you belong to the land and to the people, you feel like there's something, there's a hole. So, this irony always exists, and … I always talk about it with my family and friends."

Nature of Support

I developed this theme based on the Participant's scrapbook, her descriptions of the scrapbooking sessions, and the final interview with her. She has divided her scrapbook (Picture 10.3) into two sections: On the right, or according to her, the "East", she has illustrated Syria, and on the left, or the "West", she has depicted Canada.

Picture 10.3 Nature of support

She mentions that although using the West versus the East is a generalization, she conceptualizes her experiences this way. She feels that "there is a gap between the East and the West; the Eastern ways of living and doing things and the Western way." Accordingly, she believes that due to such a big difference, she needs "a lot of effort to cope with the neatness and the organization" of the West.

She explains that both sides reflect "urban life". However, the right side represents the collective culture of Syria, and the left side shows the individualistic culture of Canada. She mentions that building architecture impacts the dynamics of relationships, socialization, and support. Likewise, she compares the nature of support in Syria versus Canada as "organic versus organized support". She explains that in Syria, social support is "… very scattered, but it's everywhere. It's not organized, but you find people everywhere, just popping up in your life asking how you're doing; if something happened to you, you don't need to have a number there in your pocket in case something happens, you would find someone there …" However, support in Canada is "very structured, …, it's beautiful; it's there; it's strong, but it's just like this house here, it's really neat. … If you want support from someone, you need to make an appointment previously." She continues: "… in terms of friendships and social support in my home and close circle, I find that I need to do lots of efforts to bring people together, people are very busy working, figuring out how to survive, especially today. So, calling for meetings or sharing meals with people requires lots of planning and telling people in advance, and people can, and people can't. So, you find yourself working very hard. That's how I find myself working very hard to maintain this continuity and meaningful relationships." In this sense, she indicated her tendency for developing meaningful and long-lasting relationships in Canada.

She also refers to "Beit almouneh", a place in Syrians' houses to keep conserved food for winter. She recalls those days when her family and friends got together to make food to preserve them for the cold weather.

Social support for the Participant is a contributing factor to nourishment and self-love, preventing her from developing loneliness. She refers to support from various organizations in Canada and mentions her content with such assistance. She also explains that although her parents lived in Canada and were not happy with her decision to live in a different city independently, they respected and supported her decision.

In the final interview, she refers to her very limited network during COVID-19. She recalls that other than her parents, nobody reached out to her on her last birthday in 2021. She explains that none of her friends, neighbours, or extended family members remembered her birthday. She emphasizes that during the pandemic, Canadian society witnessed the importance of just sitting on the balcony and doing nothing. She believes that being forced to do so developed the ability to see the positive side of it which aligns with human nature.

Likewise, in the final interview, she explains "Social support means having people who listen to you, without judgment, understand, try to understand your history, and understand your sufferings. Social support means not putting … high expectations on … people you love, and accepting what they can give, what they can offer.

And social support means finding someone to join you in times of happiness and sorrow."

Discussion

Early findings related to the Participant and other participants demonstrate that scrapbooking is a rich research tool for data collection and an opportunity to use previously learned artistic skills. Additionally, group scrapbooking is a therapeutic and healing experience, and a space for exchanging social support. I will explain these findings as follows:

(a) A rich research tool

Participants discussed that they had control over what they were willing to disclose, to what extent and in what ways. Throughout the research project, participants used words and beyond (scrapbooking) to share their stories.

(b) An opportunity to use previously learned artistic skills

Participants could utilize their artistic skills, such as drawing, painting, or poetry in their scrapbooks.

As such, scrapbooking within groups is:

(c) A therapeutic or healing experience

Some participants refer to scrapbooking within groups as therapeutic and cathartic, an opportunity for self-expression and self-understanding and the development of a clearer self-image.

(d) A space for exchanging social support

Research participants, especially those who have been living in Canada for many years, provided support, especially in the form of emotional and informational support to the newcomers. During the scrapbooking sessions, some participants shared information on various resources, and some others reached out to me afterwards to connect them with those who live in the same city.

Conclusion

The findings related to the Participant demonstrate that various experiences, such as hope, resiliency, self-love, safety, and belonging, contribute to mental health. These findings also indicate that the conceptualization of mental health and a potentially pertinent stigma is grounded in one's culture. Thus, whether or not and with whom one may discuss mental health-related experiences and challenges is closely related to how mental health is understood and dealt with in a culture.

Likewise, the quality and quantity of support grounded in one's culture impact mental health. Given that the data with the Participant were collected in the Fall of

2022, these findings specifically show that her mental health during and after COVID-19 was impacted by her limited interactions and inadequate support. However, the support that she received from her parents and some social services, as well as her positive attitude and high resilience, protected and promoted her mental health.

Research with various ethnicities may shed light on cultural elements and how those cultural specificities contribute to mental health, either directly or indirectly through impacting social relationships and social support elicited from those relationships that further impact mental health. Such studies may be further used to tailor support to the particular needs of immigrant individuals, families, groups, and communities, in accordance with their cultural nuances.

The findings of this study also suggest elements of art and creativity to government-funded English classes (ESL/LINC) for immigrant women in Canada. Providing space for using artistic materials may increase motivation due to a sense of agency and power to help these women take the lead in their learning processes.

On the other hand, it is recommended that each session of art programs and workshops for immigrant women should have a theme to invite participants to socialize and express their experiences related to that theme. Such engaging experiences can facilitate socialization to meet psychological, emotional, and tangible needs and promote mental health. More specifically, the themes should help participants learn about each other's pre- and post-migratory journeys, and cultural and ethnic specificities. Such conversations should also pave the way for participants to gain knowledge of various support resources in Canada to smooth their resettlement in their new home.

Derived from the findings, mental health providers should also open space for clients to use creative ways for self-exploration and self-expression. Simple art supplies in counselling sessions may assist clients in navigating diverse ways, beyond words, to explain their stories, improve their self-awareness, and create new pathways for agency and resiliency to promote their mental health.

References

Charmaz, K. (2006). *Constructing grounded theory: A practical guide through qualitative analysis*. Sage Publications.

Charmaz, K. (2014). *Constructing grounded theory* (2nd ed.). Sage Publications.

Clini, C., Thomson, L. J. M., & Chatterjee, H. J. (2019). Assessing the impact of artistic and cultural activities on the health and well-being of forcibly displaced people using participatory action research. *BMJ Open, 9*, e025465. https://doi.org/10.1136/bmjopen-2018-025465

Dela Cruz, G. A., Johnstone, S., Singla, D. R., George, T. P., & Castle, D. J. (2023). A qualitative systematic review of experiences and barriers faced by migrant women with perinatal depression in Canada. *Women, 3*(1–21). https://doi.org/10.3390/women3010001

Hanania, A. (2018). A proposal for culturally informed art therapy with Syrian refugee women: The potential for trauma expression through embroidery. *Canadian Art Therapy Association Journal, 31*(1), 33–42. https://doi.org/10.1080/08322473.2017.1378516

Hudon, T. (2015). *Women in Canada: A gender-based statistical report*. https://www150.statcan.gc.ca/n1/en/pub/89-503-x/2015001/article/14217-eng.pdf?st=Cc-swu9V
Islam, F., Khanlou, N., Macpherson, A., & Tamim, H. (2018). Mental health consultation among Ontario's immigrant populations. *Community Mental Health Journal, 54*(1), 579–589. https://doi.org/10.1007/s10597-017-0210-z
Jo, E., Jo, J. S., Veblen, K. K., & Potter, P. J. (2018). Enoch Senior's College for Korean immigrant seniors: Quality of life effects. *Canadian Journal on Aging/La Revue canadienne du vieillissement, 37*(3), 345–359. https://doi.org/10.1017/S0714980818000211
Koh, E. (2018). Prevalence and predictors of depression and anxiety among Korean Americans. *Social Work in Public Health, 33*(1), 55–69. https://doi.org/10.1080/19371918.2017.1415178
Rose, E., Bingley, A., Rioseco, M., & Lamb, K. (2018). Art of recovery: Displacement, mental health, and wellbeing. *Art, 7*(4), 94. https://doi.org/10.3390/arts7040094
Turin, T., Rashid, R., Ferdous, M., Chowdhury, N., Naeem, I., Rumana, N., Rahman, A., Rahman, N., & Lasker, M. (2020). Perceived challenges and unmet primary care access needs among Bangladeshi immigrant women in Canada. *Journal of Primary Care & Community Health, 11*, 1–10. https://doi.org/10.1177/2150132720952618
Veenstra, G., Vas, M., & Sutherland, D. K. (2020). Asian-White health inequalities in Canada: Intersections with immigration. *Journal of Immigrant and Minority Health, 22*(2), 300–306. https://doi.org/10.1007/s10903-019-00898-2
Zou, P., Shao, J., Luo, Y., Thayaparan, A., Zhang, H., Alam, A., Liu, L., & Sidani, S. (2021). Facilitators and barriers to healthy midlife transition among South Asian immigrant women in Canada: A qualitative exploration. *Healthcare, 9*(182). https://doi.org/10.3390/healthcare9020182

Chapter 11
Empowering Bedouin Women in Israel: Bridging Economic Disparities Through Web Development

Nuzha Allassad Alhuzail

Abstract Israel's Bedouin population, an Indigenous ethnic minority, contends with high rates of unemployment and poverty, particularly affecting women. Bedouin women typically find employment in manual labor, such as hospital cleaning and agricultural work, and some manage small, home-based businesses through microfinance programs. The COVID-19 pandemic and the Israel–Gaza conflict severely impacted these women, stripping them of their livelihoods and their ability to support their families, leading to feelings of helplessness and mental health issues such as depression and anxiety. A unique program was created to address these concerns by teaching Bedouin women website design and development to provide an alternative income source. An exploratory qualitative study of 25 women who participated in the WIX program revealed their challenges and motivations as well as the importance of technology in empowering those living in poverty to generate income, nationally and internationally. This chapter describes the personal aspirations of the participants, who saw the course as a means for personal and professional growth and job security. Website development, which can be done from home, aligned with their cultural traditions and domestic responsibilities. They viewed this opportunity as a way to enter the national and international job market while maintaining the safety of their home environment. Participants who were working in physically and emotionally demanding jobs under rigid management viewed the program as a chance to escape harsh work conditions, achieve flexible schedules, and gain control over their work.

Keywords Bedouin women · Unemployment · COVID-19 impact · Website development · Empowerment

---

N. A. Alhuzail (✉)
Sapir Academic College, School of Social Work, National Center for Knowledge, Policy and Research on Bedouin Society in the Negev, Beersheba, Israel
e-mail: nuzhaa@mail.sapir.ac.il

D. Nyaga, M. Zangeneh (eds.), *Critical Ethics on Mental Health and Madness*, Advances in Mental Health and Addiction,
https://doi.org/10.1007/978-3-032-10166-2_11

Introduction

Women's entrepreneurship in developing countries plays a crucial role in promoting economic growth and socioeconomic development in their communities (Jamali, 2009; Panda, 2018; Teoh & Chong, 2008; Verheul et al., 2006). Empowered women can improve their families' economic status, enhance the overall well-being of future generations, and serve as role models for other women seeking new job opportunities (Garg & Agarwal, 2017; Panda, 2018; World Bank, 2014). In recent years, many women in developing nations have surpassed traditional gender-based expectations and become successful entrepreneurs (Garg & Agarwal, 2017). The motivations for women to pursue entrepreneurship in developing countries are diverse: They include economic necessity, unemployment, discrimination, and exclusion from the labor force, as well as personal aspirations to fulfill creative desires, establish a strong sense of identity, and demonstrate their capabilities (Garg & Agarwal, 2017; Malach Pines et al., 2010; Priyadarshini & Basariya, 2018; Roomi & Parrott, 2008). However, despite the significant potential of women's entrepreneurship, this form of employment has been declining (Mashapure et al., 2022). Women entrepreneurs face more significant challenges than men do (Garg & Agarwal, 2017; Mustapha, 2016; Panda, 2018; Roomi & Parrott, 2008). Because entrepreneurship relies heavily on social relations and activities, many challenges are related to women's relationships within their communities (Khayru, 2021; Panda, 2018; Steyaert & Katz, 2004). The COVID-19 pandemic (2020–2023) significantly affected small businesses, especially those that are women-owned. Lockdowns, supply chain disruptions, and decreased consumer spending led to unprecedented challenges. These difficulties disproportionately affected women entrepreneurs, especially those operating in vulnerable sectors, such as the Bedouin population in Israel. Amal, a single mother of four children who designs special-occasion dresses and evening wear for women described her experience. Like many Bedouin women, she often uses the present tense to describe what had happened. My business is thriving; [it is] my main source of income.... There are many orders, especially since the wedding season is approaching. In the last year, I hired a seamstress to help me—and suddenly everything collapsed: There are no orders, the sewing machines aren't working, women don't wear new dresses. No weddings, no events. We don't leave the house, and stay home in our pajamas. My heart beats fast, my body shakes, very stressed, I don't sleep at night, and I'm tired and nervous in the morning. I don't like any noise, [not even] the voices of my children.... I'm really scared. My savings are running out; I can only last another month incomewise. I can't cope, and the pressure is increasing. Then, I received a phone call from a friend who invited me to participate in a training program for building websites and mentoring a new business in the field. I needed clarification on what [qualifications] I have as a dress designer for web design. I asked a few questions and saw the light at the end of the tunnel. Today, I combine the two businesses, both a web designer and a dress designer, manage to market the dresses digitally, and earn more.

One needn't be an expert to understand that this woman had suffered stress, anxiety, depression, or trauma. The COVID-19 pandemic and the subsequent Israel–Gaza war not only hurt her business but hurt her personally and her family. At the policy level, there was investment in compensation programs for affected businesses, but small businesses, like A's, had no chance of compensation. Did anyone care about the state of mind she was in? Or was it easier to see and treat economic distress? Social workers may be afraid of technology or need to learn it well, and it is possible that they have not been trained in academic institutions to integrate technology into the various means of treatment and community intervention. A virtual business can be successful and profitable, a business activity that crosses borders and cultures (Kasperovica & Lace, 2021). The offer of a new occupation to meet Amal's financial and mental needs was the light in the darkness that had engulfed her, and, above all, it instilled in her hope and optimism, as we saw in the quote.

The global outbreak of the coronavirus had far-reaching consequences, deeply affecting economies and societies. Women entrepreneurs, in particular, faced unique challenges as they contended with the multifaceted implications of the pandemic (Rahayu et al., 2023). The closures and restrictions to curb the spread of the virus disrupted traditional business models, hurting women-led organizations in various sectors. Small businesses, often run by women, had to contend with closures, reduced traffic, and economic uncertainty, leading to financial, emotional, and family stress (Torres et al., 2023). The epidemic also caused a change in consumer behavior, particularly an increase in online shopping and a preference for contactless transactions. Women entrepreneurs relying on tech enterprises had to quickly adapt to e-commerce platforms or risk losing their customer base (Khayru, 2021). Service-oriented businesses, such as those in the beauty, health, and hospitality sectors, experienced significant setbacks because of social distancing measures. Women entrepreneurs in these fields faced closures, cancellations, and a drop in demand, challenging their ability to sustain their activities (Torres et al., 2023).

School closures and the need for social distancing measures disproportionately affected women, who often bear most of the caregiving responsibilities. Balancing business activity with increased caregiving duties posed a unique challenge for female entrepreneurs, requiring innovative solutions to maintain productivity (Goldberg et al., 2021). Women entrepreneurs, especially those in disadvantaged communities, faced an increased financial burden and limited access to capital and financial resources (Coleman et al., 2017; World Bank, 2014). Despite the challenges, many women entrepreneurs showed remarkable resilience and adaptability. From leading business models to embracing digital platforms, women proved their ability to navigate uncertainty, explore new avenues, and innovate in response to the evolving landscape (Kitole & Genda, 2024). Community support and collaboration proved to be essential elements in mitigating the impact of the pandemic on women's businesses. Initiatives that foster networking, mentoring, and shared resources played a vital role in helping women entrepreneurs navigate challenges and find collective solutions (Anggadwita et al., 2023).

Bedouin communities, known for their resilience and adaptability, faced unprecedented challenges with the outbreak of the pandemic and the recent conflict.

Bedouin women, in particular, have shown remarkable resilience in maintaining their businesses amid these distressing circumstances (Allassad Alhuzail, 2022). To meet the need for diversity and adaptation, an initiative was launched to train Bedouin entrepreneurs in web design. The aim is to empower Bedouin women to expand their businesses into the digital realm and provide them with a powerful tool to navigate the challenges posed by the epidemic and the recent military conflict. The initiative not only aims to preserve traditional businesses, such as clothing production, but also encourages Bedouin entrepreneurs to explore new avenues. The transition from designing dresses to designing websites for businesses symbolizes a transition toward modernization while maintaining cultural roots.

Methodology

This was an exploratory qualitative study of 25 women participants in a program to train Bedouin entrepreneurs in website building and digital marketing, a collaborative program of Israel's Ministry of Welfare and Social Affairs and a nonprofit organization. Fifty women joined the program; some dropped out initially, and 30 women entrepreneurs completed the course. The participants were aged 25 to 30; 20 were single and 5 were married. Ten were undergraduate students; the rest had completed 12 years of study. All had worked prior to the pandemic and the war.

Data Analysis

The research data underwent thematic analysis in accordance with the approach outlined by Patton (2002) and Braun and Clarke (2006). The initial phase involved a sequential reading of all interviews by the researcher, who recorded first impressions and identified key themes within the data to gain a comprehensive understanding (Braun & Clarke, 2006). In the subsequent stage, each interview was analyzed using grounded theory principles (Creswell & Poth, 2016). Open, inductive coding was employed to identify units of meaning emerging from each interview, followed by the identification of recurring patterns across multiple interviews. In the third step, the researcher connected categories and organized them thematically. Connections between categories were established, and thematic groupings were constructed.

Findings

The findings section describes three themes that emerged from the data analysis: Empowering Hope: A Transformative Journey from Despair to Entrepreneurial Optimism; Starting in a Safe Environment; and the Challenges of the Initial Experience.

Empowering Hope: A Transformative Journey from Despair to Entrepreneurial Optimism: Almost all the participants came to the program from a dark place, from despair, depression, stress, and a sense of loss of their source of livelihood. The program illuminated a horizon of hope for them, hope that was important to them in the complex reality in which they found themselves, hope that created optimism that the situation could be changed, an alternative source of income could be created, and the difficult period could be faced. The optimism motivated them to escape their stagnation—to act and not be passive—to create a business alternative. This was evident in Kothar's words:

It was a difficult time; the office was closed, no work, no income, a feeling of ...pain, depression...and a feeling of helplessness. The crisis was difficult, and the plan was the light of hope that appeared on the horizon. That's what I lacked ...[hope] to move towards the light and get out of the terrible darkness I was in. (Kothar).

The combination of the Ministry of Welfare and Social Affairs and a nonprofit organization specializing in business and technology was successful: The social workers who accompanied the participants aimed to meet the emotional need as well as the economic needs of the women, and this colored the program with the colors of hope and not just the colors of a regular training program, as can be seen from the words of one of the participants.

This is not a normal training program. There have been many programs; it is something different. This is a program that opens doors for us to a big world and, above all, gives us hope, and that is what helped all the participants and me to dream and step toward the realization of our dream.

Starting in a Safe Environment Building a personal website: All the participants who advanced to the program's second stage experienced building a personal website that presents the service they offer and the person behind the site. This experience is significant in a traditional society that keeps women behind the scenes. On the personal website, the graduates put themselves in the front. Some put a personal photo, and some put their first name, their uniqueness, and what they offered customers, as is evident in the quote below from one of the graduates: I built my website, told about myself, and put a picture of myself. There were objections at first; they said the name was enough, but I insisted that the time to hide was over. If I wanted to succeed, I had to be in the front.

Building a website for family members and friends: All the graduates of the second phase experienced building a website for family members or friends, gratis. This experience enabled them to continue practicing what they had learned and continue influencing their environment. One of the graduates built a website for a company that deals in construction nails and also helped it improve the visibility of its Facebook and Instagram pages. This experience made the participants appreciate the environment and recognize the importance of creating a personal website for business, as one of the participants described it: I built a website for my friend. She does special work in the field of [finger]nails. She has more than one method and adapts the colors to the client's event. I offered to build her a website for free. It helped her a lot in marketing, and she reached new clients. It was an excellent lesson for me on how to work with the person; it's not just [a matter of] building a website for [them].

Building a website for existing businesses: The significant challenge that the graduates encountered was recruiting business clients and building a website for their businesses. Only three graduates experienced this. One completed the construction of the website of a company she worked for. The second built a website for a successful business, and this was the only experience for her. A third graduate managed to build three websites, but for two of them she did not complete the process because of a lack of cooperation on the part of the clients. Construction of websites for existing businesses was offered at a nominal price, some by graduates who were partial owners of the business, out of a desire to market themselves and gain experience, as can be seen from the quote below.

At the tourism office where I work, I improve the website of the tourism office. I helped them with digital marketing, Instagram, TikTok, Facebook. I put everything in one place. When women arrive, they ask the manager of the office, "Who does marketing for you?" He says, "Kothar." And then they turn to me and they ask me to market for them. It's very flattering and helps me. The challenges of the initial experience, the initial experience in building websites, both for themselves and for family members and business owners, exposed the program's participants to challenges and complexities that must be considered in order to succeed in the field. First, it is important to register the business with the tax authorities, prepare invoices, make inquiries, invest time, have high mobility, and increase awareness of the environment and among entrepreneurs who run small businesses. Because the graduates had not yet established a business, they had not registered it with the tax authorities and therefore had no invoices, which created an obstacle, as can be seen from the words of one of the graduates: I haven't registered my business yet; I'm still at the beginning. I had a client who asked from the beginning if I could issue an invoice, and when he realized I couldn't, he stopped the process. I know I have to register the business, but after it is established, I will be free to invest in it.

Knowledge of Negotiation

The initial experience increased the graduates' awareness of the importance of developing their negotiating skills. Self-marketing and the marketing of their businesses require knowledge and skills in managing negotiations with various layers of the population. Being a young woman who owns a business in an unpopular field creates a situation in which the burden of proving professionalism and uniqueness falls on her shoulders, and some of the participants did not have these skills, as can be seen in the words of one participant:

I encountered a problem regarding the design of the logo. I am a computer science graduate without the ability to deal with customers. I know how to talk to a computer but don't know how to talk to customers and negotiate.

Gender Discourse

The program graduates described the beginnings of initiatives to build websites for businesses owned by men, in addition to those owned by women. They conducted a discourse from a feminine place that reflects their values and Bedouin society's values, giving respect and a place of honor to the man. Bedouin society is patriarchal; the man is still at the top of the pyramid. In a dialogue between mature women and businessmen, gender is in the background and cannot be ignored. Men try to hire women's services at a lower cost or disconnect during the process. Awareness of the dynamics between the genders in the business world is essential for graduates. One of them described the shock she experienced in this context: I had a problem at first regarding a price quote. Someone brought it from the West Bank. You can't compare my price to the one in the West Bank. The truth is that it shook me at first: Is it because I'm a woman? Or is it his character? I sent him my price quote but did not consider the West Bank offer. I sent him a detailed file regarding the increases; I asked for 50% of the price; It is not right to ask for less for your work, but it is acceptable initially [in order] to market myself and gain experience.

Self-Marketing

Self-marketing is part of the process that graduates experience. For some it is easy; for others, it is a considerable challenge. Self-marketing requires courage, boldness, belief in one's ability, patience, and faith that the investment will pay off. About half of the female graduates have invested in self-marketing and tried to reach a wider audience; the rest have not yet started, possibly because of personal and social barriers. Graduates who started self-marketing and marketing their businesses were aware of the enormous potential of building and designing websites, as can be seen from the comment of the graduate below: I hunt for opportunities. For example, I would sit at a coffee shop regularly to study. They refused to take money from me. In the end, I brought them a gift, a scent diffuser. I gave them the business of my friend, and told them I market for her. If you want me to market for you, too, here is my card. And it worked.

In conclusion, the initiative to train Bedouin entrepreneurs in web design is a strategic response to the challenges posed by the pandemic and the recent conflict.

By harnessing the power of technology, businesses led by Bedouin women can survive and thrive in the face of adversity. This approach preserves the cultural heritage and fosters economic resilience and empowerment within the Bedouin communities. Through joint efforts and ongoing support, technology training has the potential to shape a brighter and more sustainable future for Bedouin entrepreneurship.

Discussion

Entrepreneurial Bedouin women, like many women in the world, have long been characterized by their ability to adapt to changing situations. Their businesses, ranging from production of traditional clothing to various other ventures, embody a unique flexibility that has allowed them to weather the storm of the COVID-19 pandemic and the recent conflict (Kitole & Genda, 2024). Entrepreneurial women have consistently shown exceptional adaptability and flexibility, which proved invaluable during the COVID-19 pandemic. As the crisis unfolded, many female entrepreneurs swiftly adapted their business models to meet market demands and lockdown constraints. They transitioned to online sales, remote work, and virtual services, ensuring business continuity. These women also demonstrated resilience by diversifying products, entering new markets, and innovating offerings. Their quick response to disruptions and their embrace of new opportunities sustained their businesses and contributed to economic recovery. This adaptability underscores their pivotal role in fostering resilience and innovation during global uncertainty (Anggadwita et al., 2023; Donga & Chimucheka, 2024). The findings of the current study reveal that the program attracted participants who were grappling with deep despair, including depression, stress, and a sense of loss related to their livelihoods. The program served as a beacon of hope in their complex reality, fostering optimism and changing their perspective on the potential for change. This newfound hope empowered them to believe they could create alternative sources of income and navigate the challenging times ahead. Their optimism motivated them to pursue business alternatives and break free from stagnation rather than remain passive. Recent studies have demonstrated that such programs significantly impact participants' mental health and entrepreneurial success, highlighting the role of hope and optimism in overcoming economic hardship (Ayala & Manzano, 2014; Hartmann et al., 2022; Stephan, 2018). The current findings show that women typically initiate business ventures with small, cautious steps. This approach allows them to minimize risk while gaining experience and confidence in their entrepreneurial abilities. By starting small, women can better manage their resources and gradually expand their operations as they become more adept and their businesses grow. This strategy helps reduce potential financial losses and enables them to test the market and refine their business models before making significant investments. Studies elsewhere have shown that this incremental approach often leads to sustainable growth and long-term success, as it builds a solid foundation for the business and fosters resilience against market fluctuations (Buttner & Moore, 1997; Mukherjee, 2023). The current study's findings highlight the critical need for Bedouin women to acquire knowledge in negotiation and gender discourse in order to succeed in building websites. This need stems from the unique cultural and societal challenges they face, including traditional gender roles that often limit their participation in economic activities. By gaining skills in negotiation, these women can better advocate for fair business practices, secure favorable contracts, and navigate the complexities of the marketplace. Additionally, understanding gender discourse equips them to challenge and redefine societal norms, fostering an environment in which their contributions are valued and respected. Empowering Bedouin women with these skills enhances their business success and promotes broader social change by challenging gender inequalities and supporting women's empowerment within their communities (Author, 2023; Kulik & Olekalns, 2012).

Conclusions

Social workers address clients' essential needs during crises and conflicts, but equally crucial is their focus on mental well-being. The most significant aspect of their role is to instill a sense of hope, guiding clients toward positive change. Interdisciplinary collaborations, particularly between business sectors and nonprofit organizations, are essential in providing comprehensive support and fostering resilience in affected communities. These partnerships enhance resource availability, introduce innovative solutions, and ensure a holistic approach to client care, ultimately contributing to more sustainable and effective interventions.

References

Allassad Alhuzail, N. (2022). The meaning of the marital relationship in the lives of three generations of Bedouin women. *Journal of Cross-Cultural Psychology, 53*(6), 683–702. https://doi.org/10.1177/00220221221099593

Anggadwita, G., Permatasari, A., Alamanda, D. T., & Profityo, W. B. (2023). Exploring women's initiatives for family business resilience during the COVID-19 pandemic. *Journal of Family Business Management, 13*(3), 714–736.

Ayala, J. C., & Manzano, G. (2014). The resilience of the entrepreneur. Influence on the success of the business. A longitudinal analysis. *Journal of Economic Psychology, 42*, 126–135. https://doi.org/10.1016/j.joep.2014.02.004

Braun, B., & Clarke, V. (2006). Using thematic analysis in psychology. *Qualitative Research in Psychology, 3*(2), 77–101. https://doi.org/10.1191/1478088706qp063oa

Buttner, E. H., & Moore, D. P. (1997). Women's organizational exodus to entrepreneurship: Self-reported motivations and correlates with success. *Journal of Small Business Management, 35*(1).

Coleman, S., Robb, A., & Sagieva, G. (2017). Access to finance for women-led SMEs in developing countries. *International Journal of Gender and Entrepreneurship, 9*(3), 262–285.

Creswell, J. W., & Poth, C. N. (2016). *Qualitative inquiry and research design: Choosing among five approaches*. Sage.

Donga, G., & Chimucheka, T. (2024). Challenges and opportunities of the COVID-19 pandemic on women entrepreneurs operating in the informal food sector: A post COVID-19 analyses. *International Journal of Research in Business and Social Science (2147-4478), 13*(2), 216–228. https://doi.org/10.20525/ijrbs.v13i2.3168

Garg, S., & Agarwal, P. (2017). Problems and prospects of woman entrepreneurship—A review of literature. *IOSR Journal of Business and Management, 19*(01), 55–60. https://doi.org/10.9790/487X-1901065560

Goldberg, A. E., McCormick, N., & Virginia, H. (2021). Parenting in a pandemic: Work–family arrangements, well-being, and intimate relationships among adoptive parents. *Family Relations, 70*(1), 7–25.

Hartmann, S., Backmann, J., Newman, A., Brykman, K. M., & Pidduck, R. J. (2022). Psychological resilience of entrepreneurs: A review and agenda for future research. *Journal of Small Business Management, 60*(5), 1041–1079. https://doi.org/10.1080/00472778.2021.2024216

Jamali, D. (2009). Constraints and opportunities facing women entrepreneurs in developing countries: A relational perspective. *Gender in Management: An International Journal, 24*(4), 232–251. https://doi.org/10.1108/17542410910961532

Kasperovica, L., & Lace, N. (2021). Factors influencing companies' positive financial performance in digital age: A meta-analysis. *Entrepreneurship and Sustainability Issues, 8*(4), 291. https://doi.org/10.9770/jesi.2021.8.4(17)

Khayru, R. K. (2021). Opinions about consumer behavior during the Covid-19 pandemic. *Journal of Social Science Studies, 1*(1), 31–36.

Kitole, F. A., & Genda, E. L. (2024). Empowering her drive: Unveiling the resilience and triumphs of women entrepreneurs in rural landscapes. *Women's Studies International Forum, 104*, 102912. https://doi.org/10.1016/j.wsif.2024.102912

Kulik, C. T., & Olekalns, M. (2012). Negotiating the gender divide: Lessons from the negotiation and organizational behavior literatures. *Journal of Management, 38*(4), 1387–1415. https://doi.org/10.1177/0149206311431307

Malach Pines, A., Lerner, M., & Schwartz, D. (2010). Gender differences in entrepreneurship: Equality, diversity and inclusion in times of global crisis. *Equality, Diversity and Inclusion: An International Journal, 29*(2), 186–198. https://doi.org/10.1108/02610151011024493

Mashapure, R., Nyagadza, B., Chikazhe, L., Msipa, N., Ngorora, G. K. P., & Gwiza, A. (2022). Challenges hindering women entrepreneurship sustainability in rural livelihoods: Case of Manicaland province. *Cogent Social Sciences, 8*(1), 2132675. https://doi.org/10.1080/23311886.2022.2132675

Mukherjee, S. (2023). The business model canvas of women owned micro enterprises in the urban informal sector. *Journal of Enterprising Communities, 17*(2), 398–418. https://doi.org/10.1108/JEC-05-2021-0068

Mustapha, M. (2016). Challenges and success factors of female entrepreneurs: Evidence from a developing country. *International Review of Management and Marketing, 6*(4), 224–231.

Panda, S. (2018). Constraints faced by women entrepreneurs in developing countries: Review and ranking. *Gender in Management: An International Journal, 33*(4), 315–331. https://doi.org/10.1108/GM-01-2017-0003

Patton, M. (2002). *Qualitative research evaluation methods* (3rd ed.). Sage.

Priyadarshini, S., & Basariya, S. R. (2018). Women entrepreneurs—Problems and prospects in India. *International Journal of Civil Engineering and Technology, 9*(4), 96–102.

Rahayu, N. S., Masduki, & Ellyanawati, E. N. (2023). Women entrepreneurs' struggles during the COVID-19 pandemic and their use of social media. *Journal of Innovation and Entrepreneurship, 12*(1), 51. https://doi.org/10.1186/s13731-023-00322-y

Roomi, M. A., & Parrott, G. (2008). Barriers to development and progression of women entrepreneurs in Pakistan. *The Journal of Entrepreneurship, 17*(1), 59–72. https://doi.org/10.1177/097135570701700105

Stephan, U. (2018). Entrepreneurs' mental health and well-being: A review and research agenda. *Academy of Management Perspectives, 32*(3), 290–322. https://doi.org/10.5465/amp.2017.0001

Steyaert, C., & Katz, J. (2004). Reclaiming the space of entrepreneurship in society: Geographical, discursive and social dimensions. *Entrepreneurship & Regional Development, 16*(3), 179–196. https://doi.org/10.1080/0898562042000197135

Teoh, W. M. Y., & Chong, S. C. (2008). Improving women entrepreneurs in small and medium enterprises in Malaysia: Policy recommendations. *Communications of the IBIMA, 2*, 31–38.

Torres, J., Maduko, F., Gaddis, I., Iacovone, L., & Beegle, K. (2023). The impact of the COVID-19 pandemic on women-led businesses. *The World Bank Research Observer, 38*(1), 36–72. https://doi.org/10.1093/wbro/lkac002

Verheul, I., Stel, A. V., & Thurik, R. (2006). Explaining female and male entrepreneurship at the country level. *Entrepreneurship & Regional Development, 18*(2), 151–183. https://doi.org/10.1080/08985620500532053

World Bank. (2014). *World development report 2014: Risk and opportunity - Managing risk for development*. World Bank Publications.

Chapter 12
Marginalized Homeless Youth: Exploring the Relationship Between Identity and Mental Health with Youth Who Self-Identify with Marginalized Identities and Have Experienced Precarious Housing/Homelessness in a Time of COVID-19

Dawn Onishenko and Marco Giuliani

Abstract This qualitative study investigates the compounded impacts of COVID-19 on marginalized youth experiencing homelessness or precarious housing in the Greater Toronto Area. Research with 17 youth and 20 service providers explored how interlocking oppressions based on race, Indigeneity, 2SLGBTQ+ identity, and mental health intersected with housing, policing, and violence. Findings reveal increased hardships, including over-policing, decreased mental wellness, and exclusion from services. The analysis highlights the nonlinear, entangled nature of mental health, addiction, homelessness, and identity-based exclusion. This evidence advocates for structural policy responses that address these multifaceted, systemic inequities to better support youth.

Keywords COVID-19 · Marginalized youth · Oppression · Identity-based exclusion · Homelessness · Mental health

Introduction

This chapter highlights findings from a qualitative research study investigating the compounded impacts of COVID-19 on youth who *self-identify* as part of a marginalized community and, at the time of the study, were experiencing homelessness or

D. Onishenko · M. Giuliani (✉)
Toronto Metropolitan University, Toronto, ON, Canada
e-mail: donishenko@torontomu.ca; marc.giuliani@torontomu.ca

D. Nyaga, M. Zangeneh (eds.), *Critical Ethics on Mental Health and Madness*, Advances in Mental Health and Addiction,
https://doi.org/10.1007/978-3-032-10166-2_12

were precariously housed in the Greater Toronto Area. The study explores realities that marginalized homeless youth encounter in relation to housing, particularly as it intersects with substance use, mental health, policing, bullying, and harassment to uncover the layers of discrimination present within social policies and practices (Abramovich, 2016; Abramovich & Kimura, 2021; Boyd et al., 2016; Cénat et al., 2022; Gaetz, 2020; Kidd, Thistle, et al., 2019; Kidd, Vitopoulos, et al., 2019). In this chapter, we parse out the unique lived experiences of Black, Indigenous, and 2SLGBTQ participants and their intersection with these elements, and then we weave our findings back together to explore the impacts and commonalities that cross intersectional and interlocking identities, particularly as to how this relates to mental wellness. The connection between interlocking oppression and identity politics is critical as we explore the lived reality of youth homelessness during the pandemic. As identity awareness is vital in exposing the specifics of structural exclusion, understanding interlocking oppression highlights the multifaceted nature of these experiences and provides space to argue for policies and structural responses that reflect the diverse and similar realities of those who are excluded.

In addition to 17 youth (ages 16–29) who self-identified as homeless or precariously housed (i.e., living in a shelter, living rough, couch surfing, and no fixed address) and as racialized, Black, Indigenous, 2SLGBTQ+, dis/abled, girls/women, criminalized, living with mental health, and/or religious faiths, nine shelter managers/executive directors serving youth and the homelessness sector, and 11 frontline workers directly responding to youth and homelessness were engaged to deepen our understanding of their lived experiences of "the systems," such as shelter/housing, social services, and metal health, in the time of COVID-19.

Drawing on theoretical underpinnings and real-world examples, findings reveal the complexities, such as over-policing, increased violence, decreased mental wellness, and exclusion from stable housing and services experienced by youth that are disproportionately excluded from housing due to structural oppression (Abramovich et al., 2024; Baker Collins et al., 2018; Kidd, Thistle, et al., 2019; Kidd, Vitopoulos, et al., 2019; Petering, 2016), the significance of community in fostering improved mental health during pandemic health directives, and tensions between immediate/emergency responses and sustainable permanent solutions. This chapter uses an interlocking analysis to understand the various forms of systemic oppression that homeless and other marginal youths face (i.e., a queer Black youth who describes the *hypervisibility* they experience in over-policing but the *invisibility* they experience, allowing for increased violence at the hands of the police)—highlighted during the pandemic—and how this lived reality contributes to mental health and addictions.

In our research, we asked youth about aspects of their identity that *they* felt created "exclusion" or "marginalization." *All* youth interviewed reported some form of experience with mental health as a *factor of exclusion.* Compounded with other identity factors, mental health emerges as an interlocking reality that is discursive and interconnected with other aspects of their identity. Indeed, so intertwined is it that we began to try and decipher what occurred first: mental health/addictions, homelessness, or identity-based exclusion in order to validate strong policy recommendations. This exercise proved somewhat futile in practice; these elements remain fully entangled and iterative in nature rather than linear. By exposing the interlocking nature of these challenges, we can advocate for a more equitable and supportive policy environment for all youth, ensuring that they have the resources to thrive in the post-pandemic world.

Literature Review

While youth are over-represented in the homeless population in Canada (A Way Home, 2022; Gaetz et al., 2016b), youth with compounding identities based on race (A Way Home, 2022; Gaetz et al., 2016b; May, 2015), Indigeneity (A Way Home, 2022; Gaetz et al., 2016a), disability (Baker Collins et al., 2018), sexual orientation (Abramovich, 2016; A Way Home, 2022), gender (Berman et al., 2009; Tutty et al., 2014), and citizenship (Berman et al., 2009; Forchuk et al., 2022; Walsh et al., 2016), as well as those experiencing other marginal social constructions and interlocked oppressions, are disproportionately impacted by homelessness due to multifaceted factors. For example, while gender and sexual minority youth continue to be subject to homophobia/biphobia/transphobia, cisgenderism, and heterosexism within a variety of settings associated with everyday life such as school and family (Durso & Gates, 2012; Taylor et al., 2015), they remain highly invisible and are more likely to become homeless (Whittington et al., 2020) and Trans identified youth face unique and unrecognized barriers (Forbes et al., 2016); racialized homeless youth experience racial erasure within social service settings leading to increased social exclusion (May, 2015); Indigenous youth experience greater victimization due to colonization (Ansloos & Wager, 2020; Kidd, Thistle, et al., 2019); and youth living with differing abilities are often overlooked and underreported within homelessness services (Collins & Schormans, 2021). Further, racialized (Boyd et al., 2016; Cénat et al., 2022; Petering, 2016), 2SLGBTQ+ (Abramovich, 2016; Goodyear et al., 2024), Indigenous (Kidd, Thistle, et al., 2019), and homeless youth with disabilities (Baker Collins et al., 2018) are more likely to experience bullying, harassment, justice involvement, over-policing, anxiety, depression, addiction, self-harm, suicide, and school exclusion; they are also more likely to engage in survival sex, have contracted HIV, and be victims of violence (Statistics Canada, 2019; Taylor et al., 2015). These experiences contribute to increased levels of mental health and substance use among these populations in relation to the general population. Due to differential experiences pertaining to racism, colonization, homophobia/biphobia/transphobia, ableism, heteropatriarchy and other forms of structural oppression, erasure, and violence, there is no doubt that the global pandemic did not cause homelessness and marginalization, but rather *compounded and magnified issues encountered by homeless/precariously housed youth*, making this moment in time a critical opportunity to explore the relationship between identity and mental health and addictions.

The COVID-19 pandemic exposed and exacerbated existing inequalities within Canadian society, disproportionately impacting marginalized populations. Indeed, one does not have to dig very deep to see that, while a discourse of the pandemic being a "boat we were *all* in" was a prevalent one, that was indeed **not** the case, and in reality, had very heightened consequences for already excluded populations. The Medical Officer of Health reported, "Racialized populations are being disproportionately affected by the novel coronavirus"; "Black people account for 21 per cent of reported cases in the city, while making up only nine per cent of the overall population. Further, Arab, Middle Eastern and West Asian people represent 11 per cent of the city's COVID-19 cases, while only making up 4 per cent of the total population." "Racialized, Immigrant and Indigenous youth, as well as youth with disabilities, continue to be disproportionately affected by the COVID-19 pandemic". Kwame McKenzie reminded that "[the pandemic] magnified existing issues in marginalized communities." COVID-19 is not an equalizer but rather exacerbates already glaring disparities and perpetuates systemic discrimination. Thus, this chapter seeks to communicate some of these gaps from the perspective of excluded youth, provide a space of discussion regarding these unique and interlocking disparities, and examine policy and social responses that demonstrate positive outcomes for homeless youth.

Findings from the Research

As critical anti-oppressive researchers seeking to explore the experience of marginalized precariously housed youth, the more we heard the profound insights of our participants, the more important it became for us to allow the voices of participants to speak for themselves when presenting data on the interplay between mental health, homelessness, and marginalized identities. Indeed, in the pandemic context, wherein a discourse of "all in the same boat" and "COVID-19 as the great equalizer" masks the very real disparity experienced by already excluded populations, the voices of homeless youth, who are already disregarded by society, are negligible. However, COVID-19 also prompted unprecedented state and social responses; for example, funding for social supports, opportunities for services delivered in a variety of ways (i.e., use of technology and virtual approaches), and new resources were employed, and some agencies described increased tolerance and awareness by the public of the lived realities of homeless youth. However, one cannot help but notice that these were responses done *to* and *for* youth rather than *with* youth.

The COVID-19 pandemic has shed light on the interlocking oppression that young people face, highlighting the urgent need for a holistic and inclusive response. Thus, from an organizational standpoint, we will begin by exploring some of the key experiences of Black, racialized, Indigenous, and 2SLGBTQ+ youth, as told in their voices. We will then look at the culmination of their experiences as they pertain to mental health and addiction and begin to reimagine the question of more inclusive and equitable approaches to addressing youth homelessness, including mental health and crisis intervention, amid the complexities of societal structures.

Black, Indigenous, and Racialized Youth

Existing research shows that racism embedded in various Canadian institutions, including child welfare, the criminal justice system, and the education system through the school-to-prison pipeline, exacerbate existing disparities that disproportionately impact Black, Indigenous, and racialized youth through heightened surveillance, criminalization and incarceration rates, experiences of violence, and trauma (Boyd et al., 2016; Cénat et al., 2022; Gaetz et al., 2016a; Glogowski & Rakoff, 2019; Kidd, Thistle, et al., 2019; Owusu-Bempah & Jeffers, 2021; Radebe, 2024; Sanders, 2024). This/these racism(s) played out for research participants in a notable way in their relationship to the police. Several workers discuss the targeting of Black, Indigenous, and racialized youth by police. Sometimes, to their own surprise!

> So, the violence that they [Black, Indigenous, racialized youth] experience from the police, whether or not they were under arrest, is shocking to most people that don't experience police violence, and not shocking to people that do, you know, and that are from communities that do. So having not experienced a lot of police violence myself, I have been close to it with clients over the years and you can't deny it, you know. You can't deny the systemic nature of this and who gets followed by police and who gets taken to alleys by police.—Denise, Street Outreach Worker

While many shelters have Community Liaison Officers who engage with residents, Black, Indigenous, and other racialized youth report having negative interactions with the police outside of shelter settings. Youth themselves talk about their interactions with police and their experiences trying to make a living or just engaging in survival. Demir (28), a racialized youth living in a hotel shelter during the pandemic, was out collecting cans to sell and was stopped by the police. He remarks:

> I collect beer cans to sell them, and I was passing by somewhere. I was walking and a police car was driving behind me and was calling me. But the officer was really terrible. He was really mean, oh my God. He asked me are you drunk? They stopped me for 15-20 minutes they asked for my ID. I didn't have ID, but they asked my name and then called the head office to inquire about me, like if they have a warrant or something. The officer just, I felt like I was marginalized there.

Farah (23), a youth who identifies as Black, conveys similar experiences waiting outside their workplace during the pandemic:

> I'm just standing there and they [police] always come and question, like, "hey, what are you doing, why are you here?", and like, "I'm waiting for my boss to get here with my supervisor", 'cause I always get there [to work] a bit early. On the days that the supervisor wasn't there early, I'd get questioned by cops. When I told my manager, she kind of scheduled me to come in, like, after they opened.

While participants acknowledge that Black and other racialized youth are vulnerable to police surveillance, restrictions brought about by the pandemic become a means of legitimizing this targeting.

For Indigenous youth, loss of culture and intergenerational trauma intersect with anti-Indigenous racism, including policing as well as other Canadian institutions, such as child welfare, the criminal justice system, health care, and education, contributing to pathways into homelessness and suggesting a need for culturally appropriate and trauma-informed responses (Alberton et al., 2023; Blackstock, 2019; Cesaroni et al., 2019). Patty, a frontline housing worker, identifies the importance of having Indigenous workers in mitigating these barriers for Indigenous youth:

> So, when I used to work with youth on the Indigenous reserve, they were very excited that I wasn't white. They were very, they were more easily, accepted me more easily, told me things about them, because we had kind of an understanding. Like my people were colonized, they were colonized, there was a little bit of understanding of the history of racism all of that, so I feel like I haven't had any issues with working with marginalized populations, because my population is already, like the population I come from is also marginalized. So, it's much easier for people to accept me and to open up to me.

Teresa, an 18-year-old Indigenous youth experiencing homelessness, reflects on their experience working with an Elder and the importance of cultural connection:

> She gives us like teachings and stuff so it's like I get to learn a little more about like my people and, like my roots, and I think that's very important for me because, personally, I have lost that little bit of connection when I was younger.

Workers point to the unique intersection of Indigenous youth—especially as they carry trauma—when facing exclusion in social systems. Melissa, a youth worker at an Indigenous organization, explains:

> So, a lot of my youth that I work with have come out of like the child welfare system Or have had intergenerational trauma where they haven't had access to their culture and that's usually done in Community and at pow wows, it's done at friendship centers. And it's really hard for youth to sit at home by themselves and say okay I'm going to start smudging, I'm going to start learning about my culture, because they don't have those natural social connections, or they can't join a group. And I'm finding that like especially like my LGBTQ youth are really craving community and are really having trouble with that isolation being at home.

Thus, findings reveal the mental health impacts of youth homelessness are intensified by experiences of racism, colonial violence, homophobia/biphobia/transphobia, and other forms of oppression, necessitating trauma-informed approaches to care that recognize the unique intersecting traumas of marginalized identities.

Gender and Sexual Minority Youth

Gender and sexual minority youth are significantly overrepresented in the homeless youth population, accounting for an estimated 20–40%, three to four times greater than the total estimated 2SLGBTQ+ population in Canada (Abramovich & Shelton,

2017). Homophobia, biphobia, transphobia, and other forms of discrimination based on gender and sexual identity are linked to disproportionate rates of mental health issues, including anxiety, depression, suicidality, addiction, school dropout, and rejection from family, peers, and communities, contributing to pathways into homelessness (Abramovich & Shelton, 2017; Taylor et al., 2015). This was reflected by our participants, with approximately half of our youth identifying under the 2SLGBTQ+ umbrella. Several participants express that they felt safer in 2SLGBTQ + -specific residences and shelters. Demir (26), a youth living at an emergency hotel shelter, exposes the prevalence of homophobia and recounts having to keep his identity secret while living there. He shares his interactions with other residents and contemplates feeling unsafe: "They are swearing, saying like faggots and stuff." Bree (24) talks about a COVID outbreak at a queer shelter and having to go to a non-identity specific hotel shelter to quarantine: "So pretty much the lot of us got shipped off to the hotel and you would think because it's a hotel, it's nice, but it's really not, because the staff, especially if you're queer like this, the staff just constantly misgender you."

Echoing the lived reality of Black, Indigenous, and racialized youth, workers and youth alike describe increased surveillance and harassment of 2SLGBTQ+ youth by those in positions of authority, such as the police. Lillian, a worker at a youth shelter, remarks: "We've had officers come onto the, onto the site making transphobic comments. 'Oh, [scornfully] I thought this was a women's shelter'." Zola, a trans youth (25) confirms: "I've noticed that the police out here in Ontario really have no respectful care of gender identity. They will like look at your ID and they're like, okay, well that's who you are, so you better suck it up while you're interacting with me." Almost unanimously, 2SLGBTQ+ participants describe frequent incidents of increased surveillance, harassment, and discrimination due to their sexual and gender identities. This surveillance results in both a sense of hypervisibility, where they are negatively singled out, while simultaneously having their identities ignored, rendering them invisible; both tactics significantly contribute to their harm, suggesting a need for increased cultural awareness training and identity-specific interventions.

Intersectional Experiences: Invisible/Hypervisible

Identities are not mutually exclusive, with many participants identifying with more than one marginalized identity. CJ (22) shares powerful insight into his intersecting identities:

> I get kind of nervous, like, mainly 'cause of my racialized identity, I think is, like, more of, like, a, like, a danger to the police, but yeah, also my, my identity as, as a gay man. I think they're, they're more willing to, to use, to use violence, and then to not follow their, like, rules because they think it's, like, a homeless person, they're not going to be able to say anything about it, and there's no one watching.

CJ acknowledges that his intersectional identity as a racialized gay man makes him hypervisible in one context, as he is targeted by police, yet invisible in another, as his homelessness renders him overlooked by the public—deemed unworthy of protection and outside the law's safeguarding—leading to heightened surveillance, policing, and violence.

Mental Health

Research shows that 85.4% of homeless youth have experienced a mental health crisis, 42% reported at least one suicide attempt, and 35.2% reported at least one drug overdose requiring hospitalization (Gaetz et al., 2016b). These alarming figures underscore the critical necessity for trauma-informed approaches to addressing multiple intersecting systems, including crisis intervention, to effectively support marginalized youth (Schwan et al., 2017). Several youth confirm feeling unsafe when accessing crisis services. Teresa (18) shares:

> I have had some interactions with the police, kind of like medical. Instead of like someone that's you know specialized in mental health, it was just like the police dealing with the like mental health, which normally it's a different outcome because they can't really evaluate what's going on. If you don't go by ambulance, you have to go into the police car, and they will handcuff you because that's a mental health apprehension. I just don't have a very good experience with police in the past, so it's a little overwhelming. And it kind of just like makes things a little more intense.

Workers confirmed that when they call for mental health crisis services, the response is problematic:

> In 18 years, I think, maybe twice, TWICE, I've actually got the mental health response that I've asked for. And every other time it's just been you know whichever cops are on duty at the time, whichever cop picks up the call and it's often not skillful. Thankfully that's not always the case, and I have seen just you know two police who arrived in a crisis call at our youth drop-in where I work and respond incredibly well to a young Black man in a mental health crisis who was violent, and they de-escalated and there was no hands-on. It was brilliant. So, there's a spectrum.—Melanie, Shelter Manager

Gwen, a manager at another shelter, contemplates the inconsistencies of the current system:

> Sometimes when we call dispatch or request the impact team, they'll send police officers right away, and sometimes there's push back and they're saying like, oh no, the police officers, only they can request the impact team. We need the youth's consent to request for impact team. And there's just, it's not consistent.

In identifying this fractured relationship with the police, one must consider what it means in terms of the safety of marginalized youth. Linda, a frontline housing worker, shares:

> You know, Black youth, Indigenous youth, racialized youth, who have had terrible experiences with the police and don't feel safe calling the police that's an issue for their own safety because they don't know who to call. So, they might be in a very abusive relationship

> or they might be, you know, and again, like dealing with sex trafficking, drug trafficking, survival sex, unit takeovers, all those things, and they don't have anyone one to call.

Findings indicate inconsistencies in treatment, as discussed by workers, and the harm expressed by youth and workers alike reveal a need for reimagining crisis responses, particularly for youth with marginalized identities who have historically and continue to experience violence by police.

Safe, Stable Housing Critical to Supporting Marginalized Youth

Research suggests that prolonged homelessness correlates with increased risk of trauma and likelihood of transitioning into chronic homelessness in adulthood, underscoring the need for early intervention (Gaetz et al., 2016b). Melanie, a shelter manager, discusses the experiences of youth finally getting stable housing in relation to mental health: "I would say, maybe 70% do have this unraveling, this kind of what they call decompressing that happens because basic needs are finally taken care of. And then it's like here comes the mental health that I've been suppressing all this time." Linda, a frontline housing worker, also shares:

> I know like LGBTQ youth, youth who are marginalized and are experiencing a lot of discrimination and racism and oppression, I think, understanding that and coming from that lens of trauma-informed care. Because once you're housed, then you can start to you know, put the puzzle pieces back together and start to recover.

And Denise, a street outreach worker, reflects:

> It's the ones that can't maintain housing, for whatever reason, because their mental health or addiction stuff, or trauma stuff, and yeah, I mean the violence that people experience as homeless youth is, you wouldn't believe the stories we hear . . . I don't meet with very many youth that don't have some kind of physical, mental or sexual trauma from their family of origin or wherever they were raised, caretakers, caregivers. That's not usually part of the discourse of homeless youth, right? Trust me -- no one likes my answers at a party where they say, 'so, what causes youth homelessness, you know, is it guns, is it gangs?' and there's a little bit more awareness now - but I'm like, actually it's systemic inequities that cause youth homelessness... and then everyone glazes over.

Youth corroborate safe, stable housing as the singular most important support that they can receive in terms of responding to their mental health. Martin (26) shares how stable housing has made space for addressing his mental health concerns: "I've had a place for a year and a half now and been dealing with my mental health. It's taking time, but I'm figuring it all out. I've got a good therapist still." Similarly, Maria (26) contemplates how stable housing has contributed to their well-being:

> Because I was either going back and forth, like, staying with family or going back to shelters, and then, you know, got mixed up in different things, and just back and forth. Like, it was never, like, permanent, but it was always back, like I always ended up falling back to being homeless. But now I'm good, I've had this place for a bit now, and things are good here and I'm away from all the negative and stuff.

And finally, Tyler (19) considers how stable housing has contributed to a decrease in substance use: "So when I feel sick, like I'm tired or desperate, or like, I start feeling very, very bad. I smoke cigarettes, but right now, for example, that I get stabilized [housed], I don't. I don't need to smoke anything. I don't, I don't drink alcohol."

Youth experiencing homelessness and/or living in shelters are more likely to experience mental health challenges and addiction due to discrimination, lack of safety, and the stresses of engaging in survival, exacerbating their marginalization, and making stable housing a necessity for addressing the impacts of trauma and improved mental health.

Conclusion

Learnings from hidden injustices unmasked during COVID-19 can offer the opportunity to provide insight toward unravelling the historical disparities of colonization, racism and anti-Black racism, homophobia/biphobia/transphobia, ableism, heteropatriarchy, and other oppressions through multifaceted exploration, to generate more inclusive and equitable approaches in addressing youth homelessness and mental health amid the complexities of societal structures. This chapter aims to foster informed dialogue among stakeholders to deepen understanding of the unique needs and experiences of marginalized youth experiencing homelessness in a world of pandemics. Through presentation and dialogue with participants and policymakers we seek to engage with the structural issues facing historically excluded communities in ways that are intersectional and complex.

References

A Way Home. (2022). Youth homelessness in Canada. *A Way Home Canada*. https://awayhome.ca/youth-homelessness/#:~:text=YOUTH%20HOMELESSNESS%20IN%20CANADA.%20For%20thousands%20of%20young%20people%20across

Abramovich, A. (2016). Preventing, reducing and ending LGBTQ2S youth homelessness: The need for targeted strategies. *Social Inclusion, 4*(4), 86–96. https://doi.org/10.17645/si.v4i4.669

Abramovich, A., & Kimura, L. (2021). Outcomes for youth living in Canada's first LGBTQ2S transitional housing program. *Journal of Homosexuality, 68*(8), 1242–1259. https://doi.org/10.1080/00918369.2019.1696102

Abramovich, A., Marshall, M., Webb, C., Elkington, N., Stark, R. K., Pang, N., & Wood, L. (2024). Identifying 2SLGBTQ+ individuals experiencing homelessness using point-in-time counts: Evidence from the 2021 Toronto street needs assessment survey. *PLoS One, 19*(4), e0298252–e0298252. https://doi.org/10.1371/journal.pone.0298252

Abramovich, A., & Shelton, J. (2017). *Where am I going to go?: Intersectional approaches to ending LGBTQ2S youth homelessness in Canada & the U.S. Canadian observatory on homelessness*. https://homelesshub.ca/wp-content/uploads/2024/04/Where-Am-I-Going-To-Go.pdf

Alberton, A. M., Gorey, K. M., & Williams, N. G. (2025). Individual and community predictors of arrests in Canada: Evidence of over-policing of indigenous peoples and communities. *Journal of Ethnic & Cultural Diversity in Social Work, 34*(1), 5–17. https://doi.org/10.1080/15313204.2023.2211785

Ansloos, J. P., & Wager, A. C. (2020). Surviving in the cracks: A qualitative study with indigenous youth on homelessness and applied community theatre. *International Journal of Qualitative Studies in Education, 33*(1), 50–65. https://doi.org/10.1080/09518398.2019.1678785

Baker Collins, S., Schormans, A. F., Watt, L., Idems, B., & Wilson, T. (2018). The invisibility of disability for homeless youth. *Journal of Social Distress and Homeless, 27*(2), 99–109. https://doi.org/10.1080/10530789.2018.1480892

Berman, H., Mulcahy, G. A., Forchuk, C., Edmunds, K. A., Haldenby, A., & Lopez, R. (2009). Uprooted and displaced: A critical narrative study of homeless, aboriginal, and newcomer girls in Canada. *Issues in Mental Health Nursing, 30*(7), 418–430. https://doi.org/10.1080/01612840802624475

Blackstock, C. (2019). Revisiting the breath of life theory. *The British Journal of Social Work, 49*(4), 854–859. https://doi.org/10.1093/bjsw/bcz047

Boyd, J., Fast, D., & Small, W. (2016). Pathways to criminalization for street-involved youth who use illicit substances. *Critical Public Health, 26*(5), 530–541. https://doi.org/10.1080/09581596.2015.1110564

Cénat, J. M., Hajizadeh, S., Dalexis, R. D., Ndengeyingoma, A., Guerrier, M., & Kogan, C. (2022). Prevalence and effects of daily and major experiences of racial discrimination and microaggressions among black individuals in Canada. *Journal of Interpersonal Violence, 37*(17–18), NP16750–NP16778. https://doi.org/10.1177/08862605211023493

Cesaroni, C., Grol, C., & Fredericks, K. (2019). Overrepresentation of indigenous youth in Canada's criminal justice system: Perspectives of indigenous young people. *Australian & New Zealand Journal of Criminology, 52*(1), 111–128. https://doi.org/10.1177/0004865818778746

Collins, S. B., & Schormans, A. F. (2021). Making visible the prevalence on self-identified disability among youth experiencing homelessness. *Journal of Social Distress and Homelessness, 32*(1), 16–24. https://doi.org/10.1080/10530789.2021.1940719

Durso, L. E., & Gates, G. J. (2012). Serving our youth: Findings from a national survey of service providers working with lesbian, gay, bisexual and transgender youth who are homeless or at risk of becoming homeless. *Policy File*. Williams Institute. http://williamsinstitute.law.ucla.edu/wp-content/uploads/Durso-Gates-LGBT-Homeless-Youth-Survey-July-2012.pdf

Forbes, C., Clark, L. F., & Diep, H. (2016). Positive attributes and risk behaviors in young transgender women. *Psychology of Sexual Orientation and Gender Diversity, 3*(1), 129–134. https://doi.org/10.1037/sgd0000148

Forchuk, C., Russell, G., Richardson, J., Perreault, C., Hassan, H., Lucyk, B., & Gyamfi, S. (2022). Family matters in Ontario: Understanding and addressing homelessness among newcomer families in Canada. *Canadian Journal of Nursing Research, 54*(1), 27–39. https://doi.org/10.1177/0844562121998206

Gaetz, S. (2020). Making the prevention of homelessness a priority: The role of social innovation. *The American Journal of Economics and Sociology, 79*(2), 353–381. https://doi.org/10.1111/ajes.12328

Gaetz, S., Dej, E., Richter, T., & Redman, M. (2016a). *The state of homelessness in Canada 2016*. Canadian Observatory on Homelessness Press. https://homelesshub.ca/sites/default/files/SOHC16_final_20Oct2016.pdf

Gaetz, S., O'Grady, B., Kidd, S., & Schwan. K. (2016b). *Without a home: The national youth homelessness survey*. Canadian Observatory on Homelessness Press. https://homelesshub.ca/sites/default/files/WithoutAHome-final.pdf

Glogowski, K., & Rakoff, A. (2019). *Mistrust and low expectations: Educational disadvantage and black youth in Ontario*. Pathways to Education Canada. https://youthrex.com/report/research-spotlight-mistrust-and-low-expectations-educational-disadvantage-and-black-youth-in-ontario/

Goodyear, T., Knight, R., Fast, D., Oliffe, J. L., Jensen, M., Kia, H., & Jenkins, E. (2024). Navigating and negotiating "outness" among 2S/LGBTQ+ youth experiencing homelessness. *Children and Youth Services Review, 164*, 107830. https://doi.org/10.1016/j.childyouth.2024.107830

Kidd, S. A., Thistle, J., Beaulieu, T., O'Grady, B., & Gaetz, S. (2019). A national study of indigenous youth homelessness in Canada. *Public Health (London), 176*, 163–171. https://doi.org/10.1016/j.puhe.2018.06.012

Kidd, S. A., Vitopoulos, N., Frederick, T., Leon, S., Karabanow, J., & McKenzie, K. (2019). More than four walls and a roof needed: A complex tertiary prevention approach for recently homeless youth. *American Journal of Orthopsychiatry, 89*(2), 248–257. https://doi.org/10.1037/ort0000335

May, J. (2015). Racial vibrations, masculine performances: Experiences of homelessness among young men of colour in the greater Toronto area. *Gender, Place and Culture: A Journal of Feminist Geography, 22*(3), 405–421. https://doi.org/10.1080/0966369X.2013.817970

Owusu-Bempah, A., & Jeffers, S. K. (2021). *Black youth and the criminal justice system: Summary report of an engagement process in Canada*. https://www.justice.gc.ca/eng/rp-pr/jr/bycjs-yncjs/index.html

Petering, R. (2016). Sexual risk, substance use, mental health, and trauma experiences of gang-involved homeless youth. *Journal of Adolescence, 48*(1), 73–81. https://doi.org/10.1016/j.adolescence.2016.01.009

Radebe, P. (2024). Anti-black racism in the Ontario public school system: Problematizing the labeling of young black students as troublemakers. *Journal of Black Studies, 55*(6), 513–532. https://doi.org/10.1177/00219347241245365

Sanders, J. E. (2024). "I think the teachers should really connect more with the students": The influence of systemic racism, inequity, school, and community violence on connection for high school students who are suspended or expelled. *Youth & Society, 56*(7), 1191–1211. https://doi.org/10.1177/0044118X231226396

Schwan, K., Kidd, S., Gaetz, S., O'Grady, B., & Redman, M. (2017). *Mental health care for homeless youth: A proposal for federal, provincial, and territorial leadership, coordination, and targeted investment - Executive summary*. Canadian Observatory on Homelessness Press. http://hdl.handle.net/10315/41254

Statistics Canada. (2019). *Survey of safety in public and private spaces*. https://www23.statcan.gc.ca/imdb/p2SV.pl?Function=getSurvey&Id=412124

Taylor, C., Peter, T., Campbell, C., Meyer, E., Ristock, J., & Short, D. (2015). *The every teacher project on LGBTQ-inclusive education in Canada's K-12 schools: Final report*. Manitoba Teachers' Society. https://egale.ca/wp-content/uploads/2016/01/Every-Teacher-Project-Final-Report-WEB.pdf

Tutty, L. M., Ogden, C., Giurgiu, B., & Weaver-Dunlop, G. (2014). I built my house of hope: Abused women and pathways into homelessness. *Violence Against Women, 19*(12), 1498–1517. https://doi.org/10.1177/1077801213517514

Walsh, C. A., Hanley, J., Ives, N., & Hordyk, S. R. (2016). Exploring the experiences of newcomer women with insecure housing in Montréal Canada. *Journal of International Migration and Integration, 17*(3), 887–904. https://doi.org/10.1007/s12134-015-0444-y

Whittington, C., Hadfield, K., & Calderon, C. (2020). *The lives and livelihoods of many in the LGBTQ community are at risk amidst COVID-19 crisis*. https://www.hrc.org/resources/the-lives-and-livelihoods-of-many-in-the-lgbtq-community-are-at-risk-amidst

Chapter 13
Policing Black Emotions: Dissecting the Intersections of Racism and Mental Health Challenges Experienced by Young Black Men (16–29 Years) in Canada

Dion LaFleur and Donna Richards

Abstract This chapter examines the over-policing and criminalization of young Black men's mental health in Canada through the theoretical lens of critical anti-Black racism, a combination of critical race and anti-Black racism theories. The recent police killings of young Black men experiencing mental health crises serve as a consistent reminder of the potential consequences that Black men, particularly young Black men, may experience when they publicly express symptoms of mental distress. Often, acknowledging the mental health challenges of young Black men leads to criminalization, leaving their challenges unaddressed and often worsened by injury at the hands of the carceral state and the deepening of the social and economic realities that may have contributed to their unfavourable mental state. The ongoing policing of young Black men living with mental health challenges demonstrates the precarity and devaluation of Black lives. Utilizing both historical and contemporary examples through an in-depth literature review, the authors will chart the experiences of young Black men living with mental health challenges under the ever-present and punitive surveillance of the criminal justice system. The chapter will conclude with recommendations for improvement to policies, research, and social work practices that directly impact understandings of and responses to the mental health challenges faced by young Black men. These improvements are necessary to ensure that young Black men living with mental health challenges can live full lives free of the threat of criminalization and lives in which their mental health needs are met.

Keywords Over-policing · Criminalization · Young Black men · Mental health · Anti-Black racism

---

D. LaFleur · D. Richards (✉)
Trent University, Social Work Department, Durham, GTA, ON, Canada
e-mail: iandionlafleur@trentu.ca; donnarichards@trentu.ca

D. Nyaga, M. Zangeneh (eds.), *Critical Ethics on Mental Health and Madness*, Advances in Mental Health and Addiction,
https://doi.org/10.1007/978-3-032-10166-2_13

Introduction

This chapter explores how the mental health challenges of young Black men in Canada are often met with control and not care. Through an anti-Black racism framework, we examine how emotional distress in Canadian Black communities, particularly among young Black men aged 16–29, is often misread as danger and, therefore, is responded to with force. These reactions lead to greater levels of surveillance, force, and criminalization—and they are not random. Rather, they reflect long-standing patterns that are deeply rooted in their historical antecedents, which continue to shape how institutions respond to Black pain.

This discussion draws on historical accounts, contemporary examples, and scholarly literature from Canada, the USA, and beyond. In Section 1, we frame the issue by demonstrating how Black mental health is frequently treated as a threat rather than a need for care. Section 2 uncovers the deeper history of anti-Black racism in Canada and how this history continues to shape the present. Section 3 focuses on how Black identity is defined, both by external forces and within Black communities. Section 4 closely examines the mental and emotional toll of the constant pressure experienced by young Black men, with a specific focus on how Black masculinity is shaped by silence and survival. Section 5 examines community-based responses, which offer examples of healing through Afrocentric and Afro-Indigenous practices. Section 6 closes with implications, offering clear steps that social workers, educators, policymakers, allies, and peers can take to support change.

Framing Questions

- What is your understanding of how racism shapes the mental health experiences of young Black men?
- How do cultural narratives about strength and masculinity affect emotional expression and help-seeking?
- What role does education, health care, and policing play in causing harm or healing?
- What are some community-led and culturally grounded approaches that support wellness through care, not punishment, for young Black men?

Theoretical Approach: Anti-Black Racism and Black Mental Health

To better understand young Black men's experiences of mental health and racism with law enforcement, we centre anti-Black racism (ABR) within mental health systems to show how this discrimination impacts their lives. The impact of racism on the mental health of Black communities is well documented in research from the United States and the United Kingdom, and to a much lesser extent in Canada (Williams & Mohammed, 2013). Clarke et al. (2018) define ABR as follows:

> ABR is that pervasive, overarching climate of attitudes, beliefs, institutional practices, and policies that are embedded in Canada's White supremacist history and culture that denigrate people of African descent, and it is manifested in various forms of structural violence and racialized inequities in multiple social systems, including education, health and mental health, housing, racialized poverty, workplace, and criminal justice (p. 44).

ABR helps us to understand the "particular type of systemic and structural racism in Canadian society" (Benjamin, 2003, p. ii) as it is leashed upon young Black men in all contexts.

Section 1: Framing the Issue—Criminalizing Black Mental Health

Canada's mental health systems are failing Black men, and this is not a coincidence. This failure goes far deeper than stretched budgets or medical oversights. It reflects the very ideas that shape our institutions, where racism, control, and surveillance are literally baked into the foundation. As a result, Black suffering is not understood as a sign that someone needs help, but it is viewed as a problem that needs to be controlled.

Critical Race Theory (CRT) tells us that racism is not unusual in Canadian institutions, but rather it is built into their very foundations. This means that the unequal treatment of Black men in mental health crises is not a mistake or an oversight, but it is a result of how power is instrumentalized and is maintained and protected (Delgado & Stefancic, 2017). Systemic anti-Black racism takes this further, arguing that Black people are often seen not just as outsiders to care for, but as active threats to social stability, particularly when they are in distress or asking for help (Maynard, 2017). This perspective helps explain why, as Williams et al. (2022) demonstrate, Black men's emotional distress is so often misinterpreted as dangerous. Instead of being met with compassion or clinical support, they are met with surveillance, suspicion, and significant levels of force. In many cases, when a Black man is in crisis, the first person to arrive is not a nurse or social worker, but the police.

The link between mental health and policing is not only found in abstract research, but in the experiences of people. For example, D'Andre Campbell called 911 for help and was killed by police in his own home. Latjor Tuel, a refugee from South Sudan and a former child soldier living with PTSD, was killed during a wellness check in Calgary. Abdirahman Abdi, a Somali-Canadian man with known mental health issues, died after being beaten by police outside his apartment, and a 19-year-old Nigerian student was shot and killed by Winnipeg police while experiencing a mental health crisis (Nasser, 2020; Puzic, 2024; & The Canadian Press, 2024).

Even beyond mental health cases, Black youth are less likely to have formal charges reduced or dismissed and are more likely to face the criminal justice system for the same minor offences as White youth (Samuels-Wortley, 2019). This is a pattern that reveals how racial bias in discretionary decisions can turn minor offences into significant legal consequences, a risk that becomes even more severe when mental health is involved. The examples noted above should not be considered as anomalies or rare tragedies; rather they point to a larger pattern. Osman et al. (2024) explain how racism shapes every stage of the mental health system. Their work demonstrates that Black men, particularly younger men, are often misdiagnosed, ignored, or treated like criminals instead of being offered the care that fits their cultural and emotional needs.

When distress is understood as danger, it ceases to be a medical concern and becomes a police matter. For instance, the Mental Health Commission of Canada (2024) found that Black people are more likely to be referred to mental health care through the police or justice system and not through voluntary or community support. This route to care deepens mistrust and keeps care rooted in a place of force and policing, and not compassion. Uwamahoro et al. (2024) refer to this phenomenon as part of a "disciplinary architecture". Canada's mental health systems are less about healing and more about control, especially when it comes to Black people. In particular, young Black men are often viewed as risky, deviant, and dangerous, which means the system's first instinct is to restrain and not to help.

Federal institutions have recognized the reality of this systemic bias that is rooted in discrimination and racism. For example, in 2021, the House of Commons Standing Committee on Public Safety and National Security found that racial discrimination remains deeply rooted in Canadian policing and called for major investment in culturally appropriate crisis response services (House of Commons, 2021).

At its core, this section brings the truth into focus, and that is in Canada, Black mental health is not just overlooked, it is policed, surveilled, and harshly disciplined. When viewed from this perspective, Black emotional pain and distress are seen as dangerous and in doing so, it builds a system where care is withheld, and punishment is the norm. If we want change, we have to name this reality, and that starts here.

Section 2: The Hidden History of Anti-Black Racism in Canada

Canada's Foundational Myths and the Realities They Conceal

Canada often presents itself as a multicultural, post-racial society that is a friendly, warm, and inviting contrast to the racial struggles of the United States. This national myth paints Canada as a welcoming haven, celebrating the Underground Railroad and Black Loyalists, while simultaneously ignoring the 200 years of slavery and the white supremacist structures that are a result of it (Beals & Wilson, 2020; Maynard, 2017). This so-called multicultural colour blind revisionist version of history does not just omit the truth, it actively misleads the history and contemporary reality in its representation of the country as a whole. Anti-Black racism in Canada is not new or borrowed; it has always existed, from the very beginning. In point of fact, Canada was founded on the principles, ideology, knowledge, and deeply established foundations that actively favour whiteness above all else.

Black people have lived in what is now Canada for over four centuries. Enslaved Africans were brought to the country through the transatlantic slave trade to Nova Scotia and to New France, which is now Quebec, starting in the 1600s. Slavery was legal in Canada for more than 200 years and only ended in 1834 when British law abolished the practice. However, the end of slavery did not mean the end of anti-Black racism. It continues to permeate society through legislation, policies, systems, structures, and institutions that perpetuate its existence.

The historian Robin Winks stated that racism in Canada tends to be "quiet", happening under the surface in the form of polite avoidance rather than public outbursts (Winks, n.d.). However, silence is not neutral; it allows harm to continue, and as CRT theorists remind us, the over racist does not need to exist for racial bias to flourish. Canada's silence about the existence and reality of its slaveholding past has aided in the continuation of anti-Black racism to this very day. Anti-Black racism exists and persists in the structural arrangements that comprise society and various institutions. For example, the inequities that currently exist in education, housing, health care, employment, child welfare, the criminal justice system, and policing are not outliers. Rather, they are the direct result of a nation built on stolen land, the genocide of Indigenous peoples, forced labour, systemic and institutionalized racism, and other forms of discrimination, and systematic exclusion of those considered to be undesirable who are pushed to the margins. These structures do not just shape the world around Black communities; they also shape their internal experiences. Over time, external oppression becomes something we feel inside. The impact of racist legislation, policies, and narratives does not simply exist in the world; they have a direct impact on people. The experience of external oppression is manifested through emotional fatigue, anxiety, self-doubt, and grief. When systems keep perpetuating the message that Black lives *do not matter*, that message takes root in Black people, even when unspoken.

The following sections explore how these patterns that produce and reproduce inequality, racism, exclusion, and violence continue in the present and how the weight of this history affects the mental health of Black communities across generations.

Institutionalized Anti-Black Racism: Policy in Practice

The segregation of Black Canadians has a long history in Canada in both policy and practice, particularly in relation to education, housing, the law, and child welfare. For example, in some Canadian schools, Black children in Ontario and Nova Scotia were legally segregated until the 1960s. In fact, Nova Scotia's last segregated school closed in 1983 (The Walrus, 2023). Today, Black students in Ontario are still suspended twice as often as their White classmates, and often for subjective reasons that can reflect teacher bias (Ontario Human Rights Commission, 2020).

In regard to housing, Black Canadians were deliberately shut out of certain areas by racial covenants. These policies prevented Black families from purchasing homes in parts of cities such as Toronto, Vancouver, and Halifax. A powerful example of how anti-Black racism shaped housing is the destruction of Africville, a Black community in Halifax, Nova Scotia, that was denied basic city services, such as running water and garbage removal, yet remained strong and self-sustaining. In the 1960s, the city forcibly removed the residents and demolished the neighbourhood in the name of urban renewal. Some families were moved in garbage trucks. Compensation was minimal or absent. A formal apology came in 2010, but the displacement left lasting scars (Clairmont & Magill, 1999; Halifax Regional Municipality, 2010).

Similar stories exist across the country. For example, in Vancouver, the Black community of Hogan's Alley was targeted by city officials in the 1960s and 1970s for urban renewal. Despite its vibrant cultural and social life, it was demolished to make way for the Georgia Viaduct. The destruction displaced generations of Black families and erased a vital cultural space from the city's landscape. No meaningful reparations have been made to displaced families. In Alberta, Amber Valley was a rural farming settlement founded by Black homesteaders in the early twentieth century. Despite their significant contributions and attempts to live peacefully, residents faced exclusion and systemic racism, including government policies that later limited Black immigration. Over time, the community dwindled due to systemic barriers and lack of support, and today few Canadians know it ever existed (Foggo, 2020).

Anti-Black racism was also written into immigration law. In 1911, Canada passed an Order-in-Council banning Black immigrants, stating that "the Negro race" was not suited to Canada's climate or economy. This policy reflected Canada's self-image as a white settler state, a view that shaped immigration rules until the points-based system was introduced in 1967.

In the child welfare system, racism continues to hide behind protective language. In Ontario, Black children are just 8% of the population but make up 40% of those in government care in some regions (Turner, 2016). In Nova Scotia, Black families are also far more likely to have their children removed.

Together, these systems and institutions have caused deep harm and distrust among Black Canadians. Social work scholar Akua Benjamin wrote that anti-Black racism is not just one form of discrimination; rather it is built into the very design of Canadian institutions. This means Black people are not only underserved but also watched, surveilled, ignored, and shut out from a multiplicity of decisions that directly affect their lives (Benjamin, 2003).

The Politics of Erasure

Even with this long history described above, Black stories are still missing from most classrooms. In 2023, the Alberta Teachers' Association criticized schools for skipping over lessons about Black slavery and resistance. As a result, many students graduate without ever knowing that slavery ever existed in Canada. The Walrus (2023) found that most Canadians do not even know Black segregation was legal well into the twentieth century.

In Canadian classrooms, Black history is often reduced to stories about the Underground Railroad. This limited view frames Black people as grateful escapees who have arrived in the land of milk and honey rather than key figures who shaped this country. This approach shifts focus to White benevolence, casting Canada as a safe and welcoming haven that distorts history, while ignoring the centuries of Black presence, resistance, and contribution that came before and after. Furthermore, Poole (2012) argues that Canadian history textbooks from 1950 to 1985 largely excluded the experiences and contributions of Black Canadians, making it difficult for Black students to see themselves as part of the national identity.

When Africa is mentioned, it is usually through narrow and negative frames: war, poverty, and crisis. Rarely do students learn about the continent's rich cultures, scientific advances, or intellectual legacies. Even less often are they taught how colonial powers, multinational corporations, and Western governments have disrupted African nations, extracting resources, staging coups, and driving instability. These gaps in the curriculum not only erase Black histories but also excuse the West's role in creating the suffering it claims to mourn. This type of omission leaves many Black youth with stories that start in violence and disappear in silence, narratives that diminish rather than affirm who they are as people. This erasure is repeated in political statements that claim racism does not belong in Canada. In a 2025 interview, psychologist Jordan Peterson said: "We basically, what would you say, imported and invented racism in Canada … this obsession with race that wokeism has reinserted, well, invented even".

The current federal Conservative leader, Pierre Poilievre, publicly agreed, stating that conversations about racism had led to a 250% increase in reported hate crimes. These comments do not simply deny history; they actively rewrite it, and in doing so, they allow institutions to carry on as if race, racism, and the violence they produce were never actually real in the first place. This is a form of racial gaslighting, one that invalidates and alienates every Black, Indigenous, and racialized person who has experienced racial discrimination and its intersectionalities in this country. When two White public figures, with considerable influence, claim that racism does not exist in Canada, it does more than distort the truth; it devalues lived experience, casts doubt on those who speak out, and reinforces the idea that racial harm is either exaggerated or imagined. For those already navigating systems that minimize or criminalize their pain, this denial deepens the psychological toll in a profound manner.

From Historical Erasure to Mental Health Inequity

The scholar Robin Maynard (2017) reminds us that, "The past is not past. It lives on through policies that continue to surveil, punish, and silence Black lives disproportionately." We can see the results today. For example, in Toronto, Black people are 20 times more likely to be fatally shot by police than White people (Ontario Human Rights Commission, 2020). A report from the House of Commons Standing Committee on Public Safety and National Security affirmed that systemic racism remains embedded in Canadian policing and called for investment in culturally appropriate, community-based mental health supports. In Ontario's schools, Black students are disproportionately streamed into applied or non-academic programs, a practice that significantly limits their future educational and career opportunities. For instance, a 2022 study analysing TDSB data revealed that 39% of Black students were enrolled in applied courses compared to 16% of White students, highlighting a significant racial disparity in course placement. This disproportionate placement narrows Black students' access to post-secondary pathways and directly contributes to the cyclical reproduction of inequality.

Canada's mental health systems did not grow out of care. They were created to control people who did not fit the norms, including those who were poor, racialized, or disabled. The lack of mental health services that are trauma-informed, culturally safe, and anti-racist is not a recent oversight. It comes from a long history of treating Black people as problems to be managed instead of individuals who deserve care.

Section 3: Who Defines Blackness?

External Definitions: Colonialism, Whiteness, and Cultural Control

In Canada, Black identity has rarely been shaped by Black people. From slavery and immigration laws to mainstream media and classroom content, Blackness has long been filtered through a White colonial lens. This lens does not simply observe, but it reduces, restricts, and distorts.

As Hrabovsky (2013) notes, Black identity is only validated when it fits into White expectations, usually in forms that are non-threatening and easy for the dominant culture to accept. "Good" Blackness is seen as polite, thankful, quiet, and unpolitical. Expressions that do not match this, like anger, pride, or grief, are often rebranded as dangerous or unstable. This pattern is easy to spot in the media, wherein Black people are boxed into roles: the athlete, the artist, the criminal, and the refugee. These narrow portrayals take away their full humanity. Meanwhile, Black culture is often praised and consumed, and its music, fashion, and language are used in marketing, even as the people behind it are stereotyped or erased—this is cultural appropriation in action. White audiences widely embrace Black creativity, but when Black people express the same things, they are often punished, ridiculed, or seen as threatening. Blackness becomes a product to sell, while Black people remain marginalized. Greene et al. (2022) note that for many Black youth in Toronto, media-fuelled stereotypes and constant exposure to racialized policing contribute to chronic stress and emotional suppression. When popular culture celebrates Blackness, but institutions punish Black presence and existence, the contradiction itself becomes traumatic.

What is missing is a broader societal understanding of how systems like slavery, immigration controls, and surveillance have shaped who is seen as a full citizen and who is not. Without this history, Black identity in Canada is often constructed by others and then judged for not fitting a mould it never created.

Internal Policing: Respectability, Gatekeeping, and the Fight to Belong

The pressure to meet outside definitions does not just stay outside. Over time, it seeps into Black communities, thus creating unspoken rules about what it means to be "Black enough". Within these spaces, identity can become a test. For example, how someone talks, dresses, listens, or expresses themselves can be used to measure authenticity. Those who do not match are sometimes told they are "acting White" or are out of touch. Instead of building unity, this kind of gatekeeping creates division. Samuels-Wortley (2019) explains that these pressures are not only social, but they often stem from the need to survive.

Many Black youth adjust or conceal aspects of their identity to avoid being criminalized, particularly in schools and communities where they are already heavily monitored and surveilled. Hooks (2004) referred to this phenomenon as the "psychic trauma of domination", wherein systems built to exclude you end up shaping how you see yourself and others. In this space, identity becomes a balancing act. You can be too much or not enough, depending on who is watching. Frantz Fanon (1952), in *Black Skin, White Masks*, described this very same split, the self you know and the version you must perform to survive. This is not just theory; it weighs on mental health, causing exhaustion, fear, and a deep sense of not belonging. Respectability politics adds to this burden, as staying safe means being quiet, polite, overly agreeable, and being real and authentic starts to feel risky and quite possibly dangerous. Still, this is the tightrope that many Black people are forced to walk every single day. This tightrope is not imagined, as federal policy agencies have acknowledged how constant surveillance contributes to distress and have emphasized the need for culturally grounded supports for Black Canadians (Public Health Agency of Canada, 2021; Public Health Agency of Canada, 2025).

The idea of the "Black card" reflects this tension as it is both a measure and a weapon. It sets the rules about who qualifies, how to behave, and who gets excluded. When identity depends on meeting shifting standards, true belonging becomes uncertain, and that uncertainty runs very deep. This struggle is not just social; it affects mental health, too. For Black youth balancing the layered identities of Canadian and immigrant, African and Caribbean, city and rural, the constant pressure to perform can lead to anxiety, hyper-awareness, and emotional numbness. It builds over time, quietly but powerfully.

To ask the question of "Who defines Blackness?" is really to ask "Who is allowed to just be?" And when neither society nor community offers a clear answer, what is left is silence, stress, and a very heavy toll on the soul.

Section 4: The Psychological Toll and Mental Health Impact

Everything described above: the gatekeeping, the historical denial, the criminalization, and the constant pressure to prove one's humanity takes a heavy psychological toll. For young Black men, moving through Canadian systems and institutions often requires one to hold back emotions, hide pain, and adjust to environments where showing vulnerability can lead to being seen as a threat. The effects are far-reaching and become visible in the emotional and physical exhaustion that one experiences when enduring racism, the quiet self-doubt that grows when lived experiences are dismissed, and the long-term impact of racial trauma reaches beyond the mind and moves into the body.

The Burden of Black Masculinity: Silencing, Surveillance, and Survival

Black masculinity in Canada causes significant pressure. For example, from an early age, many Black boys learn to hold back their emotions and appear strong, even when they are hurting. This approach is not about pride, but rather it is about survival in a world that often sees their feelings and emotions as something to fear. At school, work, and in public, showing sadness or fear, or distress can lead to serious consequences. Crying, speaking out, or getting upset is often not read as distress but as danger, and over time, this silence becomes a shield to protect oneself.

Majors and Billson (1992) refer to this phenomenon as the "cool pose". It is a way of demonstrating confidence and control in a society that expects Black men to be strong and punishes them when they openly display their vulnerability. This pose might protect on the outside, but inside, it can leave people feeling alone, isolated, and worn down. However, not everyone responds by acting tough. Stuart and Benezra (2018) found that many young Black men do the opposite in an effort to seem less threatening. Some walk with a girlfriend, carry a basketball, smile more, or wear glasses. These are not random choices; they are calculated efforts to reduce suspicion from police or others in power. Stuart and Benezra refer to this as "cover strategies", that is, ways to look harmless in order to avoid being targeted.

This pressure not only affects how someone feels, but it also shapes how they move through the world. Each step, glance, or outfit becomes part of a strategy to stay safe. Stuart and Benezra describe this as policing and not just behaviour, but also identity. The presence of authority teaches young men what types of masculinity are permitted and which ones will get them punished.

Mental health professionals often overlook this phenomenon when engaging with young Black men. When Black men talk about anxiety, sadness, or stress, they are sometimes dismissed or misdiagnosed. Hammond (2012) establishes that when Black men feel they have to live up to narrow expectations of toughness, they experience deeper emotional pain, especially in the face of racism. The more they are expected to contain everything, the heavier the burden becomes.

The realities described above have a long history. For generations, Black men have been treated as a threat before they are treated as people with complex feelings and emotions, and this negative perception has not gone away over time. Rather, it is always present and evident in everyday experiences that young Black men face in classrooms, hospitals, and traffic stops, to name but a few examples. Hooks (2004) reminds us that real strength is not about hiding pain, it is actually about being able to feel and to speak honestly, and about having people around who will listen and support you.

If we truly want to support young Black men, we need to stop asking them to hold all of their feelings in. They need space to feel what they feel, and they deserve care from people who listen and do not make them prove that they are worthy of help.

Racial Battle Fatigue and Its Consequences

Systemic racism creates what scholars call Racial Battle Fatigue (RBF). This refers to the emotional, mental, and physical exhaustion that racialized people face from the constant exposure to racism, microaggressions, and hostile spaces. Williams et al. (2022) describe how Black men in Canada often live in a state of constant alertness, always expecting judgment or harm. This constant stress takes a significant toll, draining emotional energy and putting strain on the body.

The burden of RBF is increased by the myth of the "Strong Black Man", which is the idea that Black men must always appear tough, silent, and unbreakable. It teaches that showing sadness or fear is weakness and that vulnerability is not safe, but is potentially very dangerous. However, this is not strength; it is survival disguised as control, and it isolates people, telling Black men to carry pain quietly and alone.

hooks (2004) reminds us that holding back emotion is not resilience, it is unhealed trauma, passed down, and is mistaken for pride. When pain goes unspoken, it does not go away; it remains in the body, relationships, and how people move through the world.

Racial Gaslighting and Its Impact

Racial gaslighting is trauma that is both personal and institutional. When Black men seek support, they are often met with disbelief or treated with suspicion. Osman et al. (2024) demonstrate how Black men are regularly misdiagnosed or criminalized during mental health crises. Many Black men often have interactions with police officers before they ever meet a therapist. This is due to the fact that the fear experienced by Black men is often mistaken for a threat, and therefore, asking for help becomes a risk. From this perspective, the system punishes pain instead of helping to heal it.

Racial gaslighting exacerbates the experience of mental health challenges. For example, when care providers or institutions deny the racism that someone has experienced, it breeds self-doubt that can cause individuals to question whether their experience was truly about race or if they were just imagining what happened. Over time, this erodes trust in oneself and others. Uwamahoro et al. (2024) highlight that such invalidation is a major reason many Black Canadians withdraw from mental health services, as the system not only fails to support them but also makes them feel like their pain is not real or legitimate.

Somatic Symptoms of Racial Trauma

Racial trauma is also experienced in the body as well as the mind. Chronic exposure to racism not only causes emotional distress, but it also creates physical symptoms. Research demonstrates that long-term exposure to racial stress raises cortisol, increases inflammation, and contributes to high blood pressure, insomnia, and digestive issues (Uwamahoro et al., 2024). The effects experienced are often sleepless nights, headaches, racing heartbeats, shortness of breath, and extreme levels of exhaustion. However, too often, these symptoms are treated without determining their underlying cause. As a result, constant racial trauma is frequently misread as individual bodily dysfunction instead of a mind and body reaction to living in a hostile environment.

When healthcare providers do not connect these symptoms to racism, they pathologize the person rather than the system. Unfortunately, this ultimately leads to more misdiagnoses, mistrust, and people walking away from care that does see them.

Section 5: Resistance & Solutions—What Needs to Change

Even with the harm, the silence, and the weight described above, we are still here, still resisting, creating, and imagining better futures. However, imagining alone is not enough. The mental health crisis that we speak of needs more than awareness, it requires action. The mental health crises must stop being treated as a criminal matter. While the call to "defund the police" has sparked wide debate, it is not and never was about the abandonment of the requirement for law enforcement. Rather, it is actually about a reallocation of funds whereby resources are reallocated from punishment to care, from control to compassion, and from enforcement to healing. In both Canada and the USA this requirement reflects long-standing demands to address over-policing in racialized communities and the chronic lack of investment in services that actually support well-being (Eaglin, 2021; Wortley, 2021). As Maynard (2017) argues, reform is not enough; we need to rethink how the systems work.

Reallocation means building a crisis response that centres on care and not coercion or discipline. Imagine a world where distress does not bring a 911 dispatcher but activates a community network. Where a knock at the door means a peer support worker, a cultural healer, or a trauma-informed responder, and not law enforcement. This is not idealism at all; it is harm reduction, and such programs already exist through services like Toronto's Gerstein Centre, a 24/7, non-police mental health crisis program rooted in community care (Gebremikael et al., 2022).

We need to prioritize Black-led, culturally grounded, trauma-informed support. Mullings et al. (2021) show that Afrocentric care is not just about treatment; it is about transformation that rests on dignity, spirituality, community, and connection. It tells a fuller story: that Black people are not broken, the systems that they are navigating are broken.

In addition, Afro-Indigenous support and care furthers this vision by rooting healing in the land, ceremony, kinship, and ancestral wisdom. These approaches care for the spirit, the mind, the body, and the collective. From this perspective, mental and physical health are not viewed as separate, but rather are intimately connected. The individual is not isolated, but rather is connected to restorative relationships. This approach meets trauma with tradition and separation with connection.

Ubuntu, the Southern African philosophy meaning "I am because we are," reminds us that healing is a collective experience. It shifts focus from surviving as individuals to thriving as a community. As Ginwright (2018) notes, justice cannot stop at being trauma-informed. It must be healing-centered. It must make space for joy, belonging, and true change.

However, these practices need more than praise; they require funding. A reallocation of law enforcement funds must reach the places that have always held us: the barbershops, the community halls, the kitchens of aunties, the faith circles, the peer-led programs, and the art collectives. These are not extras; they are essential elements.

In education, the shift must start early in primary school. This means ending zero-tolerance discipline policies, stopping the streaming of Black students into non-academic programs, and embedding an anti-racist, culturally relevant curriculum. Programs like One Vision One Voice, Afrocentric schools, and youth mentorship projects show what becomes possible when schools honour who students are and where they come from.

Mentorship is not an additional idea, but it is central to providing care. When Black youth are surrounded by those who see them, believe in them, and walk beside them, healing does not just become possible; it becomes inevitable.

Section 6: Implications and Conclusion

Black communities should not be left to carry this burden alone. Understanding the mental health impacts of anti-Black racism on young Black men is only the beginning. Recognition must lead to responsibility, and responsibility must lead to action. People in authoritative roles can play an instrumental role in affecting change, regardless of whether you are a policymaker, social worker, educator, student, or community member.

Social workers and mental health professionals need to go beyond clinical neutrality. Culturally grounded, anti-racist, and healing-centred care must become the norm. Afrocentric approaches, like those practiced by the TAIBU Community Health Centre in Toronto, focus on care rooted in Black communities' values and lived experiences (Gebremikael et al., 2022). Research shows that when care aligns with a client's cultural framework, trust improves, and outcomes strengthen (Public Health Ontario, 2023).

Educators and school leaders must end disciplinary practices that disproportionately target Black students. Instead, they must create schools that reflect, affirm, and uplift their Black students. This includes culturally responsive teaching, hiring more Black educators, and Black people for leadership roles in order to help shape safe and inclusive learning spaces.

Policymakers must direct funding toward long-term, community-led, Black-focused mental health supports. That means investing in prevention, not just reacting to crises. Studies across Canada show that when communities are given resources to lead their own care, intervention happens earlier, and reliance on institutional responses, including the police, decreases (Public Health Ontario, 2023).

Peers, colleagues, friends, and allies, especially those with privilege, must speak up when anti-Blackness occurs. Silence allows harm to continue, irrespective of whether it is in the form of a joke, a hiring process, a curriculum decision, or a staff meeting. Real and effective allyship is active and informed.

Furthermore, to Black youth, especially young Black men navigating these challenges, hear this: the system was never designed for you. But that does not mean you are broken. You are whole, even when the world fails to see it. You deserve more from life than just getting by and accepting the status quo—you deserve rest, love, joy, connection, and care.

Ginwright (2018) argues that healing-centred engagement requires a shift from viewing trauma as an individual experience to recognizing collective care and joy as forms of resistance. This work does not require perfection, but it does require that we all show up, speak when it is hard, make new choices, challenge old systems, and refuse to look away from what needs to be changed.

Justice is not a single act. It lives in the choices we make every day, in the budgets that are created, the conversations we start, the structures we rebuild, and the communities we support. Black mental health is not a side issue; it is an issue of justice and healing, a community issue, a future-building issue, and it calls for nothing less than our full commitment.

Glossary

Anti-Black racism (ABR) Prejudice, attitudes, beliefs, stereotypes, and distrust that is directed against Black people. This type of systemic racism is deeply entrenched in Canadian institutions, policies, and practices.

Black masculinity A complex concept that speaks to diverse experiences, identities and expressions of Black men that is informed by intersectionality of race, gender and culture. This concept is heavily influenced by both historical and contemporary events such as slavery and systemic anti-Black racism, that shapes perceptions and expectations of Black men in general.

Respectability politics Involves adhering to dominant cultural standards of behaviour, appearance, and morality, often those associated with white, middle-class values.

Additional Resources

Black Health Alliance

https://www.blackhealthalliance.ca/

A community-led charity organization working closely with other partners to support Black Canadians in reducing the impacts of mental health challenges, addiction, and other health inequities.

Amani Mental Health & Substance use Program (Centre for Addiction and Mental Health)

https://www.camh.ca/en/patients-and-families/programs-and-services/amani-mental-health-and-substance-use-program

The AMANI Mental Health & Substance Use Program (formerly known as the Substance Abuse Program for African Canadian and Caribbean Youth or

"SAPACCY") offers culturally responsive and affirming mental health and substance use health support for Black youth, ages 12–25, alongside their families and caregivers. We provide a safe and welcoming space for Black, African, and Caribbean youth to talk about mental health and substance use health issues.

Caribbean African Canadian Social Services
https://cafcan.org/
CAFCAN provides culturally appropriate social services that enrich the lives of the African, Caribbean, and Diaspora (ACD) communities in the Greater Toronto Area.

TAIBU Community Health Centre
https://www.taibuchc.ca/en/
TAIBU Community Health Centre provides Black-identifying individuals across the Greater Toronto Area with access to primary care, health promotion, and disease prevention services in a culturally affirming and supportive environment.

Wanasah
https://wanasah.ca/
Wanasah is a new non-profit mental health agency created to address the urgent mental health needs of Black youth and their families in Regent Park and neighbouring areas, in downtown Toronto. We are a space where Black youth and their families recognize themselves.

Videos & Podcast

Black Youth Mental Health and Well-being
https://youthrex.com/video/black-youth-mental-health-wellbeing-ft-namarig-ahmed/

How to Support BIPOC Youth Mental Health
https://www.youtube.com/watch?v=Obk90mwb9CY

References

Beals, A. M., & Wilson, C. L. (2020). Mixed-blood: Indigenous-Black identity in colonial Canada. *AlterNative, 16*(1), 29–37. https://doi.org/10.1177/1177180119890141

Benjamin, A. K. (2003). Anti-Black racism in Canadian social policy. In D. V. Mullings et al. (Eds.), *Africentric social work*. Fernwood Publishing.

Canadian Press. (2024, January 2). 19-year old student shot by Winnipeg police was having mental-health crisis, lawyer says. *Winnipeg News*. https://winnipeg.citynews.ca/2024/01/02/student-shot-police-mental-health-crisis/

Clairmont, D., & Magill, D. (1999). *Africville: The life and death of a Canadian Black community*. Canadian Scholars' Press.

Clarke, J., Hasford, J., Gudge, L., & Mills-Minster, S. (2018). Imagining a community-led, multi-service delivery model for Ontario Child Welfare: A framework for collaboration among African Canadian community partners. *Journal of Law and Social Policy*, *28* (1&2), 42–66.
Delgado, R., & Stefancic, J. (2017). Chapter I. Introduction. *In Critical Race Theory* (Third Edition) (pp. 1–18). NewYork University Press.
Eaglin, J. M. (2021). Beyond criminal justice reform: Procedural justice and legitimacy in the movement to defund the police. *Stanford Law Review Online, 73*, 120–129.
Fanon, F. (1952). *Black skin*. Grove Press.
Foggo, C. (2020). *Pourin' down rain: A Black woman claims her place in the Canadian West*. Brush Education.
Gebremikael, L., Sicchia, S., Demi, S., & Rhoden, J. (2022). Afrocentric approaches to disrupting anti-Black racism in health care and promoting Black health in Canada. *Canadian Medical Association Journal, 194*(42), E1448–E1450. https://doi.org/10.1503/cmaj.220456
Ginwright, S. (2018). The future of healing: Shifting from trauma-informed care to healing-centered engagement. *Medium*. https://ginwright.medium.com/the-future-of-healing-shifting-from-trauma-informed-care-to-healing-centered-engagement-634f557ce69c
Greene, C., Urbanik, M.-M., & Samuels-Wortley, K. (2022). "It stays with you for life": The everyday nature and impact of police violence in Toronto's inner-city. *International Journal of Environmental Research and Public Health, 19*(17), 10503. https://doi.org/10.3390/ijerph191710503
Halifax Regional Municipality. (2010). *Africville apology*. https://www.halifax.ca/africville
Hammond, W. P. (2012). "Taking it like a man": Masculine role norms as moderators of the racial discrimination–depressive symptoms association among African American men. *American Journal of Public Health, 102*(S2), S232–S241. https://doi.org/10.2105/AJPH.2011.300485
House of Commons. (2021). *Systemic racism in policing in Canada: Standing Committee of Public Safety and National Security* (Report No 6). https://www.ourcommons.ca/Content/Committee/432/SECU/Reports/RP11434998/securp06/securp06-e.pdf
hooks, b. (2004). *We real cool: Black men and masculinity*. Routledge.
Hrabovsky, P. (2013). *The concept of Blackness in theories of race: A historical review* [Conference presentation, University of Toronto].
Majors, R., & Billson, J. M. (1992). *Cool pose: The dilemmas of Black manhood in America*. Simon & Schuster.
Maynard, R. (2017). *Policing Black lives: State violence in Canada from slavery to the present*. Fernwood Publishing.
Mental Health Commission of Canada (MHCC). (2024). *Experiences with suicide: African, Caribbean and Black communities in Canada*. https://mentalhealthcommission.ca/resource/experiences-with-suicide-african-caribbean-and-black communities-in-canada/
Mullings, D. V., Clarke, J., Bernard, W. T., Este, D., & Giwa, S. (Eds.). (2021). *Africentric social work*. Fernwood Publishing.
Nasser, F. (2020, June 12). D'Andre Campbell fatally shot by police in Brampton home after calling for help, family says. *Global News*. https://globalnews.ca/news/7058201/dandre-campbell-family-peel-regional-police-shooting/
Ontario Human Rights Commission. (2020). *A disparate impact: Second interim report on the inquiry into racial profiling and racial discrimination of Black persons by the Toronto Police Service*.
Osman, A., Lewis, T., & Kaba, M. (2024). Dual pandemics: The intersecting impacts of anti-Black racism and the COVID-19 crisis on Black Canadians' mental health. *Canadian Journal of Public Health, 115*(1), 101–117. https://doi.org/10.1177/08445621241253116
Poole, C. (2012). "Not of the nation": Canadian history textbooks and the impossibility of an African-Canadian identity. *Southern Journal of Canadian Studies, 5*(1–2), 81–102.
Public Health Agency of Canada. (2021). Mental health of Black Canadians—Question period note. *Government of Canada*. https://www.canada.ca/en/public-health/corporate/transparency/corporate-management-reporting/question-period-notes/mental-health-black-canadians.html

Public Health Agency of Canada. (2025). Promoting health equity: Mental Health of Black Canadians Fund. *Government of Canada.* https://www.canada.ca/en/public-health/services/funding-opportunities/mental-health-black-canadians-fund.html
Public Health Ontario. (2023). *Mental health services and programs with, and for, Black communities.* https://www.publichealthontario.ca/-/media/Documents/M/2023/mental-health-services-programs-black-communities.pdf
Puzic, S. (2024, December 19). Jury finds Abdirahman Abdi's death a homicide; Makes recommendations. *Ottawa CityNews.* https://ottawa.citynews.ca/2024/12/19/jury-finds-abdirahman-abdis-death-a-homicide-makes-recommendations/
Samuels-Wortley, K. (2019). Youthful discretion: Police selection bias in access to pre-charge diversion programs in Canada. *Race and Justice, 12*(2), 387–410. https://doi.org/10.1177/2153368719889093
Stuart, F., & Benezra, A. (2018). Criminalized masculinities: How policing shapes the construction of gender and sexuality in poor Black communities. *Social Problems, 65*(2), 174–190. https://doi.org/10.1093/socpro/spx017
The Walrus. (2023). Canadian education is steeped in anti-Black racism.
Turner, T. (2016). *One vision one voice: Changing the Ontario Child Welfare System to better serve African Canadians.* Practice Framework Part 1: Research Report. Ontario Association of Children's Aid Societies.
Uwamahoro, M.-C., Idowu, J., Chowdhury, N., et al. (2024). Defining the Black population in Canadian health research: A scoping review protocol. *BMJ Open, 14*, e081296. https://doi.org/10.1136/bmjopen-2023-081296
Williams, D. R., & Mohammed, S. A. (2013). Racism and health I: Pathways and scientific evidence. *American Behavioral Scientist, 57*(8), 1152–1173. https://doi.org/10.1177/0002764213487340
Williams, M. T., Metzger, I. W., Leins, C., & DeLapp, R. (2022). The traumatizing impact of racism in Canadians of colour: A review of racial trauma research and policy implications. *Journal of Racial and Ethnic Health Disparities, 9*(1), 102–120. https://doi.org/10.1007/s40719-022-00225-5
Winks, R. W. (n.d.). *The Blacks in Canada: A history.* Yale University Press.
Wortley, S. (2021). Race, police stops, and perceptions of anti-Black police discrimination in Toronto, Canada over a quarter century. *Policing: An International Journal, 45*(4), 570–585. https://doi.org/10.1108/PIJPSM-11-2021-0157

Chapter 14
Mental Health First Aid Certification to Build Capacity in Black, Caribbean, and African Communities

Noah Boakye-Yiadom, Mary Akuamoah-Boateng, and Ebba Gifty Amakye

Abstract The disproportionate impact of COVID-19 on Black, Caribbean, and African communities is not a new phenomenon. It is deeply rooted in the historical oppression and marginalization of our communities. The legacy of slavery, colonialism, and racial discrimination has led to systemic inequalities that have contributed to the unequal distribution of resources and opportunities. The lack of Mental Health resources and the COVID-19 pandemic exacerbate the problems in the communities of people of African descent or Black, Caribbean, and African communities. Despite the disproportionate impact of COVID-19 on the Black, Caribbean, and African communities, these communities have shown remarkable resilience. The pandemic has brought attention to the strength and resilience of these communities, highlighting the importance of addressing the needs and working to eliminate systemic inequality.

Strategic enhancement of mental health resources within communities is a crucial step toward addressing these systemic inequities. Acquiring certification in Mental Health First Aid (MHFA) represents a substantial leap towards creating inclusive and supportive environments. MHFA empowers individuals with the understanding and skills to offer immediate assistance to those facing mental health challenges. Having MHFA certification allows individuals to reduce the stigma surrounding mental health and advocate for recovery and overall well-being. Additionally, MHFA empowers individuals to recognize the signs and symptoms of mental health issues, provide appropriate support, and facilitate connections with

N. Boakye-Yiadom (✉)
University of Calgary, Cumming School of Medicine, Community Health Sciences, Calgary, AB, Canada
e-mail: Noah.boakyeyiadom@ucalgary.ca

M. Akuamoah-Boateng
Ghanaian Canadian Association of Ontario, North York, ON, Canada
e-mail: vp@gcaocanada.org

E. G. Amakye
Northern Alberta Institute of Technology, Learning Services, Edmonton, AB, Canada
e-mail: giftya@nait.ca

D. Nyaga, M. Zangeneh (eds.), *Critical Ethics on Mental Health and Madness*, Advances in Mental Health and Addiction,
https://doi.org/10.1007/978-3-032-10166-2_14

professional resources when necessary. It is also beneficial to individuals who want to make a positive impact on their communities by promoting mental health awareness and providing support to those in need, and it is crucial to take into account the cultural background of the individuals and the community.

The Public Health Agency of Canada (PHAC) extended COVID-19 relief funding to the Ghanaian Canadian Association of Ontario (GCAO) to facilitate the training of instructors from Black, Caribbean, and African communities. This initiative also aimed to enhance the cultural relevance and responsiveness of the MHFA program by incorporating case studies pertinent to these communities. The project received funding for a duration of thirteen (13) months, resulting in the successful training of 24 instructors. These instructors are now poised to deliver MHFA certification training within their respective communities, with the collaborative support of agencies and organizations dedicated to serving the Black, Caribbean, and African populations.

Keywords Oppression · Marginalization · COVID-19 · Black · Caribbean · African

Introduction

The specific challenge of mental health awareness and stigma in the Black, Caribbean, and African community during the COVID-19 pandemic is multifaceted in nature. It involves the intersection of pre-existing social and structural inequalities, the disproportionate impact of the pandemic on Black populations, and the exacerbation of stigma and discrimination (Miconi et al., 2021; Okoro et al., 2022). The pandemic has not only heightened health concerns but also intensified issues related to family, finances, and education, which are significant stressors affecting mental health in the Black community (Okoro et al., 2022). Moreover, the stigma associated with COVID-19 has compounded social stigmas, further complicating the community's ability to cope with the pandemic's mental health implications (Ponder et al., 2023). Interestingly, despite the greater exposure to stressors, Black Americans have shown resilience in mental health outcomes, which may be attributed to protective factors such as higher self-esteem and in-group identity (LaMotte et al., 2023). However, this does not negate the urgent need for culturally sensitive mental health services and interventions, as evidenced by the positive impact of tailored interventions in Black faith communities (Codjoe et al., 2013). The challenge is also evident in the reluctance of the Black community, especially its young adults, to seek professional help due to stigma and limited mental health literacy (Siby & Vijayan, 2021).

The challenge of mental health awareness and stigma in the Black, Caribbean, and African community calls for culturally responsive public health interventions, advocacy against discrimination, and the integration of mental health services into the broader public health response to the pandemic (Codjoe et al., 2013; Muttathody

& Sathyanath, 2020). Addressing this challenge is critical for the well-being of the Black, Caribbean, and African communities and for mitigating the long-term mental health consequences of the pandemic.

The disproportionate impact of COVID-19 on Black, Caribbean, and African communities underscores the urgent need for strategic enhancement of mental health resources. This initiative focuses on addressing stigma, the lack of mental health literacy, and promoting resilience using the Mental Health First Aid (MHFA) Standard certification program with tailored case studies for the Black Caribbean and African communities.

The legacy of slavery, colonialism, and racial discrimination has created systemic inequalities that continue to disproportionately affect Black, Caribbean, and African communities (Este et al., 2018). These historical injustices have led to unequal distribution of resources and opportunities, exacerbating the impact of crises like the COVID-19 pandemic on mental health within these communities. Acquiring certification in MHFA represents a proactive step towards creating inclusive and supportive environments within Black, Caribbean, and African communities. MHFA equips individuals with the necessary understanding and skills to offer immediate assistance to those facing mental health challenges, thereby reducing stigma, promoting recovery, and fostering overall well-being (Bonnar, 2015; Monette, 2012).

Initiatives such as the collaboration between the Public Health Agency of Canada (PHAC) and the Ghanaian Canadian Association of Ontario (GCAO) highlight the importance of enhancing the cultural relevance and responsiveness of mental health programs. By incorporating case studies pertinent to Black, Caribbean, and African communities, MHFA training becomes more effective and accessible, empowering instructors to deliver tailored support within their respective communities.

Project Background and Objectives

This project builds on the GCAO's existing relationships with numerous Black, African, and Caribbean associations and the established evidence that affirms Mental Health First Aid as a means of fostering capacity building to decrease stigma and augment mental health literacy to promote the well-being of community members.

Ghanaian Canadian Associations (GCAs) exist primarily to support and unify the Ghanaian diaspora in Canada, promoting cultural heritage, mutual aid, and socio-economic advancement. These organizations aim to preserve Ghanaian traditions and foster a sense of community among members. They serve as platforms for networking, cultural exchange, and advocacy, addressing issues such as immigration, integration, and youth engagement. GCAs operate through various means, including organizing cultural events, educational programs, and social gatherings. They also provide resources and support services to assist with challenges related to settlement and adaptation in Canada. Funding for these associations often comes from membership dues, fundraising events, grants, and community donations, allowing them to sustain their activities and initiatives. According to Owusu (2000), these associations play a critical role in maintaining cultural identity and providing a support network that helps Ghanaians in Canada navigate their new environment while staying connected to their roots.

MHFA is an essential tool for capacity building, aimed at decreasing stigma and enhancing mental health literacy. By training individuals to recognize early signs of mental health issues, provide initial help, and guide those affected towards appropriate professional support, MHFA fosters a more informed and supportive community. Research by Kitchener and Jorm (2002) demonstrates that MHFA significantly improves participants' knowledge of mental health conditions and reduces negative attitudes towards those experiencing mental health problems (Kitchener & Jorm, 2002). Moreover, a study by Morgan et al. (2018) highlights that MHFA training leads to increased confidence in providing assistance and a greater willingness to engage with individuals experiencing mental health crises (Morgan et al., 2018). This approach not only equips people with the skills to address mental health challenges effectively but also promotes a culture of empathy and understanding. Consequently, MHFA contributes to breaking down barriers of stigma, thereby facilitating a more inclusive and supportive environment for mental health.

The program, supported by the Public Health Agency of Canada's Promoting Mental Health in the Black Communities Canada initiative, aimed to offer culturally focused MHFA training to Black, Caribbean, and African communities in Canada. This program was developed in response to a pressing need within these communities, which is influenced by a multitude of factors.

According to studies, African individuals and those of African heritage often confront substantial cultural obstacles when seeking support for mental health concerns (Kirmayer et al., 2011). These barriers are rooted in the widespread stigma surrounding mental illness, entrenched cultural beliefs regarding mental health, and the scarcity of resources that are culturally relevant (Boyle et al., 2007; Khanlou, 2004; Salami et al., 2019). Moreover, access to mental health services remains restricted for many Black, Caribbean, and African Canadians due to various impediments, including language barriers, insufficient knowledge about accessible services, and financial constraints (Woodgate et al., 2017; Yohani et al., 2020). Furthermore, the underrepresentation of African Canadians in mental health research, programs, and services exacerbates the issue, resulting in a dearth of culturally appropriate interventions tailored to their unique needs.

Moreover, the COVID-19 pandemic further magnified the mental health challenges faced by the target audience, disproportionately affecting them in several ways. The pandemic-induced stress and anxiety permeated deeply within African Canadian communities, stemming from concerns about health, employment, finances, and the well-being of loved ones. Social distancing measures and lockdowns exacerbated feelings of social isolation and loneliness, particularly among those living alone or separated from family and community support networks. Compounding the issue, many community organizations and support services had to curtail or suspend their operations due to the pandemic, resulting in a loss of vital resources and support for mental health and well-being. Additionally, individuals with pre-existing mental health conditions experienced worsening symptoms due to the heightened stress and uncertainty of the pandemic, coupled with disruptions to their regular treatment and support systems.

By tailoring MHFA training to the cultural context of African diaspora communities, this project acknowledges the unique challenges these individuals face and empowers them with culturally relevant knowledge and strategies to navigate mental health challenges effectively. This approach not only fosters greater awareness and understanding of mental health issues within these communities but also enhances their capacity to provide timely and appropriate support to those in need. This project seeks to bridge the gap in mental health support capacity by utilizing the networks of various organizations and training competent frontline workers and community leaders as MHFA Instructors.

Given these complex challenges, the implementation of culturally focused MHFA training emerges as a timely and imperative intervention. By addressing cultural barriers to mental health support and equipping individuals with the knowledge and skills to recognize and respond to mental health challenges, this initiative fills a crucial gap in existing services. It also fosters resilience and empowerment within African diaspora communities in Canada, mitigates the stigma surrounding mental illness, and promotes greater awareness and acceptance of mental health issues within these communities with the following objectives:

1. To train community members to become MHFA Instructors competent in delivering a culturally appropriate course
2. To increase the effectiveness of MHFA for the Black Caribbean and African communities and create a toolkit with relevant case studies and examples
3. To increase the capacity of mental health support in the Black community, trained instructors will conduct MHFA sessions free to their various communities

Actions Taken to Achieve Objectives

The recruitment process for instructors of MHFA training encompassed a comprehensive strategy to attract a varied and competent pool of candidates. This approach entailed employing email communication, in-person and virtual gatherings, and meetings to connect with 150 Black organizations and associations located across Canada. These endeavours aimed at identifying individuals who could be trained as MHFA instructors. To be eligible, nominees were expected to have a minimum of two years of hands-on experience in providing support to individuals struggling with mental health issues, ensuring that the selected instructors possessed substantial practical knowledge. Prospective instructors were asked to submit resumes and comprehensive forms detailing their experiences with various mental health problems. This rigorous application process was designed to evaluate their suitability and commitment to the MHFA program. By setting high standards and engaging with community organizations, the recruitment strategy aimed to build a robust team of instructors capable of effectively delivering MHFA training and contributing to the overall goal of enhancing mental health literacy and reducing stigma within their communities.

The development of a culturally relevant Case Study toolkit was a collaborative effort designed to enhance the effectiveness of MHFA training for African descent communities. A working group composed of MHFA instructors, social workers, counsellors, psychologists, and psychiatrists of African descent was established to create the content. This diverse group brought together a wealth of expertise and cultural insights, ensuring that the toolkit was both comprehensive and culturally sensitive. The toolkit incorporated culturally relevant case studies and examples, which were added to the instructor's manual by the MHFA. These case studies and examples were designed to reflect the unique experiences and challenges faced by African descent communities, making the training more relatable and effective. By integrating these culturally specific elements, the toolkit aimed to improve the relevance and impact of MHFA training, fostering better understanding and support for mental health issues within these communities.

The MHFA facilitator training was meticulously organized to ensure comprehensive preparation and support for participants from various provinces. Two in-person training sessions were held in Toronto, each spanning five days. These sessions aimed to equip facilitators with the necessary skills and knowledge to effectively deliver MHFA training in their communities. The project covered all expenses associated with the training, including accommodation, travel, and meals, thereby removing financial barriers for participants and ensuring that the focus remained on the learning experience. The training was conducted under the auspices of the Mental Health Commission of Canada's Opening Minds initiative, which provided a robust framework and resources for the facilitators. This support underscored the commitment to enhancing mental health literacy and reducing stigma through well-trained MHFA facilitators equipped to serve diverse communities across Canada.

Community training sessions were a key component of the MHFA initiative, aimed at broadening the reach and impact of the program across Canada. Utilizing a train-the-trainer model, 24 trained MHFA facilitators conducted monthly training sessions nationwide. This approach enabled the facilitators to pass on their knowledge and skills to new participants, thus exponentially increasing the number of individuals equipped to provide mental health support in their communities. Promotion of these training sessions was achieved through the distribution of flyers at community meetings, church gatherings, and recreational events, ensuring wide visibility and engagement. The training sessions were offered both in-person and virtually, accommodating participants from different provinces and catering to diverse preferences and needs. This dual approach enhanced accessibility and allowed more individuals to benefit from the MHFA training, further fostering mental health literacy and reducing stigma across Canadian communities.

Results

The results of the MHFA initiative demonstrated significant success and positive community engagement. Initially, outreach efforts received favourable responses from 57 organizations, with 32 of these organizations nominating 35 individuals to become facilitators. This enthusiastic response underscored the community's recognition of the importance of mental health training and support.

Through the program, 24 individuals were successfully trained as MHFA facilitators. These facilitators went on to conduct training sessions with over 150 cultural, community, and religious organizations across Canada, thereby extending the program's reach and impact significantly. A key development in enhancing the program's effectiveness was the creation of a culturally relevant case study toolkit, specifically designed to address the unique mental health needs and challenges within the Black Caribbean and African communities.

The initiative also saw the recruitment of 18 professional mental health care workers of African descent to form a dedicated working group. This group's expertise was instrumental in ensuring the cultural relevance and sensitivity of the training materials and approach. The program trained over 400 community members across Canada to become mental health first aiders, significantly boosting the capacity for community-based mental health support.

Moreover, the initiative obtained access codes for an additional 400 individuals from the Mental Health Commission of Canada, potentially doubling the initial target of trained mental health first aiders. This expansion was facilitated by a snowball recruitment approach, which proved highly effective, resulting in a larger-than-anticipated pool of 27 mental health professionals. This comprehensive and inclusive approach not only met but exceeded the project's initial objectives, fostering a robust network of trained individuals capable of supporting mental health within their communities.

Discussion

The project demonstrated remarkable adaptability and flexibility in navigating challenges and evolving circumstances, particularly amidst the COVID-19 pandemic. Despite potential disruptions, the project remained agile, implementing innovative solutions such as virtual training sessions and remote collaboration to ensure continuity and accessibility. Central to the project's success was its unwavering commitment to cultural sensitivity and relevance. The development of a culturally relevant Case Study toolkit, informed by the expertise and insights of mental health professionals of African descent, ensured that MHFA training addressed the unique cultural barriers and challenges faced by African diaspora communities.

The project made significant strides in education and awareness, equipping over 400 community members with the knowledge and skills to become mental health first aiders. Through monthly training sessions facilitated by trained MHFA facilitators, the project raised awareness about mental health issues and promoted destigmatization within African diaspora communities. By engaging community leaders and organizing public events, the project also aimed to increase access to mental health resources and support services for individuals in need.

In doing so, the project not only promoted mental well-being but also fostered a socially inclusive environment where mental health was openly discussed and addressed. As a result, many individuals who were previously hesitant to seek help for their mental health concerns were empowered to do so, leading to better outcomes and improved quality of life. The project's success in promoting mental health awareness and access to resources serves as a model for other communities seeking to address this critical issue. By working together and leveraging the power of community engagement, we can create a world where mental health is prioritized and everyone has access to the support they need to thrive.

Conclusion

The project was a significant step towards promoting mental health awareness and providing support to those most affected by the COVID-19 pandemic. Through community engagement and public events, the project was able to bring attention to the issue of mental health and connect individuals with the resources they needed to improve their well-being. By fostering collaboration between local organizations and community members, the project was able to create a lasting impact on the community and pave the way for future initiatives. Overall, the project was a valuable investment in the health and well-being of the community and a testament to the power of collaboration and advocacy.

The project's efforts to involve community leaders and organize public events were crucial in promoting mental health awareness and breaking down the stigma surrounding mental health issues. Through these initiatives, the project was able to reach a wider audience and provide them with the necessary resources and support to maintain positive mental health. By engaging with the community in this way, the project was able to make a meaningful impact on the lives of many individuals in need and pave the way for future initiatives aimed at improving mental health care. In conclusion, the project was a great success and demonstrated the power of collaboration and community engagement in promoting mental health and well-being.

References

Bonnar, F. (2015). Mental health first aid: Triage for the mind. *British Journal of Nursing, 24*(14), 724–724. https://doi.org/10.12968/bjon.2015.24.14.724

Boyle, F. M., Donald, M., Dean, J. H., Conrad, S., & Mutch, A. J. (2007). Mental health promotion and non-profit health organisations. *Health & Social Care in the Community, 15*(6), 553–560.

Codjoe, L., Byrne, M., Lister, M., McGuire, P., & Valmaggia, L. (2013). Exploring perceptions of "wellness" in black ethnic minority individuals at risk of developing psychosis. *Behavioural and Cognitive Psychotherapy, 41*(2), 144–161. https://doi.org/10.1017/S1352465812000707

Este, D., Lorenzetti, L., & Sato, C. (2018). *Racism and anti-racism in Canada*. Fernwood Publishing.

Khanlou, N. (2004). Immigrant youth mental health promotion in transnationalizing societies. *Revista Brasileira de Enfermagem, 57*(1), 11–12. https://doi.org/10.1590/S0034-71672004000100002

Kirmayer, L. J., Narasiah, L., Munoz, M., Rashid, M., Ryder, A. G., Guzder, J., Hassan, G., Rousseau, C., Pottie, K., & for the Canadian Collaboration for Immigrant and Refugee Health (CCIRH). (2011). Common mental health problems in immigrants and refugees: General approach in primary care. *Canadian Medical Association Journal, 183*(12), E959–E967. https://doi.org/10.1503/cmaj.090292

Kitchener, B. A., & Jorm, A. F. (2002). Mental health first aid training for the public: Evaluation of effects on knowledge, attitudes and helping behavior. *BMC Psychiatry, 2*(1), 10. https://doi.org/10.1186/1471-244X-2-10

LaMotte, M. E., Elliott, M., & Mouzon, D. M. (2023). Revisiting the black-white mental health paradox during the coronavirus pandemic. *Journal of Racial and Ethnic Health Disparities, 10*(6), 2802–2815. https://doi.org/10.1007/s40615-022-01457-6

Miconi, D., Li, Z. Y., Frounfelker, R. L., Santavicca, T., Cénat, J. M., Venkatesh, V., & Rousseau, C. (2021). Ethno-cultural disparities in mental health during the COVID-19 pandemic: A cross-sectional study on the impact of exposure to the virus and COVID-19-related discrimination and stigma on mental health across ethno-cultural groups in Quebec (Canada). *BJPsych Open, 7*(1), e14. https://doi.org/10.1192/bjo.2020.146

Monette, M. (2012). The boundaries of mental health first aid. *CMAJ : Canadian Medical Association Journal = Journal de l'Association Medicale Canadienne, 184*(17), E891–E892. https://doi.org/10.1503/cmaj.109-4298

Morgan, A. J., Ross, A., & Reavley, N. J. (2018). Systematic review and meta analysis of mental health first aid training: Effects on knowledge, stigma, and helping behaviour. *PLoS One, 13*(5), e0197102. https://doi.org/10.1371/journal.pone.0197102

Muttathody, S., & Sathyanath, S. (2020). Stigma reduction and provision of mental health services in the public health response to COVID-19. Indian. *Journal of Community Health, 32*(2 (Supp)), 269–272. https://doi.org/10.47203/IJCH.2020.v32i02SUPP.019

Okoro, O., Vosen, E. C., Allen, K., Kennedy, J., Roberts, R., & Aremu, T. (2022). COVID-19 impact on mental health, healthcare access and social wellbeing—a black community needs assessment. *International Journal for Equity in Health, 21*(1), 137. https://doi.org/10.1186/s12939-022-01743-z

Owusu, T. Y. (2000). The role of Ghanaian immigrant associations in Toronto, Canada. *International Migration Review, 34*(4), 1155–1181.

Ponder, M. L., Gardner, T. E., & Sun, W. (2023). "Just one more thing on our plate that makes it undesirable to be around": African Americans' experiences during COVID-19. *Howard Journal of Communications, 34*(4), 372–391. https://doi.org/10.1080/10646175.2023.2191806

Salami, B., Salma, J., & Hegadoren, K. (2019). Access and utilization of mental health services for immigrants and refugees: Perspectives of immigrant service providers. *International Journal of Mental Health Nursing, 28*(1), 152–161. https://doi.org/10.1111/inm.12512

Siby, M., & Vijayan, D. D. (2021). Mental Health Knowledge, Attitude towards Seeking Help, and Perceived Stigma among College Students. *International Journal of Indian Psychology, 9*(2).

Woodgate, R. L., Busolo, D. S., Crockett, M., Dean, R. A., Amaladas, M. R., & Plourde, P. J. (2017). A qualitative study on African immigrant and refugee families' experiences of accessing primary health care services in Manitoba, Canada: It's not easy! *International Journal for Equity in Health, 16*(1), 5. https://doi.org/10.1186/s12939-016-0510-x

Yohani, S., Salami, B., Okeke-Ihejirika, P., Vallianatos, H., Alaazi, D., & Nsaliwa, C. (2020). "If you say you have mental health issues, then you are mad": Perceptions of mental health in the parenting practices of African immigrants in Canada. *Canadian Ethnic Studies, 52*(3), 47–66. https://doi.org/10.1353/ces.2020.0016

Chapter 15
Post Pandemic Perspectives on Mental Health and Addiction

Dionisio Nyaga

Abstract This volume takes an anti-racism focus to look at the ways in which COVID-19 affected racialized communities in terms of mental health and addiction. Such a racial focus on mental health and COVID 19 brings to bear the social issues that racialized people faced and the ways in which they were able to resist and negotiate themselves. In the middle of the pandemic, it became clear that Black and other racialized bodies were faced with compounded effects of the pandemic. While narratives of 'we are on this together' became a clarion call for facing the COVID-19 pandemic, Black Lives found themselves closed out of this togetherness. This is because many Black people had to contend with major historical trauma and structural modes of anti-Black racism. While the rest of the world was sheltering in isolation, Black women and men were out there working to make sure they had enough to sustain themselves. To isolate was a privilege many Black people could not afford. If they do not work, they die. If they work, they die. This had an immense mental health effect on Black essential service workers and contributed to disproportionate deaths in many Black households.

This chapter seeks to engage with the effects of COVID-19 on marginalized communities and the ways in which various quantitative interventions (Hass, Being human during COVID. University of Michigan Press, 2021; Van Oorschot et al., Production and Operations Management 32:1345–1361, 2023) that were employed to flatten the curve work in complex ways to disremember marginalized communities; more so Black Lives (Hassoun Ayoub et al., Journal of Social Issues 79:667–693, 2023; Yang et al., Infant and Child Development 32, 2023). Such quantified measures to COVID-19 disremembered the various ways through which marginalized communities faced catastrophic impacts of the pandemic and how they employed their community resources and spiritual power to navigate the challenges brought about by the pandemic (Hass, Being human during COVID. University of Michigan Press, 2021). Marginalized communities faced the pandemic in disproportionate,

D. Nyaga (✉)
School of Social Work, Algoma University, Sault Ste. Marie, ON, Canada
e-mail: dionisio.nyaga@algomau.ca

D. Nyaga, M. Zangeneh (eds.), *Critical Ethics on Mental Health and Madness*, Advances in Mental Health and Addiction,
https://doi.org/10.1007/978-3-032-10166-2_15

compounded, and unique ways, all informed by their values, realities, and histories (Gaynor and Wilson, Public Administration Review 80:832–838, 2020). Of course, the key element of quantifying the measures to flatten the curve was business-oriented and meant to return the world to normal life. That normal had already impacted marginalized communities in various ways, ranging from police brutality, unemployment, and many other institutionalized forms of violence against marginalized communities such as Black Lives (Collins, The Hastings Center Report 52:S63–S65, 2022). These forms of anti-Black violence seemed to escalate even amid the pandemic. Case in point was the death of George Floyd under a police chokehold. This is one of the many forms of anti-Black racism that continued to exist throughout the pandemic, making it more disproportionate for Black communities to navigate the pandemic compared to other communities. On top of historical injustices against Black communities, they had to contend with the consequences brought about by the pandemic. This made it harder for Black communities to exist as part of what seemed to be a normalized sentiment of being "in this together". Our existence was in question before, during, and post-pandemic. Even with what seems to be regarded as post-pandemic, Black life continues to exist with the after effects of the pandemic. The trauma of slavery and other historical anti-Black hate continues to be compounded by COVID-19. Black trauma was and continues to be compounded in various ways and forms.

Keywords COVID-19 · Racialized communities · Mental health · Addiction

Race and Space in Pandemic Regimes

History is replete with examples of historical racism, sexism, homophobia, and other forms of prejudice and discrimination meted out to marginalized groups. In this regard, quantification of the pandemic helped compound and forget historical racial oppression meted out to marginalized communities in ways that were colonial and violent and seemingly sanctioned by the law (Merritt, 2021). Colonialism informs the science of quantification through the process of mapping spaces. Race as space helps us to understand how COVID-19 scientific data helped map new and complex forms of racial disparities while helping forget histories, values, and realities of Black communities (Razack, 2002). Flattening of the curve was a form of mapping the space meant to stop the spread of the COVID virus. It is in flattening the curve that we must pay attention to the ways in which particular bodies, mostly those marked as Black, became collateral damage meant to pay the price for a world seeking to return to normal. Flattening the curve meant some people had to disappear for the rest to survive the pandemic. Foucault et al.'s (2003) concept of biopolitics may help explain this phenomenon and yet we are failed by the limited reach of this concept in understanding Black life during and after the COVID-19 pandemic. This may help us understand how Black women had to sacrifice themselves to work as care providers knowing well that they were putting themselves in danger of contracting COVID-19. They had to work in person since they could not afford to live without a paycheck. This is living in the intersection of life and death, whereby to live is to die. This is well elaborated and demonstrated by Mbembe's necropolitics in which he discusses Black life and internment (Foucault Mbembe, 2019). Black life is the uninsured population whose worth mattered less than the rest of humanity.

An uninsured population is devalued and is expendable. It is a population that is left to die, and yet its deaths must not be remembered. To mark a population as uninsurable is to say that it cannot exist and that its life is simultaneously its death. The flattening of the curve simultaneously meant the burying of the history of anti-Black racism, sexism, transphobia, and other forms of discrimination. The COVID-19 pandemic became the graveyard upon which Black Lives and other marginalized were again devalued and reminded of their expendability. In a neoliberal society, marked by market and property values, there is a price to be paid for being Black. Being Black is summed up in the market and sold as a property to the highest bidder. To sum, Blackness is to make proper that which is outside the scope of normality. Normalization became a process of dismembering those who fail to add up. Normalization of Black becomes the very essence of anti-Black racism. This and many other factors help understand why race is a space of exploration.

On Blackness and Spirituality

The chapter seeks to imagine the opportunities and challenges presented by the COVID-19 pandemic and the ways in which we can learn and unlearn our quantitative social life. Put differently, can we rethink our quantified selves to start looking at ourselves as beyond the numerical understanding of science? At the height of the pandemic, it was clear that social life was quantified, reducible, and represented in ways that fail to imagine our spiritual self. In the process of quantifying our social lives and the haste to return to normal, we forgot our spiritual selves. In moments of emergency, the spirit fails to normalize quantifying methods. During the pandemic, it became easy and simple to forget and disregard spiritual aspects of life. Psychic abilities are discarded and replaced with numbers. In psychic terms, numbers are spiritual and yet we work hard to deplete their spirits' energy, all in the name of being rational thinkers. Within the Black tradition, spirits keep many of us breathing even in moments of crisis (Martin & Martin, 2002). When numbers are denied spaces of spiritual strength, they cease to exist. It is this Western belief in singular quantifiable life that informs numbers and from which, in the height of the pandemic, Black people were being forced to exist and embrace. During the pandemic, life became singular and divorced from the spirit, making it possible to forget such traditions that inform realities and values of Black Lives.

Numerical Mediations, White Hegemony and the Art of Black Disappearance

In the midst of the pandemic, most media outlets presented to the world the number of people we were ready and prepared to lose for us to return to normal (Ghosh, 2023). Numbers helped us to spiritually detach ourselves from others in ways that affected our physical and mental health. I would argue that the return to normal created an environment of individualism and atomization. The spirit meant to connect and lessen the distance between us and them was exponentially accelerated spatially and exponentially. To make such a claim around social distancing is not to claim such a health measure meant to protect and flatten the curve was wrong, but rather saying they were not equally right when it came to Black Lives. They failed to account for historical evidence perpetrated on Black Lives and the ways in which numerical metrics employed during the COVID-19 pandemic helped compound and complicate Black recovery post-pandemic. The spirit that helps Black existence and expressed through breathing was disregarded, making social distancing more of a physical exercise rather than a spiritual practice. Within the Black tradition, to be spiritual is to exist beyond the physical experience. To breathe is to speak life to the lifeless. Breathing is resistance to every form of violence expressed against Black Lives.

During the COVID period, normalization was presented as the only way to live a livable life. That life never heeded the fact that Black people needed to breathe again to recover from historical and economic oppression brought about by colonialism and imperial domination. Life became more of a numerical calculation, such that those who came close to us were marked as encroaching on our space and therefore putting us in danger. We therefore marked territorial boundaries between ourselves, meant to protect ourselves from the enemy without. We became a separated property living and inhabiting life in calculated, controlled, and proper terms and conditions. Numbers helped to collapse the lived realities of people, the majority of whom were marginalized and for which we were told we should lose them in order that we could return to normal. Normal was constructed as a model that must be sustained in order for the world to exist and breathe again. In a nutshell, there were lives that had to be lost for us to breathe and live in ways that were quantifiable and numerical.

In a world made of numbers, it is the marginalized communities who must bear the brunt of natural disasters. This was explicitly clear during the COVID 19-pandemic, wherein many Black, Asian, and other marginalized women came to be understood as strong to overcome Covid-19 and therefore expected to serve as essential service. They were placed at the forefront of the pandemic, serving as nurses, store employees, and caretakers. The key was to employ them so that they could be used to help return the world to normal. These racialized women, most immigrants, had to work in person and put themselves in harm's way for them to exist (Biswas et al., 2024). Their existence was grounded in choosing to live by sacrificing life itself. Here, distance was reduced to the level of exposing them to the pandemic while increasing the distance of those who can bear to seclude themselves in their house. This may sound like a cliché, but what remains is the reality of most marginalized racialized immigrant women whose families had to endure the trauma of losing their loved one who had chosen to work in person during the COVID-19 pandemic. Many of these women suffered the pandemic in disproportionate ways (Biswas et al., 2024), and that was made possible by the failure to pay attention to their everyday lived realities, values, and histories of oppression they continue to face.

Before the pandemic, immigrant women had continued to face issues of discrimination in ways that were various and complex (Biswas et al., 2024). COVID-19 compounded that discrimination in ways that could not be quantified and verified, and therefore had to be forgotten in the process of returning to normal. Normalization became the site of disappearance for these immigrant women, some of whom had left their countries in search of a better life in the West (Biswas et al., 2024). These immigrant women became the site of neoliberal violence and exploitation that was made real through everyday gendered social life. To speak of gendered life in neoliberal society is to be reminded of how normal is calculated in profit margins and that, to achieve that normal, women of colour must be exploited and return to their spaces of exception. Private space must therefore be considered as a space of exception wherein violence is suppressed by law (Razack, 2002). This gendered and raced space is constructed in ways where women of colour are seen as caretakers who are obedient and submissive to the law (Nyaga & Torres, 2017). The law must be employed to violently order and normalize their existence. It is in this gendered normalization of care that helps demarcate their space as worth less pay, allowing corporations to make more profits. This devaluation of care was clear during COVID-19 where immigrant women continued to be lowly paid, and when their pay was improved, it was to help further normalize women as expendable bodies. That normalization helps force immigrant women to sacrifice their lives for them to exist.

Existing in and with Pandemics

Around 2023, the World Health Organization announced that we were coming to the end of the COVID-19 pandemic. That said, the organization cautioned that while there was clear sign that we were entering a post-COVID pandemic era, a couple of things had to be paid attention to. One was that COVID-19 will continue to evolve over time and space and that we should not let our guard down. What that meant is that we should continue with the same measures that had been employed over the COVID pandemic period. This meant washing hands, wearing masks in congested spaces, and monitoring the spread of the virus. The second cautionary note was that COVID-19 may not be the last pandemic and that there will be more pandemics sooner. This aspect of the post-pandemic era has clearly shown us several things. The call was that the world will never be the same again, and the question of normal was far-fetched. This meant that we would need to live a life of hesitation, and that normal will take a different grammatical direction away from what we were used to. This means that normal will never be assured and therefore we cannot be assured of any catastrophes. We were made to open our perspective to social life to allow other forms of life that had been forgotten in normalized social life. Post-pandemics provide a new grammar to imagine life in ways that are fluid and tentative. Post-pandemics allow us to think of multiple worlds existing on this planet and that allows us to exist and habituate in ways that consider life beyond numbers. In this perspective, the post-pandemic era allows us to see the life of immigrant women beyond their quantified self and see how their service is beyond profit. This perspective on life helps imagine those others who are not us as lives that must be protected from catastrophes such as the pandemic. What that means is that we must pay attention to the various unique lives of those others who may be at a distance from us in terms of their race, gender, citizenship, and other social markers.

Conclusion

Distance may not be the physical one but rather holistic. What that means is that those who are at a distance can equally be near and that we have the ethical responsibility to care beyond distances. COVID-19 pandemic helped us to imagine ways in which the world is interconnected in complex ways whereby what belongs here is equally manifested in other places and in ways that are both global and local. It is never far off from there. We are human beings who feed into each other beyond the distanciation employed in science. We are porous beings who breathe into each other. The fact that the pandemic made it impossible for people to breathe. But such forms of breathability were not shared equally. Rather, what we saw was a compounded form of metrics of measuring breathability, such that Black people had to worry about their life in the context of COVID as well as the ever-present racial profiling and carding. This had severe effects on the mental health of marginalized communities, and for which quantified COVID-19 measure to flatten the curve became a form of curving out Black and other marginalized communities. This chapter, therefore, calls for a more humane form of understanding the pandemic beyond the present-day form of reductionism supported by science (Chassmen & Cohen, 2020; Hewitt & McGregor, 2020).

References

Biswas, U. N., Leach, B., Jijina, P., & Niraula, A. (2024). Lived experiences of skilled Indian women immigrants (SIWI) navigating the COVID-19 pandemic: Immigration trajectories to Canada. *Journal of International Migration and Integration, 25*(2), 595–619. https://doi.org/10.1007/s12134-023-01078-w

Chassmen, D., & Cohen, J. (Eds.). (2020). *The politics of care. Boston Review.*

Collins, M. (2022). Black and waiting: Bioethics and care during the Covid-19 pandemic. *The Hastings Center Report, 52*(S1), S63–S65. https://doi.org/10.1002/hast.1374

Foucault, M., Bertani, M., Fontana, A., Ewald, F., & Macey, D. (2003). *Society must be defended : lectures at the Collège de France, 1975–76*. Picador.

Gaynor, T. S., & Wilson, M. E. (2020). Social vulnerability and equity: The disproportionate impact of COVID-19. *Public Administration Review, 80*(5), 832–838. https://doi.org/10.1111/puar.13264

Ghosh, B. (2023). *The virus touch : theorizing epidemic media*. Duke University Press.

Hass, K. (2021). In K. A. Hass (Ed.), *Being human during COVID*. University of Michigan Press. https://doi.org/10.3998/mpub.12136619

Hassoun Ayoub, L., Partridge, T., & Gómez, J. M. (2023). Two sides of the same coin: A mixed methods study of black mothers' experiences with violence, stressors, parenting, and coping during the COVID-19 pandemic. *Journal of Social Issues, 79*(2), 667–693. https://doi.org/10.1111/josi.12526

Hewitt, J. G., & McGregor, D. (2020). In C. M. Flood, V. MacDonnell, S. Thériault, S. Venkatapuram, & J. Philpott (Eds.), *Vulnerable : the law, policy and ethics of COVID-19*. University of Ottawa Press.

Martin, J. M., & Martin, E. P. (2002). *Spirituality and the black helping tradition in social work*. National Association of Social Workers.

Mbembe, A. (2019). *Necropolitics* (S. Corcoran, Trans.). Duke University Press.

Merritt, D. (2021). George Floyd's death and COVID-19: inflection points in the Anthropocene era? *Journal of Analytical Psychology, 66*(3), 750–762. https://doi.org/10.1111/1468-5922.1267

Nyaga, D., & Torres, R. A. (2017). Gendered citizenship: A case study of paid Filipino male live-in caregivers in Toronto. *International Journal of Asia-Pacific Studies, 13*(1), 51–71. https://doi.org/10.21315/ijaps2017.13.1.3

Razack, S. (2002). Race, space, and the law : unmapping a white settler society. Between the Lines.

Yang, Y., Emmen, R. A. G., Bruijn, Y., & Mesman, J. (2023). Crisis and bias: Exploring ethnic prejudice among Chinese-Dutch children before and during the COVID-19 pandemic. *Infant and Child Development, 32*(6). https://doi.org/10.1002/icd.2462

Van Oorschot, K. E., Van Wassenhove, L. N., & Jahre, M. (2023). Collaboration–competition dilemma in flattening the COVID-19 curve. *Production and Operations Management, 32*(5), 1345–1361. https://doi.org/10.1111/poms.13709

Part IV
Theme: Anti-oppressive Perspectives to Mental Health and Addictions

Chapter 16
Power and Politics in the Provision of Anti-oppressive Harm Reduction and Low Barrier Services to People Experiencing Multiple Mental Health Diagnoses, Active Addiction, and Homelessness in Kingston, Ontario, Canada: A Case Study of Sisyphus and His Rock

Candice Christmas-Krumreich and Claudia McNulty

Abstract This chapter provides a case study of how people who experience mental health and substance use challenges, as well as homelessness, can be treated with extreme prejudice by the community service providers who are responsible for their care, despite knowledge of harm reduction best practices and local community-based research to determine needs.

In 2020, the Integrated Care Hub (ICH) was created in Kingston, Ontario, Canada, to provide low-barrier services to people experiencing homelessness who were also in active substance use. This day-drop-in and overnight shelter also housed the region's safe injection site. This was at the intersection of the housing crisis, the worsening drug poisoning crisis, and the COVID-19 pandemic, which saw a closure of most social services for the community's most vulnerable and marginalized.

A community-based qualitative study entitled *Crystal Meth, Opiates, Overdose and Housing in Kingston, Ontario: 2021 Rapid Assessment and Response Community Needs Assessment for the Integrated Care Hub* was foundational to achieving a $1.5 million grant from Health Canada's Substance Use and Addictions Program (SUAP) to launch the "Support Not Stigma" initiative, a series of projects

C. Christmas-Krumreich
Independent Researcher, Queen's & York University Alumnus, Montreal, QC, Canada

C. McNulty (✉)
Master's Student, Factor-Inwentash Faculty of Social Work, University of Toronto, Toronto, ON, Canada
e-mail: claudia.mcnulty@mail.utoronto.ca

D. Nyaga, M. Zangeneh (eds.), *Critical Ethics on Mental Health and Madness*, Advances in Mental Health and Addiction,
https://doi.org/10.1007/978-3-032-10166-2_16

developed from the recommendations for policy and program delivery devised through consultation with service users. The programs ran from the summer of 2022 to the spring of 2024.

However, the political climate in Ontario that sought to close services like safe injection sites over concerns with public safety, along with local political pressure from the City of Kingston that sought to eliminate a homeless encampment adjacent to the ICH, and finally growing public opinion that the ICH was a dangerous place, led to a complete reversal of harm reduction based, low barrier services at that location by fall of 2024. A highly publicized stabbing at the site in September of 2024 led to a rapid dismantling of the encampment, and the ICH fell under the new management of Addictions and Mental Health Services which has adjusted the term "low barrier" to mean case management and treatment services. With no true low-barrier shelter services available, many people experiencing homelessness who are also in active substance use have been forced back to the streets.

Keywords Anti-oppressive · Harm reduction · Homelessness · Mental health

Introduction

In 2020, the Integrated Care Hub (ICH) was created in Kingston, Ontario, Canada, at the intersection of the housing crisis, the drug poisoning epidemic, and the COVID-19 pandemic. Co-housed with the region's safe injection site as a day-drop-in and overnight shelter, "the Hub" as it was known to clients and staff provided low-barrier services to people experiencing multiple mental health diagnoses, active addiction, and homelessness.

This case study outlines how this vulnerable and marginalized population was treated with extreme prejudice—including discrimination and stigmatization—leading to denied access to health and harm reduction services and emergency housing by Kingston health and community service providers. Paradoxically, this occurred in parallel to programs of knowledge dissemination of harm reduction best practices through a Health Canada-funded anti-stigma campaign called Support Not Stigma, informed by client-centred community-based research.

By 2023, the Ontario Government sought to close harm reduction services like safe injection sites over concerns for public safety. Combined with local political pressure from the City of Kingston to eliminate a homeless encampment adjacent to the ICH, and growing public opinion that the ICH was a dangerous place, a complete reversal of harm reduction-based, low barrier services occurred. A highly publicized stabbing at the ICH in September 2024 led to a rapid dismantling of the encampment, and the ICH fell under new management which has adjusted the term "low barrier" to mean case management and treatment services. With no true low-barrier shelter services available for many people in active substance use, experiencing homelessness with multiple mental health diagnoses, many have been forced back into the streets.

Framing Question 1 How are people experiencing multiple mental health diagnoses, active addiction, and homelessness portrayed by institutions as posing a threat to public life and safety?

Framing Question 2 How are people experiencing multiple mental health diagnoses, active addiction, and homelessness deprived of their humanity?

Framing Question 3 How does the power and influence of institutions, health care, and social service providers trump best practice around the provision of harm reduction and low-barrier shelter services for people experiencing multiple mental health diagnoses, active addiction, and homelessness?

Framing Question 4 How are harm reduction front line workers experiencing trauma and moral injury as a result of the public and institutions stigmatizing and discriminating against the patrons/clients experiencing multiple mental health diagnoses, active addiction and homelessness that they serve?

Key Study

At the nexus of the COVID-19 pandemic, the drug poisoning epidemic, and the housing crisis in 2021, a rapid needs assessment was commissioned in Kingston, Ontario, Canada, with funding from several health and community service agencies, including the Kingston United Way and leadership from [then] Kingston, Frontenac, Lennox and Addington Public Health (KFL & A)'s Community Drug Strategy Group. Entitled "Crystal Meth, Opiates, Overdose and Housing in Kingston, Ontario" (Christmas, 2021), the report sought to build capacity, compassion, and community across sectors that served people experiencing multiple mental health diagnoses, active addiction, and homelessness using the newly created Integrated Care Hub (ICH) by better understanding the thoughts, feelings, and needs of these clients.

The ICH's needs assessment involved consultations with 32 stakeholders who had used/use crystal meth and/or opioids. Challenges to social, health, criminal justice, and education systems were identified, many beyond the scope and operations of the ICH. Six major assumptions on how to better the lives of people who frequented the ICH were articulated, providing a "spirit of moving forward" for community and health care organizations serving this population:

1. Health and social justice for all citizens of KFL & A is the shared goal we are collectively striving for as service providers, friends and family members, neighbours, and society at large.
2. Stigma and discrimination exist in society at large and in our institutions that have caused harm.

3. People served at the ICH have very complex conditions——cognitive, mental health, and substance use challenges——what we refer to as "tri-diagnosis".
4. People who use substances have a specialized community of their own but long for a "second chance" to reintegrate into employment and reconnect with their families.
5. An integrated care model could be the key to their healing.
6. There is a lack of decent, safe, affordable housing in Kingston, particularly for individuals living in low-income, and/or dealing with physical, cognitive, mental health, and/or substance use challenges.

Introduction

This chapter provides a case study of how people experiencing multiple mental health diagnoses, active addiction, and homelessness, can be treated with extreme prejudice—including discrimination and stigmatization—leading to denied access to health and mental health services, harm reduction services, and emergency housing by the health and community service providers who are responsible for their care as citizens. This account takes place in Kingston, Ontario, Canada, with a population of about 135,000 people, from early 2020 and the onset of COVID-19 lockdowns, to a highly publicized stabbing in September 2024. The mistreatment of this vulnerable and marginalized population occurred despite extensive knowledge dissemination of harm reduction best practices to community health and social service providers through a Health Canada-funded anti-stigma campaign called Support Not Stigma. The campaign was informed by local, community-based research to determine needs and maximize relevancy.

In response to the rising opioid overdose mortality rates across Canada, Ontario, and the region, the [then] Kingston, Frontenac, Lennox & Addiction Public Health Unit (KFLA Public Health) showed early leadership, forming a Community Drug Strategy Advisory Committee (CDSAC) in March 2017. Membership included people with lived and living experience (PWLLE), social service agencies, law enforcement, Corrections Canada (prison system), local municipalities, and primary care practitioners. In 2019, following community consultations, opioids and crystal methamphetamine were identified as the main causes for concern. As the COVID-19 pandemic hit in early 2020 and community partners refined their responses, it became clear that the real challenge was the poor treatment people who used substances were experiencing in the community. A newly formed Stigma and Education subcommittee designed and implemented a Collective Impact Stigma Reduction Strategy, including an anti-stigma campaign.

Meanwhile, in 2020, the Integrated Care Hub (ICH) was created in Kingston to provide low-barrier services to people experiencing multiple mental health diagnoses, active addiction, and homelessness. This day-drop-in and overnight shelter also housed the region's safe injection site. The intersection of the housing crisis, the worsening drug poisoning epidemic, and the COVID-19 pandemic led to the closure of most social services for the community's most vulnerable and marginalized. Politically, it was a "hot potato" issue from the start because the public and politicians were concerned about the fifty-plus people who had settled into an encampment near the ICH at Belle Park and the KP Trail on public lands. These "homeless" persons had become very "visible", many of whom were substance users and were perceived as a threat to public safety. Ironically, many of them had been experiencing homelessness for some time, but had been dispersed within the city over time and space. It was the concentration of so many "addicts and junkies" that fuelled a public imagination of fear, and subsequent stigma and discrimination. This became more amplified through the media and social media over time. However, incredible actions of empathy and solidarity from the community were also witnessed, as people rallied to provide support to the residents of the encampment. Divisions on what to do about the situation were palpable, so a study was undertaken.

Funded by the Kingston United Way in 2021, the ICH Needs Assessment for People who Use Crystal Meth & Opioids was conducted by Ms. Christmas-Krumreich as primary investigator and author with assistance from ICH management and staff. The results of the Needs Assessment were presented to the KFLA Public Health Board of Directors on 27 April 2021, who unanimously approved the report and its recommendations on how to better support people experiencing multiple mental health diagnoses, active addiction, and homelessness. Then, Trellis HIV & Community Care stepped forward as the lead organization to apply to Health Canada's Substance Use Addictions Program (SUAP). The report was foundational to achieving a $1.5 million grant from Health Canada to launch the "Support Not Stigma" (SNS) initiative, a series of projects developed from the recommendations for policy and program delivery devised through consultation with service users. The programs ran from the summer of 2022 to the spring of 2024. In Summer 2022, the KFLA CDS was awarded $20,000 from Innoweave. Combined with a portion of the SUAP grant, the cross-community anti-stigma education campaign was launched on International Overdose Awareness Day, 31 August 2023.

However, the political climate in Ontario that sought to close services like safe injection sites over concerns with public safety, along with local political pressure from the City of Kingston that sought to eliminate a homeless encampment adjacent to the ICH, and finally growing public opinion that the Hub was a dangerous place, led to a complete reversal of harm reduction based, low barrier services at that location by fall of 2024. A highly publicized stabbing at the site in September of 2024 led to a rapid dismantling of the encampment, and the ICH fell under the new management of Addictions and Mental Health Services, which has adjusted the term "low barrier" to mean case management and treatment services.

The authors wrote this case study to demonstrate that despite intensive community consultations to inform best practices for harm reduction services, and funding to achieve innovative programs for people with multiple mental health diagnoses, in active substance use and experiencing homelessness, it was the politicization of this population as a threat to public safety that led to the dismantling of several years of important work and progress. Not only were clients negatively impacted by the loss of services they had helped to build, but harm reduction front-line workers experienced significant moral injury as their work and supports were dismantled by the organizations whose mandates it was to serve this vulnerable and marginalized population. Candice Christmas-Krumreich, PhD, was the main researcher and the Community Engagement Project Manager for Support Not Stigma. Claudia McNulty was the Community Support Coordinator, a front-line worker managing the employment program at the ICH.

Co-creation of Care Model: The Inception of the ICH and Support Not Stigma

People in the Kingston community were dying from drug poisoning at alarming rates. The lives of the people served at the ICH were very complex, and the COVID-19 pandemic revealed how the health and social service systems struggled to deal with their needs within multiple intersecting crises: public health, accidental overdoses due to drug poisoning, and growing homelessness. The need for specialized care for our most vulnerable and marginalized citizens was paramount. Our findings around the heightened vulnerability of this population are consistent with a study done by McCann et al. (2022). The findings of the rapid needs assessment report were not to lay blame on service providers, but rather, to acknowledge that we could do better, starting with listening to the people we serve.

Conceptualizing "Care" at the ICH was underpinned by the work of the National Harm Reduction Coalition and its eight guiding principles. "Harm reduction is a set of practical strategies and ideas aimed at reducing negative consequences associated with drug use. Harm Reduction is also a movement for social justice built on a belief in, and respect for, the rights of people who use drugs." The "vision" for care was to bake the eight guiding principles of harm reduction into an anti-oppressive practice to be used across all policies and programs at the ICH. The study results called for six policy platforms:

1. Health and social justice for all citizens of KFLA as the shared goal to collectively strive for as service providers, friends and family members, neighbours, and society at large.
2. Stigma and discrimination exist in society at large and in Kingston institutions that have caused harm.
3. People served at the ICH have very complex conditions——cognitive, mental health and substance use challenges——referred to as "tri-diagnosis".
4. People who use substances have a specialized community of their own, but long for a "second chance" to reintegrate into employment and reconnect with their families.
5. An integrated care model could be the key to their healing.
6. There is a lack of decent, safe, affordable housing in Kingston, particularly for individuals living in low-income and/or dealing with physical, cognitive, mental health, and/or substance use challenges.

One of our immediate successes was consultation with PWLLE around equitable hiring practices, competitive wages (at the time), and accessibility for community members. This led to the successful implementation of the Community Support Program, offering paid work for residents of the ICH (even if they were in active substance use). It was unique in Canada as sobriety was not a necessary criterion for inclusion in the work program. We also developed a specialized training program for everyone in the community working with ICH clients. Using a Social Justice framework, we sought to engage workers in Dialogical Action, to expose the stigma against people experiencing mental health and substance use challenges who find themselves housed or homeless, and to critically reflect on the systems change needed to address potentially morally injurious events in our work and as experienced by our clients. For seven sessions, we engaged with a keynote expert, people with lived and living experience, and each other through focus groups and a plenary discussion focused on acknowledging the challenges we face and then problem-solving. We hoped to provide workers with the knowledge, skills, and tools to build positionality, reflexivity, and compassion, to work together in solidarity with the people we serve, and to "be hard on the problem, not on the person". Three of the keynote presentations are still available at www.SupportNotStigma.ca.

Marginalized Citizens: Multiple Mental Health Diagnoses in Active Substance Use

For the *Crystal Meth, Opiates, Overdose and Housing in Kingston, Ontario—Rapid Community Needs Assessment* (Christmas, 2021), we used an anti-oppressive lens on the psycho-social profiles of clients using crystal meth and/or opiates to better understand who was being served. Information gathered guided the development of effective responses and drug policy to support people who use crystal meth and opiates, and prevent overdose. To qualify, clients had to be 18 years of age or older, use crystal meth and/or opiates, and frequent the ICH.

Thirty-two individuals aged 18 and over participated in one-hour semi-structured interviews. One of the limitations was a smaller female sample of 11 as compared to 21 males. In terms of self-identified ethnicity, 47% of males were Caucasian and 36% of females; 33% of males had mixed Indigenous ancestry and 33% of females; 19% were of males and 18% of females were Indigenous, and one female self-identified as being of mixed African descent. This highlights the over-representation of Indigenous people in the homeless population.

The health needs of the clients were complex, with 90% of males and 91% of females having sustained a significant head injury. Mental health and trauma have been, and continue to be, significant barriers to wellness in the ICH community. Ninety-five percent of males and 91% of females indicated having had multiple mental health diagnoses. Five of 11 females lost a parent or close loved one by age twenty, one male lost his grandmother and father in the same year, and he dropped out of college, one male lost his mother to overdose at the age of 18, and 3 males have not spoken to their family members in over 20 years.

Fifty-two percent of males completed high school, while only one female did (half had dropped out by grade 10). From a developmental health lens, it is important to note that 56% of participants cited having a learning disability that impaired their schooling. Ninety percent of males had been incarcerated, of which 57% indicated charges were drug-related. For females, 73% had been incarcerated and 64% indicated charges were drug related.

Early incarceration due to drug use dramatically changed people's lives. Many individuals had suffered immensely at the hands of the child welfare system (intergenerational trauma), the youth justice and criminal justice systems, the healthcare system, and the housing system.

Only 24% of males and 45% of females indicated having a family doctor. In the space of one year, males made an average of 3.7 trips to the hospital, females 4.9.

Of a total of 134 trips to the hospital, mental health issues accounted for 38 trips, overdose 22, physical issues 18, and infections 8 (and another 2 for endocarditis). Six males cited having had negative experiences in the health care sector and another three avoid care altogether because of the stigma and discrimination they had endured.

A study on emergency department care experiences among people who used substances in Kingston (2023) proposed three recommendations: (1) integration of an equity-oriented approach into the ED; (2) widespread training on substance use; and (3) investment in expert resources and services to support people who use substances (Rajab et al., 2023, p. 1).

The evidence indicates that safe supply would save lives and visits to the hospital. On average, males indicated they knew of 50 people who had overdosed, females an average of 57. Males had lost an average of 18 people close to them to death by overdose, females an average of 20. An average of 10 males had overdosed in the past year, 2.8 females. Of these, 53% had been revised by friends, 34% by ICH staff, 28% by CTS staff, 19% by emergency responders, 9% by strangers, and only one person had been resuscitated in the hospital. This indicates that it is the community itself that is responding to overdose, an incredibly traumatic phenomenon that leaves them in constant worry. As one respondent described what safe supply could do: "It would change my life. I could be productive, not chase dope, not die… just live life!" Staff at the ICH and CTS are lifesavers, calling for the addition of self-care and counselling for them in these traumatic roles, in the same way that we provide support to first responders.

Also significant is the evidence around substances used and links to overdose. People using crystal meth daily (and marijuana to sleep) overdosed 17 times. People using a combination of crystal meth and opioids (to sleep) daily, or binging on them, overdosed 56 times. People using Fentanyl daily (and crystal meth to "get things done") overdosed 132 times. While the prevalence of crystal meth as the first drug of choice for daily use (44%) is only slightly higher than that of Fentanyl (37.5%), the risk of overdose is almost double, and Fentanyl is tainting the crystal meth supply. If these people could be treated for their physical and mental pain through pharmacology, and crystal users had access to clean products and marijuana for sleeping, the overdose crisis would be dramatically reduced.

Overall, it was discovered that programs need to align with a more person-centred philosophy. Services need to be more relationship-focused and violence and trauma-informed care-based. Increased support is needed that engages people in meaningful activity and supports life skills; and *effective* community integration supports are needed to prevent ongoing homelessness. The Support Not Stigma initiative sought to operationalize these findings.

A Different Kind of Ghetto: Place-Based Oppression

The Integrated Care Hub (ICH) moved to its "permanent" location, 661 Montreal Street, on 1 November 2020, after operating for 4 months at a local community centre closer to the downtown core that had been closed due to COVID lockdowns. Construction had started on the new facility months sooner, but the renovation to a former industrial sanitation building and site led to several delays to the move-in date. When the doors finally opened at the "new" facility, scaffolding still surrounded the East side of the building, so management had to find creative ways of facilitating access to the drop-in space until construction was completed.

The building selected was, at its best and newest, a contaminated site inadequate in size for the number of people it hoped to serve, nor was it equipped to do so. From the first day the "Hub" staff and patrons entered the space, the experience would be tainted by the ever-apparent message that echoed through the walls of the building—this is what we *deserve*. Everything about the space suggested squalor. Rats were sighted in communal spaces around the building regularly. There was rarely a time when the building was not experiencing a serious plumbing problem, which sometimes resulted in sewage spilling into the basement where the safe injection site operates. The land itself is polluted with chemicals, with unknown side effects of prolonged exposure (the smell of burning wood from this area is particularly unpleasant). In the first few months, overnight shift front-line workers caught bats that flew around the sleeping quarters and brought them to an animal rescue the next morning. Another day, another health and safety concern for both occupants and staff.

The site and the land in the surrounding area have documented high concentrations of pesticides and heavy metals that register above the provincial limit. It is true that the City of Kingston took some measures to prepare for the use of the building as a shelter. However, a report on the status of the efforts was published and recommended that the basement and main floor not be resided in due to the lingering contamination levels (Federation of Canadian Municipalities, n.d.). This raised questions as to whether clients sleeping on the concrete floor of the main level every night for months, or working 40 hours a week on these floors, could be potentially harmful exposures. Answers were not forthcoming from the City of Kingston who interacted with the Landlord. The state of the property and building post-renovation sent a clear message about the deservingness of the population that would inhabit it. Historically, and in Canada, there is no shortage of examples of politicians and decision-makers perpetuating the oppression of a group by isolating them in poorer-maintained and harmful environments. The Aamjiwnaang First Nation in Ontario is an example of how forced exposure to pollutants can have serious negative impacts on health (McIntosh, 2025).

When individuals are exiled to spaces that are harmful to them, unsafe, and/or unsanitary, this communicates that the individuals in this location are here because they, too, are unsafe/unsanitary. This was an especially salient message at this time, given how contrastingly unwelcome the rest of Kingston had become to people experiencing homelessness and mental health issues. The downtown core, which in many cities sees an increased number of unhoused individuals, facilitated the high visibility of homelessness since they were the only group of people not isolating at home. Businesses became upset at the "loitering" and use of public bathrooms, ultimately contributing to new anti-loitering bylaws implemented in 2023 in Kingston. With shelters closed or operating at half-capacity, and the buffer of the public missing, unhoused citizens were targeted and made to feel unwelcome in their own city.

The "First", First Responders: Positionality, Trauma and Grief

The people in the community with those who use drugs, almost always individuals who use drugs themselves, have historically been the first group to intervene in crises experienced by their peers. Whether drug poisonings, violence, or death, the first responders to these events and the first to attend have long been the individuals experiencing these events themselves. Due to stigma and discrimination experienced by unhoused folks who use drugs at the hands of police and emergency service providers (EMS), this group has developed its practices of intervention to avoid contacting EMS if necessary. Additionally, there is a higher degree of trust and interpersonal solidarity amongst unhoused people who use/used drugs, and who have experienced homelessness/incarceration in the context of service delivery at a program. At the Integrated Care Hub, the early days of operations were characterized by a staff team that was largely comprised of individuals who, at one time in their lives, endured very similar circumstances to the people served. It was a known priority of the management team to embody the practice of aiding service delivery through community membership.

The positionalities of these front-line workers were foundational to the methods of service delivery and approaches taken in building connections with the people we served. Many of the staff were individuals who had experienced a substance use disorder or addiction at some time in their lives, while some were still quietly struggling. Some had experienced bouts of incarceration or suffered from mental health challenges. Some employees had never had "legitimate" (meaning tax-paying and legal) employment before the ICH. Some were young people who had recently graduated from college programs, primarily white women. A significant number of the staff, particularly in leadership roles, were members of the 2SLGBTQIA+ community. Most of the employees were white. None of these were mutually exclusive categories, and if one thing was undoubtedly shared amongst the group members, it was the collective trauma and grief we carried due to the ongoing drug poisoning crisis. We were pained and strung out, trying to take care of ourselves, one another, and the people we served.

The grief was hard to carry on some days. A number of times, a person accessing services passed away in the building or on the property. When this happened, there was no respite or space for grief because the other individuals accessing the Hub still needed care, support, and services. We practiced and mastered the skill of working around emergency service providers. Even if someone was actively overdosing or experiencing a medical emergency in their pod, we still needed to conduct 5-minute checks and make sure everyone else was okay. This is a fairly normal occurrence in a workplace like a hospital or in emergency services, but these are occupations where the hazard of patients dying is expected and trained for, and the act of trying to save the patient is considered noble and heroic by society. The work of providing emergency shelter to people who are experiencing homelessness, by definition, would not necessarily have to include giving life-saving services. However, for people using a toxic drug supply, it was where we were at, and the public didn't understand why we did it. Some thought we shouldn't!

Our grief was compounded by the fact that our mission was not unconditionally accepted as noble, but was needed work in the broader community. Facebook pages, Reddit threads, and visits from concerned or outraged community members repeatedly reinforced that our grief-filled and traumatic work was not only devalued, but was a nuisance to our neighbours who were fearful of the "addicts" and "junkies". The community of people who use drugs has been comprised of the responders to one another's health crises when outsiders did not understand——and were not committed to preserving their lives. They are not only the ones who pioneered the movement of progressive drug policy and carried the boots on the ground labour, but they are also the ones who energized the front-line workers to keep going when the work was challenging. They were humorous, hopeful, and modelled how to endure while carrying tremendous grief for their community members. There were times we lost multiple peers in the same week.

It did not take long for workers or service users at the ICH to realize that in the most strained operation periods, our priorities could not be around the traditional obligations of an emergency shelter/mental health service. In this time of constant death and crisis, we did not have the luxury to make our mission anything other than the maintenance of the clients and the preservation of their lives. In some special moments, our mission was to create and share joy through pranks, music, and doing activities together. We did not complete very many referrals in peak periods, we sloppily rushed through the intake, and note-taking/client documentation was sparse. We simply could not work in any other way, and while service users were unable to move through the housing/mental health systems, our responsibility shifted to incubating them until a time when services and more intensive support resumed.

Our ability to respond to emergencies was a critical and valued skill. Overdoses happened everywhere and regularly: in the bathrooms, in the sleeping pods, in the adjacent woods, in the community. We had staff who were ready for each of these occurrences, and several practiced peers who would often accompany the staff and support the response. Occasionally, there would be accompanying injuries/illnesses that complicated the response procedures, such as a fight, a seizure, or, in one case, an active fire. These had to be handled in a particular way that prioritized the most imminent health crisis first. Sometimes a response would involve being outside in the rain and the mud, trying to get someone's heart to start beating again while waiting for paramedics to arrive. The community always did its best and worked together in the worst of times. Not all attemps were successful, and then it was time to hold one another.

The lives that were lost during this time were celebrated as often as they could be. In the summer months, folks gathered outside and spoke about how meaningful that person had been to each of them. Stories were shared, and favourite songs were played. Tremendous love could be found in the ways the community treated one another when a loss happened. The ICH was the safest place for workers and service users to exist, in more ways than one. The patrons were less likely to die due to a poisoned supply of illicit drugs if they used them on the property or in the safe consumption site, and they were more likely to have their dignity preserved and emotions validated than in the rest of the community. Front-line providers were more likely to have their work understood by others who work in the same place, who validate its importance and saw value in the service users in the same way. In all of the instances of interpersonal conflict, the ICH was a safe place for the hearts of people carrying a lot of hurt.

COVID 19: "Othering" and Ostracization

People who use substances, who were already seen as hazards to the public for experiencing misunderstood mental health challenges, were uniquely targeted in the early years of the COVID-19 pandemic. Congregate living spaces, including prisons and shelters, see understandably high rates of transmission of infection and illness; however, nothing required so much preparation and accommodation as managing COVID-19 in a shelter. In the time of a drug poisoning crisis, where it is safest for people who use drugs to be with one another in case of emergency or overdose, the pandemic demanded that people isolate and stay apart. This was nearly impossible to achieve in one of the only fully operational shelters in the city, where people were prone to sharing drug use supplies like mouthpieces and pipes. The front-line workers and proactive service users did their best to encourage safe protocols for cohabitating in these numbers, but the ostracization of the population served by the ICH was severe and unrelenting. The ICH was open just a few short months before experiencing its first full-scale COVID-19 outbreak.

Despite that the ICH was the only shelter providing full-capacity services to unhoused individuals, the City of Kingston did not offer any tangible support to the organization as front-line staff and service users attempted to care for sick community members. Not only did managing people sick with COVID-19 severely overextend the capacity of front-line workers (many of whom were not comfortable working during active outbreaks) but there was seemingly no relief. Precariously housed or unhoused individuals in Kingston had the option to isolate at a motel in the West end of the city. However, the eligibility requirements of the isolation program stated that individuals who use opiates (including fentanyl) were not permitted to access this service and had to find elsewhere to isolate and recover. One young man, one of the first individuals staying at the ICH who contracted COVID-19, was denied isolation at the hotel due to fentanyl use and was thereby forced to isolate in a shack that was built on the property of the ICH. It had no heat, no running water, and worst of all, the community internalized the ostracization shown to them and projected this onto him for the ten days he isolated in the shed. This was not a dissimilar experience to solitary confinement, with the exception that the shed provided virtually no protection from the elements as the temperature continued to drop over the ten days, and he spent each night huddled under blankets alone, dope-sick, and severely ill with COVID-19.

As more people fell ill with COVID-19 as the weeks went on, the city surrendered and provided two trailers to the Integrated Care Hub to isolate individuals from the unsick population. After a short time, tall metal fences were erected around the trailers. The fences, along with the trailers filled with cots but lacking running water, bathrooms, and food, established an extremely inhumane way to treat people who were experiencing social ostracization, oppression, and illness. The only respite from this treatment was if someone was hospitalized, or if they lied about their substance use to access the hotel site service. Both of these options carried significant risk.

While all of this transpired, persons served were also under-served by Housing Case Managers, paramedics, firefighters, and individuals delivering medication from pharmacies. The public perception (exasperated by the appearance of the compound constructed on property) of people at the ICH during this time was that they were extremely dangerous to the broader public and were a cesspool of illness and disease. There were so few cases of individuals being adequately supported in a multi-faceted way. Very few people obtained housing at this time. It was an impossible, frustrating, losing battle while we waited for the storm to pass and for people to enter the sweet, three month "safe" period in which they could not contract COVID-19 again.

Support Not Stigma?

With generous Health Canada funding, the Support Not Stigma initiative was taking root. This included several components, which because of space limitations, we cannot fully describe. There was a Low Barrier Vocational Training and Paid Employment program as already described, a Building Community through Creativity weekly arts program, a Family Support and Repair program with psychotherapists, the Specialized Training for People who Work with People who use Substances already described, and a city-wide Anti-stigma and Education Campaign with regional public health.

Objectives of the Support Not Stigma campaign included increasing the community's knowledge of substance use stigma and how it impacts people who use substances (PWUS); increasing the community's knowledge about who PWUS are; That PWUS are not always visible and no one is immune; knowledge about how to support PWUS; and that PWUS are not all the same. Each has an individual story. On an individual level, stigma fosters isolation, shame, the belief that you will not receive help when you ask for it, and feeling unheard, unseen or uncared for. On an interpersonal level, stigma can be perpetuated through healthcare providers, law enforcement, business owners, family members, etc.

Juxtaposing the increasing public vitriole against the ICH and its clients was the launch of the Support Not Stigma campaign in the spring of 2023. It featured seven stories of people impacted by substance use. These were diverse and included themes related to resilience, parenthood, intergenerational impacts of substance use, trauma, etc. Stories demonstrated that those impacted by substance use are diverse; that substance use is not always visible; that stigma has been experienced interpersonally and within systems meant to support; and how to be kind and compassionate to those impacted by substance use. These can be found at www.SupportNotStigma.ca.

Despite the tremendous forward motion of the campaign against stigma towards addiction and people who use drugs, the public perception of "the Hub" and the people who accessed services there was scathing. Other citizens who resided in Kingston, specifically in the downtown/Belle Park area where the ICH was located, had significant reactions to the operation of the Hub; during this time, Reddit threads (Reddit, 2023) were made for people to complain about the "eye sore" that was the site, community members shared videos of individuals experiencing psychosis and mental health crises on Facebook, and there was even a website that pushed the narrative of wanting to "save" the Belle Park neighbourhood from the "Crime Hub." This social interpretation of a service that provided care to marginalized individuals is predictable—services that cater to individuals who do not behave in socially acceptable ways face tremendous scrutiny and judgment. Additionally, the lingering sentiments of the War on Drugs and the labelling of drug users as deviant made the operations of the ICH akin to coddling dangerous criminals.

The impact of this narrative on the community of people we served at the ICH was profound. It was clear that the persons served felt marginalized, unwanted, and generally unsafe in most other parts of the city. If the risk was not being labelled a danger or nuisance in public by fellow community members, then it was of persecution or violence by police. Some individuals felt this more deeply than others, often based on their own internalized relationship to substance use and shame. For some folks, this meant that they did not leave the ICH property for months. One gentleman in particular did not leave the property for over a year, aside from highly resisted hospital visits when he entered a deep psychosis and was a danger to himself. Despite the ever-present threat of theft, interpersonal violence (occasionally), and a shortage of support available due to a lack of resources, folks served at the ICH still felt more comfortable and welcomed in this space than in the rest of their city.

This phenomenon reinforced to the front-line staff of the ICH the necessity of ensuring that the persons served felt welcomed and deeply loved, starting the very moment they began accessing the service. While the ICH was not able to shelter the community of service users from the harm they faced in the community, the mission inside the four walls was to do things differently and more softly. The trauma could not be undone, and further trauma could not be prevented in all cases. However, there was a reliable group of individuals who supported this community as they did what they could to survive.

"Care" and "Healing"

A specialized training program devised for front-line workers, including emergency first responders, harm reduction workers, housing workers, social workers, etc., was very popular and much needed. Called "Specialized Training for People Who Work with People Who Use Substances: Unpacking Substance Use & Stigma to Better Understand Moral Injury," its learning objectives included: Unpacking substance use; Surfacing stigma to identify and dismantle; Learning how systems interconnect; Knowledge exchange on tools to help prevent moral injury; Building critical thinking skills; Acknowledging different roles, and how people approach their work; How to build solidarity together vs. blame/shame and/or hot potato games; Building compassion for each other and how we are all impacted by moral injury; Working with the people we serve from a place of compassion; Staff wellness as more than just "self-care"; and Mobilizing for a better future.

The program was underpinned by the knowledge that front line workers were experiencing moral injury (MI) through their work in a system ill-equipped to handle the challenges of serving with this vulnerable and marginalized population. MI is a multi-disciplinary, evolving construct, described as a form of psychological distress, an interpersonal crisis, a character wound, the undoing of character, or a spiritual wound in response to the learning about, bearing witness to, failure to prevent, or perpetration of any event that transgresses one's belief about subjective moral standards or deeply held personal beliefs. MI can also result from the betrayal of justice by a person of authority.

Over time, in having open dialogue and unconditional positive regard for the expertise of the people served at the ICH, some new ways of caring for one another emerged. We needed creative solutions to support people in managing their Post-Traumatic Street Disorder (PTSD) and MI. This was not without error; some strategies devised to support folks had the unintended consequence of reproducing harm. It is the responsibility of the service provider to learn from these occurrences, too. As previously mentioned, addressing traumatic losses and grief became a necessary facet of service delivery at the ICH. Grief and trauma were treated as medical ailments that required significant accommodation and support, as well as ongoing care from community members as a whole.

One of the ways grief and loss were validated was by issuing medical exemptions for people so they could maintain access to a sleeping pod for at least a few days, sometimes up to a few weeks, depending on the individual. Each of the accommodations issued was tailored specifically to the needs and behaviour of the person provided the accommodation. If someone processing grief could not get out of bed, or did not have a safe place to store sentimental items associated with the person lost, the use of a private space (although small) with consistent access to rest was sometimes very helpful. When the individual was no longer consistently accessing the rest pod, a conversation would take place between front-line workers and the service user to determine if the pod could be "flipped" and used for another individual. This sometimes became harmful because individuals who have not had access to a safe place to sleep for some time often will not willingly surrender it. There were hard situations of forcibly removing personal items from a space when folks became too overwhelmed or hurt to "move out" themselves. This sometimes felt like an eviction and served as a significant potential morally injurious event.

Another way we showed compassion and love for one another was by respecting and upholding the autonomy of the grieving individuals, not forcing them to participate in particular forms of celebration or memorialization. We spoke kind words about the individuals we lost into the universe and listened to their favourite music. Not everyone could handle group spaces like this- for some, their emotions were more comfortably processed independently, and this often included substance use. It was understood that it was not our jurisdiction to instruct folks on how to feel pain; we simply offered an opportunity to process in community with others who felt the same. Additionally, front-line workers and peers alike made sure to check on and comfort those who were struggling, bringing tea, spending time talking, gifting clothing or snacks, or making artwork. Emotions can be hard to talk about for individuals who have been chronically traumatized, but there was space made for sitting in silence while quietly caring for one another.

The building of the ICH became rife with memorials of well-known and influential community members. This was another way that we honoured the individuals impacted by these crises; by demonstrating the mark they left on the space in their final days. What an honour it was—that these individuals spent their last few weeks/months with us. Entire lives of parents, children, siblings, and citizens concluded at this very site at the intersection of catastrophes. One gentleman who frequented the Consumption Treatment Services had a locker for personal items named after him that was covered with hearts. An older gentleman who spent a lot of his time reading and talking about books had his name hung above a bookshelf that lived in the rest area, memorializing his "library" forever.

Healing was redefined through various measures implemented at the ICH. It is important to make the distinction between what we were "supposed" to be healing, which is what the broader community would deem treatment to cure substance use disorders and mental health conditions, and what was being healed in this space. At the Hub, the healing that took place was from the persistent estrangement of the community of service users from the rest of their city's population. Through the love and commitment to the autonomy of the patrons of the ICH, steps were taken towards healing the hurt that accompanied the War on Drugs and the social ostracization of people who use drugs in a time of late-stage capitalism.

The majority of services available to people experiencing substance use challenges and homelessness are geared towards "recovery", usually connoting abstinence from drugs or alcohol. Service restrictions, eligibility requirements, and programming at various social services in Kingston revolved around encouraging sobriety and punishing drug use. From the individuals that we served at the ICH, we learned about lengthy restrictions from other shelters that were doled out to people who used drugs in the bathroom or on the property. The sole detoxification facility in Kingston required not only identification, but also occasionally mandated a pre-existing period of sobriety before accessing the service. Transitional housing programs overwhelmingly required sobriety as a condition of staying housed or permitted individuals who used substances, but mandated participation in therapy groups to stay in housing. These barriers to care led to individuals experiencing a "revolving door" of not only support services, but also of the basic human right to housing and shelter. Front-line staff at the ICH saw the same faces over and over, and heard the same stories of marginalization and punishment. They were surveilled, penalized, and the power dynamic between "in need of help" and "helper" was exacerbated.

At the ICH, these dynamics were acknowledged, and there were ongoing attempts to dismantle the power imbalance, restoring some autonomy and sense of dignity to the service users. For example, while substance use could not be "permitted" in the communal spaces that were not the Supervised Consumption Site, people were minimally or not punished for using drugs in these non-allocated areas as often as possible. Not only would the punishment for using drugs inside the building be a faulty way for individuals to be deterred from doing so (positive punishment has been proven an ineffective method of deterrence from unwanted behaviour), but issuing harsh consequences without helping the individuals understand *why* this conduct was harmful to themselves and others broke trust between patron and service. The understanding amongst the leadership team who guided the development of these policies (sometimes with significant concerns raised by front-line staff who were familiar with the procedures of other services) was that to punish people for the use of substances that eased their suffering and pain was to communicate to them that their respite, their medicine, was undeserved. The goal, instead, was to aid in the understanding of the potential risks of this conduct and suggest a better choice.

Other measures taken in the space also recreated a decolonial narrative around the necessary division between service users and service providers. This was a fundamental truth about nearly all aspects of service delivery; almost all spaces in the ICH building were open and communal spaces accessible to all people. The drop-in, rest zone, and Consumption Treatment Services were the primary spaces where clients spent time and could exist without requirements of participation or engagement. However, there were also many "staff" spaces where persons served could access their own goods and services as needed, and often they acted in ways that supported staff, such as entering the kitchen space to help serve meals at the busy dinner hour, going to the laundry storage to help distribute bedding, etc. They would also grab an extra blanket for a friend if they were dopesick or cold. They would get extra Naloxone for staff if they were preoccupied responding to a drug poisoning. The people served at the ICH were, from day one, an integral part of operations running smoothly and they were welcomed into the spaces where they could participate in the care of their community members.

Additionally, the staff office space became a site where private conversations could be held with service users, phone calls could be made, and individuals who required additional support were welcomed to spend more time one-on-one with staff. This was another example of the boundaries of a traditional work/shelter space being flexed and expanded - most shelter and social services have specific "client" spaces and "employee" spaces in which patrons are not permitted. This was not the reality at the ICH; front-line staff were consistently "working in the grey" regarding their professional boundaries.

In the documentary "5B" about the healthcare providers who supported people dying of AIDS at the height of the epidemic, nurses were described as violating all social protocol by holding hands with, hugging, and lying with their patients as they died. At the time, it was a radical expression of love and human connection to prioritize the experience of the dying individual over a need for self-preservation and social conformity. This community is not so different; unhoused individuals and people who use drugs are deemed dangerous, dirty, and infected—some of them living with the same virus that was killing people by the thousands in the 1980s.

The front-line staff at the ICH knew, collectively, that the people we were working with had not been shown love or acceptance for some time; whether they were ostracized from their family, ejected from other services, etc. We continued this behaviour of radically loving them. Phrases like "stay safe", "I love you", and "we're so glad you're here" echoed towards our clients regularly. People hugged on hard days or to greet one another after the weekend. They were gentle with one another, and there was an unspoken understanding (especially amongst the people who used fentanyl) that you may not see that person again, so kind words mattered and love was an infinite resource. This was a deeply decolonial way of shifting our understanding of "professionalism" to be "the capacity to determine what is needed from the people you serve, and providing it", rather than it meaning the rigid upholding of boundaries that are inherently paternalistic and colonial.

Sisyphus and His Rock

Defending against the ongoing War on Drugs and hatred of people who use drugs, while attempting to provide shelter services in the midst of a housing crisis with seemingly no way to exit homelessness, and trying to establish connection and healing during a global pandemic, was no small undertaking for the community of people who lived and worked at the ICH. The pain, sadness, grief, and ostracization experienced by this community was profound. The sharing of these challenging experiences expedited the community's ability to build trust with one another and connect people who would not have typically had anything in common. Fighting this fight at this critical time was a bonding experience unlike anything the people in the space had experienced in their lives before.

There was acceptance of one another in their most raw, honest forms. People who did not have close relationships still developed the skill of reading one another's emotions. Everyone who had ever felt like the "black sheep" in their families or communities of origin felt seen and validated in the space, because if nothing else, we knew that we shared the same goal and the same vision for the future; a thriving community where each person has their needs met and brings something unique and valuable to the lives of others. Some people were artists, some were singers or rappers, some were the providers or caretakers of others. This community had "mothers" and "fathers" who took care of those they were not related to because they held power and influence within the community. In this space that operated outside the traditional modus operandi of capitalism (drugs, clothing, and other material goods were the currency), what became visible was the stripped-down, honest version of human community building. There was conflict, inevitably, and often. One even ended in death. But undeniably, there was love to be shared and acceptance to be offered to one another.

This is where the hope came from. Tremendous love and compassion for one another, seeing each other exactly as they were (for some at the lowest points in their lives) and still recognizing the value inherent in human life is how we endured. The pursuit of the good thing was fighting the war against stigma. Seeing ICH service users achieve stability in their everyday lives was the purpose. The motivation to endure in the work was not dependent on the likelihood of seeing the desired purpose achieved. The pursuit was what made it meaningful.

In this pursuit, there were beautiful things. There were love letters written to one another on the walls of the bathroom and the walls of the sleeping pods. There were moments of really, truly seeing each other and crying together through the exhaustion of enduring oppression. There were BBQs, practical jokes, games, movie nights, dancing, and so much laughter. Joy was our fuel and working to create these moments was to know that we were investing in our resolution. Even more impressive, this joy was established inside the walls of the ICH despite the fact that the world around us continued to spiral into an individualistic, public-safety-obsessed opposition to our mission and the work.

Examples of human deprivation continued at a variety of services across the city, and the positive influences of radical compassion and new ways of healing began to be pushed further to the sidelines. Despite the occasional illusion of progress, such as new housing facilities opening to address the shortage of deeply affordable housing, these programs opened with stringent rules around substance use and "criminal activity". Some behaviours that are woven into the survival strategies of unhoused people were demonized and used as justification to remove individuals from housing—such as ongoing use of drugs, selling substances for income, or collecting and keeping bike parts (frequently used as a form of transportation for people that are street-involved). These services, such as new shelters and housing programs, also collaborated more with the municipality than their fellow service providers, leading to more rigorous implementation of oppressive and high-barrier rules.

The popularity of the ICH as a place that maintained its low-barrier approach meant that more service users found solace and community in the adjacent encampment in Belle Park, as staying in tents in the forest seemed to some like a more tolerable option than accessing stigmatizing shelters. This increasing population of "campers" facilitated an increased politicization of the encampment, leading to ongoing conflict with the City of Kingston, the Kingston Police Department and By-Law officers. Trespassing notices, public nuisance tickets, and bylaw tickets were issued frequently, and residents of the encampment targeted repeatedly for trying to stay close to the services they needed most.

This presented an interesting parallel between the attempted forced displacement of encampment residents and ongoing anti-Indigenous racism in Canada. All of Canada and its land originally belonged to the original peoples, Indigenous communities, before colonization and the genocide of Indigenous people and culture. In the present day, the Belle Park encampment sees a higher population of Indigenous individuals than the rest of the city, highlighting the intersecting oppressions experienced by Indigenous communities now steeped with intergenerational trauma. Not only have people with Indigenous ancestry been over-represented in systems such as the criminal justice and mental health due to systemic racism, but they are now being told (once again) that their way of life (camping) and preservation of their community members is dangerous, hazardous to the public, and "incorrect".

The "correct" way to exist on historically Indigenous-owned land (including the land of Belle Park) is documented through signage, the enforcement of municipal By-Law, and the conduct of (mostly) white people who use the trail for leisure and exercise. Living on the land, using its materials for warmth or shelter, and leaving evidence of human life on the land are examples of the incorrect ways that encampment residents occupy space on this now privately-owned land (by a white developer and landlord, no less). The tickets, fines, and other legal ramifications solidify the same message ICH service users and unhoused folks have been receiving for years: *you do not belong here.*

The battle against this narrative that took place on a daily basis within the ICH service was noble and justified. People deserve better. People, especially those who have repeatedly been neglected by their communities and abandoned by those who are supposed to care for them, deserve to know that they are worth fighting for. The healers, the ones who will lead the battle, are the ones who will find joy in the journey of helping. They find satisfaction and enjoyment in the process, regardless of the outcome. The people that the healers support do not have to "achieve" anything to be worthy of the work. They are a pleasure to support simply by virtue of being a human who requires it, even when it feels like a losing battle—when progress is slow, or regresses, or when more pain comes. People deserve a relentless pursuit of the good thing. Thus, we endure—we push the rock up the hill, and we love on each other, we make joy in our plight, and above all else, we do not stop.

Conclusion

In 2020, the Integrated Care Hub (ICH) was created in Kingston, Ontario, Canada, at the intersection of the housing crisis, the drug poisoning epidemic, and the COVID-19 pandemic. Co-housed with the region's safe injection site as a day-drop-in and overnight shelter, it provided low-barrier services to people experiencing multiple mental health diagnoses, active addiction, and homelessness. This case study outlines how this vulnerable and marginalized population was treated with extreme prejudice—including discrimination and stigmatization—leading to denied access to health and harm reduction services, and emergency housing by Kingston health and community service providers. People experiencing multiple mental health diagnoses, active addiction, and homelessness were portrayed by institutions and the public as posing a threat to public life and safety. They are deprived of their humanity by being ghettoized and then tormented by cat calls and insults by people driving by the ICH. Despite having done community-based research to develop solutions that work for these clients, the power and influence of institutions, health care, and social service providers did not embrace best practices around the provision of harm reduction and low-barrier shelter services for people experiencing multiple mental health diagnoses, active addiction, and homelessness. Harm reduction front-line workers experienced moral injury as a result of the public and institutions stigmatizing and discriminating against their patrons/clients. Ironically, all of this occurred in parallel to knowledge dissemination of harm reduction best practices through a Health Canada-funded anti-stigma campaign called Support Not Stigma, informed by client centred community-based research.

After the highly publicized stabbing at the ICH in September 2024 and the rapid dismantling of the encampment, the ICH fell under new management, which has adjusted the term "low barrier" to mean case management and treatment services. Many of the harm reduction front-line staff were laid off, and the Community Support Program was terminated. With no true low-barrier shelter services available, many people experiencing homelessness who are also experiencing multiple mental health diagnoses and active substance use have been forced back into the streets. The moral injury experienced by those of us who worked at the ICH and within the Support Not Stigma initiative has been devastating. We have lost too many friends already and wonder what the future holds for so many others. We hope the recounting of this case study will show the good that is possible when one co-creates policies and programs with vulnerable and marginalized persons with multiple mental health diagnoses who use substances and may be experiencing homelessness. It is an over-simplification to think that our work was done in vain because the "system" reverted away from the low barrier model we implemented and many of our clients faced the same challenges as before we began. The experience demonstrates how radical love in the face of deep stigma positively transforms our relationship to care work and the people we serve.

References

Christmas, C. M. (2021). *Crystal Meth, Opiates, Overdose and Housing in Kingston, Ontario: 2021 Rapid Assessment and Response Community Needs Assessment for the Integrated Care Hub.* https://supportnotstigma.ca/wp-content/uploads/2023/01/Community-Needs-Assessment-V2.pdf

Federation of Canadian Municipalities. (n.d.). Burton Sanitation Redevelopment – Risk Assessment and Risk Management Plan, BPE Development/City of Kingston. Green Municipal Fund. https://info.gmf-fmv.ca/en-US/projectdetails/?id=ee191d5b-17dd-ec11-bb3c-0022486da190

McCann, V., Allen, R., & Purkey, E. (2022). Exploring the impact of COVID-19 on substance use patterns and service access of street involved individuals in Kingston, Ontario: a qualitative study. *BMC Public Health, 22*(1), 571.

McIntosh, E. (2025). *How Ontario could have cracked down on Chemical Valley pollution — but chose not to.* The Narwhal, June 26. https://thenarwhal.ca/chemical-valley-sarnia-pollution-delays/

Rajab, D., Fujioka, J. K., Walker, M., Bartels, S. A., MacKenzie, M., & Purkey, E. (2023). Emergency department care experiences among people who use substances: a qualitative study. *International Journal for Equity in Health, 22*(1), 248.

Reddit. (2023). Staff at ICH [Comment on the thread]. Reddit, March 31. https://www.reddit.com/r/KingstonOntario/comments/1e9uw1v/staff_at_ich/

Chapter 17
Increasing the Effectiveness of Social Work Practice in a Pandemic World with Marginalized People Experiencing Mental Distress Who Access Spiritual or Religious Resources

Julia Read and Stewart J. Smith

Abstract The COVID-19 pandemic further isolates marginalized people from general contact with others and, in particular, community resources and agencies, including spiritual and/or religious resources. Given this exacerbated isolation, known here as "COVID-19 isolation," it is important for social workers to examine how we contribute to and/or assist in finding solutions to people's compounded distress. In this chapter, we deconstruct how general counseling has taken up the Euro-western medicalized model of "mental illnesses." Informed by insights from various social justice frameworks, including Mad studies, we examine and challenge problematic mainstream assumptions about dominant "mental illness" narratives. Mad studies present the less stigmatizing term "mental distress" as a more useful understanding and way of working with marginalized people. Furthermore, we advocate that "mental distress" and holistic healing are paradigms in harmony with social justice-centered interventions. Using empowering ideas related to "COVID-19 isolation," we specifically reflect on examples concerning spiritual or religious resources that marginalized people experiencing mental distress may access. Working with spiritual or religious people going through mental distress can be complex for therapists. When spirituality or religion is added to the mix, some might presume the complications to be outside of their social work practice skill set. Acknowledging these complexities, we present practical strategies for working with spiritual and religious people experiencing mental distress. These considerations can contribute to increasing the general effectiveness of work done in a pandemic world with people in mental distress who access spiritual or religious resources.

J. Read · S. J. Smith (✉)
Wilfrid Laurier University, Faculty of Social Work, Kitchener, ON, Canada
e-mail: Jread@wlu.ca; read4080@mylaurier.ca; smit0020@wlu.ca

D. Nyaga, M. Zangeneh (eds.), *Critical Ethics on Mental Health and Madness*, Advances in Mental Health and Addiction,
https://doi.org/10.1007/978-3-032-10166-2_17

Keywords COVID-19 isolation · Spirituality/Religion · Mental distress · Mental illness

Introduction

The COVID-19 pandemic further isolates marginalized people from general contact with others and, in particular, community resources and agencies, such as spiritual and/or religious resources. Given this exacerbated isolation, known here as "COVID-19 isolation," it is important for social workers to examine how we contribute to and/or assist in finding solutions to people's compounded mental distress. In this chapter, we lay the groundwork for a robust practice grounded in social justice principles and practices that underpin Critical Disability Justice and Mad Studies. It is imperative that the expertise on mental distress experienced by folks seeking support from social workers is privileged. Next, we explore how counsellors have taken up the dominant medical model narrative on mental illness and provide an analysis through a Mad Studies lens (LeFrançois et al., 2013). We then discuss the implications the "mental illness" narratives have on people from marginalized communities struggling with mental distress who are seeking spiritual or religious guidance. Workers informed by the dominant medical model often understand spiritual or religious practices as either not helpful or exacerbating mental health issues (Garfield et al., 2013). Folks in mental distress who practice spiritual or religious rituals or prayers often find they are protective factors; however, they are told that religious resources have no place within mental health services (Lee & Baumann, 2013).

Following the analysis and deconstruction of "mental illness" hegemony that bolsters the dominant and harmful medical model narratives that align with the Neoliberal risk mitigation agenda and austerity measures. We explore how spiritual and religious experiences and resources are typically avoided by social work clinicians, as it is widely viewed as out of their scope of practice. Finally, we offer guidelines and recommendations to social work practitioners to address the area of clinical work, which are underpinned in social justice principles and anti-stigma language. As authors, we have taken up the anti-stigma language from people with lived mental distress experience (Lee, 2013).

The Issue at Hand

The problem identified during the pandemic was the lack of access and accessibility to religious and spiritual services and/or guidance for marginalized communities who experienced compounded mental distress caused by COVID isolation. In a review of the literature, we found that generally, spirituality is understood as subjective, individual, and experiential. Whereas religion is presented as objective, communal, and codified (Gasker, 2019; Kvarfordt & Herba, 2018). These terms sometimes overlap in that some folk find their spiritual experiences within a religion (Saucier & Skrzypinska, 2006). Others identify as spiritual but not connected to religion (Armstrong, 2013). Still others use the terms synonymously (Koenig, 2009). In this chapter, both terms are used with the intention of identifying the various ways people access spirituality.

Thesis Statement

Using social justice frameworks such as Mad Studies, social workers and clinicians can support religious and spiritual people from marginalized communities experiencing mental distress brought about by COVID isolation, using the guidelines we recommend.

What do Critical Theory, Social Justice, and Mad Studies all have in common? They are all built upon a common lynch pin which is "emancipatory action" (Dumbrill & Yee, 2019; Sharma, 2022). Critical Theory offers social agents time and space to open up a critical way of dismantling or critiquing what is normally taken for granted as truth (Dumbrill & Yee, 2019). It also promotes self-determination and liberation on a societal level and holds space to re-examine the notion of "normal," including "normal mental health" and what systems and structures hold power to disqualify those who are deemed outside of "normal" (Macy, 2000). Social work has adopted much of what critical theory has to offer and infuses it into clinical practice, community capacity building, research, and theory.

Social justice in the mental health field aligns with the basic attributes of critical theory and anti-oppressive practice that comes from a place that is guided by human rights principles and practices. Social justice is the idea that all people have equal access to all resources and that all needs are met across all communities all over the world. According to Morrow and Malcoe (2017), "…material resources must be distributed to ensure participants independence and voice… and that the institutionalized cultural patterns of interpretation and evaluation must express equal respect for all participants and ensure equal opportunity for achieving social esteem" (p. 9).

Where does Mad Studies fit into all of this? Mad Studies is a body of literature written by those with lived experience of mental distress and experience of being psychiatrized (Beresford & Russo, 2021). Some Mad Studies scholars identify their own lived experience, while some identify as allies, advocates, and activists (Costa et al., 2012). Mad Studies' first official text *Mad Matters: A Critical Reader in Canadian Mad Studies* was published in 2013; this field is relatively new. The collection of works can be found in Critical Disabilities Studies and is influenced by anti-psychiatry, radical therapy, critical psychiatry, psychiatric survivors, and mad communities (LeFrançois et al., 2013). Mad Studies was founded from the Mad movement, where the patient story from within the horrors of the asylums needed to be exposed (Starkman, 2013). Mad Studies has blossomed into an international conversation about the act of resistance, taking back power, and talking back to the medical/psychiatry industry (Beresford & Russo, 2021; Starkman, 2013). Breseford (2016) conceptualizes power from the Mad Studies lens as "the enormous political and economic power of psychiatry" (p. 31). Furthermore, power refers to the control the medical system, particularly the psy-industry holds to label folk as dangerous, rewrite human experiences as diagnoses, and determine who and when folk deemed "mentally ill" can be locked up or institutionalized against their will (Burstow, 2013; Smith & Read, 2024). Mad Studies offers a robust critique of the medical model, especially the harms caused by the "mental illness" dominant narrative (Burstow, 2013). Many Mad scholars highlight the problematic issues of the medical model's disempowerment narrative, deficit perspective, essentializing through diagnosis, lack of scientific proof of such diagnoses, discounting of "other" cultures that are not Euro-western centric, and the violence caused by the harmful storying of people's mental health experiences which also include spiritual or religious experiences (Lee, 2013; Liegghio, 2013; Voronka, 2013). Liegghio uses the term epistemic violence as an application to explore the "denial of being" through the process of psychiatrization. More specifically, "Epistemic violence refers to the way certain persons… are disqualified as legitimate knowers at a structural level through various institutional process an practices" (Liegghio, 2013, p. 123).

One of the many emancipatory and liberatory practices of Mad Studies is their diligent work on destigmatizing language (Beresford & Russo, 2016; Poole, 2011). This is where we, the authors, picked up the language of mental distress, rather than "mental illness." Mental distress is about everybody's experiences on a micro and macro level, not just the "crazy person" discourse. Another attribute of Mad Studies is the bolstering of other ways of knowing and being (Liegghio, 2013). Rather than referring to someone as a schizophrenic, through the lens of Mad Studies, we understand the person as someone who hears voices (Hearing Voices Network, n.d.; Sweeney, 2016). Who are we to judge that a person who is experiencing mental distress is not hearing legitimate voices, and who are we to say those voices are not ancestors, angels, or any other form of spiritual or religious experiences. According to the Hearing Voices Network (n.d.) website, 75% of the world may have a single incident where they hear voice(s) such as a name being called out when it is not. Highlighting this fact aids in normalizing the experience of hearing voices, this aids in breaking down the walls of stigma that prevents people from reaching out for support.

Madness can refer to a range of experiences, such as thoughts, moods, and behaviors, that are outside of normal conventionalism (Liegghio, 2013). The dominant psy-industry discourses construct "normal mental health" and decide who fits within or outside of it (Rose, 2000). Mad people's identities are essentialized by the psy-industry by a process of symptom identification and categorization, then diagnosed, and then pathologized that devalues and denies their humanity and cultural context (LeFrançois et al., 2013; Liegghio, 2013). People who hear voices or have visions often have their experiences delegitimized as they become diagnosed with "psychosis" (Beresford & Russo, 2021). Mad studies opens dialogues to critically question what mental health is and who has the power to decide who is included and who is excluded. Rose (2000) extends the work of Foucault (1978) and further articulates the power dynamics among the psy-industry and the techniques and tactics used to decipher circuits of exclusion where marginalized people are marked for incarceration or rehabilitation (Garland, 1997; Voronka, 2013). Clients in such situations access spirituality/religion for support and benefit from these resources being included in social work assistance.

Spirituality/Religion and Holistic Social Work Practice

There are numerous critical frameworks within critical theory that can be applied to issues related to spirituality/religion as related to social work practice (Gardner, 2016). Inclusion of all aspects of clients' lives is one aspect of effective social justice-informed social work practice. To accept people for who they are, and to respectfully work towards understanding their worldviews embodies the acceptance and celebration of diversity. Varied worldviews often include spiritual/religious practices as evidenced in First Nation, Metis, and Inuit communities, Black, People of Color, as well as settler populations in Canada. Indigenous spiritualities generally do not make this kind of distinction between spirituality and religion, but rather focus on the "interconnectedness and interrelationship with all life" (Baskin, 2011, p. 171). Indigenous spiritualities are commonly rooted in the traditions of their communities (Absolon, 2011; Baskin, 2016). To effectively work with Indigenous peoples is to respectfully include their spiritual traditions (Baskin, 2016; TRC, 2015). This working principle can apply to non-Indigenous folk as well.

Canada's population includes many new immigrants who identify with a form of spirituality/religion (Connor, 2009; George & Ellison, 2015; Reitz et al., 2009). In one census of the overall population in Canada, 75% identified as having a religious affiliation (Statistics Canada XE "Statistics Canada", 2011). Working with the whole person in a respectful helping relationship enhances the therapeutic alliance. This working relationship should include clients' spiritualities/religions.

Although there are variations in definitions, generally, the literature identifies spirituality and religion as differing terms. Spirituality is identified as individual subjective experiences of spirit, transcendence, meaning, and/or purpose (Crisp, 2017; Provis, 2023). Religion is identified as a communal understanding of spirituality rooted in theology, expressed in particular rituals and practices (Crisp, 2017; Provis, 2023). For many, there is an interconnection or overlap in ideas related to spirituality and religion, with some form of religion informing their spirituality (Wong & Vinsky, 2009). When considering these terms as applied to social work practice, it is important to recognize the "complexity and multiplicity of spirituality and religion" (Wong & Vinsky, 2009, p. 1357). The lived experiences of spiritual/religious clients have a direct impact on well-being.

Holistic practices related to mental health note that all aspects of a person need to be considered when assessing well-being (Baskin, 2016; Wilkinson, 2022). Often spirituality is identified as part of what it is to be human, and as needing attention when optimizing well-being (Wilkinson, 2022). Holistic health components can be identified in Indigenous medicine wheels and in Western holistic wellness wheels (Sasakamoose et al., 2016). One aspect of work with spiritual/religious clients is identifying the impact of their practices on their overall well-being.

General well-being can be enhanced for clients who pray, meditate, gather in community, and/or review spiritual readings (Scheffert et al., 2023). Religiously informed mental health practices, like mindfulness, can also increase positive well-being (Michalski & Smith, 2023). It is essential to also recognize that well-being can also be harmed by spiritual/religious ideas (Ellison & Lee, 2010). It has been our experience that often the impact of spirituality/religion has multiple impacts on clients. For example, in our work with spiritual/religious gay couples, they may identify the negative aspects of their religion, including being homophobic, as well as the positive impacts, which might include spiritual and family connections. The social worker can assist clients in identifying these nuanced impacts, as well as the connection with holistic health and spirituality/religion. This subjectivity can be one reason to celebrate "diversity" and hold a "wide acceptance of spirituality in all its expressions" (Gardner, 2016, p. 183). Among clients' multiple identities, there is the possibility of their spiritual/religious identity. If this is identified by clients, social workers need to be prepared to respectfully engage with these elements of people's lives. This has several implications for social work practice.

Discussion: Implications for Practice

Effective social work, informed by social justice principles, can be helpful to spiritual/religious clients. There are three principles presented below that will enhance the therapeutic alliance that are: systemic analysis, client-centeredness, and ethical practices.

Client-centered social work re-situates the client as the central focus of services. When working with spiritual/religious clients, social workers need to be pragmatic. If this area of their lives is important to clients, social workers work with them to identify how the spiritual/religious aspects of clients' lives are helpful (Gokani & Smith, 2020). It has been our experience that being curious about how service users understand spirituality/religion can strengthen the working therapeutic relationship. Appreciating spirituality/religiosity as part of complex multiple identities demonstrates respect. Working respectfully with clients' individual subjective experiences of spiritual/religious experiences includes considering structural and systemic concerns.

Systemic analysis includes evaluation of individual practices within larger systems (Dumbrill & Yee, 2019). This might include oppression by the dominant culture of particular religious groups. It might also invite evaluation of particular spiritual/religious communities. Challenging oppression from the larger society and/or within faith communities is part of social work for change in social systems that negatively impact health. Promoting Human Rights related to freedom of spirituality/religion is related to this aspect of social justice work. Social work advocacy includes the recognition of the right to practice spirituality/religion (Gardner, 2016; Lundy, 2011). Being social justice advocates demands we stand in solidarity with spiritual/religious people, which includes challenging oppression from the dominant culture and/or within religious organizations. The principles related to structural considerations, as well as client-centered services, are examples of social work ethics in practice.

Within the code of ethics for social workers are principles that guide those in the profession as to what can and cannot be done with clients (CASW, n.d.). Ethical behavior in social work creates sound professional boundaries (Banks, 2021). We maintain that the inclusion of clients' spirituality/religion is an example of working within ethical principles of respect, social justice, and sound practice principles.

Social work principles of working with a person in the environment, client-centered service, and ethical considerations have been explored earlier. How this may impact our interactions with spiritual/religious clients is something social workers need to consider.

Conclusion

The authors offer that critical reflexive practice be informed by the social justice principles in mad studies and an openness to clients' spirituality/religion. Critical reflection in social work analysis invites reflection on the subjective experiences of the social worker, which includes accessing critical theories in the analysis (Gardner, 2016). The use of critical theory in reflexive practice is to identify privilege and bias within social workers, to the end that oppression is not reproduced, and social justice is promoted (Béres & Fook, 2020; Gardner, 2016). Gardner (2016) explains that "Reflective practice affirms the value of experience, including subjective experience. In relation to spirituality, this reinforces the centrality of our own subjective and individual experience of the spirit" (p. 183).

Curiosity about clients' worldviews must include explorations of what they believe, what their beliefs mean to their lives, and how they understand the impact their beliefs have on their lives. Social work involves all aspects of people's lives, including micro (individuals, families, or small groups), mezzo (community-based social service agencies, community groups), and macro (social policy development, social work program design, human rights legislation) (Dumbrill & Yee, 2019; Wu & Greig, 2022). Being cognizant of these aspects helps social workers to view the person through a holistic lens while remaining curious about how the pandemic has impacted everyone differently.

References

Absolon, K, E. (2011). *Kaaandossiwin: How we come to know*. Halifax, NS: Fernwood.

Armstrong, N. T. (2013). Spiritual but not religious. *Journal for the Scientific Study of Religion, 52*(2), 258–278. https://www-jstor-org.libproxy.wlu.ca/stable/24644008

Banks, S. (2021). *Ethics and values in social work* (5th ed.). Red Globe Press.

Baskin, C. (2011). *Strong helpers' teachings: The value of Indigenous knowledges in the helping professions*. Canadian Scholars' Press.

Baskin, C. (2016). Spirituality: The core of healing and social justice from an Indigenous perspective. *New Directions for Adult and Continuing Education, 2016*(152), 51–60.

Beresford, P., & Russo, J. (2016). Supporting the sustainability of mad studies and preventing its co-option. *Disability & Society, 31*(2), 270–274.

Béres, L., & Fook, J. (Eds.). (2020). *Learning critical reflection: Experiences of the transformative learning process*. Routledge.

Beresford, P., & Russo, J. (Eds.). (2021). *The Routledge international handbook of mad studies*. Routledge.

Beresford's. (2016). The role of survivor knowledge in creating alternatives to psychiatry. In Russo & Sweeney (Eds.), *Searching for a rose garden: Challenging psychiatry, fostering mad studies* (pp. 25–34). PCCS Books.

Burstow, B. (2013). A rose by any other name: Naming the battle against psychiatry. In Menzies, Lefrancois, & Reaume (Eds.), *Mad matters: A critical reader in Canadian mad studies*. Canadian Scholars' Press.

(CASW) Canadian Association of Social Workers. Code of Ethics. https://www.casw-acts.ca/en/Code-of-Ethics%20and%20Scope%20of%20

Connor, P. (2009). Immigrant religiosity in Canada: Multiple trajectories. *International Migration & Integration, 10*, 159–175. https://doi.org/10.1007/s12134-009-0097-9

Costa, L., Voronka, J., Landry, D., Reid, J., McFarlane, B., Reville, D., & Church, K. (2012). Recovering our stories: A small act of resistance. *Studies in Social Justice, 6*(1), 85–101.

Crisp, B. R. (Ed.). (2017). *The Routledge handbook of religion, spirituality and social work* (1st ed.). Routledge. https://doi.org/10.4324/9781315679853

Dumbrill, G. C., & Yee, J. Y. (2019). *Anti-oppressive social work: Ways of knowing, talking, and doing*. Oxford University Press.

Ellison, C. G., & Lee, J. (2010). Spiritual struggles and psychological distress: Is there a dark side of religion? *Social Indicators Research, 2010*(98), 501–517. https://doi.org/10.1007/s11205-009-9553-3

Foucault, M. (1978). Governmentality. In J. D. Faubion (Ed.), *Power* (pp. 201–222). New Press.

Gardner, F. (2016). Critical spirituality in holistic practice. *Journal for the Study of Spirituality, 6*(2), 180–193. https://doi.org/10.1080/20440243.2016.1235185

Garfield, C. F., Isacco, A., & Sahker, E. (2013). Religion and spirituality as important components of men's health and wellness: An analytic review. *American Journal of Lifestyle Medicine, 7*(1), 27–37. https://doi.org/10.1177/1559827612444530

Garland, D. (1997). "Governmentality" and the problem of crime: Foucault, criminology, sociology. *Theoretical Criminology, 1*(2), 173–214.

Gasker, J. (2019). *Generalist social work practice*. Sage Publications.

George, M., & Ellison, V. (2015). Incorporating spirituality into social work practice with migrants. *British Journal of Social Work, 2015*(45), 1717–1733. https://doi.org/10.1093/bjsw/bcu035

Gokani, R., & Smith, S. J. (2020). A brief comment on theoretical and clinical implications of a pragmatic approach to religion and spirituality in social work. *Journal of Religion & Spirituality in Social Work: Social Thought, 2020, 39*(1), 73–89. https://doi.org/10.1080/15426432.2019.1701614

Hearing Voices Network. (n.d.). https://www.hearing-voices.org/#content. National Hearing Voices Network: London.

Koenig, H. G. (2009). Research on religion, spirituality, and mental health: A review. *The Canadian Journal of Psychiatry, 54*(5), 283–291. https://doi.org/10.1177/070674370905400502

Kvarfordt, C. L., & Herba, K. (2018). Religion and spirituality in social work practice with children and adolescents: A survey of Canadian practitioners. *Child Adolescent Social Work Journal, 35*(2), 153–167. https://doi.org/10.1007/s10560-017-0513-5

Lee, J. (2013). Mad as hell: The objectifying experience of symbolic violence. In Menzies, Lefrancois, & Reaume (Eds.), *Mad matters: A critical reader in Canadian mad studies* (pp. 130–140). Canadian Scholars' Press.

Lee, E., & Baumann, K. (2013). German psychiatrists' observation and interpretation of religiosity/spirituality. *Hindawi Publishing Corporation Evidence-Based 347, Complementary and Alternative Medicine, 2013*., Article ID 280168, 1–8. https://doi.org/10.1155/2013/280168

LeFrançois, B. A., Menzies, R., & Reaume, G. (Eds.). (2013). *Mad matters: A critical reader in Canadian mad studies*. Canadian Scholars' Press.

Liegghio, M. (2013). A denial of being: Psychiatrization as epistemic violence. In Menzies, Lefrancois, & Reaume (Eds.), *Mad matters: A critical reader in Canadian mad studies* (pp. 122–129). Canadian Scholars' Press.

Lundy, C. (2011). *Social work, Social Justice & Human Rights: A structural approach to practice* (2nd ed.). University of Toronto Press.

Michalski, E. W., & Smith, S. J. (2023). The use of mindfulness in group work. *Social Work With Groups*. https://doi.org/10.1080/01609513.2023.2257755

Morrow, M., & Malcoe, L. H. (2017). Introduction: Science, social (in)justice, and mental health. In *Critical inquiries for social justice in mental health* (pp. 3–30). University of Toronto Press.

Poole, J. (2011). *Behind the rhetoric: Mental health recovery in Ontario*. Fernwood Publishing.

Provis, C. (2023). Spirituality: Definition, religion and ethics. *Humanistic Management Journal, 8*(3), 399–420. https://doi.org/10.1007/s41463-023-00162-8

Reitz, J. G., Banerjee, R., Phan, M., & Thompson, J. (2009). Race, religion, and the social integration of new immigrant minorities in Canada in. *International Migration Review, 43*(4), 695–726. https://doi.org/10.1111/j.1747-7379.2009.00782.x

Rose, N. (2000). Government and control. *British Journal of Criminology, 40*, 321–339.

Sasakamoose, J., Scerbe, A., Wenaus, I., & Sandrett, A. (2016). First nation and metis youth perspectives of health: An indigenous qualitative inquiry. *Qualitative Inquiry, 22*(8), 636–650. https://doi.org/10.1177/1077800416629695

Saucier, G., & Skrzypinska, K. (2006). Spiritual but not religious? Evidence for two independent dispositions. *Journal of Personality, 74*(5), 1257–1292. https://doi.org/10.1111/j.1467-6494.2006.00409.x

Scheffert, A. H. M., Harper, A. W., & Yancey, G. (2023). Coping behavior changes in Christian congregations in the United States: A National Survey. *Social Work & Christianity, 50*(3), 218–238. https://doi.org/10.34043/swc.v50i3.340

Sharma, P. (2022). Navigating voices, politics, positions admits peers. In *The Routledge international handbook of mad studies* (pp. 340–350). Routledge.

Starkman, M. (2013). The movement. In Menzies, Lefrancois, & Reaume (Eds.), *Mad matters: A critical reader in Canadian mad studies* (pp. 27–37). Canadian Scholars' Press.

Statistics Canada. (2011). *Table 32-10-0198-01 Number of persons in the total population and the farm population, classified by religious affiliation*. https://www150.statcan.gc.ca/t1/tbl1/en/tv.action?pid=3210019801

Sweeney, A. (2016). Why mad studies needs survivor research and survivor research needs mad studies. *Intersectionalities: A Global Journal of Social Work Analysis, Research, Polity, and Practice, 5*(3), 36–61.

TRC. (2015). Truth and Reconciliation Commission of Canada, (2015). *Honouring the truth, reconciling for the future: summary of the final report of the Truth and Reconciliation Commission of Canada. 2015*. http://www.trc.ca/websites/trcinstitution/index.php?p=7

Voronka, J. (2013). Rerouting the weeds: The move from criminalizing to pathologizing "troubled youth" in *the review* of the roots of youth violence. In Menzies, Lefrancois, & Reaume

(Eds.), *Mad matters: A critical reader in Canadian mad studies* (pp. 309–322). Canadian Scholars' Press.

Wilkinson, B. D. (2022). Holistic irreducibility: Humanistic practice as the gateway to phenomenal mind. *Journal of Counseling and Development, 100*(2), 215–224. https://doi.org/10.1002/jcad.12415

Wong, Y. L. R., & Vinsky, J. (2009). Speaking from the margins: A critical reflection on the 'spiritual-but-not-religious' discourse in social work. *British Journal of Social Work, 2009*(39), 1343–1359. https://doi.org/10.1093/bjsw/bcn032

Wu, H., & Greig, M. (2022). Adaptability, Interdisciplinarity, Engageability: Critical reflections on green social work teaching and training. *Healthcare, 10*(7), 1245. https://doi.org/10.3390/healthcare10071245

Chapter 18
Critical Ethics in Mental Health in Iranian Adolescents

Roghieh Nooripour, Ainaz Shateri, and Sepideh Safarpoor Dehkordi

Abstract This chapter critically examines the ethical challenges in mental health care for Iranian adolescents, focusing on the complicated relationship among global psychological approaches, Islamic ethics, and Iranian socio-cultural realities. Iran's ethnic diversity, encompassing groups such as Kurds, Arabs, Baluchs, Turks, Lors, and nomadic tribes, creates distinct mental health challenges shaped by cultural traditions, social inequities, and historical marginalization. The chapter foregrounds the necessity of critically conceptualizing "culture" and "cultural sensitivity," moving beyond their superficial use as mere markers of diversity. In today's global order, culture is often commodified—packaged and sold—risking new forms of exclusion and racism, including anti-Muslim bias. Understanding how culture is defined, by whom, and for whose benefit reveals underlying power struggles that shape mental health practices in Iranian communities. The concept of "inclusion" is similarly interrogated. While often portrayed as a benevolent ideal, inclusion can mask dominant Western epistemologies that marginalize or erase indigenous healing traditions and local knowledge systems. This chapter warns against uncritical acceptance of inclusion, highlighting the political and ethical complexities involved in genuinely respecting and preserving local ways of healing. Resilience, within this ethical framework, is conceptualized not as an individual trait but as a culturally embedded, collective process shaped by social, religious, and familial contexts. It requires navigating structural constraints and cultural expectations unique to Iranian adolescents. Gender issues are examined through an intersectional lens, acknowl-

R. Nooripour (✉)
Department of Counseling, Qa.C, Islamic Azad University, Qazvin, Iran
e-mail: nooripour@iau.ac.ir

A. Shateri
Department of Psychology, Florida International University, Miami, FL, USA
e-mail: Ashat010@fiu.edu

S. S. Dehkordi
Department of Educational Management, Shi.C., Islamic Azad University, Shiraz, Iran
e-mail: sa.safarpoor@iau.ac.ir

D. Nyaga, M. Zangeneh (eds.), *Critical Ethics on Mental Health and Madness*, Advances in Mental Health and Addiction,
https://doi.org/10.1007/978-3-032-10166-2_18

edging how gendered pressures intersect with systemic inequalities, including gendered racism. The framework challenges reductive stereotypes and emphasizes narratives of cultural resistance and empowerment.

Finally, the chapter calls for caution when employing mixed methods in mental health research and practice. It highlights the risk that global agendas might superficially embrace local knowledge while simultaneously appropriating or erasing it. Ethical mental health care needs constant awareness of power relationships and careful plans to combine global psychological ideas with the protection and support of local cultural and religious traditions.

Keywords Critical ethics · Iran · Mental health · Culture

Introduction

Understanding ethical dimensions of mental health practices for Iranian adolescents requires a nuanced exploration of intersections between psychological approaches, religious beliefs, and cultural norms (Estrada et al., 2019). The unique socio-cultural context of Iran provides a critical framework for examining how adolescents perceive, address, and treat mental health challenges. Ethical frameworks commonly derived from universal standards often fail to adequately consider the regional and cultural variations that shape these practices (Dehghani et al., 2015).

Mental health care for adolescents is universally recognized as a priority; however, its ethical application varies significantly across cultural, religious, and socio-political contexts. In Iran, applying international standards to adolescent mental health reveals a complex set of moral dilemmas shaped by the intersection of global psychological paradigms with the country's distinctive cultural, religious, and societal dynamics(Mianji & Kirmayer, 2020). Core factors such as cultural collectivism, Islamic ethical teachings, strong familial obligations, and entrenched gender norms influence how mental health is perceived, expressed, and treated. These influences often clash with universal ethical frameworks that may fail to consider local values, expectations, and lived realities. There is a pressing need to critically reassess and adapt global ethical models to ensure they are culturally responsive, contextually grounded, and ethically appropriate for Iranian adolescents.

The variety of ethnic groups in Iran, like Kurds, Arabs, Baluchs, Turks (including Azeris and Turkmens), Lors, Gilaks, Mazandaranis, and nomadic tribes such as Qashqais and Bakhtiaris, makes it hard to address mental health issues for these communities. Marginalized groups, particularly Kurds, Arabs, and Baluchs, often experience compounded mental health difficulties not only due to cultural norms and social inequities but also as a result of linguistic barriers. These barriers become especially problematic when mental health services—including clinical interventions, psychoeducational resources, and therapeutic communication—are predominantly offered in Persian, the official language of the country. For individuals whose first language is not Persian, especially those with limited fluency, these linguistic obstacles can lead to miscommunication with mental health professionals, diminished cultural sensitivity in diagnosis and treatment, and reduced trust in healthcare systems. Moreover, the lack of linguistically and culturally appropriate services can heighten feelings of exclusion, identity confusion, and reluctance to seek help. As a result, linguistic marginalization can significantly exacerbate psychological distress and contribute to poorer mental health outcomes within these communities.

These intersecting factors—such as ethnicity, socioeconomic status, gender, and linguistic background—interact within broader systems of oppression and structural inequalities that operate within and beyond individual experiences. Intersectional systems of oppression, like institutional racism, economic marginalization, and cultural discrimination, create unequal access to resources and opportunities, which greatly affect how Iranian adolescents view, experience, and handle their mental health. This framework highlights that mental health challenges cannot be fully understood or addressed without considering the complicated relationship among overlapping social identities and systemic power imbalances. The combination of ethnicity, religion, and social class in these groups shows the weaknesses of Western mental health models, which mainly focus on individual problems, standard diagnoses, and one-size-fits-all treatments. Such frameworks often overlook the collectivist orientations, spiritual traditions, and sociopolitical contexts that influence mental health in non-Western settings. Given Iran's cultural complexity—marked by ethnic, religious, and economic diversity—these models fall short in capturing the lived realities of adolescents, indicating the importance of culturally grounded and contextually relevant strategies. By bridging global psychological paradigms with localized approaches, we aim to develop inclusive mental health care that respects the unique needs of each community. Iran's rapid sociocultural evolution further complicates this landscape. Adolescents today encounter rapid transformations driven by technological advancements, evolving youth culture, and shifting political landscapes. These changes challenge established social norms, including parental authority, religious adherence, traditional gender roles, and community expectations. Such disruptions complicate ethical decision-making for mental health professionals, who must carefully balance respect for indigenous cultural values with the emerging psychological needs and identities of Iranian adolescents. These transitions create tensions between traditional values rooted in collective well-being and the growing influence of globalized mental health paradigms, which often emphasize individual autonomy. In this context, mental health care for adolescents must balance respect for Iran's cultural heritage with the need for innovative, adaptive approaches (Rosenbaum et al., 2023).

Gender roles, family dynamics, and educational pressures also play pivotal roles in shaping adolescent mental health(Dittman et al., 2023). In a culture that prioritizes familial and social obligations over individual aspirations, these interconnected factors shape the expression, perception, and resolution of mental health challenges. The complexity of these dynamics highlights the ethical dilemmas faced by mental health practitioners in reconciling indigenous Iranian cultural values with evolving psychological needs of adolescents.

This chapter explores how ethical ideas from Islamic ethics, Iranian cultural values, and proven psychological methods can help Iranian teenagers, who are about 12 to 18 years old, in ways that respect their culture and situation. Key concepts include Islamic ethics, which emphasize compassion and family-centered decision-making; Iranian cultural values, highlighting collectivism and social harmony; and evidence-based psychology, focusing on scientifically supported yet culturally adapted interventions. By examining these critical intersections, the discussion aims to establish a foundation for addressing the ethical challenges in adolescent mental health care in Iran, setting the stage for more profound investigation into specific questions and practical approaches in the chapters that follow.

How Do Iranian Cultural Norms and Religious Beliefs Influence Ethical Questions Regarding Adolescent Mental Health?

Addressing adolescent mental health within the Iranian context requires a nuanced understanding of the country's cultural norms and religious beliefs, which deeply influence the ethical landscape surrounding mental health care. Iran's socio-cultural framework is characterized by a unique interplay of collectivist values, family-centered traditions, and Islamic ethics (S. Jafari et al., 2009). These factors significantly shape societal attitudes toward mental health and inform the ethical dilemmas faced by practitioners who work with adolescents. This chapter explores how Iranian cultural and religious values intersect with adolescent mental health, examines the ethical tensions that arise in clinical practice, and proposes an integrated model for ethical care.

Cultural Norms and Their Ethical Implications

Collectivism and Family-Centered Values

Iranian culture is profoundly collectivist, prioritizing the needs and well-being of the family over individual desires (Joshanloo, 2013). Family expectations often encourage adolescents to conform, thereby limiting their autonomy and discouraging open discussions about mental health struggles. For example, adolescents experiencing anxiety might avoid seeking help to protect their family's reputation(Razavieh & Hosseini, 1972). This cultural emphasis on familial harmony can create ethical challenges for mental health practitioners, who must navigate the delicate balance between respecting family dynamics and advocating for the adolescent's needs.

In addressing such challenges, culturally sensitive approaches are essential. In the Iranian context, where family plays a central role in adolescents' lives, involving family members in the therapeutic process can significantly enhance understanding, emotional support, and treatment adherence. However, this involvement must be structured and continuous. Merely providing information to family members is not sufficient; practitioners must remain actively engaged to guide, monitor, and support both the adolescent and their family throughout the therapeutic journey. Such involvement ensures that the responsibility for change does not fall solely on the family and that the adolescent's autonomy and well-being remain at the center of care. Ethical practice requires practitioners to educate families about mental health in ways that respect their cultural values while ensuring the adolescent's well-being(Valizadeh et al., 2018). For instance, family psychoeducation programs that frame mental health as a collective issue rather than an individual failure can help reduce stigma and promote open dialogue.

Honor and Social Expectations

The concept of honor ("āberu") plays a central role in Iranian society, shaping how mental health challenges are perceived and addressed. Often, societal norms expect adolescents to uphold the family's honor ("āberu"), which can intensify feelings of shame and isolation when they encounter psychological difficulties(Abbaszadeh & Dabbagh, 2024). For instance, Iranian adolescents experiencing depression may fear being perceived as weak—a perception often shaped by gender norms that discourage emotional expression, particularly among boys. Cultural values tied to family reputation and honor further compound this stigma, underscoring the importance of intersectional and culturally responsive interventions.

Practitioners face ethical dilemmas when attempting to dismantle stigma while respecting cultural norms. One effective strategy is community-based psychoeducation, which normalizes mental health discussions without directly challenging traditional values. Collaborating with community leaders, including religious scholars, can enhance the acceptance of mental health initiatives by aligning them with locally embedded cultural and religious values that are widely acknowledged and respected within the community itself.

Respect for Authority and Hierarchical Relationships

Iranian culture deeply instills respect for authority across various social contexts, including the family, educational institutions, and local social networks that form the basis of communal interactions.

Often, these hierarchical structures discourage adolescents from questioning authority, limiting their ability to advocate effectively for their mental health needs. The process of empowerment is inherently complex and involves ongoing power negotiations. Some practitioners, consciously or unconsciously, may impose

Western values under the guise of empowerment, which introduces ethical dilemmas regarding cultural sensitivity and autonomy. Therefore, truly ethical empowerment requires practitioners to adopt culturally attuned strategies that respect local norms while fostering adolescents' gradual development of agency. In this dynamic, adolescents are active agents who navigate the tensions between culturally ingrained expectations of obedience and their own emerging mental health needs. They do so by strategically choosing when and how to express their concerns, seeking trusted support networks, and negotiating boundaries within their familial and social contexts. Through these actions, adolescents assert their perspectives in ways that honor their cultural background while challenging restrictive norms, embodying a negotiated balance between compliance and self-advocacy (Shahhosseini et al., 2012).

To address this issue, therapists can use culturally congruent methods that encourage self-expression within acceptable boundaries. For example, therapeutic approaches that frame self-advocacy as a means of strengthening family bonds can resonate with Iranian values. This approach allows adolescents to explore their mental health needs without feeling they are betraying cultural expectations.

The Role of Islamic Beliefs in Ethical Decision-Making

Theological Interpretations of Mental Health

Islamic teachings significantly influence the understanding and treatment of mental health in Iran(Hamidi et al., 2010). People often view psychological struggles as interconnected with spiritual well-being, interpreting conditions like anxiety or depression as tests of faith. While this perspective can give adolescents a sense of purpose and coping mechanisms, viewing mental health issues solely as spiritual challenges may delay professional intervention.

Ethical care requires integrating psychological and spiritual approaches. For instance, therapy sessions can incorporate Quranic verses or Islamic teachings that align with psychological principles, fostering a holistic approach to healing(Keshavarzi & Ali, 2019). This integration not only respects the adolescent's religious beliefs but also bridges the gap between traditional and modern mental health practices.

Family Involvement in Ethical Decision-Making

Islamic ethics emphasizes the collective good, often involving family members in decisions that affect an individual's well-being. While this can create a supportive environment for adolescents (Rizvi & Pasha-Zaidi, 2021), it may also limit their autonomy, particularly when families prioritize traditional values over adolescents' mental health needs.

To navigate this tension, practitioners can adopt a collaborative approach that respects family involvement while prioritizing the adolescent's voice. Structured family therapy sessions can facilitate open communication, allowing adolescents to express their concerns in a supportive setting. By framing these discussions within Islamic principles of compassion and collective responsibility, therapists can foster understanding and cooperation among family members.

Gender Dynamics in Islamic Ethics

Cultural and religious norms shape gender roles, which significantly influence the perception and treatment of mental health challenges in Iran. Cultural and religious norms often expect boys to demonstrate emotional resilience, encouraging them to suppress displays of vulnerability. While girls are generally encouraged to prioritize modesty and familial obligations, they are also expected to embody strength, albeit defined differently within their social context. For example, a girl facing academic pressure might suppress her struggles to avoid disappointing her parents, reflecting how cultural expectations influence emotional expression (Mir-Hosseini, 2021). This shared expectation of "strength," while expressed differently for each gender, can limit adolescents' ability to openly express their emotions or seek help, which may worsen mental health struggles. Therefore, cultural expectations shape gender-specific ideals of strength that apply to both boys and girls, limiting their emotional expression and help-seeking behaviors.

Ethical care requires addressing gender-specific pressures in culturally sensitive and contextually relevant ways. For example, interventions targeting adolescent boys can focus on reconstructing traditional notions of masculinity to embrace emotional expressiveness and vulnerability. Such efforts may include implementing psychoeducational group therapy programs that create safe spaces for boys to explore and verbalize their emotions, challenging cultural stigmas around male emotional restraint. Mentorship initiatives led by respected male figures can model alternative masculine behaviors that value empathy and interpersonal connection. For adolescent girls, empowerment programs can be designed to foster assertiveness and self-advocacy skills within the framework of Islamic teachings. For instance, workshops combining religious education with communication skills training can equip girls to negotiate familial and social expectations while maintaining cultural and religious congruence. These programs may also involve collaboration with community and religious leaders to ensure acceptance and reinforce the legitimacy of girls' agency in various social domains. Incorporating religious principles of equity and compassion into these interventions can enhance their acceptance and effectiveness.

The Relationship between Ethnicity, Religion, and Socioeconomic Status Intersects

Ethnic and Linguistic Barriers

Iran's diverse ethnic landscape includes groups such as Kurds, Arabs, Baluchs, Turks (including Azeris and Turkmens), Lors, Gilaks, Mazandaranis, and nomadic tribes like Qashqais and Bakhtiaris, who often face systemic inequities that exacerbate mental health challenges. Linguistic barriers, limited access to resources, and social marginalization create unique hurdles for adolescents in these communities(Elling, 2015).

Practitioners must advocate for culturally and linguistically inclusive care. This process involves not only offering therapy sessions in local languages but also engaging community leaders at multiple levels—both within therapeutic contexts to foster trust and enhance client engagement and at the policy level, where they can serve as advocates for systemic mental health reforms that reflect cultural values and community needs. These efforts must be grounded in a thorough understanding of each group's cultural context to avoid perpetuating stereotypes or biases.

Socioeconomic Inequities

Economic disparities further compound challenges faced by adolescents, particularly in rural or underprivileged areas. Limited access to education, healthcare, and social support systems disproportionately affects their mental health outcomes(Seddighi & Mousavi, 2019).

Ethical considerations include prioritizing interventions that address these inequities. Schools in underprivileged areas can serve as hubs for mental health services, offering accessibility and a familiar environment for adolescents. Partnerships with government and non-governmental organizations (NGOs) can help fund and sustain these initiatives, ensuring long-term impact.

Navigating Ethical Tensions Between Tradition and Modernity

The Impact of Social Change

Global paradigms that emphasize individual autonomy, self-expression, and personal choice—such as those promoted by Western liberal thought—are increasingly influencing Iranian adolescents through social media, digital platforms, and globalized education. These values, including gender equality, freedom of thought, and self-determination, often stand in stark contrast to traditional cultural and religious norms, creating psychological tensions that may manifest as identity confusion, internal conflict, or a sense of social alienation (Delvecchio Good & Good, 1988).

Therapists must support adolescents in reconciling their aspirations with societal expectations by developing interventions that promote adaptability and resilience. While preserving core aspects of identity is vital for psychological well-being, it is also important to recognize that some elements may need to be reshaped or relinquished to accommodate evolving cultural and social realities (Jong, 2024). For example, integrating global mental health practices with culturally relevant approaches can empower adolescents to embrace change while staying connected to their roots.

Integration of Global and Local Frameworks

Western-centric mental health models often dominate the field, but their applicability in the Iranian context can be limited. Ethical care requires adapting evidence-based practices to align with local cultural and religious values.

For instance, Iranian adolescents can find cognitive behavioral therapy (CBT) more relatable and effective when it incorporates Islamic teachings. Similarly, mindfulness practices can be restructured to align with Islamic meditative traditions, such as dhikr (remembrance of God). This integration ensures that interventions resonate with adolescents while maintaining their cultural and religious identity.

Proposed Ethical Model for Adolescent Mental Health Care in Iran

Principles of the Ethical Model

In conceptualizing an ethical framework for adolescent mental health care in Iran, it is essential to first clarify how the term "ethics" is understood within this context. Ethics here is regarded as a systematic reflection on principles and values that guide mental health professionals in making decisions that respect the dignity, rights, and welfare of adolescents. Rather than being a fixed set of rules, ethics is a dynamic, context-sensitive process that balances universal moral principles—such as justice, autonomy, and beneficence—with the cultural, social, and religious realities of Iranian society. Within this framework, empathy is conceptualized as a genuine, culturally informed understanding of adolescents' lived experiences, emotions, and social contexts. It involves more than simply feeling what another person feels; it requires an active effort to perceive the adolescent's perspective within their own cultural and social realities. This empathy is carefully practiced to guard against the risk of imposing external, particularly Western, values onto Iranian adolescents. Instead, it encourages practitioners to continuously reflect on their beliefs and be humble about different cultures, making sure that the adolescent's opinions are prioritized and not influenced by any unintentional biases. Based on these fundamental understandings, the proposed ethical model is organized around three interconnected principles that steer mental health care for Iranian adolescents:

Compassion and Collective Well-Being This principle emphasizes the importance of compassion as an ethical imperative grounded in both emotional responsiveness and active engagement to alleviate suffering. Reflecting core Islamic values, it extends beyond individual care to include a commitment to the collective well-being of families and communities. Recognizing that adolescents exist within a broader social fabric, mental health professionals are encouraged to balance individual needs with communal responsibilities, fostering social harmony and support networks that are integral to mental health.

Cultural Sensitivity This model understands cultural sensitivity as a continuous, dialogical process that tailors interventions to the socio-cultural realities of Iranian adolescents. This principle acknowledges the diversity within Iranian society and the multiplicity of adolescent identities shaped by ethnicity, religion, socioeconomic status, and family structures. Mental health care must therefore avoid one-size-fits-all approaches or uncritical adoption of Western frameworks. Instead, it requires collaborative engagement with adolescents and their families to co-construct culturally meaningful interventions that respect local values and lived experiences.

Equity and Inclusivity This principle stresses the ethical obligation to ensure fair and equitable access to mental health services for all adolescents, particularly those who belong to marginalized or underserved groups. Equity goes beyond formal equality to actively address systemic barriers, such as economic hardship, social stigma, or geographic limitations that hinder access to care. Inclusivity demands that mental health programs be designed and implemented with sensitivity to the needs of ethnic minorities, girls and young women, and other vulnerable populations, thus promoting social justice and empowerment within the mental health system.

These principles form a comprehensive ethical foundation that acknowledges the complexity of adolescent mental health care in Iran. They invite practitioners to engage thoughtfully and critically with ethical challenges, fostering a practice that is both culturally grounded and responsive to the evolving needs of adolescents.

Application of the Model

Gender-Sensitive Interventions Mental health care for adolescents in Iran must account for the distinct and often unequal social expectations placed on boys and girls. Gender-sensitive interventions go beyond simply acknowledging differences; they require an in-depth understanding of how gender roles, shaped by cultural, religious, and familial contexts, affect emotional development, self-expression, access to resources, and help-seeking behaviors. For instance, girls may face restrictions in mobility or expression, while boys may be discouraged from showing vulnerability. Effective interventions should aim to create safe therapeutic spaces where gendered experiences are validated without reinforcing stereotypes. This requires a careful balance between respecting cultural norms and challenging harmful expectations that compromise mental well-being.

Integration of Religious Practices Given the central role of religion in Iranian society, particularly Islam, incorporating religious values and practices into mental health care can significantly enhance therapeutic acceptance and effectiveness. However, this integration must be handled thoughtfully. It is not about turning therapy into religious instruction but about recognizing the psychological resources that Islamic teachings, such as concepts of patience (sabr), trust in God (tawakkul), and communal duty, can provide. Collaborating with religious scholars and understanding spiritual concerns enables therapists to provide culturally resonant and ethically grounded care. Crucially, therapists should incorporate religious content based on clients' preferences and respect the diverse levels of religiosity among adolescents.

Community Engagement Adolescents in Iran do not exist in isolation; their mental health is deeply intertwined with their relationships with family, school, and the broader community. Thus, ethical mental health care must involve key stakeholders—including parents, caregivers, teachers, and local leaders—not merely as informants but as active partners in supporting the adolescent's well-being. Community engagement fosters greater trust in mental health services, helps reduce stigma, and ensures that interventions align with collective values. However, practitioners must be mindful of potential conflicts between individual and community interests, ensuring that the adolescent's voice remains central in all decision-making processes.

Iranian cultural norms and religious beliefs profoundly shape the ethical questions surrounding adolescent mental health care (Ahmadi et al., 2018). The interplay of collectivism, familial values, Islamic ethics, and socioeconomic factors creates a complex ethical landscape that demands culturally sensitive approaches. By integrating global psychological paradigms with localized practices, mental health practitioners can navigate these challenges effectively (Malekan, 2015). The integration of culturally respectful frameworks ensures that adolescents experience mental health care that is not only effective but also deeply aligned with their cultural, familial, and religious values. This approach fosters trust between adolescents, their families, and practitioners while addressing the unique challenges posed by Iran's socio-cultural and religious context.

Such frameworks can empower adolescents by promoting resilience, adaptability, and self-awareness, enabling them to navigate the complexities of modern life while remaining rooted in their cultural identity. Mental health interventions tailored to the Iranian context must prioritize not just the individual but also the collective well-being of families and communities, reinforcing the ethical responsibility of mental health practitioners to honor cultural diversity and inclusivity.

Ultimately, the proposed ethical model bridges the gap between tradition and modernity, ensuring that adolescents receive comprehensive care that respects their heritage while embracing the potential of contemporary psychological practices. By addressing the ethical tensions inherent in this process, practitioners can contribute to a healthier, more equitable future for Iran's adolescents, fostering their growth into confident, emotionally balanced individuals capable of contributing positively to their families, communities, and society at large.

Universal Ethical Principles in Global Mental Health and Their Cultural Challenges in Iran

International mental health standards, such as those outlined by the World Health Organization (WHO) and the American Psychological Association (APA), emphasize four foundational ethical principles: autonomy, confidentiality, beneficence, and non-maleficence. These principles serve as cornerstones of ethical mental health care worldwide, yet their application must be critically examined and adapted to diverse cultural contexts.

Autonomy highlights the importance of individual decision-making and self-determination. Confidentiality ensures privacy and trust between the patient and the practitioner. Beneficence directs professionals to act in the best interest of the patient, while non-maleficence requires them to avoid causing harm.

However, using these principles in Iranian society, which values community, strong family ties, and deep religious and cultural beliefs, creates complicated ethical issues. These universal principles may not align neatly with the lived realities and expectations of Iranian culture.

For example:

- Autonomy, emphasizing individual decision-making, may clash with family-oriented models that frequently make collective decisions, particularly concerning adolescents.
- Confidentiality can be difficult to maintain in tight-knit family systems where transparency is expected.
- Beneficence and non-maleficence are often interpreted through religious and communal lenses, requiring practitioners to consider what is “good” or “harmful” based on cultural or spiritual definitions rather than purely clinical ones.

Therefore, rather than applying these universal principles in a rigid or prescriptive manner, they must be critically re-evaluated, adapted, and contextualized within the Iranian sociocultural landscape. The following section proposes a more culturally grounded ethical framework based on this approach.

Proposed Ethical Model for Adolescent Mental Health Care in Iran

In conceptualizing an ethical framework for adolescent mental health care in Iran, it is essential to first clarify how ethics is understood in this context. Ethics is not treated as a static or universal code but rather as a dynamic process of reflection that balances universal values, such as justice, autonomy, and beneficence, with local cultural, religious, and social realities.

Within this framework, empathy is conceptualized not merely as emotional resonance but as a culturally grounded, critical awareness of the adolescent's lived experience. Practitioners must avoid using empathy as a subtle tool to impose Western values. Instead, empathy must be practiced with humility, respect, and reflexivity, ensuring that interventions are co-constructed with adolescents and their communities.

Based on this foundation, the following principles guide ethical mental health care for Iranian adolescents:

Compassion and Collective Well-Being

Rooted in Islamic ethics and communal values, this principle emphasizes both emotional responsiveness and active engagement to reduce suffering, not only at the individual level but also across families and communities. Mental health professionals are urged to balance individual care with social responsibility, recognizing the adolescent's embeddedness in a broader social fabric.

Cultural Sensitivity

Cultural sensitivity is treated as an ongoing dialogical process, not a checklist. It requires an awareness of the diverse identities of Iranian adolescents shaped by ethnicity, gender, religion, and socioeconomic status. Practitioners must co-construct meaningful and relevant practices with adolescents and their families instead of applying universal interventions or importing Western therapeutic models.

Equity and Inclusivity

Equity goes beyond surface-level equality by actively addressing systemic barriers to access, such as poverty, stigma, rurality, or gender-based discrimination. Inclusivity involves designing services that are sensitive to the needs of marginalized groups—including girls, ethnic minorities, and those in underserved areas—while ensuring that no group is unintentionally excluded.

(a) **Autonomy versus Collectivism**

Western frameworks emphasize individual autonomy as a cornerstone of ethical mental health care (Bernal & Adames, 2017), encouraging adolescents to make independent decisions about their mental health, free from external pressures. In contrast, Iranian culture places significant value on collectivism, where the family's well-being often supersedes individual desires (Mostafavi et al., 2017). Adolescents are often expected to demonstrate emotional resilience and limit displays of vulnerability. These cultural expectations can hinder their willingness to seek help for mental health issues such as anxiety or depression. For instance, an Iranian adolescent experiencing such challenges may be hesitant to seek therapy or openly express emotional distress due to concerns about family reputation and potential social stigma. This divergence creates moral dilemmas for practitioners who must balance respect for cultural values with the need to provide effective mental health care. Ethical tensions arise when practitioners must decide whether to prioritize the adolescent's autonomy or involve the family in the therapeutic process(Chaichian, 1997). While involving the family may align with cultural norms, it could compromise the adolescent's confidentiality and sense of agency. Families imposing decisions that undermine therapeutic progress further compound these challenges, forcing practitioners to balance the cultural importance of familial unity against the adolescent's mental health needs. Practitioners must carefully navigate these cultural dimensions, ensuring the adolescent's emotional well-being without violating cultural expectations.

(b) **Beneficence and Non-Maleficence in a Cultural Context**

The principles of beneficence (promoting well-being) and non-maleficence (avoiding harm) take on culturally embedded dimensions within Iranian society. For example, a treatment method that encourages adolescents to express their personal needs might inadvertently disrupt family relationships shaped by long-standing authority patterns rooted in religious, cultural, and historical traditions, rather than imposed colonial frameworks. However, it is important to acknowledge that today's views on these family structures are still affected by colonial ideas, which have often supported male-dominated and hierarchical relationships in non-Western societies. A nuanced ethical approach must therefore consider both indigenous sources of familial structure and the subtle effects of global power dynamics on how mental health norms are constructed and practiced. Practitioners must navigate these cultural sensitivities to ensure that their interventions do not unintentionally exacerbate familial tensions or social ostracism. The cultural misunderstandings between families and practitioners can lead to resistance, requiring practitioners to employ culturally adapted interventions that balance ethical imperatives with respect for traditional norms(Plöckinger & Auga, 2022). Practitioners may need to train themselves in culturally sensitive practices to avoid inadvertently causing harm while promoting the adolescent's mental well-being.

Navigating Gender Norms and Expectations

Gender plays a significant role in shaping the ethical landscape of adolescent mental health care in Iran. Islamic teachings and cultural traditions prescribe distinct roles and expectations for boys and girls, influencing the perception and treatment of mental health challenges.

(a) **Emotional Resilience versus Vulnerability**

Iranian culture often expects boys to exhibit emotional resilience and avoid displays of vulnerability. Practitioners face moral dilemmas when addressing these deeply ingrained gender norms. Encouraging boys to express their emotions openly may conflict with societal expectations, potentially exposing them to ridicule or marginalization(Mohammadkhani et al., 2024). The societal pressures to conform to traditional masculinity can lead to internalized stigma, making it crucial for practitioners to adopt approaches that validate boys' emotional experiences while challenging harmful stereotypes in a culturally sensitive manner. The stigma surrounding mental health for boys, in particular, may require tailored strategies to create a safe space where they feel validated and supported without fear of judgment.

(b) **Modesty and Familial Obligations for Girls**

Girls often prioritize modesty and familial obligations over their individual needs. Adolescent girls experiencing mental health challenges may feel compelled to prioritize their family's expectations over their well-being (Niroomand et al., 2024). The gender-specific interventions that align with Islamic principles of modesty, such as all-female therapy groups or the inclusion of maternal figures in therapy sessions, may provide a culturally sensitive avenue for supporting adolescent girls. However, ensuring that these interventions don't inadvertently limit their self-expression or agency is a critical consideration for practitioners.

Addressing Stigma and Confidentiality Concerns

Mental health stigma is a significant barrier to care in Iran. People often perceive psychological struggles as indicators of personal or familial weakness, posing ethical challenges for practitioners who must strike a balance between maintaining confidentiality and promoting broader societal education.

(a) **Confidentiality versus Family Involvement**

Confidentiality is a core tenet of international mental health standards, but it can be difficult to uphold in a collectivist society where family involvement is paramount. For instance, a practitioner treating an adolescent with suicidal ideation may feel compelled to involve the family for support. However, disclosing the adolescent's struggles without their consent could violate their confidentiality and undermine their trust in the therapeutic process. These dilemmas become more pronounced in cases of abuse or neglect, where the practitioner must weigh the adolescent's safety against potential familial retaliation or legal repercussions. Ensuring the adolescent's well-being while navigating familial dynamics and potential repercussions presents a challenge that requires nuanced ethical decision-making.

(b) **Reducing Stigma through Community Engagement**

Reducing mental health stigma requires community-wide education, but this can conflict with the need for privacy. For example, organizing public workshops on adolescent mental health might inadvertently expose participants to judgment or gossip. Practitioners must carefully design these initiatives to balance awareness-raising with the protection of individual privacy. Utilizing trusted community figures, such as teachers or religious leaders, can also enhance the credibility and acceptance of such programs, creating a supportive environment for addressing stigma collectively. Community engagement initiatives must be tailored to the cultural context, ensuring that privacy concerns are respected while addressing the larger issue of stigma.

The Influence of Islamic Ethics on Mental Health Practices

Islamic ethics significantly shape the moral framework for mental health care in Iran. While these principles often align with international standards, their application can create unique ethical dilemmas.

(a) **Spiritual Interpretations of Mental Health**

Sometimes, people interpret mental health challenges as spiritual tests or faith deficiencies. This perspective can delay professional intervention, as adolescents and their families may prioritize religious coping mechanisms over psychological treatment (Fallahi et al., 2022). Practitioners must navigate the ethical tension between respecting these beliefs and advocating for evidence-based care. Integrating Islamic teachings with psychological principles, such as incorporating Quranic verses into therapy, can help bridge this gap. However, practitioners must also remain vigilant to avoid reinforcing misconceptions that mental health struggles stem solely from spiritual failings, fostering a more holistic understanding of well-being. The practitioner's role may involve helping families reconcile spiritual beliefs with modern mental health treatment in a way that promotes psychological and spiritual healing.

(b) **Family-Centered Decision-Making**

Islamic ethics emphasize collective well-being, often involving family members in decisions about an individual's care. While this approach can create a supportive environment, it may also limit the adolescent's autonomy. For example, a family might prioritize traditional remedies over modern therapy, potentially compromising the adolescent's mental health (Joshanloo, 2014). Practitioners must adopt a collaborative approach that respects family dynamics while ensuring the adolescent's needs are met. In order to create a comprehensive care plan, this collaboration often necessitates mediating between divergent perspectives within families. Practitioners must be sensitive to the complexities of family decision-making, facilitating communication and understanding between the adolescent and their family.

Ethical Challenges in Marginalized Communities

Iran's ethnic diversity, including Kurds, Arabs, Baluchs, Turks (including Azeris and Turkmens), Lors, Gilaks, Mazandaranis, and nomadic tribes like Qashqais and Bakhtiaris, and other groups, adds another layer of complexity to mental health care. Marginalized communities often face systemic inequities that exacerbate mental health challenges, creating ethical dilemmas for practitioners (Atabaki, 2005).

(a) **Linguistic and Cultural Barriers**

Adolescents from marginalized groups may struggle to access mental health care due to linguistic and cultural barriers. For instance, a Kurdish adolescent could experience alienation during a Persian-language therapy session. Practitioners must advocate for inclusive care by offering therapy in local languages and incorporating culturally relevant approaches. However, these efforts require resources that may not always be available, creating ethical tensions around equitable care. The practitioners must address the mistrust that often exists between marginalized communities and healthcare systems, fostering a sense of safety and inclusion in therapeutic settings.

(b) **Addressing Socioeconomic Disparities**

Economic inequities further compound the challenges faced by marginalized adolescents. Limited access to education, healthcare, and social support systems disproportionately affects their mental health. Practitioners must prioritize interventions that address these disparities, such as school-based mental health programs in underprivileged areas. Balancing resource allocation across diverse communities presents an ongoing ethical challenge(Doshmangir et al., 2019). Advocacy for systemic change, such as lobbying for government policies that address socioeconomic inequities, is essential to creating sustainable solutions for these communities. Practitioners must adopt a holistic approach that acknowledges the broader societal determinants of mental health.

Reconciling Tradition and Modernity

Iran's rapid socio-cultural evolution has created tensions between traditional values and modern mental health paradigms. Globalized ideals of individualism and self-expression increasingly expose adolescents today, often clashing with Iran's collectivist norms.

(a) **Identity Crises and Psychological Tensions**
   Adolescents navigating these cultural shifts may experience identity crises, characterized by feelings of confusion or alienation. Practitioners must work to reconcile these conflicting cultural pressures, encouraging adolescents to explore their identities while respecting the cultural norms that shape their lives(A. Jafari, 2007). This delicate balance requires practitioners to facilitate discussions about cultural change, self-acceptance, and the negotiation of personal values. Supporting adolescents through these crises is vital, as they are at a formative stage in their development.

(b) **Modernizing Mental Health Practices**
   As Iran integrates more modern mental health practices, practitioners face ethical dilemmas in adapting these approaches to fit the country's cultural and religious context. Iranian cultural values must resonate with the presentation of evidence-based therapies, despite their potential high effectiveness. Adapting practices such as Cognitive-Behavioral Therapy (CBT) to account for religious and familial considerations can enhance their effectiveness, but doing so requires careful thought and cultural sensitivity(Pirhekayaty, 2022).

By exploring these ethical dilemmas in depth, practitioners can better navigate the complexities of adolescent mental health care in Iran, ensuring that their interventions are effective and culturally sensitive. These considerations emphasize the importance of ongoing cultural competence training for mental health professionals and the need for a nuanced approach that respects the rich tapestry of Iranian cultural, religious, and societal values while adhering to international standards of mental health care.

How Can We Ethically Integrate Modern Psychological Techniques and Traditional Healing Methods?

The integration of modern psychological techniques and traditional healing methods represents an evolving challenge and opportunity in adolescent mental health care, particularly in Iran's complex socio-cultural landscape. As the world increasingly embraces global psychological paradigms, it is crucial to understand how these approaches intersect with traditional cultural and religious frameworks, particularly in countries like Iran, where values and social structures differ markedly from Western contexts. Iranian adolescents, navigating a world of rapid change, face mental health issues deeply embedded in their cultural context, family obligations, and societal expectations (Zamani-Farahani & Musa, 2012). Modern psychological approaches, while evidence-based, often present challenges in aligning with the community-oriented, collectivist nature of Iranian society, creating potential tensions between therapeutic goals and cultural values.

The significance of bridging these global psychological practices with Iran's rich cultural and religious heritage cannot be overstated. Islamic teachings profoundly shape Iran's identity, providing ethical and spiritual guidelines that influence daily life, including the perception and management of mental health. This chapter seeks to deepen the understanding of these challenges and explore practical ways to create an integrated approach to adolescent mental health that respects and incorporates modern psychological practices and traditional healing methods. This intersection of disciplines is particularly important as Iran's rapidly evolving social environment demands mental healthcare solutions that resonate with local experiences while incorporating the benefits of scientifically validated psychological practices.

Theoretical Foundations of Modern Psychological Techniques

Modern psychological techniques such as Cognitive Behavioral Therapy (CBT), Mindfulness-Based Stress Reduction (MBSR), and resilience-building interventions are grounded in empirical research and emphasize individual empowerment, emotional regulation, and cognitive restructuring. These methods have shown promising results in treating a range of psychological conditions, including anxiety, depression, and PTSD, especially in adolescents. However, their focus on individual autonomy and self-expression may conflict with the collectivist ideals predominant in Iranian society(Yang, 2024). Adolescents in Iran are often raised in family-centered environments where respect for authority, collective decision-making, and social cohesion are prioritized. This cultural emphasis on interconnectedness may pose a challenge for therapeutic models that emphasize personal autonomy as the path to healing.

For instance, CBT encourages adolescents to independently challenge and reframe their negative thoughts. However, in Iranian culture, where collective well-being often supersedes individual needs, an approach that emphasizes personal autonomy could feel alienating. CBT could adapt to include family sessions, where the adolescent and their family collaborate on emotional regulation and problem-solving, thereby strengthening the collective support system.

While Western therapeutic frameworks aim to empower individuals to manage their own mental health through structured, self-directed interventions, this model may not always resonate with Iranian adolescents, particularly those from marginalized ethnic communities who experience compounded challenges in accessing mental health care and educational resources(Havighurst et al., 2022). For these adolescents, traditional family or community-based support systems may be more appropriate, as they provide a collective framework for addressing emotional distress. Modern psychological interventions, when introduced in isolation from traditional practices, may not fully address the cultural nuances of identity, social relations, and community-oriented values. Thus, integrating contemporary psychological methods with local healing practices ensures that these interventions can meet adolescents where they are, taking into account their cultural identities and social environments.

Principles of Traditional Healing Methods

Traditional healing methods in Iran often draw from a rich tapestry of religious, cultural, and historical influences, combining spiritual practices with physical healing. Islamic ethics, in particular, provide a foundation for these methods, emphasizing compassion, collective well-being, and a holistic approach to health. Practices such as Quranic recitation, prayer, and spiritual rituals play central roles in supporting emotional and mental health, especially in times of distress. Family and community support systems, deeply embedded in Iranian society, are crucial in the healing process(Haque & Keshavarzi, 2014). Collective efforts emphasize a shared responsibility for mental well-being and understanding the individual's struggles within the larger family or social unit.

For example, when an adolescent is struggling with mental health issues, the family may engage in collective prayer, reflecting on Quranic verses for healing. This collective practice not only provides spiritual comfort but also reinforces the importance of family unity and mutual support, which is vital in Iranian culture. Similarly, traditional healers in rural areas may combine spiritual rituals with herbal remedies, offering a comprehensive approach that integrates the physical, psychological, and spiritual well-being of the individual.

The role of traditional healers, who often combine spiritual, physical, and psychological approaches, is particularly significant in rural or underserved areas where access to modern mental health services may be limited. Folk medicine, including the use of herbal remedies, has also been an important part of the Iranian cultural landscape, with many communities continuing to rely on these practices alongside or even instead of clinical treatments. While these methods have a deep cultural resonance, they can present challenges in terms of their scientific validation and standardized application. This creates a dilemma for mental health practitioners: balancing respect for cultural practices while adhering to the scientific principles required for effective treatment. Nevertheless, these traditional healing practices can offer valuable insights into how best to integrate modern psychological approaches in a way that is culturally relevant and sensitive to the needs of Iranian adolescents.

Ethical Challenges in Integration

The ethical integration of modern psychological techniques with traditional healing practices in Iran presents multiple challenges. One of the foremost issues is the balance between cultural sensitivity and scientific rigor. Modern psychological approaches are often based on empirical data and standardized interventions, which prioritize measurable outcomes such as symptom reduction or improved cognitive function. In contrast, traditional healing methods tend to focus more on the holistic, subjective experience of individuals, with less emphasis on objective measurement or scientific validation(Messick, 1989). This difference in approach raises questions about how to ensure that traditional methods are not only culturally appropriate but also effective in the therapeutic context.

The tension between individual autonomy and collective values creates ethical dilemmas for practitioners working with Iranian adolescents. Western psychological practices tend to emphasize self-autonomy and the individual's right to make decisions regarding their mental health care. In contrast, Iranian culture places a significant emphasis on family and community responsibility in the mental health process, which may lead to conflicts about personal agency. Therapeutic interventions that promote self-reliance may pose a challenge for adolescents caught between the pressure to meet societal expectations and the desire to assert their autonomy(Atari et al., 2020). For instance, when an adolescent wishes to pursue therapy alone, but the family insists on being involved in the treatment process, the therapist must navigate these tensions carefully to balance the adolescent's autonomy with the cultural importance of family engagement.

Integrating religious beliefs with secular psychological techniques necessitates a careful approach to ensure that therapeutic interventions do not undermine or conflict with an adolescent's religious practices, which are central to their identity and well-being. A mindful integration of Quranic principles with psychological interventions like mindfulness-based stress reduction (MBSR) can create a harmonious balance between spiritual and psychological well-being, fostering an integrated therapeutic approach.

Ethical Principles for Integration

To ethically integrate modern psychological techniques with traditional healing methods, practitioners must first embrace cultural competence. This involves gaining a deep understanding of the values, customs, and beliefs that shape the mental health experiences of Iranian adolescents. Understanding the role of family, religion, and community in the healing process is essential for creating interventions that resonate with the cultural identity of the individual(Mehran, 1989). At the same time, adolescent autonomy must be respected to allow them to make informed care decisions. Culturally appropriate psychoeducation can help adolescents and their families understand the potential benefits of integrating modern therapeutic practices with traditional approaches.

Another key ethical principle is evidence-based adaptation. Modern psychological interventions should not be applied in a vacuum but rather adapted to fit the specific cultural and religious context in which they are being used. For instance, mindfulness-based interventions can incorporate spiritual practices from Islam, such as reflection on Quranic verses, which can deepen the therapeutic experience. The interventions should be inclusive, ensuring that all adolescents, including those from marginalized communities, have access to care that respects their cultural values while addressing their mental health needs. Mental health practitioners can ground their interventions in the community's cultural realities, enhancing their acceptability and effectiveness by collaborating with local healers and religious leaders.

Strategies for Ethical Integration

Practical strategies for integrating modern psychological techniques with traditional healing methods involve a multifaceted approach. One such strategy is to incorporate religious and spiritual dimensions into modern therapeutic practices. By blending mindfulness practices with Quranic recitations or reflections on Islamic teachings, mental health practitioners can create a culturally relevant therapeutic experience that resonates with the adolescent's spiritual beliefs while also addressing psychological distress. Family-centered interventions are another key strategy. Given the importance of family in Iranian culture, mental health interventions should actively involve family members in the treatment process, incorporating modern family therapy techniques and traditional approaches to conflict resolution, mutual respect, and collective decision-making(Alizadeh Zarei et al., 2024).

Community engagement is also vital for effective integration. By working closely with community leaders, traditional healers, and religious figures, mental health professionals can ensure that interventions are culturally relevant and accepted by the community. This collaboration fosters a shared sense of responsibility for adolescent mental health, which can lead to greater engagement and improved therapeutic outcomes. The training and education for mental health professionals on cultural competence and the ethical integration of traditional practices is essential. By equipping professionals with the skills and knowledge needed to navigate the complex intersection of modern and traditional healing methods, they can better serve the needs of Iranian adolescents and their families(Salmani et al., 2015). Finally, the development of culturally tailored interventions that incorporate elements of traditional storytelling, rituals, and resilience-building can further enhance the effectiveness of mental health programs.

Integrating modern psychological techniques with traditional healing methods presents a unique opportunity to enhance adolescent mental health care in Iran, a country with a rich cultural and religious heritage. By addressing the ethical challenges associated with this integration, practitioners can develop holistic, culturally competent approaches that respect the scientific principles of modern psychology and the values embedded in Iranian traditions. This approach not only offers a more inclusive model of care but also ensures that Iranian adolescents receive the support they need to navigate the challenges of adolescence in a culturally relevant and effective manner.

What Ethical Framework Meets the Unique Needs of Iranian Adolescents in a Rapidly Changing Culture?

Adolescence is a critical developmental stage marked by significant emotional, cognitive, and social changes(Nooripour et al., 2023). Various influences, such as family dynamics, peer interactions, cultural values, religious beliefs, and societal expectations, shape these transformations. Iran's unique socio-cultural context, which combines traditional Islamic values with the pressures of modernity and rapid sociocultural change, further complicates these factors for Iranian adolescents. As such, providing effective mental health care requires an ethical framework that not only addresses the psychological needs of adolescents but also respects their cultural, religious, and familial contexts.

Given the complexity of Iranian society, mental health practices must navigate the tension between individual well-being and collective values. In this respect, a one-size-fits-all, Western-centric approach to mental health is insufficient. An ethically sound framework for Iranian adolescents must integrate Islamic principles, respect for traditional values, and evidence-based psychological practices while addressing gendered pressures, ethnic diversity, and the ever-evolving socio-political climate(Shamshirian et al., 2021). This chapter provides an in-depth exploration of the ethical framework that best meets the unique needs of Iranian adolescents in a rapidly changing cultural environment, proposing a comprehensive model that balances global psychological principles with local cultural realities.

The Role of Cultural Sensitivity in Mental Health Care

Cultural sensitivity is a cornerstone of any ethical framework for mental health care, particularly in a society as diverse as Iran. Iranian society is characterized by its multi-ethnic makeup, with ethnic groups such as Kurds, Arabs, Baluchs, Turks, Lors, Gilaks, Mazandaranis, and nomadic tribes, each possessing distinct cultural traditions, languages, and social structures(Ahmady, 2022). These ethnic groups experience mental health challenges in unique ways, influenced by their specific historical experiences, socio-economic conditions, and cultural practices. For instance, marginalized groups such as the Kurds, Arabs, Baluchs, Turks (including Azeris and Turkmens), Lors, Gilaks, Mazandaranis, and nomadic tribes like Qashqais and Bakhtiaris may face compounded mental health struggles due to linguistic barriers, limited access to mental health resources, and socio-political marginalization.

An ethical framework for mental health care in Iran must acknowledge these ethnic and cultural differences and avoid the imposition of uniform therapeutic practices that do not consider local contexts. It must provide flexibility to adapt interventions to the needs of different ethnic groups while ensuring that they remain culturally appropriate and effective. For example, mental health interventions aimed at Baluch adolescents may need to involve community-based approaches, such as the inclusion of local elders and religious leaders in the therapeutic process, to foster a sense of trust and acceptance.

The ethical model must underscore the significance of cultural competence in mental health professionals, guaranteeing their training to acknowledge and honor the diverse cultural backgrounds of their clients. This involves understanding the cultural norms, values, and beliefs that shape adolescents' mental health understanding, along with the social and familial dynamics that shape their help-seeking behaviors. In this way, mental health practitioners can provide more effective care that aligns with the adolescent's cultural context, leading to better therapeutic outcomes.

Islamic Ethical Principles as Guiding Framework

Iran is an Islamic Republic, and the principles of Islam play a central role in shaping the moral, social, and psychological landscape of the country. For Iranian adolescents, Islamic values provide not only spiritual guidance but also a framework for understanding and managing mental health. Islamic ethics emphasize compassion, respect for others, and the importance of community well-being. Concepts such as *rahmah* (compassion), *sabr* (patience), *Tawakkul* (trust in God), and *ihsan* (doing well) form the basis of a moral code that guides individuals in their interactions with others and in managing personal adversity (Ebrahimi & Yusoff, 2017).

These Islamic principles can help adolescents navigate the psychological challenges they face in the context of mental health care. Therapeutic interventions can incorporate *sabr* to help adolescents develop resilience in the face of stress, trauma, or personal setbacks. *Tawakkul* emphasizes the importance of trusting in God's plan, which can offer comfort and hope to adolescents dealing with feelings of helplessness or despair. The *rahmah* and *ihsan* provide a moral foundation for mental health professionals to approach their work with compassion and a commitment to the well-being of their clients(Rassool, 2024).

Islamic teachings also emphasize the close connection between mental health and spiritual well-being. For Iranian adolescents, who are likely to perceive mental health struggles through a religious lens, addressing spiritual concerns alongside psychological ones is crucial. Incorporating spiritual practices like prayer, Quranic reflection, and mindfulness into therapeutic interventions can achieve this. For example, incorporating *dhikr* (remembrance of God) or guided Islamic meditation into therapeutic practices can enhance their cultural resonance and effectiveness in reducing stress and promoting emotional well-being.

The Islamic ethics emphasize the importance of family and community in the well-being of individuals. In Iranian society, where family plays a central role in adolescent life, involving family members in the therapeutic process can be an essential component of mental health care. However, the approach must respect the adolescent's autonomy and acknowledge the family's role in supporting the adolescent's mental health. This balance is critical in maintaining respect for individual and collective values.

Gender and Ethical Considerations

Gender plays a significant role in shaping the mental health experiences of Iranian adolescents. In Iranian society, gender roles are deeply entrenched, and societal expectations often place different pressures on boys and girls. Boys typically demonstrate strength, independence, and financial responsibility, while girls typically adhere to strict norms regarding modesty, obedience, and family roles(Rahmani et al., 2015). These gendered expectations can contribute to the development of mental health issues, as adolescents struggle to reconcile their personal desires with societal demands.

Iranian adolescents require an ethical framework that responds to gendered dynamics and tailors interventions to meet the unique needs of boys and girls. For example, programs aimed at girls may need to focus on issues such as body image, self-esteem, and educational pressure, as these are often sources of distress for girls in Iran. Conversely, interventions for boys may need to address issues related to emotional expression, resilience-building, and managing societal expectations of masculinity.

It is also crucial to recognize that gendered experiences of mental health may intersect with other factors, such as socio-economic status, ethnicity, and religious beliefs. For instance, girls from marginalized ethnic groups may face compounded challenges due to gendered and ethnic discrimination. An ethical framework must consider these intersecting factors and offer interventions that are equitable and sensitive to the unique experiences of different groups.

Autonomy and Collectivism: Ethical Tensions

One of the central ethical challenges in providing mental health care for Iranian adolescents is the tension between individual autonomy and collective values. Iranian society places a high value on family cohesion, social harmony, and respect for authority, all of which can sometimes conflict with the adolescent's desire for personal autonomy. Adolescents may find themselves in a difficult position when their personal goals, such as pursuing a career or lifestyle that differs from their family's expectations, come into conflict with familial or societal values(Dastmalchian et al., 2001).

An ethical framework for mental health care in Iran must navigate these tensions by promoting a balanced approach that respects the adolescent's rights and the collective values of their family and community. Shared decision-making processes involving the adolescent and their family members can achieve this. Family therapy models that engage adolescents and their parents in the therapeutic process can help facilitate open communication, mutual understanding, and support.

In practical terms, this implies that mental health professionals need to receive training to identify instances where family dynamics hinder the adolescent's mental health and to provide the required support. Practitioners must also possess the necessary skills to assist families in navigating the adolescent's autonomy while upholding their cultural values.

Evidence-Based Practices and Local Adaptation

An ethical framework must also integrate evidence-based psychological practices while adapting them to the cultural context of Iran. Western psychological interventions, such as Cognitive Behavioral Therapy (CBT), Mindfulness-Based Stress Reduction (MBSR), and Family Therapy, are effective in addressing various mental health issues, including depression, anxiety, and trauma. However, their direct application in Iran may not always be appropriate unless modified to reflect the cultural, religious, and social realities of Iranian adolescents.

For example, CBT can be adapted to incorporate Islamic teachings and cultural values, such as emphasizing the importance of hope, faith, and resilience in the face of adversity. Similarly, Iranian adolescents can enhance the relevance and effectiveness of MBSR techniques by incorporating Islamic mindfulness practices like reciting Quranic verses or prayers.

Family therapy, which emphasizes the involvement of family members in the therapeutic process, can be particularly beneficial in Iranian society, where family plays a central role in an adolescent's life. However, family therapy must be adapted to reflect the hierarchical nature of Iranian families, where parents typically hold significant authority. This may involve working with the adolescent and their parents to foster a healthy balance between individual autonomy and family cohesion.

Cultural, religious, social, and political factors uniquely shape the mental health needs of Iranian adolescents. To address these needs effectively, an ethical framework must be culturally sensitive, gender-responsive, and adaptable to the rapid changes occurring in Iranian society. This framework must integrate Islamic ethical principles, respect for traditional values, and evidence-based psychological practices while navigating the ethical tensions between individual autonomy and collective values.

By adopting an inclusive and culturally relevant approach, this ethical model ensures that mental health care in Iran is effective and respectful of the cultural realities of Iranian adolescents. This framework is not only an ethical imperative but also a practical necessity for fostering the well-being of Iranian adolescents in a rapidly changing cultural environment. In this way, it provides a path forward for addressing the mental health challenges facing Iranian youth in a manner that is culturally resonant and therapeutically sound.

Summary

In light of the complex socio-cultural dynamics of Iran, this chapter has explored the unique ethical framework necessary to address the mental health needs of Iranian adolescents in a rapidly changing cultural context. A multitude of influences, such as family dynamics, peer interactions, cultural values, and societal expectations, shape adolescence, a critical developmental phase. In Iran, where traditional Islamic values intertwine with modern pressures, an ethical approach to adolescent mental health must balance individual psychological needs and collective societal values. The discussion highlighted the importance of cultural sensitivity, particularly when working with Iran's diverse ethnic groups, such as Kurds, Arabs, Baluchs, Turks (including Azeris and Turkmens), Lors, Gilaks, Mazandaranis, and nomadic tribes like Qashqais and Bakhtiaris. These groups face distinct challenges that demand tailored interventions that respect their cultural, linguistic, and religious backgrounds. The chapter emphasized the ethical tension between individual autonomy and familial and societal values. Mental health professionals in Iranian society, which deeply values family cohesion and social harmony, must navigate this tension by respecting adolescents' personal goals while maintaining alignment with collective familial expectations. The role of Islamic ethical principles, such as compassion (rahmah), patience (sabr), and trust in God (Tawakkul), was underscored as essential in guiding therapeutic practices that resonate with adolescents' spiritual beliefs and cultural values.

The integration of evidence-based practices, such as Cognitive Behavioral Therapy (CBT) and Mindfulness-Based Stress Reduction (MBSR), into the Iranian context was discussed, with a focus on necessary adaptations to incorporate Islamic values and cultural relevance. These modifications enhance the efficacy of Western therapies, making them more effective for Iranian adolescents.

In conclusion, the chapter proposes a comprehensive ethical framework that combines global psychological principles with local cultural and religious considerations, ensuring that mental health care for Iranian adolescents is culturally sensitive and therapeutically sound. This framework is essential for addressing the unique mental health challenges faced by Iranian youth in a dynamic socio-cultural environment.

References

Abbaszadeh, E., & Dabbagh, A. (2024). "You have no right!": Conceptualizations of Iranian women in the dialogues and visuals of a local film. *International Journal of Language and Culture*. https://doi.org/10.1075/ijolc.00063.abb

Ahmadi, F., Khodayarifard, M., Zandi, S., Khorrami-Markani, A., Ghobari-Bonab, B., Sabzevari, M., & Ahmadi, N. (2018). Religion, culture and illness: A sociological study on religious coping in Iran. *Mental Health, Religion & Culture, 21*(7), 721–736. https://doi.org/10.1080/13674676.2018.1555699

Ahmady, K. (2022). Ethnicity and identities in Iran: Progress and equality. *International Journal of Kurdish Studies, 8*(2), 238–272. https://doi.org/10.21600/ijoks.1148638

Alizadeh Zarei, M., Hassani Mehraban, A., & Shahbazi, M. (2024). An umbrella review on family oriented adaptive functioning for neurodevelopmental disorders. *Occupational Therapy in Mental Health*, 1–29. https://doi.org/10.1080/0164212X.2024.2427712

Atabaki, T. (2005). Ethnic diversity and territorial integrity of Iran: Domestic harmony and regional challenges. *Iranian Studies, 38*(1), 23–44. https://doi.org/10.1080/0021086042000336528

Atari, M., Graham, J., & Dehghani, M. (2020). Foundations of morality in Iran. *Evolution and Human Behavior, 41*(5), 367–384. https://doi.org/10.1016/j.evolhumbehav.2020.07.014

Bernal, G., & Adames, C. (2017). Cultural adaptations: Conceptual, ethical, contextual, and methodological issues for working with ethnocultural and majority-world populations. *Prevention Science, 18*(6), 681–688. https://doi.org/10.1007/s11121-017-0806-0

Chaichian, M. A. (1997). First generation Iranian immigrants and the question of cultural identity: The case of Iowa. *International Migration Review, 31*(3), 612. https://doi.org/10.2307/2547288

Dastmalchian, A., Javidan, M., & Alam, K. (2001). Effective leadership and culture in Iran: An empirical study. *Applied Psychology, 50*(4), 532–558. https://doi.org/10.1111/1464-0597.00072

Dehghani, A., Mosalanejad, L., & Dehghan-Nayeri, N. (2015). Factors affecting professional ethics in nursing practice in Iran: A qualitative study. *BMC Medical Ethics, 16*(1), 61. https://doi.org/10.1186/s12910-015-0048-2

Delvecchio Good, M.-J., & Good, B. J. (1988). Ritual, the state, and the transformation of emotional discourse in Iranian society. *Culture, Medicine and Psychiatry, 12*(1), 43–63. https://doi.org/10.1007/BF00047038

Dittman, C. K., Sprajcer, M., & Turley, E. L. (2023). Revisiting gendered parenting of adolescents: Understanding its effects on psychosocial development. *Current Psychology, 42*(28), 24569–24581. https://doi.org/10.1007/s12144-022-03536-7

Doshmangir, L., Bazyar, M., Majdzadeh, R., & Takian, A. (2019). So near, so far: Four decades of health policy reforms in Iran, achievements and challenges. *Archives of Iranian Medicine, 22*(10), 592–605.

Ebrahimi, M., & Yusoff, K. (2017). Islamic identity, ethical principles and human values. *European Journal of Multidisciplinary Studies, 6*(1), 325. https://doi.org/10.26417/ejms.v6i1.p325-336

Elling, R. C. (2015). Tribal hands and minority votes: Ethnicity, regionalism and elections in Iran. *Ethnic and Racial Studies, 38*(14), 2534–2550. https://doi.org/10.1080/01419870.2015.1061135

Estrada, C. A. M., Lomboy, M. F. T. C., Gregorio, E. R., Amalia, E., Leynes, C. R., Quizon, R. R., & Kobayashi, J. (2019). Religious education can contribute to adolescent mental health in school settings. *International Journal of Mental Health Systems, 13*(1), 28. https://doi.org/10.1186/s13033-019-0286-7

Fallahi, F., Anoosheh, M., Foroughan, M., Vanaki, Z., & Kazemnejad, A. (2022). Raising adolescent children as a developmental task of Iranian middle-aged mothers: A qualitative study. *International Journal of Community Based Nursing And Midwifery, 10*(2), 120–133. https://doi.org/10.30476/IJCBNM.2021.90710.1726

Hamidi, F., Bagherzadeh, Z., & Gafarzadeh, S. (2010). The role of islamic education in mental health. *Procedia – Social and Behavioral Sciences, 5*, 1991–1996. https://doi.org/10.1016/j.sbspro.2010.07.402

Haque, A., & Keshavarzi, H. (2014). Integrating indigenous healing methods in therapy: Muslim beliefs and practices. *International Journal of Culture and Mental Health, 7*(3), 297–314. https://doi.org/10.1080/17542863.2013.794249

Havighurst, S. S., Choy, R., Ulker, A., Otterpohl, N., Aghaie Meybodi, F., Edrissi, F., Qiu, C., Kar-Man Shum, K., Radovini, A., Hosn, D. A., & Kehoe, C. E. (2022). A preliminary evaluation of the cultural appropriateness of the tuning in to kids parenting program in Germany, Turkey, Iran and China. *International Journal of Environmental Research and Public Health, 19*(16), 10321. https://doi.org/10.3390/ijerph191610321

Jafari, A. (2007). Two tales of a city: An exploratory study of cultural consumption among Iranian youth. *Iranian Studies, 40*(3), 367–383. https://doi.org/10.1080/00210860701390497

Jafari, S., Movaghar, A., Craib, K., Baharlou, S., & Mathias, R. (2009). Socio-cultural factors associated with the initiation of opium use in Darab, Iran. *International Journal of Mental Health and Addiction, 7*(2), 376–388. https://doi.org/10.1007/s11469-008-9176-y

Jong, A. (2024). Social theory and navigating indeterminacy: A configurational analysis of Iranian youth's identity construction in contemporary Iran. *Societies, 14*(3), 32. https://doi.org/10.3390/soc14030032

Joshanloo, M. (2013). Mental Well-being in Iran: The importance of comprehensive well-being in understanding the linkages of personality and values. In C. L. M. Keyes (Ed.), *Mental well-being: International contributions to the study of positive mental health* (pp. 177–207). Springer. https://doi.org/10.1007/978-94-007-5195 8_9

Joshanloo, M. (2014). Differences in the endorsement of various conceptions of well-being between two Iranian groups. *Psychology of Religion and Spirituality, 6*(2), 138–149. https://doi.org/10.1037/a0035510

Keshavarzi, H., & Ali, B. (2019). Islamic perspectives on psychological and spiritual well-being and treatment. In H. S. Moffic, J. Peteet, A. Z. Hankir, & R. Awaad (Eds.), *Islamophobia and psychiatry* (pp. 41–53). Springer. https://doi.org/10.1007/978-3-030-00512-2_4

Malekan, M. (2015). Islam and Iranian women: Determining the level of religious beliefs in Muslim Iranian women. In E. Rodriguez & B. Wejnert (Eds.), *Research in political sociology* (Vol. 23, pp. 195–215). Emerald Group Publishing Limited. https://doi.org/10.1108/S0895-993520150000023014

Mehran, G. (1989). Socialization of schoolchildren in the Islamic Republic of Iran. *Iranian Studies, 22*(1), 35–50. https://doi.org/10.1080/00210868908701724

Messick, S. (1989). Meaning and values in test validation: The science and ethics of assessment. *Educational Researcher, 18*(2), 5–11. https://doi.org/10.3102/0013189X018002005

Mianji, F., & Kirmayer, L. J. (2020). The globalization of biological psychiatry and the rise of bipolar spectrum disorder in Iran. *Culture, Medicine, and Psychiatry, 44*(3), 404–432. https://doi.org/10.1007/s11013-019-09665-2

Mir-Hosseini, Z. (2021). *Islam and gender: The religious debate in contemporary Iran*. Princeton University Press. https://doi.org/10.1515/9781400843596

Mohammadkhani, M., Nakhaee, N., Goudarzi, R., Nekoei-Moghadam, M., & Aminizadeh, M. (2024). Living on the slum areas in the shadow of drought: A qualitative analysis of lived experience of migrant households facing drought in southeast of Iran. *BMC Public Health, 24*(1), 3241. https://doi.org/10.1186/s12889-024-20455-3

Mostafavi, H., Ziloochi, M. H., Delavari, S., Rezaei, S., & Homaie Rad, E. (2017). Mental health, family orientation, and individualism: A systematic review and meta-analysis in Iranian students. *Mental Health and Social Inclusion, 21*(5), 289–296. https://doi.org/10.1108/MHSI-07-2017-0030

Niroomand, S., Gholizadeh, L., & Baird, K. (2024). Iranian immigrant women's experiences of intimate partner violence: A literature review. *Journal of Immigrant and Minority Health, 26*(5), 905–924. https://doi.org/10.1007/s10903-024-01610-9

Nooripour, R., Ghanbari, N., Hosseinian, S., Lavie, C. J., Mozaffari, N., Sikström, S., & Hosseini, S. R. (2023). Psychometric properties of persian version of escapism scale among Iranian adolescents. *BMC Psychology, 11*(1), 323. https://doi.org/10.1186/s40359-023-01379-w

Pirhekayaty, T. (2022). Cognitive behavioral therapy in Iran. In M. D. Terjesen & K. A. Doyle (Eds.), *Cognitive behavioral therapy in a global context* (pp. 267–284). Springer. https://doi.org/10.1007/978-3-030-82555-3_17

Plöckinger, U., & Auga, U. (2022). The "Four Principles" of western medical bioethics and the bioethics of Shīʿī Islam in Iran—is the claim of universality by both justified? *Religions, 13*(11), 1118. https://doi.org/10.3390/rel13111118

Rahmani, A., Merghati-Khoei, E., Moghaddam-Banaem, L., Zarei, F., Montazeri, A., & Hajizadeh, E. (2015). Sexuality research in Iran: A focus on methodological and ethical considerations. *Iranian Journal of Public Health, 44*(7), 979–986.

Rassool, G. H. (2024). Exploring the intersection of Islāmic spirituality and psychotherapy: Healing the Soul. Springer Nature Switzerland. https://doi.org/10.1007/978-3-031-72724-5.

Razavieh, A. A., & Hosseini, A. A. (1972). Family, peer, and academic orientation of Iranian adolescents. *The Journal of Psychology, 80*(2), 337–344. https://doi.org/10.1080/00223980.1972.9924811

Rizvi, S., & Pasha-Zaidi, N. (2021). Health and wellbeing: Bridging secular and Islamic worldviews. In N. Pasha-Zaidi (Ed.), *Toward a positive psychology of Islam and Muslims* (Vol. 15, pp. 183–206). Springer. https://doi.org/10.1007/978-3-030-72606-5_9

Rosenbaum, L. L., Bhakta, S., Wilcox, H. C., Pas, E. T., Girgis, K., DeVinney, A., Hart, L. M., & Murray, S. M. (2023). Cultural adaptation of the teen mental health first aid (tMHFA) program from Australia to the USA. *School Mental Health, 15*(2), 637–655. https://doi.org/10.1007/s12310-023-09576-z

Salmani, Z., Zargham-Boroujeni, A., Salehi, M., K Killeen, T., & Merghati-Khoei, E. (2015). The existing therapeutic interventions for orgasmic disorders: Recommendations for culturally competent services, narrative review. *Iranian Journal of Reproductive Medicine, 13*(7), 403–412.

Seddighi, H., & Mousavi, M.-T. (2019). Status of health, education and income inequality in Iran. *Journal of Community Health Research*,. 10.18502/jchr.v8i3.1561.

Shahhosseini, Z., Simbar, M., Ramezankhani, A., & Majd, H. A. (2012). Supportive family relationships and adolescent health in the socio-cultural context of Iran: A qualitative study. *Mental Health in Family Medicine, 9*(4), 251–256.

Shamshirian, S., Halldorsson, V., & Sigmundsson, H. (2021). Passion, grit and mindset of Iranian wrestlers: A socio-psychological approach. *New Ideas in Psychology, 62*, 100871. https://doi.org/10.1016/j.newideapsych.2021.100871

Valizadeh, L., Zamanzadeh, V., Rassouli, M., & Rahkar Farshi, M. (2018). Concerns of parents with or raising adolescent children: A qualitative study of Iranian families. *Journal of Caring Sciences, 7*(1), 27–33. https://doi.org/10.15171/jcs.2018.005

Yang, Z. (2024). "I Gain a Resilient Self": Exploring disaster identity communication and post-traumatic growth of young adults in Chinese culture. *Communication Studies, 75*(5), 733–751. https://doi.org/10.1080/10510974.2024.2374641

Zamani-Farahani, H., & Musa, G. (2012). The relationship between Islamic religiosity and residents' perceptions of socio-cultural impacts of tourism in Iran: Case studies of Sare'in and Masooleh. *Tourism Management, 33*(4), 802–814. https://doi.org/10.1016/j.tourman.2011.09.003

Chapter 19
Let Us Confront "Agonistic Life" Lived Experience, Mental Health, and Taking "Care of the Self'

'nob' Doran

Abstract This chapter critiques the external, detached perspective dominant in social science mental health research. Instead, it advocates for a methodology that begins with the embodied, "lived experience" of individuals struggling with unintelligible aspects of their own lives. It argues that scholarly inquiry originating from this personal "agonism" can generate powerful new discourses to make sense of one's self and social world, ultimately challenging and talking back to inadequate dominant frameworks. The argument is exemplified through the intellectual journeys of Michel Foucault and Dorothy E. Smith, who each constructed new scholarly selves to explain their lived realities.

Keywords Agonistic life · Mental health · Lived experience

Introduction

Modern social science often understands issues regarding mental health from a standpoint outside the lived experience of the embodied individuals who are seen as having such issues. And this remains the case with regard to the recent COVID-19 pandemic (Chen et al., 2024). In contrast, this chapter seeks to carry out an almost opposite task. It wants to demonstrate what may be learnt when one starts from the "lived experience" of someone who has aspects of their life which they do not fully understand and with which they struggle, but who then tries to make these (and other related issues) intelligible in some scholarly fashion. In other words, when one starts one's scholarly life from a somewhat unintelligible situation of agonism (Foucault, 1983: 222–3), this can lead to interesting results. For example, this way

'nob' Doran (✉)
Department of Social Science, University of New Brunswitch,
Saint, New Brunswick, Canada
e-mail: doran@unb.ca

D. Nyaga, M. Zangeneh (eds.), *Critical Ethics on Mental Health and Madness*,
Advances in Mental Health and Addiction,
https://doi.org/10.1007/978-3-032-10166-2_19

of "making sense" can eventually produce a means of talking back to the "dominant discourses" (Miller, L., 1993) which were previously available for making sense of that person's "lived experience," but which are now shown to be inadequate.

For the purpose of this chapter, I will exemplify my argument by following the careers of two individuals who used such an approach, and who went on to construct scholarly selves (of themselves) which made sense of their own lives (and their social worlds), albeit in quite different ways. That is, they assembled new discourses[1] to explain both themselves and the agonistic social relations in which they lived. These two individuals started their lives as Paul-Michel Foucault and Dorothy Place, but went on to convert themselves into "Dorothy E. Smith—feminist sociologist" and "Michel Foucault—philosopher and fellow of the college de france."

Although both of them are now extremely well known for their scholarly contributions, especially regarding questions of knowledge (e.g., Foucault, 1970, 1972, 1975), power (e.g., Foucault, 1977,1980), ideology (e.g., Smith, 1974a, 1990a, 1990c), the self (e.g., Foucault, 1985, 1988, Smith, 1990b), etc., their scholarly starting points in concerns with the problem of "madness, of lunacy, of mental illness" for Smith (1959:15) and of "madness, dementia, insanity" for Foucault (Preface to the 1965 version of Madness and civilization) are often passed over quickly, in favor of their more mature work. In contrast, this chapter wants to argue that these authors' early embodied concerns are important to consider, as they reveal insights about the construction of their (scholarly and embodied) "selves," each of them producing a "self" which "talks back" (hooks, 1989, Jeffrey and McDonald 2007). Moreover, questions about the assembling of scholarly selves are rarely asked. This process is typically seen as a product of prior socialization, rather than one of confronting the agonistic relations into which one is born, and within which one grows up and lives (Smith, 1994; Miller. J., 1993; Eribon, 1991).

Having said that, it should be readily observable that Smith's scholarly "self" was not solely informed by her academic socialization. She openly acknowledged the influence of the "women's movement" with regard to her converting herself into a feminist one (Smith, 1974b), and one which organized its subsequent scholarship around the prioritization of women's embodied selves. However, the same cannot be said for how Foucault has typically been received in the western social sciences. He has conventionally been understood as a product of the elite French education system (Eribon, 1991: 15–40), becoming a major theorist on power/knowledge, governmentality, sexuality, etc. In contrast, one aim of this chapter is to display Foucault's final few lecture courses, and especially his explicit theorizing of life-long "care of the self" (Foucault, 2005). And it will also highlight the implicit application of these practices to Foucault's own embodiment, so as to suggest a quite different understanding of his scholarly self. And by doing this, one simultaneously draws attention to what Foucault calls the relations of "agonism" in which we are

[1] Although some might want to call them "theories," both Foucault and Smith would have probably balked at such a term.

all embroiled, and out of which selves agentively form themselves. Furthermore, Foucault is particularly concerned with the agonism of everyday life, and not just the agonistic struggles traditionally associated with the realms of the economy and the polity. Consequently, his excavation of "care of the self" documents the practices available for confronting this agonism of the lifecourse.

I will also suggest that, in the case of these scholars, Smith and Foucault, their early challenges to the conventional meanings of "mental illness" and "madness" were exemplifications of the agonistic struggle in which they found themselves, and especially with the then-dominant discourse of psychiatry. As a result, and perhaps more explicitly for Smith, this struggle was part of a more general struggle with dominant (often social scientific) discourses, and led to a very straightforward reversal of our understanding of the scholarly "self." For her, it is one who starts from their own lived embodied experience, rather than textual materials (Smith, 1974b). But as will be discussed later in this chapter, Foucault's mature understanding of the "self" that talks back understands the "self" as the endpoint of analysis, rather than its starting point (Foucault, 2010, 2011).

Early Days: Embodied Individuals Struggling with Texts

So let us begin by looking at Dorothy Smith's early writings on what she calls "mental illness, depression, etc." And by drawing attention to this rather marginalized aspect of her work, it allows us, today, to better understand how she constructed her scholarly self, and the importance of situating it in its socio-historical context. This is important, because today, she is somewhat pilloried for her essentialist standpoint, as we are now in an era where embodied standpoints based on other notions of sexuality (queer, trans, etc.) get prioritized, but which do not fully appreciate the specific agonistic relations in which Smith grew up.[2]

Most importantly, there was no discourse of feminism to be utilized, by Smith. For example, her first scholarly publication was concerned with the "state mental hospital" in 1959. And this writing reflects her academic socialization. There is no language yet to situate the issue in a feminist context. Instead it is informed by one of the dominant scholarly discourses of that time. In fact, her approach resembles a rather conventional and traditional sociological consideration of mental illness.[3] But she subsequently endeavors to convert herself. It is in 1975 that we get her first quasi-feminist approach to mental illness when she examines the statistics on mental illness and provides a critique similar to the ones that ethnomethodologists were

[2] In a very different context, Williams suggests that we examine these generational differences in cultural expression, via the exploration of generational styles (1977:131).

[3] In this early work, she situates her work within the dominant Parsonian theorizing of that time (Smith, 1959: 16).

compiling of official statistics, at that time.[4] In other words, her familiarity with this new language of critique proposed by ethnomethologists like Cicourel allowed her to produce a powerful condemnation of the official statistics on women and illness, one which was not premised on the question of their "accuracy." And the title of the book in which her chapter appeared was equally revealing, as it hinted at the emergence of this new standpoint from which to confront dominant discourses. It was simply called "women look at psychiatry."

Subsequently, her concern with mental illness was then extended to the precise and specific textual analysis of how a medical doctor may construct an ideological narrative of someone as "depressed," because of the professional's ability to cherry-pick only certain pieces of evidence in order to construct an ideological narrative out of a primary narrative (Smith, 1990c). Of course, for Smith, the "primary narrative" reflects the "actualities" of a woman's life; the hard work and the strains imposed on her. Yet the ideological narrative ignores that work component and instead highlights only the features that point to depression.

So as we can see, Smith's early work is very much concerned with issues which can be understood within a colloquial language game (Wittgenstein, 1974), concerned with "depression." But perhaps as importantly, Smith has also pointed to the fact that there is an experiential connection between this scholarly interest in mental illness (and related issues) and her own lived experience. She openly discusses the fact that she too, like some of the women she writes about, had spent significant amounts of time in therapy, especially when she was in graduate school and a young mother (Smith, 1994). Thus her early work displays this movement from a concern with "mental health," which begins from a textual standpoint, to one whereby the stance adopted for beginning analysis resides in women's lived experience, including her own.

In contrast, Foucault's work is not usually remembered as prioritizing "lived experience" at all. But, in some ways similar to Smith, his early career was concerned with what might colloquially be called "mental illness." Published originally in 1954 in French as "Maladie Mentale et Personnalite," and then largely rewritten for a 1962 release date as "Maladie Mentale et Psychologie," Foucault was still not happy with it, as he forbade its reissue and tried unsuccessfully to prevent it getting published in English, with its title directly and literally translated as "mental illness and psychology." However, this frustration did not extend to his other publication of the early 1960s. In 1961 (the edited English version appeared in 1965), he published what he went on to call "his first book"—on "madness and civilization," which began with the following startling comment: "in the midst of the serene world of mental illness, modern man no longer communicates with the madman" (1965:xii), and he then proceeds, at length, to display the "history of madness" which documents this split.

[4] She cites Garfinkel, 1967; Zimmerman, 1969; Cicourel, 1968 as exemplars of this approach (Smith, 1975:116–7).

One can discover another similarity to Smith at this time. It was not just that they both start their careers with writings on "mental illness." It is that Foucault's "lived experience" as a student was also bound up with embodied issues, such that, at one point, his father arranged a consultation for his son with Professor Delay an "eminent psychiatrist" in Paris. Foucault's biographer, Eribon (1991), also mentions Foucault's suicide attempt in 1948, and his being found lying on a floor having cut his own chest with a razor, and other attempts at suicide. Not surprisingly, perhaps Eribon states that Foucault's schoolmates "all remembered Foucault as precariously balanced on a tightrope between sanity and madness" (1991:27). So what we can conclude from this is simply that both these scholars struggled with their "lived experience," and sought, in part, to confront such an agonistic experience, through their early scholarly writings.

Maturing as Scholars

Despite these early concerns with challenging the dominant social scientific discourses' understandings of "mental illness," "mental health," etc., these individuals' scholarly importance is, in no way, premised on these early beginnings. In fact, as already noted, much of this early work is seen as only of marginal importance to their mature writings. Smith's development was to convert herself into a "social theorist" with an implicit introduction of the importance of "lived experience" and the associated concept of the feminist standpoint. Moreover, she constructed her theory/method[5] of institutional ethnography in the late 1980s (Smith, 1987) and then formed a school of researchers who still follow her lead in analyzing the "ruling relations" (e.g., see Smith ed. 2006; Smith & Turner eds 2014) from this vantage point from below (one which begins from one's lived experience, and the sense of disjuncture that should motivate one's research) (Campbell & Gregor, 2008:48).

Foucault also left behind his early focus on mental illness, but applied himself to the more wide-ranging analysis of the "ignoble origins" (Sheridan 1980; 157) of other human sciences. And this approach, especially with regard to his conceptualizations of genealogy and of governmentality, was taken up rapidly by social scientific researchers in several locations, outside of France. (e.g., Garland, 1987; Rose, 1979; Dean, 1992). But the later stages of his career saw him returning to his earliest concerns. Concretely, he began examining the practices of the self in Antiquity, but he recognized that the origins of this work lay in the frustrations he had encountered when writing "Mental Illness and Psychology." As he said in the early 1980s, with regard to this final project, "to study forms of experience in this way—in their history—is an idea that originated in an earlier project" (Foucault, 1991:334) but it was one that had left him unsatisfied.

[5] In 2022 she (and Alison Griffith) reflected on "institutional ethnography's perceived status, and insisted it is not a qualitative method; it is more than that. It is a sociology" (Smith & Griffith, 2022:3).

These final explorations not only dealt with aspects of the sexual which appear in his last publications before his death, but they went well beyond practices of sexuality, and ended up examining the lifelong "care of the self" which he also found in ancient Greece, but which had the potential to produce the parrhesian[6] individual as an end product (Foucault, 2001, 2010, 2011); that is, the underdog who speaks the truth to power, from an embodied standpoint. So let us turn to what Foucault means by this lifelong care of the self.

Care of the Self in Antiquity[7]

Despite the massive transformation in the content of his analyses (from analyses of modernity to everyday practices in antiquity) between 1980 and 1985, Foucault certainly acknowledges the connection between the two. Specifically, he admits that his newly found concern with the "self" came from his prior analyses of power/knowledge, and especially that of "pastoral power." Moreover, in his mundane observations of contemporary social life, he noticed that resistances often seemed to be directed against a pastoral power which "categorises the individual, marks him by his own individuality, attaches him to his identity, imposes a law of truth on him which he must recognize" (Foucault, 1983:212). And such observations led him to respecify the power–resistance relationship, so as to incorporate the "one over whom power is exercised… a person who acts" (1983:220), because "at the very heart of the power relationship and constantly provoking it are the recalcitrance of the will and the intransigence of freedom" (1983: 221–2). In other words, for Foucault, this relationship is always one of struggle, or agonism. And not surprisingly, using his usual methodological approach, Foucault begins to genealogically excavate the practices of the self that resist pastoral power.

Perhaps not surprisingly, this led him back to the era before the emergence of pastoral power in the fourth century, it led him back to Greek antiquity, where he eventually, and rather surprisingly[8] came upon a rather subjugated phenomenon "the principle that one should tell the truth about oneself in all of ancient morality, and in Greek and Roman culture" (Foucault, 2011: 4). But this approach, which is constitutive of "care of the self" has been subjugated by the Cartesian moment, he asserts. That is to say, the Cartesian approach of modern philosophy has been successful in "discrediting the principle of care of the self and in excluding it from modern philosophical thought" (2005:14). This Cartesian moment also marginal-

[6]Although Foucault does not use this adjective in his own writings, I coined it to emphasize the Foucauldian understanding of "parrhesia"; and, as the rest of this chapter will argue, to suggest that it extends beyond Greek Antiquity.

[7]Much of the rest of this paper is taken from Doran, 2015. For fuller details on this argument please consult the original analysis.

[8]He acknowledges that this discovery came about while studying the practices of aphrodisia in Ancient Greece.

ized another aspect of care of the self, whereby one's access to the truth comes about via spirituality and a conversion of the self. That is to say, "there can be no truth without a conversion or a transformation of the subject." (2005:15).

Although care of the self originates with Socrates, it is not just about knowing yourself. It needs to be practiced throughout one's life. And this is because the problems to be overcome are seen as being so deep-rooted. They are found in early childhood with the "famous nursery tales that already obliterate and destroy the child's mind" (2005: 95), and also in the family milieu with the "set of values it transmits and lays down... the 'family ideology'" (2005:96) and in "the training given by masters of what we call primary education .... The teachers of rhetoric" (2005:96).

For Foucault, a major problem is with the individual who is "blown by the wind...someone who lets all the representations from the outside world into his mind... without examining them... and constantly changes his viewpoint" (2005:131–2). So, to counter this problem (which the Greeks called "stultitia"), one has to aim for salvation. But of course, this is not a Christian type of salvation. It is totally different. It is not dramatic, it is about building up defenses for oneself. Just as "a city is saved by building the necessary defences" (2005:183–4), an individual has to "save" her/himself in a similar fashion. But it is not easy work, and many are not able to do it. A "lack of courage, strength or endurance, an inability to grasp the importance of the task to see it through; such is the destiny of the majority" (2005:118).

Thus, this conversion necessitates a long process, a self-subjectivation (2005:214) consisting of "exercise, practice and training" (2005:210), such as is involved with the practices of athletes. And this long process requires assistance from a guide or master; someone who already has parrhesia (2005:399) and someone who tells the truth rather than engaging in rhetoric or flattery (2005:373–83). And the distinguishing feature of the parrhesian is that they are a person who can be identified by the harmony between what they say and what they do (2005:402–9). In other words, their embodied way of life must harmonize with what they say. Foucault, later on, sums up this entire process when he concludes that the parrhesian displays the "standpoint... which constantly brings the question of the moral subject back to the question of the true discourse in which this moral subject constitutes itself and to the question of the relation of power in which this subject is formed" (2011:68).

Foucault Taking Care of Himself

So, having begun this mature analysis of the self (because of his observation about the form contemporary resistances were taking), Foucault's subsequent genealogical analyses eventually ended up displaying how "care of the self" in antiquity sought to produce a truth-teller, a "frank speaker." But my own long-term immersion in Foucault's intellectual journey made me realize that he himself had been engaging in somewhat similar practices throughout his career. Let me clarify.

Earlier, Foucault had suggested that "exercise, practice, and training" were necessary for the actual work of "self on self" in antiquity, but he elaborates on this and clarifies the "askesis" needed for this task.[9] This is not the ascetic practices found in several religions; this instead requires an "athletic kind of concentration" (2005:222) as found in those preparing for races, or when an archer focuses on her/his target (2005:222). In other words, it involves "keeping before our eyes, in the clearest way, that towards which we are striving and having…a clear consciousness…of the possibility of our achieving it" (2005:220).

In addition, it requires useful knowledge (2005:232); not causal knowledge but relational knowledge which takes into account "things of the world on the one hand and ourselves on the other" (2005:235). Moreover, this type of knowledge is "immediately translatable" (2005:235) into prescriptions for the individual. In other words, useful knowledge helps produce an ethical individual. That is to say, "knowledge is useful when it has a form and functions in such a way that it can produce ethos" (2005:237) in the individual—knowledge "which is philosophically relevant for the practice of the self" (2005:238). Furthermore, this type of useful knowledge is contrasted with the poverty of the "cultural embellishment" (2005:236) type of knowledge found in the paideia (the formal education system in antiquity). Because this merely produces a "kind of boastful knowledge" (2005:239) spoken by "word spinners" (2005:239). This useful knowledge, which Foucault recommends, this "phusiologia" (2005:238), gives "the individual boldness and courage a kind of intrepidity which enables him to stand firm… against the many beliefs that others wish to impose upon him" (2005:240). Moreover, it is the type of knowledge which can transform the subject "into a free subject" (2005:241). Finally, this care of the self is an extremely long process, often life-long. It is something of an odyssey (2005:249), "the dangerous journey of life" (2005:250), which has an outward journey and then a safe return home (2005:248).

But once one completes this odyssey and returns to one's beginnings, one obtains a crucial standpoint. It allows us to see the world and our own situatedness within it. As Foucault says, it allows us to "situate ourselves so high that from this point and below us, we can see the world in its general order, the tiny space we occupy within it and the short time we remain there… it is the self's view of itself from above which encompasses the world of which we are a part and which ensures the subject's freedom within this world" (2005:282). In other words, this long journey of conversion culminates in a standpoint on both oneself and the world we inhabit.

And when one reflects upon Foucault's own lifelong journey, we can propose that he has taken "care of himself." He even suggests that this is the case when, in one of his final publications before he died, his words strikingly resembled those in Antiquity who had taken care of themselves. As he said, in the introduction to "The Use of Pleasure," "sure of having travelled far, one finds that one is looking down on oneself from above. The journey rejuvenates things and ages the relationship with oneself. I seem to have gained a better perspective on the way I

[9] See McGushin (2007) for a thoughtful introduction to Foucault on askesis.

worked—gropingly, and by means of different or successive fragments—on this project whose goal is a history of truth" (1985: 11).

Conclusion: the Importance of Harmony

Such a statement allows us to reflect upon Foucault's career and suggest that perhaps, he too, displays the harmony of the parrhesian speaker in Antiquity. That is to say, one might examine the content of his career's work, which led to his theorizing about how individuals took care of themselves in order to become "frank speakers"; and the practices they had to engage in to accomplish that. But one might also examine his own embodied practices over his lifetime, and identify these as ones that harmonize with those of the individuals taking care of themselves in Antiquity. In other words, his content articulates the conceptualization of "care of the self," while his embodied form, his "lived experience" actually displays this lifelong "care of the self." And such harmony, as was pointed out earlier, is the hallmark of the "parrhesian speaker" in Ancient Greece; and is someone who can guide others in obtaining access to the truth. And this journey started with Foucault's struggle with the agonistic relations in which he grew up, but which he then made intelligible in a more comprehensive and completely different fashion; eventually culminating in his conceptualization of the parrhesian underdog talking back truthfully to the dominant discourses of his/her time.

Finally, what we have seen here is the amazing potential that starting from one's own embodied experience has for producing scholarly insights.[10] Smith did this and produced a harmony between her understanding of her social world (an agonistic world of capitalism and patriarchy) but also her own situatedness within this world, a woman who converted herself so that she could talk back to these dominant discourses. And perhaps, right at this very minute, a few young scholars somewhere who are struggling with making their lived experience of "COVID-19" intelligible, may be encouraged to follow in the footsteps of these scholars and produce their own harmonious means of talking back, ones which challenge the dominant discourses' interpretations of their lives.

References

Campbell, M., & Gregor, F. (2008). *Mapping social relations: A primer in doing institutional ethnography*. University of Toronto Press.

[10] Michalko's writings (e.g., 1999, 2002) provide another excellent display of how to produce insightful scholarship from an embodied experience of "blindness," while Frank began his insights into suffering from his own embodied experience of illness (Frank, 1991).

Chen, S., Cárdenas, D., Zhou, H., & Reynolds, K. J. (2024). Positive school climate and strong school identification as protective factors of adolescent mental health and learning engagement: A longitudinal investigation before and during COVID-19. *Social Science & Medicine, 348*, 116795. https://doi.org/10.1016/j.socscimed.2024.116795
Cicourel, A. V. (1968). *The social organization of juvenile justice*. Wiley.
Dean, M. (1992). A genealogy of the government of poverty. *Economy and Society, 21*(3), 215–251. https://doi.org/10.1080/03085149200000012
Doran, N. (2015). Beyond phenomenological anti-sociologies: Foucault's "care of his self" as standpoint sociology. *Canadian Journal of Sociology, 40*(2), 131–162. https://doi.org/10.29173/cjs21786
Eribon, D. (1991). Michel Foucault (B. Wing, Trans.). Cambridge, MA: Harvard University Press.
Foucault, M. (1965). Madness and civilization. (R. Howard, Trans.) (Abridged). New York: Pantheon.
Foucault, M. (1970). *The order of things: An archeology of the human sciences*. Tavistock Publications.
Foucault, M. (1972). The archaeology of knowledge. (A. M. Sheridan, Trans.). London: Tavistock Publications.
Foucault, M. (1975). *The birth of the clinic: An archeology of medical perception*. Vintage Books.
Foucault, M. (1977). *Discipline and punish: The birth of the prison*. Vintage Books.
Foucault, M. (1980). The history of sexuality, *Volume 1: An introduction*. (R. Hurley, Trans.). New York: Vintage Books.
Foucault, M. (1983). The subject and power. In H. L. Dreyfus & P. Rabinow (Eds.), *Michel Foucault: Beyond structuralism and hermeneutics* (pp. 208–271). essay). University of Chicago Press.
Foucault, M. (1985). The history of sexuality: The use of pleasure. (R. Hurley, Trans.) (Vol. 2). New York: Pantheon.
Foucault, M. (1988). *The history of sexuality: The care of the self* (Vol. 3). Vintage.
Foucault, M. (1991). Preface to the history of sexuality, Volume II. In P. Rabinow (Ed.), *The Foucault reader* (pp. 333–340). essay). Penguin.
Foucault, M. (2001). In J. Pearson (Ed.), *Fearless speech*. Semiotext(e).
Foucault, M. (2005). Hermeneutics of the subject: Lectures at the Collège de France 1981–1982. (F. Gros, Ed.). : Palgrave Macmillan.
Foucault, M. (2010). The government of self and others: Lectures at the Collège de France 1982–83. (G. Burchell, Trans., F. Gros, Ed.). : Palgrave Macmillan.
Foucault, M. (2011). *The courage of truth: The government of self and others*. Palgrave Macmillan.
Frank, A. W. (1991). *At the will of the body: Reflections on illness*. Houghton Mifflin.
Garfinkel, H. (1967). *Studies in ethnomethodology*. Prentice-Hall.
Garland, D. (1987). *Punishment and welfare: A history of penal strategies*. Gower.
hooks, b. (1989). *Talking back: Thinking feminist, thinking black*. South End Press.
Jeffrey, L. A., & MacDonald, G. M. (2007). *Sex workers in the Maritimes Talk Back*. UBC Press.
McGushin, E. F. (2007). Foucault's askēsis: An introduction to the philosophical life. : Northwestern University Press.
Michalko, R. (1999). *The two-in-one: Walking with Smokie, walking with blindness*. Temple University Press.
Michalko, R. (2002). *The difference that disability makes*. Temple University Press.
Miller, J. E. (1993). *The passion of Michel Foucault*. Simon & Schuster.
Miller, L. J. (1993). Claims-making. In J. Holstein & J. Gubrium (Eds.), Handbook of constructionist research (pp. 251–274). essay, : Guilford Press.
Rose, N. (1979). The psychological complex : Mental measurement and social administration. *Ideology and Consciousness, 5*, 5–68.
Sheridan, A. (1980). *Michel Foucault: The will to truth*. Tavistock.
Smith, D. E. (1959). Legitimate and illegitimate deviance: The case of the state mental hospital. *Berkeley Journal of Sociology, 5*(1), 15–39.
Smith, D. E. (1974a). The ideological practice of sociology. *Catalyst, 8*, 39–54.

Smith, D. E. (1974b). Women's perspective as a radical critique of sociology. *Sociological Inquiry, 44*(1), 7–13.

Smith, D. E. (1975). The statistics on mental illness: What they will not tell us about women and why. In D. E. Smith & S. J. David (Eds.), *Women look at psychiatry* (pp. 73–119). Press Gang Publishers.

Smith, D. E. (1987). *The everyday world as problematic: A feminist sociology* (Ser. Northeastern). University of Toronto Press.

Smith, D. E. (1990a). The conceptual practices of power. : University of Toronto Press.

Smith, D. E. (1990b). Femininity as discourse. In *Texts, facts, and femininity* (pp. 159–208). Routledge.

Smith, D. (1990c). No one commits suicide: Textual analyses of ideological practices. In *The conceptual practices of power: A feminist sociology of knowledge* (pp. 141–173). University of Toronto Press.

Smith, D. (1994). A Berkeley education. In K. M. Orlans & R. A. Wallace (Eds.), *Gender and the academic experience: Berkely women sociologists* (pp. 45–56). essay). University of Nebraska Press.

Smith, D. E. (2006). *Institutional ethnography as practice*. Rowman & Littlefield Publishers.

Smith, D. E., & Turner, S. M. (2014). *Incorporating texts into institutional ethnographies*. University of Toronto Press.

Smith, D. E., & Griffith, A. I. (2022). *Simply institutional ethnography: Creating a sociology for people*. University of Toronto Press.

Williams, R. (1978). *Marxism and literature*. Oxford University Press.

Wittgenstein, L. (1974). Philosophical investigations. (G. E. M. Anscombe, Trans.). Basil Blackwell. Oxford.

Zimmerman, D. H. (1969). Record keeping and the intake process in a public welfare agency. In S. Wheeler (Ed.), On record: Files and dossiers in American life (pp. 319–345). essay, : Russell Sage Foundation.

Chapter 20
Forgiveness: An Ethical Requirement in Addressing Social Injustice

Rose Ann Torres

Abstract As an Ilokano, one of the indigenous groups in the Philippines, I have learned to appreciate the beauty and struggle in life. I chose this remark while keeping in mind that many people are suffering as a result of capitalism and liberalism, as well as the ongoing effects of colonization. I shall present the accounts of my research on capitalism, which discusses forgiveness in this chapter. This demonstrates how, despite their disagreement with the gendered violence they experience, they insist on the need to forgive. I will explore how we can find forgiveness when there is violence. I will examine the moral necessity of forgiveness in the struggle of finding peace in the midst of pain and suffering.

Keywords Social injustice · Capitalism · Liberalism · Mental health

Introduction

I owe this chapter to one of my research participants, who shared their stories with me about forgiveness. Since I personally feel that this type of subject has no place at the university, I have long avoided talking about forgiveness. This belief holds that forgiveness is not merely a human act but a dialogue with the divine, a conversation through which one may approach God and ask for forgivness (Kolnai, 1973; Murphy, 2003; Murphy, 2003; Worthington, 2009; Haikola, 2023). The essence of pain is touched by forgiveness, and discussing forgiveness maks no sense when you are in pain. We discuss forgiveness because we have experienced hurt (McGary, 1989; Holmgren, 1993; Wade et al., 2005; Hourigan, 2019; Levy et al., 2021). Who injured us and what kind of hurt are you experiencing are always the questions that linger in our minds when we think of forgiveness.

R. A. Torres (✉)
University of Toronto, ON, Canada
e-mail: rose.torres@utoronto.ca

D. Nyaga, M. Zangeneh (eds.), *Critical Ethics on Mental Health and Madness*, Advances in Mental Health and Addiction,
https://doi.org/10.1007/978-3-032-10166-2_20

When we address systematic violence, hurt becomes symbolic because we are dealing with structures, institutions, policies, and so on. Systems can refer to a wide range of concepts. For instance, the legal and institutional structures inside a nation are examples of systems (Meyer & Rowan, 1977; Edquist & Johnson, 1996; Hodgson, 2006). Finding harm within these broad systems with such an expansive scope is difficult to determine, but it does not always imply that you cannot be harmed by them. The system functions within all state-governing structures (Popkewitz, 1996; Harris, 2000; Leslie, 2004; Andersen, 2005; Kravtsova et al., 2019). The system operates within every structure that governs the state. Within this system, there are mechanisms that govern workers on how to do the work. When these forms of mechanism are not being followed in the state of neoliberalism, workers are being punished (Davies & Peterson, 2005; Braithhwaite, 2005; Wacquant, 2012; Lacey, 2013). We may ask who is often being punished? Racialized workers are being punished not necessarily because they are not doing the right thing but simply because their existence is not meant to exist (Bonacich et al., 2008; Soss et al., 2011; Reed, 2013; De Lissovoy, 2013; Dawson & Francis, 2016; Hatton, 2018; Zatz, 2020). In the consideration of their existence, that means a pseudo-existence, violence exists. In this state of existence, can forgiveness be employed for racialized people who do not consider that their existence is indeed an existence? This is the central question that helps me frame this chapter. In this chapter, I will include the narrative of one participant who speaks about forgiveness. I will analyze their narratives, then I will conclude.

Forgiveness in the Bible

There are five verses in the Bible that speak about forgiveness. I would like to include them here because the participants locate their discussion of forgiveness through these verses in the Bible. While I include and discuss the verses, we can see why forgiveness is imperative in our social justice work. Justice means fairness for all regardless of race, class, gender, and other forms of identity. The first verse, Ephesians 4:32, states, "Be kind to one another, tenderhearted, forgiving one another, as God in Christ forgave you." This verse speaks about one another, which means all of us, regardless of who we are. When we talk about tenderheartedness, it is the ability to have a living and caring heart. To be tenderhearted is a choice that we need to make. It comes with an intent to be good or not. Tenderheartedness is paramount, whether you will be kind or forgiving. The statement that "God in Christ forgave you" is a reminder that we are dependent on God and we too have committed mistakes; therefore, we have no reason not to be kind and forgiving to others, since we are all prone to make mistakes. We can achieve this by allowing ourselves to be tenderhearted, because a heart that is tender means that it has the capacity to see hate as the process of love and care.

The second verse is Matthew 6:14–15: "For if you forgive others their trespasses, your heavenly Father will also forgive you, but if you do not forgive others their trespasses, neither will your Father forgive your trespasses." This verse is a reminder of who we are. It talks about values. It is a verse that conditions us to forgive while we are also forgiven. It is a reminder that we too have gone astray, but we have forgiven. This verse teaches us to be humble and to be reflective. Though it sounds like a threat, there is a reason why it sounded like a threat, because forgiveness is the hardest thing to do when you are hurt. Therefore, we need to be shaken and reminded that if you do not forgive, you will not be forgiven as well. It is a reminder of how vulnerable we are, and because of this vulnerability (Torres & Nyaga, 2021a), we will also hurt others at some point, and when we reach this point, we also need to be forgiven.

The third verse is Colossians 3:13: "Bearing with one another and, if one has a complaint against another, forgiving each other; as the Lord has forgiven you, so you also must forgive." I really like the word "bearing" because it shows that we have the obligation to take care of each other. That I exist because you exist, and vice versa. So my existence depends on your existence. I have the responsibility to make good, so I will be good. I also have the responsibility to forgive, so you will be forgiving. The way I can make others forgiving is for me to make myself forgiving.

The fourth verse is Luke 6:37: "Judge not, and you will not be judged; condemn not, and you will not be condemned; forgive, and you will be forgiven." This verse teaches us to do what others want us to do for us. If you want respect, then you have to respect. What we do to others will also happen to us. It goes back to the third verse of being connected to one another. That my existence depends on your existence. So this verse is a powerful reminder that we have the power to determine how you are being treated and the kind of environment you want to live in.

The last verse is Matthew 18:21–22: "Then Peter came up and said to him, 'Lord, how often will my brother sin against me, and I forgive him? As many as seven times?' Jesus said to him, 'I do not say to you seven times, but seventy-seven times.'" Forgiveness is an endless commitment to one another.

Methodology

Our research is about understanding the experiences of Filipino healthcare workers in terms of the accessibility of mental services in Northern Ontario. Part of our study has been published in the Reimagining Mental Health, and my co-applicant and I coauthored a paper with our research assistant, and we discussed the methodology. According to Torres et al. (2021) that:

For this study, we interviewed Filipino frontline healthcare workers using a semi-structured and open-ended interview guide to elicit information related to the objectives of the study (Torres & Nyaga, 2021). Interviews were conducted in person and through Zoom interviews. Participation was voluntary, and participants were mandated to answer any questions they deemed inappropriate. We recruited Filipino frontline healthcare workers who have been working at a Canadian healthcare facility in Sudbury, Timmins, and Sault Ste. Marie, Ontario at the time of the interview.

I invited one of the healthcare workers, and they agreed to participate in our study. I had a copy of the consent and a list of questions to ask. The participant was given the opportunity to speak without any fear or worry that their answers were wrong. I encourage them they can speak from their heart and from their own location. Our methodology is a critical qualitative research method (Torres, 2021). Participants were also informed that they are free to withdraw or not to answer the questions if they are not comfortable. They were also told that their narratives will be published and will be used with pseudonyms.

I spoke in my Indigenous language, Ilokano, to participants who are Ilokano and Tagalog to other participants who speak the language. There were 25 participants who participated in telephone interviews, zoom, and in-person. However, for this chapter, I only include the narratives of Gloria. Gloria has been working at the dental office. She has been working in this workplace for a while. Before I asked the research questions, I informed her that she could share with me any stories of her life that she may think it is important to share. She told many things about her life and her struggles of being a Filipino woman working in the West. As a Filipino healthcare worker, she has to pray hard before she goes to the workplace. She believes that through prayers, she can face challenges that might come her way. Her faith makes her strong. She needs her strength from the pain she anticipates to experience. She speaks about anticipation because, being a Filipino, anything can happen. She belongs to a liminal space where anything can happen, and it is only through her faith that makes her live. Her faith allows her to look at the pandemic as a season of renewal, which could have meant a season to be more reflexive. According to Torres and Nyaga (2021b) that:

While it is important to interrogate the structure, it is equally imperative that we interrogate our own implicit participation in the oppression of ourselves laterally. In fact, to think and act in interrogating the structure reminds us that we are part of and embody the structure that we are investigating. Consequently, the decolonization of the structure is equally a representation of how we engage in reflexive exercise of our implication in colonization. To that extent, critical reflexivity plays the role of outhabiting us from ourselves in ways that we mourn and question the role we play in the elimination of others from national imaginaries. (p. 2)

Reflexivity is a journey that everyone is included in. It can be a difficult journey because it looks into the details of how the journey comes into being and where it is going, and how it will arrive at the destination. The destination is not the focus, but it is how it gets into the destination is the main concern of reflexivity. It is like a ring that has no end; it is a continuous process. An invitation to be more caring for one another. A season of remembering that our lives are connected to one another and therefore it is teaching us to live not for ourselves but for others (Nyaga & Torres, 2021).

Findings and Analysis

In this section, I will include the narrative of the participants who speak about forgiveness. Gloria is originally from the northern part of Luzon. A pseudonym was used to protect the participant's anonymity. Luzon is one of the major islands in the Philippines. She is an Ilokano. She works as a dental assistant. I informed her about my research and asked her about her experience in the healthcare system. I will include the narrative that was spoken in Ilokano, and then I will translate it. There is something in our language that is so deep, but for the purpose of this chapter, I will translate it in English. She states:

> *Manang Nasayaat met. Agayamank kenni Apo tayo ta innikkan na tayo to trabaho ditoy Canada. Nagadu ti agrigrigat ita, ngem inik kan na tayo ni Apo ti trabaho isu nga agayaman tayo ta ti trabaho ket blessings.*

> *My sister (we call my sister to anybody in the Philippines), I am good. I give thanks to our God for giving us work in Canada. There are many who are suffering but has given us work, so we need to be thankful to God.*

Remember, my question is focused on her expectations of the workplace, but Gloria chose to speak about being thankful to God because of the blessings that she receives from God. She reiterated that being thankful is a necessary thing to do because she is aware that many who do not have it are therefore suffering. Therefore, she cannot fail to thank God. I listened to her and tried not to interfere her while she was speaking about giving. Her answer was not necessarily what I would like to hear, but it is important to hear it. Then she continued to talk about her job:

> *Toy trabahok ket mayat ngem narigat manang. Medyo nababa ti sweldo. Adu pay ti kliyente nga bastos. Talaga nga pasenya Ken pammakawan ti kasapulan tayo isu ngarud ti bilin ni Apo tayo.*

> *My work is good, but it's difficult. The salary is a bit low. I have many clients who are rude. We need patience and forgiveness because the is what our God's asked us ask to do.*

The statement of Gloria speaks of gratitude while not forgetting the hardship that she is going through. She is making a point that the hardship cannot be the center of her being because she knows that if she centers it, it might overshadow her strength and will to work while resisting the injustice in her workplace. She knows that she is good. It is good because she is doing what she likes to do. The power of doing what you really like to do is what matters most with Gloria. While it is hard, it is also easy at the same time because she is doing what she likes doing and she chose the job and no one has told her to do it. She went to school to get a diploma in order for her to do the job and did everything on her will to finish her diploma. With this, she remembers the beauty and joy of receiving a degree in Canada. A place where she chose to migrate when her original country has failed her because of the ongoing encroachment of the Western countries. This encroachment has made the country forget its own people's needs, but instead it centers on comprising its values just to compete with others. The work of colonization in the Philippines has impacted the lives of many Filipinos to the point that many of them have sacrificed to work in another country to provide for the needs of their families.

Gloria's attitude of being grateful for the job that she has, even though it is hard, does not necessarily mean that she has become docile. In fact, it shows how strong and resilient she is because she is able to work with disrespectful clients. In the midst of working with clients who do see her worth, she employs the moral value of forgiveness. For her, forgiveness is not a matter of getting back; it is about seeing the worth of the other while they are being rude to her. Forgiveness for her means obeying what God wants her to do, not because she expects something in return. But while she is in the process of forgiving the client who chose to disrespect her, she is already healing up. In the process of healing up, she is seeing the client as someone who needs her care and service. Forgiveness comes with power. The power to go beyond what the pain is telling you to feel. The power to feel joy in the midst of pain. Forgiveness gives her the ability to see the worth of others. It gives her the ability to know the pain of others. It is the ability to respect, love, and care for others. While the other may not ask for her to do this, for Gloria to be in the state of loving, caring, and respecting is about centering the other so that she can provide the highest care that others need. This would become the turning point for the other to see that the world is not all about what they expect. Gloria knows that the other is rude; not because they want to be rude, but because of their experiences. Though Gloria is not giving the client any excuse to be rude, it is all about not wanting to judge others but to give the best that she can to her own service.

Not to forgive is to put our place in a position of revenge, pain, suffering, and denial. To revenge is a tendency of paying back. The notion of paying back is based on what the other has given to you. Since the idea of revenge comes from a violent act, we can deduce that paying it back is about being violent to the other. Gloria has narrated that the client was rude to her; this would mean that the client is not appreciative of the work of Gloria or disrespectful to her. So, if we employ the notion of revenge, which is paying back the rudeness of the other, then we become the other. When we become the other, the question is what will happen to the social justice movements. How do we do social justice work when we use the same mechanism of treating one another?

Gloria's way of responding to the client through forgiveness is a reminder that when the other person instills pain, instead of repaying it through using the same tool, we can show them the other way of treating human beings. We can only do this when we forgive the other. One might argue that forgiveness is a moral obligation that runs through beyond what we can see. Others might also argue that by forgiveness we become complicit. Instead of addressing the violence, we end up nourishing it. Gloria's way of addressing the pain is to show the client that they are important. She may not be able to see the result at that moment, but she instills goodness in the life of the client. If the clients continue to have this experience, Gloria believes that at some point she will treat Filipinos differently.

Conclusion

Forgiveness is a difficult discussion when we talk about social justice because it means that we see the act of violence as something that is not just about hate, but there is more than what we can imagine. But in this chapter, I locate forgiveness through the narrative of Gloria. Gloria is a Christian and believes in God and the Lord Jesus Christ. Social justice is about embracing people's belief systems; it is through this that we realize Gloria's notion of forgiveness is beyond what we can grasp. It is a moral obligation that Gloria has taught us, to be forgiving while embracing the pain and the ability to come out of that pain. Embracing pain does not mean that we forget and validate the violence. Instead, we acknowledge it, and through this acknowledgement, we choose how we address it. To tell Gloria not to forgive is to show her that justice does not matter because, at this point, we are erasing Gloria. Our obligation is not prioritizing what to believe; it is about listening, feeling, and understanding Gloria's way of addressing injustices. Gloria's way of dealing with hate and violence is a new form of social justice that we all can learn from.

It is hard to comprehend how we employ forgiveness when you have been erased on the basis of your race. But to argue with Gloria and not recognize where she is coming from is also a form of injustice. A way to disregard Gloria's voice is a disgrace to the fight for social justice.

References

Andersen, S. C. (2005). How to improve the outcome of state welfare services. Governance in a systems-theoretical perspective. *Public Administration, 83*(4), 891–907.

Bonacich, E., Alimahomed, S., & Wilson, J. B. (2008). The racialization of global labor. *American Behavioral Scientist, 52*(3), 342–355.

Braithwaite, J. (2005). Neoliberalism or regulatory capitalism. RegNet Occasional Paper, (5).

Dawson, M. C., & Francis, M. M. (2016). Black politics and the neoliberal racial order. *Public Culture, 28*(1), 23–62.

Davies, B., & Petersen, E. B. (2005). Intellectual workers (un) doing neoliberal discourse. *International Journal of Critical Psychology, 13*(1), 32–54.

De Lissovoy, N. (2013). Conceptualizing the carceral turn: Neoliberalism, racism, and violation. *Critical Sociology, 39*(5), 739–755.

Edquist, C., & Johnson, B. (1996). Institutions and organizations in systems of innovation. Univ..

Haikola, A. (2023). Conversations with god: How are religion and spirituality used to make sense of forgiveness? *Pastoral Psychology, 72*(5), 693–709.

Harris, K. J. (2000). Governance structures, roles and responsibilities. SEARCH, National.

Hodgson, G. M. (2006). What are institutions? *Journal of Economic Issues, 40*(1), 1–25.

Hatton, E. (2018). When work is punishment: Penal subjectivities in punitive labor regimes. *Punishment & Society, 20*(2), 174–191.

Holmgren, M. R. (1993). Forgiveness and the intrinsic value of persons. *American Philosophical Quarterly, 30*(4), 341–352.

Hourigan, K. L. (2019). Forgiving the unforgivable: An exploration of contradictions between forgiveness-related feeling rules and lived experience of forgiveness of extreme harm. *Humanity & Society, 43*(3), 270–294.

Kravtsova, Z. S., Sinkevych, O. V., & Kudriavtseva, O. M. (2019). The functions of state institutions: Constitutional legal aspect. *Journal of Advanced Research in Law and Economics, 10*(1 (39)), 285–294.

Kolnai, A. (1973, January). Forgiveness. In Wiley (Ed.), *Proceedings of the Aristotelian society* (Vol. 74, pp. 91–106). Aristotelian Society, Wiley.

Lacey, N. (2013). Punishment,(neo) liberalism and social democracy. In *The SAGE handbook of punishment and society* (pp. 260–280).

Leslie, D. W. (2004). Governance or Governing? *Metropolitan Universities, 15*(1), 17–37.

Levy, K., Grant, P. C., Clem, K., Eadie, D. S., & Rossi, J. L. (2021). Holding onto hurt: the prevalence of interpersonal hurt and need for forgiveness-focused solutions for hospice family caregivers. *Journal of Palliative Medicine, 24*(8), 1139–1146.

McGary, H. (1989). Forgiveness. *American Philosophical Quarterly, 26*(4), 343–351.

Meyer, J. W., & Rowan, B. (1977). Institutionalized organizations: Formal structure as myth and ceremony. *American Journal of Sociology, 83*(2), 340–363.

Murphy, J. G. (2003). *Getting even: Forgiveness and its limits*. Oxford University Press.

Popkewitz, T. S. (1996). Rethinking decentralization and state/civil society distinctions: The state as a problematic of governing. *Journal of Education Policy, 11*(1), 27–51.

Reed Jr, A. (2013, January). Marx, race, and neoliberalism. In New labor forum (Vol. 22, 1, pp. 49-57). : SAGE Publications.

Soss, J., Fording, R. C., & Schram, S. (2011). *Disciplining the poor: Neoliberal paternalism and the persistent power of race*. University of Chicago Press.

Wacquant, L. (2012). Three steps to a historical anthropology of actually existing neoliberalism. *Social Anthropology/Anthropologie Sociale, 20*(1), 66–79.

Torres, R. (2021). Research methodologies: History, issues, tensions. In R. Torres & D. Nyaga (Eds.), *Critical research methodologies* (Studies in critical social sciences series). Sense Brill Publisher. PA Leiden.

Torres, R., & Nyaga, D. (2021a). Critical research as inconsolable mourning. In R. Torres & D. Nyaga (Eds.), *Critical research methodologies* (Studies in critical social sciences series). Sense Brill Publisher. PA Leiden.

Torres, R., & Nyaga, D. (2021b). Critical reflexivity framework on theorizing Asian Canada. In R. Torres, K. Leung, & V. Soepriatna (Eds.), *Outside and in-between: Theorizing Asian Canadian exclusion and the challenges of identity formation* (Studies in critical social sciences series). Brill Publisher. PA Leiden.

Torres, R., & Nyaga, D. (2021). Using critical research methodologies: The significance of reflexivity, resistance, and response. In R. Torres & D. Nyaga (Eds.), *Critical research methodologies* (Studies in critical social sciences series). Sense Brill Publisher. PA Leiden.

Wade, N. G., Bailey, D. C., & Shaffer, P. (2005). Helping clients heal: Does forgiveness make a difference? *Professional Psychology: Research and Practice, 36*(6), 634.

Worthington, E. L., Jr. (2009). *Forgiving and reconciling: Bridges to wholeness and hope*. InterVarsity Press.

Zatz, N. D. (2020). Get to work or go to jail: State violence and the racialized production of precarious work. *Law & Social Inquiry, 45*(2), 304–338.

Chapter 21
Of Mental Health and Postpandemic: A Review of Literature

Dionisio Nyaga

Abstract This chapter attempts to look at the ways in which the COVID-19 pandemic affected the world. The discussions in this volume pay particular attention to the ways in which the COVID-19 pandemic affected community mental health and the ways in which communities employed various ways to cope with its aftermath. The World Health Organization has invited all countries to reflect on the various issues that affected communities and for which we can learn to be able to counter future pandemics. It is now clear that COVID-19 had an immense effect on communities. During the COVID-19 period, many people were presented with the numbers that we were ready to lose to help return to normal. What these numbers did is forgetting that those who were lost in the pandemic were not just digits but rather human lives. This does not mean that numbers were wrong or right, but rather the presentation of the numbers of those who died from COVID-19 left no doubt that some lives were more valued than others. In this regard, this volume breaks from numerical quantification of human life to start not only qualifying the lives lost in ways that provide some form of accountability for the loss. This volume is, therefore, a reorientation of the models employed to flatten the curve. The volume recalls other ways of navigating the pandemic that were community-based. These ways that were employed by marginalized communities could help resolve any future challenges brought about by future pandemics.

Keywords COVID-19 · Community · Pandemic

D. Nyaga (✉)
School of Social Work, Algoma University, Sault Ste. Marie, ON, Canada
e-mail: dionisio.nyaga@algomau.ca

D. Nyaga, M. Zangeneh (eds.), *Critical Ethics on Mental Health and Madness*, Advances in Mental Health and Addiction,
https://doi.org/10.1007/978-3-032-10166-2_21

Introduction

COVID-19 has severely affected different communities in very disproportionate and unique ways (Azevedo et al., 2022; Chang et al., 2021; Gaynor & Wilson, 2020). Among the ways that COVID-19 has affected marginalized communities in uneven ways is around the issue of mental health and addictions (Azevedo et al., 2022; Smallwood & Willis, 2021; Zhai et al., 2023). Among those affected by the pandemic in distinctive ways are the Black peoples (Gaynor & Wilson, 2020; , Indigenous peoples, Asian (Tamagawa, 2023), 2SLGBTQIIA+ (Tamagawa, 2023), those living with disabilities, and many other living marginalized communities. Some of the effects brought about by the COVID-19 pandemic are the heightened levels of mental health and addiction. Researchers and policymakers have spoken about how COVID-19 compounded an already precarious issue of mental health in ways that were unique and disproportionate (Chang et al., 2021; Gaynor & Wilson, 2020; Parrish, 2020; Smith et al., 2022). While measures to curb the spread of the pandemic, such as wearing of the musk, hand washing, and sanitizing, as well as social distancing, were initially prioritized (Chang et al., 2021; Hanna et al., 2023), it is not lost how such measures also reproduced new forms of inequalities (Javed et al., 2020). Many times, we saw marginalized workers (Smallwood & Willis, 2021), most of whom were immigrants, left to decide whether to stay at home or work to sustain life. Life to them was equally a way of precariously playing with death (Hardi et al., 2023). Many of these marginalized immigrants were summarized as essential for the growth of the economy. Nurses and other service industries, marked as essential services, were severely affected by mental health and addiction following the COVID-19 pandemic (García-Vivar et al., 2023; Kuki et al., 2021; Mercado et al., 2022; Smith et al., 2022). Such forms of essentialism helped us understand that some lives had to be sacrificed in order that businesses could continue. Such a social system encouraged people to decide which bodies were valued and which could be dispensed out with. While we discuss these issues, it is equally important to understand how the pandemic highlighted and painted clear and nuanced historical social inequalities in ways never experienced before (Chang et al., 2021; Gaynor & Wilson, 2020; Parrish, 2020; Smith et al., 2022). Some of these issues were mental health and addiction, wherein a majority of those considered as essential workers (mostly the immigrants) continue to speak of the effect of COVID-19 on their mental health. The level of mental health and addictions among the essential workers, who mostly come from Black, African, Asian, 2SLGBTQIIA+ communities, is now a living sacrifice of a society that is tailored to support and value science and profit on the backs of marginalized communities (Butler, 2022). The science of numbers was always presented to us in ways that prepared us to lose a number of people so that the economy could be maintained (Ma et al., 2023). Vaccination against the pandemic became an instrument of entrenching inequalities across the globe. This is manifested through unequal access to COVID-19 vaccines. Some countries had to hoard vaccines from other African countries, creating an artificial shortage.

It appears that the pandemic is over for some, while others must come to terms with its aftermath. In fact, studies have shown that while the COVID-19 pandemic seems to be coming to an end for some, for others, it is the start of dealing with the mental health pandemic as an aftermath of the COVID-19 pandemic (Parrish, 2020). Some of these communities, which have historically been marginalized continue to suffer from the effects of the pandemic. Issues of mental health and addiction have become prevalent and endemic as such among the marginalized communities. It is upon us to start imagining new ways of curbing future pandemics beyond quantification of pandemic if ever we want to live a just and ethical life (Hanna et al., 2023). Presently, the World Health Organization has identified that COVID-19 will be with us for a long time, so we must prepare to embrace a world of pandemics (WHO, 2022). This comes at a point where already marginalized communities must continue working toward coming out of COVID-19, and this sets another form of inequalities that will set some communities way behind others in terms of the overall world health index. Such indexing of health needs to remember the histories of colonialism that set the current inequalities experienced by those left on the edges of the world. For such inequalities to be ameliorated in ethical ways, we must interrogate quantitative pandemic responses in ways that are complex, intersectional, and that allow us to remember unique traumatic histories, values, and realities of marginalized communities.

Literature Gap

While all these studies have highlighted the issue of COVID-19 and its aftermath, it is equally important to note that issues of community capacity building, community knowledge mobilization, and social actions have not received enough focus. The studies, though qualitative, need to be grounded in the capacities of communities to build community self-determination in the age of pandemics. The "how" of building community resilience must be grounded in people's active participation in the methodologies of curbing the spread of yet-to-come pandemics. These studies have expressed the need for reimagining policy issues in the age of pandemics and yet remain driven by a heteronormative methodology that is top-down and elitist. The studies have not expressed in explicit terms some of the proposals for dealing with future pandemics for which the World health Organization is preparing us. This project plans to embrace the strengths of marginalized communities to chart the ways toward engaging with the effects of COVID-19 toward redressing policy issues in ways that are grounded in communities' histories, values, and everyday realities. This project seeks to employ conferences and seminars as platforms for social actions, capacity building, and knowledge mobilization. So far, School of Social Work at Algoma University has been running brown bag seminars, and anti-racism workshops with community organizations along Sault Ste. Marie to address issues of mental health and addiction and its connection to other social justice issues, which culminated in a widely attended International Conference on Mental

Health and Addiction, held from April 27 to 28, 2023, at Algoma University, Brampton campus. We plan to employ the same strategies to continue building awareness on mental health and addiction during the COVID-19 pandemic and other future pandemics.

It is noteworthy that minimal research has been done on the impact of COVID-19 on community health and addiction in Canada. A plethora of studies on the effect of COVID-19 and its effect on community mental health and addiction have mostly come from the United States of America, and, therefore, a Canadian-based research project is required to tell the stories of how marginalized communities in Canada navigated the effects of COVID-19 on their mental health and addiction. We plan to employ monthly brown bag seminars, workshops, and international conferences as a platform for the communities to narrate their stories of their resilience and agency in dealing with the COVID-19 pandemic and its effects on their mental health. We are in the process of publishing a book from the 2023 International Conference on Mental Health and Addictions, and we plan to do the same in ways that help build community capacities through knowledge mobilization for social awareness/preparedness in dealing with future pandemics.

Theoretical Frameworks

This project was preceded by our ongoing brown bag seminars, community workshops, and the International Conference on Mental Health and Addiction held from 27 to 28 April 2023, in Brampton. In that social engagement, community members and scholars were invited, and a key aspect of focus was to employ an intersectional perspective/approach (Collins & Bilge, 2020; Collins et al., 2021) toward imagining community mental health and addiction. This means that mental health and addiction are not singular social issues, but rather tie with other social metrics to complicate social life in ways that are beyond the quantitative system of measurement that have, over time, been employed in curbing the spread of the COVID-19 pandemic (Ma et al., 2023). An intersectional perspective on any future pandemic will have to be ethical and bring on board marginalized communities as a quintessential ethical demand in the fight against pandemics. This will mean employing a narrative perspective to allow marginalized communities to tell their stories in terms of how they navigate the pandemic. Such expression of their realities will help build knowledge centres that can help rethink the science of pandemics in ways that are human and relational. This, in essence, will help in community knowledge mobilization to complicate scientific models of curbing community spread. An intersectional perspective will allow the qualification of people's histories, values, and realities in ways that help look at quantification of the pandemics in ways that connected communities. This is an aspect of community capacity building that helps western science to come together in respectful relationships with communities that continue to face pandemics in disproportionate ways. An intersectional model looks at mental health from a community perspective, wherein everyone partakes in the construction of new ways of living with pandemics. From a social justice perspective, intersectional approaches bear witness to the kind of pain and trauma, and how it may be compounded by prevailing pandemics. Such an approach looks at social issues such as mental health and addiction as not exclusive and singular but, instead, as intersected with race. Gender, sexual orientation, disability, and other social markers. To imagine mental health and addiction from a universal indexing provides an avenue for epistemological imperialism and neoliberalism to determine which life gets to be lost and which gets to live (Butler, 2021).

Conclusion

The effect of the COVID-19 pandemic on community mental health and addiction is an area of concern. COVID-19 has affected diverse communities' mental health and addiction in various ways. Prevailing scholarship paints a grim picture of the impact of COVID-19 on marginalized communities. While the World Health Organization has marked the pandemic as not a serious threat, and subsequently called all countries to prepare for a world of pandemic; it is prudent for us, community members, government, and all stakeholders to employ an intersectional approach toward future pandemics. Western science, while having helped flatten the curve, has shown a need to bring on board other ways of dealing with future pandemics. This will mean building community capacities through social awareness/preparedness as well as knowledge mobilization.

References

Azevedo, K. J., Kalvesmaki, A. F., Riendeau, R. P., Sweet, P. A., & Holmes, S. M. (2022). Leveraging anthropological expertise to respond to the COVID-19 global mental health syndemic. *American Anthropologist, 124*(3), 622–627. https://doi.org/10.1111/aman.13747

Butler, J. (2022). *What world is this?: A pandemic phenomenology*. Columbia University Press.

Butler, J. (2021). The force of nonviolence: An ethico-political bind (Paperback edition.). Verso.

Chang, H.-Y., Tang, W., Hatef, E., Kitchen, C., Weiner, J. P., & Kharrazi, H. (2021). Differential impact of mitigation policies and socioeconomic status on COVID-19 prevalence and social distancing in the United States. *BMC Public Health, 21*. https://doi.org/10.1186/s12889-021-11149-1

Collins, P. H., & Bilge, S. (2020). *Intersectionality* (2nd ed.). Polity Press.

Collins, P. H., da Silva, E. C. G., Ergun, E., Furseth, I., Bond, K. D., & Martínez-Palacios, J. (2021). Intersectionality as critical social theory: Intersectionality as critical social theory, Patricia Hill Collins, Duke University Press, 2019. *Contemporary Political Theory, 20*(3), 690–725. https://doi.org/10.1057/s41296-021-00490-0

García-Vivar, C., Rodríguez-Matesanz, I., San Martín-Rodríguez, L., Soto-Ruiz, N., Ferraz-Torres, M., & Escalada-Hernández, P. (2023). Analysis of mental health effects among nurses working during the COVID-19 pandemic: A systematic review. *Journal of Psychiatric and Mental Health Nursing, 30*(3), 326–340. https://doi.org/10.1111/jpm.12880

Gaynor, T. S., & Wilson, M. E. (2020). Social vulnerability and equity: The disproportionate impact of COVID-19. *Public Administration Review, 80*(5), 832–838. https://doi.org/10.1111/puar.13264

Hanna, E., Martin, G., Campbell, A., Connolly, P., & Fearon, K. (2023). The impacts and implications of the community face mask use during the Covid-19 pandemic: A qualitative narrative interview study. *Health Expectations: An International Journal of Public Participation in Health Care and Health Policy, 26*(3), 1349–1357. https://doi.org/10.1111/hex.13752

Hardi, F. A., Goetschius, L. G., McLoyd, V., Lopez-Duran, N. L., Mitchell, C., Hyde, L. W., Beltz, A. M., & Monk, C. S. (2023). Adolescent functional network connectivity prospectively predicts adult anxiety symptoms related to perceived COVID-19 economic adversity. *Journal of Child Psychology and Psychiatry, 64*(6), 918–929. https://doi.org/10.1111/jcpp.13749

Javed, B., Sarwer, A., Soto, E. B., & Mashwani, Z. (2020). The coronavirus (COVID-19) pandemic's impact on mental health. *The International Journal of Health Planning and Management, 35*(5), 993–996. https://doi.org/10.1002/hpm.3008

Kuki, K., Yamaguchi, Y., Makinodan, M., Honda, M., Ueda, J., Okazaki, K., Okamura, K., Kimoto, S., & Kishimoto, T. (2021). Effects of contact with COVID-19 patients on the mental health of workers in a psychiatric hospital. *Psychiatry and Clinical Neurosciences, 75*(2), 67–69. https://doi.org/10.1111/pcn.13179

Ma, H., Chan, A. K., Baral, S. D., Fahim, C., Straus, S., Sander, B., & Mishra, S. (2023). Which curve are we flattening? The disproportionate impact of COVID-19 among economically marginalized communities in Ontario, Canada, was unchanged from wild-type to omicron. Open Forum. *Infectious Diseases, 10*(1), ofac690. https://doi.org/10.1093/ofid/ofac690

Mercado, M., Wachter, K., Schuster, R. C., Mathis, C. M., Johnson, E., Davis, O. I., & Johnson-Agbakwu, C. E. (2022). A cross-sectional analysis of factors associated with stress, burnout and turnover intention among healthcare workers during the COVID-19 pandemic in the United States. *Health & Social Care in the Community, 30*(5), e2690–e2701. https://doi.org/10.1111/hsc.13712

Parrish, E. (2020). The next pandemic: COVID-19 mental health pandemic. *Perspectives in Psychiatric Care, 56*(3), 485–485. https://doi.org/10.1111/ppc.12571

Smallwood, N., & Willis, K. (2021). Mental health among healthcare workers during the COVID-19 pandemic. *Respirology, 26*(11), 1016–1017. https://doi.org/10.1111/resp.14143

Smith, G. D., Bradbury-Jones, C., Gelling, L., Neville, S., Pandian, V., Salamonson, Y., & Hayter, M. (2022). Addressing the mental health of nurses during the COVID-19 pandemic: Time for support. *Journal of Clinical Nursing, 31*(19–20), e32–e33. https://doi.org/10.1111/jocn.16383

Tamagawa, M. (2023). *The Japanese LGBTQ+ community in the world: The COVID-19 pandemic, challenges, and prospects for the future*. Routledge, Taylor & Francis Group.

Zhai, W., Fu, X., Liu, M., & Peng, Z.-R. (2023). The impact of ethnic segregation on neighbourhood-level social distancing in the United States amid the early outbreak of COVID-19. *Urban Studies, 60*(8), 1403–1426. https://doi.org/10.1177/00420980211050183

WHO. (2022). *Imagining the future of pandemics and epidemics: A 2022 perspective.* file:///C:/Users/nyaga/Downloads/9789240052093-eng.pdf.

Chapter 22
Land Back, Indigenous Constitutionalism, and the Canadian Disability Movement

Walter Wai Tak Chan

Abstract This chapter explores the need for Indigenous leadership in the Canadian disability movement. I posit that the low level of interest among Indigenous leaders for this movement is because of differing belief systems on health and disability between settlers and Indigenous people and the movement's tacit presumption of settler privilege. It is also noted that Indigeneity is a highly intersectional identity, and there are many shared practices between Indigenous and non-Indigenous communities regarding beliefs on medicine, healing, and ways to a good life. I review the gray literature of 13 Indigenous and Canadian disability organizations and see whether the content aligns or differs from our thesis. The nine Indigenous organizations contained some consistent themes regarding the further marginalization of Indigenous folks with disabilities compared with non-Indigenous disabled people. Only one out of the four Canadian disability organizations I studied provided content on Indigenous leadership—namely, treaty and sui generis rights, Indigenous concepts of physical and spiritual difference and exceptionalities, and Indigenous views of intersectionality. The three disability organizations focused on rights based on Canadian parliamentary and civil law procedure. The implications of Indigenous leadership for the disability movement and that movement's possible role in the practice of Land Back—the restoration of Indigenous rights, laws, and relations to earth, water, air, and the plant and animal kingdoms—are explored at the end of the chapter. To start, I hope the disability movement can start to engage with Indigenous ideas and worldviews, facilitating a better, more fruitful conversation between the settler-dominated movement and Indigenous knowledge holders and community members. Paraphrasing Anishinaabe lawyer John Borrows, a better conversation can fill in the gaps between disability rights and Indigenous notions of leadership and inclusion. I conclude the disability movement should seek constitutional relationships with Indigenous polities and legal systems to be both anticolonial and for facilitating greater freedom and resiliency in the movement itself. Also, there is a

W. W. T. Chan (✉)
School of Social Work, Algoma University, Sault Ste. Marie, ON, Canada
e-mail: walter.chan@algomau.ca

D. Nyaga, M. Zangeneh (eds.), *Critical Ethics on Mental Health and Madness*, Advances in Mental Health and Addiction,
https://doi.org/10.1007/978-3-032-10166-2_22

need to clearly define Indigenous disability and quantify more precisely how many Indigenous people experience disability.

Keywords Indigenous · Disability · Leadership · Gray literature · Anticolonization · Land Back

Introduction

The Canadian disability movement arose in the second half of the twentieth century, advocating for the rights of Canadians with disabilities. Disability activists advocate for disability rights in self-care, public services, housing, employment, transportation, education, and so on, as well as building a sense of disability pride and identity (Galer, 2015). This movement has also been criticized as being dominated by White middle-class men (and increasingly White women) with disabilities and narrowly focused on Euro-American worldviews (Chan, 2019; Bell, 2010; Galloway, 2001/2012). Although this Canadian movement is located on mostly unceded Indigenous land, Turtle Island (and land ceded under duress), Indigenous leaders seem to demonstrate modest interest in it—with some important exceptions (Atherton, 2009). These included British Columbia Aboriginal Network on Disability (2017), which actively advocates at the local, national, and international levels for the rights of Indigenous people with disabilities and uplifts Indigenous perspectives on disability. They have also been key players in shaping the recent federal disability law. Doreen Demas (2010), a visually impaired Dakota woman who has since made her journey into the spirit world, was a vocal, strategic, and determined advocate for Indigenous disability rights and women's rights. Labrador Inuit women have resisted corporate and governmental resource extraction projects, which threaten Indigenous ways of life as well as the lives of women with disabilities (Stienstra, 2015). Some Labrador Indigenous individuals have resisted the label of disability but search for ways to include people with disabilities into the circle (Stienstra et al., 2018). Otherwise, this lower interest level is remarkable given the Turtle Island Indigenous overrepresentation in the prevalence of mental health problems, traumatic brain injury, diabetes, HIV/AIDS, and musculoskeletal disorders compared to non-Indigenous Canadians (Alexander, 2008; de Leeuw et al., 2018; Kirmayer, 2007).

This chapter explores why Indigenous leadership is vitally needed in the Canadian disability movement. Namely, such leadership includes how treaty and sui generis (inherent, unique) rights affect disability rights, Indigenous concepts of physical and spiritual difference and exceptionalities, and Indigenous views of intersectionality. There is little academic literature, other than Atherton (2009) on commonalities between Indigenous organizations and disability rights advocacy, Redikopp (2021) on Mad studies supporting hidden and emerging forms of White supremacy, Senier and Barker (2013) on disability themes in contemporary Indigenous stories, and Tam (2013) on psychiatric survivor usurpation of Indigenous knowledges. I posit the low interest level is because of divergent worldviews regarding disability and the movement's unstated presumptions of White settler privilege—that ethnic minorities and Indigenous communities shall come to this disability movement to be educated on their rights, premised on a Euro-American worldview. In our review of gray literature, Indigenous organizations described the multifaceted ways in which Indigenous persons with disabilities suffer greater disadvantage compared with non-Indigenous people with disabilities. In contrast, only one out of the four Canadian disability organizations provided significant Indigenous content (e.g., Indigenous concepts of physical and spiritual difference, Indigenous intersectionality).

By Indigenous people, I refer to descendants of the earliest known inhabitants of a territory, who have been displaced or unethically controlled by a now-dominant settler group (Chan, 2025). The Canadian Encyclopedia (2024) stated, "Inuit and First Nations history extends well before the arrival of Europeans in Canada, while Métis emerged as a distinct culture after intermarriage between European settlers and First Nations people."

I discuss Indigeneity as a highly intersectional identity, with many shared practices between Indigenous and non-Indigenous communities regarding beliefs on medicine, healing, and ways to a good life. Within Indigenous communities, there are centers and margins, as well, and an Indigenous individual with disabilities may move from center to margin in the Indigenous world, or they may move from margin to center in the settler world (Olsen, 2018). Such journeys are influenced by various degrees of privilege and oppression for that person. At the same time, no one is only Indigenous. There are gendered, "raced," and classed individuals, among other identities, simultaneously. Furthermore, I will discuss Indigenous intersectionality as being more complicated because colonial forces—namely, the Christian religion—specifically feared certain aspects of Indigenous personhood: sexuality, Queerness, being Two Spirit, and femininity (McNeil-Seymour, 2018). Now, silenced histories and identities are rekindling and resurging (Fiola, 2023).

The implications of Indigenous leadership for the disability movement and that movement's possible role in the practice of Land Back—the restoration of Indigenous relations to earth, water, air, and the plant and animal kingdoms—are explored at the end of the chapter (Yellowhead Institute, 2019). I conclude the disability movement should seek constitutional relationships with Indigenous polities and legal systems to be both anticolonial and for facilitating greater freedom and resiliency in the movement itself (Borrows, 2016, 2019). That is, I propose that disability organizations ought to seek out and conclude formal agreements, to be partially regulated by Indigenous polity, such as band councils, hereditary leaders, matriarchal structures, and regional organizations, as well as by international human rights law.

It comes to mind that lateral violence, quite common in both settler and Indigenous communities, may mar these agreements. Lateral violence is violence directed at one's peers. It is a realistic caution. Guided by the work of Anishinaabe lawyer John Borrows (2016), I propose these agreements be rooted in Indigenous legal orders and philosophical teachings appropriate to the geographic location and people involved to protect the proceedings from the temptations of lateral violence; Anishinaabe seven grandfather/grandmother teachings perhaps for an agreement in Winnipeg, or Wahkohtowin and the four nêhiyaw/Ininiw principles regarding another Winnipeg organization. I discuss further in the conclusion.

The chapter starts with a note on the author's social location, then a summary of the history of the Canadian disability movement. I speak about how colonialism produces Indigenous disability, followed by Indigenous and settler perspectives on disability, including the medical, social, and postmodern models. I describe a secondary data analysis of the gray literature of 13 Indigenous and Canadian disability organizations. I conclude the chapter by discussing Land Back and Indigenous constitutionalism vis-à-vis the disability movement, in terms of Indigenous oversight and permit systems, and end with a reflection on healing outbreaks of lateral violence which threaten new agreements and practices.

Positionality

The primary author is Walter Wai Tak Chan, born in Hong Kong and a settler living in Manitoba, Canada, Treaty One territory for the majority of his life. I focused on the topic of Indigenous leadership after working in Canadian disability organizations. I have noticed their predominant Whiteness and Euro-American worldviews, while many Indigenous people continued to access these organizations. Treaty One territory and Manitoba are located on the ancestral lands of the Anishinaabeg, Anishininewuk, Dakota Oyate, Denesuline, and Nehethowuk Nations. It is also the Homeland of the Red River Métis. Treaty One is an agreement regarding the sharing of land and resources, established on August 3, 1871, between the British Crown and the Anishinaabe and Mushkego Ininiw nations (Krasowski, 2019). I am a Cantonese man with a disability and a user of psychiatric services.

While writing this chapter, I have been humbled in recognizing there is so much about the topic I do not know. I acknowledge the immense help in this work graciously gifted to me from Manitoba Indigenous communities and individuals, in particular: Donna Bear Glover, Daly de Gagne, Don Cardinal, Thunderbird House, Wii Chiiwaakanak, Roger Roulette, Dawnis Kennedy, Darryl Sinclair, and Derek Sinclair.

A Brief Summary on the History of the Canadian Disability Movement

I start with a brief history of the Canadian disability movement. The movement emerged in the 1960s as people with disabilities (with physical impairments, mental illness) were released from state institutions (Chabasinski, 2012). Disabled people gained a greater capacity to share experiences and start their own organizations (Chabasinski; Enns & Neufeldt, 2003). Also, parents of Canadians with disabilities advocated for community services for their family, building parent-led organizations focusing on direct services (Chan, 2019; Neufeldt, 2003). These two wings, deinstitutionalized people with disabilities and the parents and relatives of those with disabilities, formed this nascent movement (Chan, 2025; Neufeldt). A mixture of both incremental reformism and radical thought, it often sought to cooperate with the dominant Canadian governmental and health care regime.

The deinstitutionalization of people with disabilities—although please note only a small minority of people with disabilities were ever institutionalized on a long-term basis, even during the height of institutionalization—coincided with the subsequent reinstitutionalization through processes of child welfare surveillance and incarceration through the criminalization of mental health problems, addictions, and homelessness. For Indigenous individuals, the intensity of child welfare and criminal justice intervention, even when no crimes have been committed, defined the 1960s and 1970s for their communities. It was known as the 1960s Scoop, and it tore apart families. The emerging Canadian disability movement, however, paid very little attention to the situation of their Indigenous brothers and sisters.

The 1960s were politically and culturally tumultuous. In the neighboring United States, powerful movements—anti-war, Black civil rights, feminism, Indigenous resurgence, queer liberation, and environmentalism—inspired and provided knowledge to Canadian social movements (Chan, 2019; Neufeldt, 2003; Pelka, 2012; Schweik, 2011; Staggenborg, 2012). The Canadian disability movement advocated for individual human rights, to have options and make decisions, for people with disabilities (Lord, 2010). In both countries, it is accepted that capitalism is a sufficiently good system for catalyzing human freedom and prosperity. It is believed that significant positive changes for people with disabilities can happen within the existing economic structures (e.g., Canada as a colonialist, natural resource extraction economy) (Prince, 2012). The 1960s also saw Indigenous leaders rise to combat Prime Minister Pierre Trudeau's assimilationist White Paper on so-called Indian policy and craft a pan-tribal movement for Indigenous rights (Bradburn, 2023). By the late 1970s and 1980s, Canadian government policy began to retrench and shrink the welfare state, conforming to a shift from a liberal to a neoliberal ideology (Prince, 2009, 2012). The shrinking or elimination of social programs and disability benefits—which reached an apex in the Nineties with the Chretien government—diminished the life conditions of both non-Indigenous and Indigenous individuals with disabilities.

There have been few working relationships between Indigenous communities and the Canadian disability movement (Atherton, 2009; Stienstra et al., 2018), although important exceptions exist (British Columbia Aboriginal Network on Disability, 2017; Demas, 2010; Hockman, 2010). Partly, it is the case that the White supremacist colonialist capitalist patriarchy—to employ bell Hooks (1981) term—has produced an Othering and hatred of Indigenous peoples, with the extreme marginalization ("triple jeopardy" as Demas called it) of Indigenous women with disabilities. Materially, unremitting settler wealth and the socioeconomic disparity between Indigenous communities and settler communities—again, due to colonial processes of theft, dispossession, and alienation—is another plausible root cause of a lack of working relationships (Yellowhead Institute, 2019). I will discuss these reasons in this chapter.

The Colonial Production of Disability

The low level of Indigenous interest in the Canadian disability movement contrasts with Indigenous overrepresentation in mental health problems, diabetes, HIV AIDS, tuberculosis, and musculoskeletal disorders. The high rate of Indigenous disablement results from the arguably genocidal Canadian social policy immediately post-Confederation (Daschuk, 2013; Kirmayer, 2007). Quinlan (2018) identified four current factors that increase the rates of disability for Indigenous people:

1. a lack of access to quality health care, especially mental health services
2. a high prevalence of chronic illnesses such as diabetes, and a high prevalence of infectious diseases such as HIV and TB
3. alcoholism, FASD, which are due to intergenerational trauma
4. environmental, political, and economic factors such as poverty, malnutrition, poor housing, climate change, patriarchal colonial structures, and the systemic disempowerment of Indigenous women and girls (p. 5) (also, see Brian Sinclair Working Group 2017; Edwards, 2014)

The latter factor can be considered as constituting the conditions for the genocide of Indigenous peoples, most acutely directed against Indigenous women and gender-diverse people (National Inquiry into Missing and Murdered Indigenous Women and Girls or NIMMIWG, 2019).

The astute reader may say Canadians in general also suffer from these four factors. For instance, many Canadians lack access to quality healthcare. From an intersectional view, the greater the marginalization of the individual or community, it is likely the more intense these four factors become in one's life. However, due to Indigenous communities being the original titleholders to Canadian land, and due to cultural and economic advantages immigrants to Canada enjoy, forming a settler class, the latter group inherits substantive advantages despite concurrent racism, misogyny, and class oppression. The Canadian state seems predicated on erasing Indigenous rights; indeed, a traditional interpretation of Crown sovereignty precludes Indigenous rights because those rights threaten the legal operating assumptions of terra nullius (empty land) and the Doctrine of Discovery (pagan lands are fit for conquest by European Christians) (Yellowhead Institute, 2019). Thus, structurally, Canada seems to continue to relentlessly attack Indigenous nations overtly or covertly to preserve its own majesty and unquestioned sovereignty, to accomplish the alienation of Indigenous communities from their own customary laws and ways of order (Yellowhead Institute). Such unyielding Crown hegemony is not the only path available for Canada. I shall discuss more reasonable and more gentle ways in the conclusion. However, these attacks on Indigenous communities produce greater levels of disablement, because it seems to be an ongoing policy that the Canadian state has chosen.

Indigenous Perspectives on Disability

Senier (2013) quoted Mohegan medicine woman Tantaquidgeon Zobel's claim that "traditionally, disability was not seen as such" (213). Senier suggested that, for some Indigenous communities, disabled people were not marginalized. She specified that Mohegan cultural practices allowed disability to be seen as a matter-of-fact phenomenon, even as a valued capacity.

Tallbear (2000) spoke of time and differing cultural lenses altering what one would interpret when looking at the past. It would be unrealistic to judge an Indigenous practice existing 200 years ago using contemporary ideas (Chan, 2025). Thus, appraisal of Indigenous concepts of disability must be specific to a location, time, and people, refraining from overgeneralizing (Chan, 2025). Several paths of interpretation emerge. One path is rejecting the "frozen pizza theory." This is a perspective in which Indigenous people are interpreted to cease being Indigenous the moment they heat up and sink their teeth into a pizza slice, because any exposure to modern, industrial society erases their Indigeneity. This "theory" stems from a misunderstanding, racist in nature, in which Indigenous communities are interpreted to be unchanging in culture, with technology static and fossilized. It illustrates a prejudice that interprets an Indigeneity so fragile that any encounter with industrial modernity shatters it. From the anthropological record and Indigenous knowledges, one might see Indigenous concepts of disability (or any Indigenous concept for that matter) change over time and over geographic distances (Borrows, 2016). I believe one ought to avoid predetermining certain essential traits Indigenous individuals with disabilities possess or that Indigenous communities must contain certain positive values toward people with disabilities. Indeed, John Borrows (p. 3) suggested there is no timeless, essential, categorical, or fundamental characteristic to being Indigenous, as Indigeneity is context-sensitive.

However, suggestions of certain tendencies and fulsome engagements within specific contexts are plausible. Roberta Oshkabewisens, Anishinaabe ikwe and knowledge keeper, suggested perhaps past generations saw disability as a gift (Disabled Women's Network of Canada, 2020). It is something all people may eventually have, and some do not have. It opens up many doors to see what we cannot usually see, to understand ourselves and others different from us. Sterling-Collins of the Nlha'kapmux Nation (2009), a mother of a child with autism, seemed to view Indigenous disability holistically. Her medicine wheel teachings perceive Indigenous children with disabilities as spirit beings on a journey first and foremost (Chan, 2025). They enable appreciating the emotional, intellectual, and spiritual aspects of the disability experience. Although she considered biomedicine and physical rehabilitation important, her medicine wheel teachings enabled her to remain grounded and present. She similarly suggested persons with disabilities can see what many others cannot or will not see—a unique vantage point regarding family life, dialoguing with helpers, and a doorway to the spirit world (Chan, 2025; Sterling-Collins).

Settler Perspectives on Disability

In contrast, the settler-oriented disability movement in Canada typically conceives of people with disabilities as urban dwellers. It pays little attention to the ecological interrelationships between humans, animals, land, and water (Chan, 2025; Ray & Sibara, 2018). There are, of course, regional and local relationships within disability organizations, centered on human institutions, as there would be for any group of people (Chan, 2019). Typically, many persons with disabilities flock to the city, as it is where the jobs and services are, as well as for the specialized medical services in large hospitals. Disability leaders tend to see the city as a site of many contradictions: "comforts and constraints, opportunities and oppressions" (Prince, 2008). Many Indigenous individuals, although perhaps with some agreement as well on the need for urban amenities, might favor natural ecological relationships and reciprocity. These take land, water, and air seriously, as beloved relatives, with a keen understanding that the colonial severance from the ancestral Indigenous hunting and farming lands caused starvation and ill health (Adelson, 2000; Carter, 1990). Indigenous individuals often have complex and conflicting relationships with city life. Economic and cultural opportunities beckon in a highly concentrated, multicultural setting, as well as medical services, with significant flows of capital and people back and forth between First Nations and big cities (Borrows, 2016, 2019). However, they may experience a sense of unease and a lack of belonging difficult to express, often triggered by overt episodes of racism in the city and the underlying structural discrimination (D. Glover, personal communication, April 2012; Martin & Walia, 2019; Thomas-Muller, 2021).

The disability movement typically assumes a liberal politics of citizen participation, with citizenship presumed by a history of immigration to Canada (Prince, 2012). Indigenous land title and sui generis rights, as collective rights, favored by substantial numbers of Indigenous people, make the idea of subsuming one's political status to be another minority group—initiated by newcomers no less, a disability minority—within the liberal nation-state a somewhat unattractive prospect

(Borrows, 2016; Razack, 2015). Nonetheless, for many Indigenous individuals, human rights and minority politics remain important (NIMMIWG, 2019).

Canadian settler perspectives on disability typically fall into three main ideas: the medical model, the social model, and the postmodern perspectives (Withers, 2012). All three perspectives are highly influential. All three are quite anthropocentric, eschewing natural ecological relationships. I discuss them here.

The Medical Model of Disability

The medical model defines the cause of disability as organic dysfunction in human tissue and organ systems. The model typically deems cultural representations of the body as being irrelevant to the disability experience. The model suggests that the role for non-health professionals regarding disability is sympathy and kindness, and for health professionals, curing the dysfunction causing the disability. If a cure is not possible, the health professional is to bring the person as close to normal functioning as possible. In assuming generalship of the health care system and leading the fight against disease, allopathic medicine produces in its own image a host of paramedical professions, including physical therapy, occupational therapy, speech language pathology, audiology, laboratory technology, and so on. The medical model is the worldview underlying Canada's comprehensive health care system, funded in the billions of dollars, and carrying an altruistic and benevolent aura in popular discourse. The disability movement critiques the medical model as being overly focused on disease processes, dismissive of perspectives of disabled people themselves, objectifying disabled people as an object of study and a road to the professional's career advancement, and practicing discrimination, wherein health professionals are held to be actively able-bodied, whereas disabled people are passive, weak, and in need of remediation (Zola, 1972).

Indigenous experiences of the medical model are similar but hold greater complexity because historically, medical discourse was employed as a justification for conquest. Concern about Indigenous health prompted the Canadian government in the late nineteenth century to intervene in northern and rural regions by modernizing health care, bringing in physicians and nurses, and building hospitals and nursing stations. Modernization of health care, although with intrinsic benefits, also damaged Indigenous economic and cultural capacity due to racist discourse categorizing Indigenous people a priori as ill, weak, and disabled (McCallum & Perry, 2018).

Prior to the late nineteenth century, popular discourse had, on the contrary, posited that Indigenous people were uniquely robust and hardy (MacDowell, 2012). After Confederation, government officials perceived Indigenous people to be a poor fit for a rapidly modernizing industrial society (Daschuk, 2013; Ray, 2011). Officials thought that medical intervention would forestall Indigenous groups from decline and disappearance, by bringing in modern hygiene, housing, and diet, with modern defined in English and American cultural norms and values (Mosby, 2013).

Indigenous disability, viewed through a medical model, can be remediated or cured, given advances in medical science, but a racist discourse added that a deeper disability was located within Indigenous culture and customs, so these became targets of medical intervention to modernize beliefs and eliminate traditional practices. McCallum and Perry (2018) stated that the mission of Canadian medical professionals toward Indigenous groups is that of the so-called civilizing mission, where white professionals would minister to Indigenous patients and simultaneously reinforce the superiority of English-American knowledge and culture.

The Social Model of Disability

A group of English disabled people conceptualized the social model of disability 50 years ago (Shakespeare, 2010). This group was determined to secure human rights and enact legislative reforms for people with disabilities. In the social model, disability is seen as an oppression, something ***added on top*** of impairment. Impairment in this view is the term given to a bodily dysfunction caused by a biological process, whereas disability is the process of exclusion and discrimination against people with impairments, a social phenomenon caused by an unjust society (Shakespeare). For example, a person using a wheelchair due to a spinal cord injury—the impairment—is unable to take courses at a university because the classrooms and washrooms do not accommodate wheelchairs—this is the disability. Disability here is a social construct, not an individual construct. The social model suggests that people with disabilities—that is, people with impairments—should organize, advocate for a reallocation of power so that disabled people may move closer to an equitable position in political and social life.

The social model is at the core of Canada's disability movement. The movement's founding organizations include the Council of Canadians with Disabilities and Independent Living Canada (Neufeldt, 2003). Activist narratives speak of the joy of organizing and working together, producing a movement of and for people with disabilities (Ross, 2012). A shared identity as disabled people who have survived oppression and discrimination unites the movement, and there is an emphasis on concrete, pragmatic steps to bring about incremental gains in law and government policy (Lord, 2010; Prince, 2009). I, too, worked within the disability movement informed by this social model, and I, too, have felt the joy and belonging in that shared identity and activist community.

Indigenous communities currently carry a disproportionate burden of both impairment and disability, but there seems to be little Indigenous leadership in the social model-informed disability movement (Kirmayer, 2007; Lord, 2010; McCallum & Perry, 2018). Communication between Indigenous communities and movement organizations is often minimal, at times nonexistent (Atherton, 2009). The Council of Canadians with Disabilities (2013) annual report barely mentioned Indigenous issues. Independent Living Canada's (2015) flagship vision and mission document placed Indigenous issues on the sidelines of disability policy, not the center.

Furthermore, the social model-based disability movement often inappropriately conflates the disability experience with the colonial one (Sherry, 2010). For example, some disability activists opine that mainstream society is an apartheid regime segregating people with disabilities (Howlround, 2017). Psychiatric survivors may claim that physicians colonize their bodies with psychiatric drugs (Miller, 2018). Such a discourse, I believe, reinforces settler privilege while marginalizing, even belittling, Indigenous knowledge (Tam, 2013).

Postmodern Perspectives on Disability

Postmodern perspectives on disability emerged out of European poststructuralist thought after the Second World War, with a strong influence from the nineteenth-century philosopher Nietzsche (Lyon, 2005). Postmodernity seems to oppose unitary narratives and comprehensive explanations, supposing knowledge to be unstable, provisional, and local. Postmodernity can also seem to banish disability because it seeks to destabilize all categories and unitary identities, including disability (Davis, 2002/2010). It turns the critical eye of modernity back on itself and finds what it sees inadequate (Lyon). LeFrancois (2013), for example, employed a poststructuralist critique of Canadian child welfare, an institution she felt ensnared Indigenous children and families into a settler psi complex, a prison without physical walls.

Postmodern perspectives offer an incisive intellectual critique of modernity (Tremain, 2015), but they have also exoticized and misunderstood Indigenous communities (for example, Deleuze & Guattari, 1980). Postmodernity encourages a fluid subjectivity, embracing local perspectives but simultaneously transcending the earthy, rooted, and local. It fractures categories and borders, positing that subjectivities may inhabit spaces interstitially. Disembodied subjectivity, a fluid, free-flowing transnationalism—such ideas may also be interpreted as an imperial fantasy. One would traverse borders and cultures at will, and those cultures are rendered ready for the taking (Tam, 2013).

Tam (2013) identified a peculiar psychiatric survivor trend to misappropriate and fetishize Indigenous knowledge. In American activists Jacks McNamara and Sasha DuBrul's zine, *Navigating the Space between Brilliance and Madness*, they claimed that the Hopi people's language discards linear concepts of time and space. They claim congruence with their own madness experiences, medically named as bipolar disorder (McNamara & DuBrul, 2006). The zine related mental illness to shamanism, suggesting people with mental illness are at root untutored, untrained shamans. Without reciprocal, respectful relationships with Hopi communities or a recognition that Indigenous healing practices require lengthy, rigorous training, such narratives demonstrated a serious misunderstanding and sense of conceit. They disregarded

Indigenous cultural protocols for learning and teaching, although McNamara and DuBrul (2006) seemed quite conversant with postmodern protocols.

I am not suggesting people should not use postmodern perspectives. Only, that these perspectives need to be grounded in humility. Senier (2017) cautioned that Indigenous knowledge is not a free-floating commodity, ready to be snatched by settlers, but systems intertwined with Indigenous nationhood and self-determination. Casually lifting and misrepresenting Indigenous knowledge by some psychiatric survivor groups is, I believe, an affront to dignity and a power grab.

Secondary Data Analysis of the Reports in Indigenous and Canadian Disability Organizations

To ascertain how disability movement organizations and Indigenous organizations think about Indigenous disability, I analyzed the content of 22 documents and reports from 13 Indigenous and Canadian disability organizations regarding Indigenous disability issues and policies. These reports were made available on each organization's website. They are considered gray literature.

Method

I looked for the most recent reports, analyzing the material for themes relating to Indigenous disability issues and leadership. I organized the findings into three groups: findings that demonstrate Indigenous marginalization and/or settler privilege; those that do not support my argument; and unique, unexpected findings. (My argument is that settler privilege discourages Indigenous leadership in the disability movement.) To be accountable to Indigenous community needs and Indigenous axiology(s), I asked for feedback on the findings with a number of Indigenous knowledge keepers. Given the rather narrow nature of the research topic, I carried out the process rather informally, through everyday conversation, rather than within formal appointments or sacred ceremonies. Daly de Gagne listened to me speak about the project and the secondary data analysis over an extended period, in six years of conversation. I also consulted the writings of my classmate and colleague G. Rowe (2018, 2020, 2022) (Fox Lake Cree Nation), a writer on Indigenous evaluation, for this project. Unfortunately, several other requests for assistance were unsuccessful.

Organizations Chosen

I chose the organizations by only selecting those providing documents and reports on their website. National organizations included the Council of Canadians with Disabilities, Disabled Women's Network Canada, Independent Living Canada, the National Network for Mental Health, the Assembly of First Nations (AFN), the National Inquiry into Missing and Murdered Indigenous Women and Girls, Native Women's Association of Canada, and the Truth and Reconciliation Commission of Canada. Regional or local organizations included: the Assembly of Manitoba Chiefs, British Columbia Aboriginal Network on Disability, Downtown Eastside Women's Center, Ka Ni Kanichihk, and the Southern Chiefs' Organization. Please refer to the Appendix for the list of documents.

Findings

The documents and reports contained several consistent themes. Issues of definition remained very unclear. Several reports showed creative, critical engagement with definitions of disability, but most uncritically adopted the government or medical definitions of disability. The Indigenous organizations I surveyed asserted that disability concepts ought to bear congruence with Indigenous worldviews. They often did not state what disability specifically means, in theory and practice, even when they were discussing Indigenous worldviews.

Reliable data was lacking on just how many Indigenous people identified as having disabilities. Most reports emphasized the central importance of collecting accurate data on the rates of disability for Indigenous people, especially Indigenous women, girls, and gender-diverse people. But that data was simply not available.

In particular, the Assembly of First Nations (2017b) acknowledged extremely limited disability demographic data (also, Quinlan 2018). For AFN, disability was not defined (2017b, Appendix D, 2), stating that counting the number of Indigenous persons with disabilities is extremely difficult. Because one must identify both as Indigenous and as a disabled person, these categories come attached with stigma that deters individuals from embracing those identities. The Ontario Human Rights Commission (2020) stated that Indigenous women with disabilities, seeking healthcare risks were being targeted by insults, dismissal, and even the withholding of medical treatment. It can be downright fatal to present as Indigenous and disabled in Canadian hospitals when one is dying and in need of emergent care (Canadian Broadcasting Corporation, 2014).

AFN's opinion was that Indigenous people experience a rate of disability almost twice the national average due to a higher rate of environmental (e.g., pollution) and interpersonal trauma-related disability (this was simply an opinion, without data to back it up) (Assembly of First Nations 2017b, Appendix D, 3). Indigenous persons with disabilities seem to lag behind all other Canadians in income, except for racialized persons with disabilities (Crawford, 2010).

Several reports concluded that Indigenous individuals with disabilities who reside on reserve and/or in the North experience immense difficulties accessing needed services. This situation has forced many to move to urban centers in the hope that services are available. Yet, urban-dwelling Indigenous people also experience many challenges because of the racism and discrimination present in cities and within the disability services themselves (Assembly of First Nations, 2017a, p. 28). These result in culture shock and distress. AFN (2017a) asserted that many First Nations people living off-reserve can be excluded from band funding (Chan, 2025). There appears to be a great need for Indigenous-run programs to provide culturally safe disability supports and services in both city and country. Also, Indigenous reports documented the social determinants of health (safe water, adequate housing, good education, and viable economy) that underlie the well-being of any Indigenous community, but which are grossly neglected by all levels of government.

Regarding Indigenous women, girls, and gender-diverse persons with disabilities, several reports asserted that colonization creates an environment where Indigenous women face extreme socioeconomic marginalization (Quinlan, 2018, p. 6). The crux is that settler colonization seems "largely responsible for the overthrowing of Indigenous forms of governance and self-determination, such as the dissolution of Indigenous matriarchies and the traditional positions of persons with disabilities in communities" (Quinlan, 6). Indigenous women, girls, or gender-diverse persons with a disability are systemically excluded from decision-making positions (Gehl, 2020; Martin & Walia, 2019; Quinlan, 6). Women's sociopolitical marginalization limits their access to the necessary supports and services that would have reduced the impact of disability barriers (Quinlan 2018, 6). For Indigenous women with disabilities to become empowered, reports suggest the reinvigoration of matriarchal roles and governance (Martin & Walia, 2019).

Of the four national disability movement organizations, only one, Disabled Women's Network Canada (2020), provided content on Indigenous leadership (video, several short articles). The Council of Canadians with Disabilities described the Indigenous demographics of health and impairment, confined to describing census data, with no discussion offered. Neither Independent Living Canada nor the National Network for Mental Health offered original work regarding Indigenous leadership. The latter's Indigenous content was drawn from news media. Independent Living Canada documents did not mention culture or ethnicity at all, seemingly striking a culturally neutral stance.

Contrary and Unique Findings

One finding differed from this chapter's argument regarding settler privilege. The Assembly of First Nations (2017a) emphasized the central importance of Indigenous individuals accessing the labor market (for further discussion, see Chan, 2025). In the report, the word employment was written 126 times. The message seemed to be that holding a paying job was central to the health and happiness of disabled persons, including Indigenous persons (Chan, 2025).

A unique finding was the AFN's opposition to aspects of the *Accessible Canada Act* (ACA). This was a federal disability rights legislation strongly supported by the Canadian disability movement. The crux of the argument seemed to lie in the conflict between individual rights and Indigenous peoples' collective history (Chan, 2025). The Assembly of First Nations (2022) recognized that while the ACA espoused valid legislative intentions, it was problematic because "it uses a human rights focused lens with respect to disability as distinct from First Nations' right to self-govern according to their customs, traditions, and values. This lens fails to consider the unique circumstances of First Nations underfunding and the disproportionate percent of Indigenous people with disabilities compared to the average percent of Canadians with disabilities" (p. 6). I will further discuss the AFN's approach and Canadians' lack of understanding of treaty rights in the Discussion and Conclusion.

Discussion of the AFN's Jobs Emphasis

It is interesting the AFN's jobs emphasis. The most obvious connotation may be the AFN, as funded by a liberal Ottawa, would position itself on the side of liberalism. Jobs and working are central to the good life in that view, with government programs helping a person to get back into the game, being competitive, and so on. It seems reasonable to conclude that the AFN would position itself as seeing labor market participation as one of the best ways Indigenous individuals can overcome an economic disadvantage.

Discussion and Conclusion

From reviewing gray literature, I can see the definitions of disability paired with Indigeneity as being quite uncertain (also, Chan, 2025). There is much doubt as to what one exactly means when one refers to Indigenous disability. The reports of Indigenous organizations illustrated the geographic and cultural divide between the service-scarce North and on reserves (with an Indigenous majority population) and urban Canada (with an Indigenous minority). Indigenous women and girls with disabilities seem especially marginalized, facing, as Doreen Demas (2010) said, a triple jeopardy of racism, sexism, and ableism—plus classism—within a Canadian state that has relentlessly attacked Indigenous women's political power (Chan). Canada's dissolution of Indigenous governance and legal systems also meant the displacement of people with disabilities from their traditional and valued roles in many Indigenous communities (Demas). I see disability movement organizations maintain their historic focus on disability rights and Canadian federalism, while some adhere to a façade of cultural neutrality (Chan). In comparison, the AFN would like disability rights explicitly linked to treaty rights, a very important conversation in my opinion.

Exceptionally, the following two Indigenous organizations strongly worked on disability rights: British Columbia Aboriginal Network on Disability (2017), in their work on Indigenous perspectives on the United Nations Convention on the Rights of Persons with Disabilities; and the Native Women's Association of Canada. In contrast, from the gray literature review for the Canadian disability movement, its leadership and ideas generally lack engagement with Indigenous worldviews.

We can see the Canadian disability movement steadfastly pinning its hopes on securing funding and lobbying for arrangements within a Canadian federalism that simultaneously marginalizes Indigenous aspirations. We can see this movement largely resting on a settler-focused logic of multiculturalism, market economics, and Keynesian welfare, in line with a liberal ideology (Prince, 2012; Withers, 2012). From the secondary data analysis, it is apparent that the AFN may be likewise enthused with market economics with a Keynesian social safety net, and for people with disabilities to get back into the labor market. Although the literature and our secondary data analysis suggest some Indigenous communities dislike the idea of disability, most Indigenous thought traditions would not seem to preclude participating in the disability movement (Senier, 2013). Historically, many Indigenous communities accept external traditions and perspectives, if these do not diminish individual and community freedom (Borrows, 2016; Carter, 1990; Ray, 2011). I would suggest a shared concern with materiality and physical geography bridges Indigenous communities and disability activism (Borrows; Siebers, 2008).

I argue that Indigenous people's low level of leadership has less to do with differing thought traditions about disability and more so with disparate ideas in managing our relationships with the physical and biological world. The problem raised also concerns capitalism's political economy and its ecological consequences, specifically how the relationships between human beings, non-human animals, and the land have so drastically changed. I started this chapter discussing the disability movement's social liberalism compared with the Canadian government's neoliberalism. The former is not, I would suggest, incompatible with Indigenous political aspirations (Borrows, 2016). The latter may well be incompatible (Makokis, 2008; McAdam, 2015). For example, activist Doreen Demas advocated for legal protections based on United Nations declarations and conventions, specifically the Declaration on the Rights of Indigenous Peoples. The latter centers social rights and moves away from neoliberalism's possessive individualism (Assembly of First Nations, 2017a, 19; Prince, 2009). Neoliberal societies seem to turn any aspect of land, water, and air into saleable commodities, with little regard for their environmental consequences. Also, neoliberalism has been historically racist in its assumptions. It supposes markets require a certain class of humans, typically White or White-approximating Euro-Americans, for capitalism to be successful (Whyte, 2019). Many Indigenous people resist these practices (Thomas-Muller, 2021; Thurton, 2018; Yellowhead Institute, 2019).

Moreover, the disability movement depends on the Canadian government to legitimize and fund it (Chan, 2019; Prince, 2009). The movement customarily assumes Canada to be the true sovereign, although I saw in the secondary data analysis the beginning of recognition of Indigenous sui generis rights (Disabled Women's Network Canada, 2020). I can see state-centric politics alienating many Indigenous leaders who feel Canada, far from being a benevolent ruler, is a chief cause of ill health and distress (Alfred, 2005; Cowie, 2021; de Leeuw et al., 2018). Settler colonialism has deeply wounded Indigenous cultures and families (Blackstock, 2009; de Leeuw, Lindsay, and Greenwood; Thomas-Muller 2011, 2021). To paraphrase Professors Chandler and Dunlop, cultural wounds would require cultural medicine. That is something the disability movement does not yet know how to talk about, let alone provide (Chan, 2019; Chandler and Dunlop, 2018).

Metis lawyer Chelsea Vowel suggested that when settlers and Indigenous people can speak to one another about Canadian politics and history, about issues that matter, there is hope and a common basis for action (University of Winnipeg, 2017). There would be a belief that things can get better because we can work together. Currently, the disability movement and Indigenous communities still rarely talk. The disability movement tends to play within the rules of Canadian federalism. Indigenous organizations and individuals are well attuned to those rules, including the AFN and the British Columbia Aboriginal Network on Disability, even as they may critique them. I would suggest that other Indigenous communities and individuals might be skeptical or outright oppositional regarding that game, given Ottawa's history as dominator and oppressor (Alfred, 2005; Coulthard, 2014; Cowie, 2021). For the movement to speak with Indigenous individuals and communities, I think it needs to unsettle its own claims to power, challenge liberal politics, and make its relationship to government less cozy.

It would mean entering a "discomfort zone." This could be where new understandings surface (Block et al., 2016, p. 8). Medicine and rehabilitation, for example, have reached out to the disability movement, asking: How can we learn from you (Chan, 2019; Mirza et al., 2016)? How can we correct historical wrongs? The movement may need to adopt a similar approach, approaching Indigenous individuals and communities as a humble learner. Indigenous communities are not obliged to talk to the movement but may choose according to their own notions of freedom and collective needs.

Land Back and Indigenous Constitutionalism(s)

From the gray literature review, I can see a divide, perhaps necessary, between Indigenous individuals and communities and the disability movement. Different interests are at play. Indigenous communities often have more pressing matters at hand than wrangling with a small social movement (Chan, 2019). Perhaps the approach of Land Back provides some answers. Land Back, as a legal concept, can be seen as a move toward overlapping Indigenous constitutionalism and Canadian constitutionalism. Wherein, Indigenous legal orders through mutual negotiation may have jurisdiction over settler citizens of that particular Indigenous territory. Also, Canadian constitutionalism (laws) would remain in force concurrently. The facts of the matter are such that Indigenous and non-Indigenous peoples in Canada are entwined together as two parties with shared family ancestry, economic ties, and mutual spiritual attachments, most urgently in terms of the treaty relationship (Borrows, 2016). Treaties describe exchanges where Indigenous nations agree to share some of their interests in their ancestral lands in return for various payments and promises. On a deeper level, treaties are sometimes understood, particularly by Indigenous people, as sacred covenants between nations that establish a relationship between those for whom Canada is an ancient homeland and those whose family roots lie in other countries. Treaties, therefore, form the constitutional and moral basis of the alliance between Indigenous peoples and Canada. (Albers, 2017)

It seems to me high time for these relationships to include overlapping legal responsibilities, albeit for two very different legalities. That is, Canadian laws are in force regarding Indigenous Canadians, which they currently are. Indigenous laws can also be viewed as increasingly having jurisdiction for non-Indigenous communities (Borrows, 2016). In the secondary data analysis, we saw the AFN strongly criticize the new Canadian federal disability law for being out of touch with Indigenous history and First Nations' economic capacity to realistically fulfill the proposed disability support standards. The AFN, at the same time, agreed with the ACA's human rights approach. It seems to me that this critique and conversation are fruitful. It may help bring Indigenous legal orders into closer alignment with settler-oriented perspectives like the ACA that have significant merits as well as gaps. Neither Indigenous nor settler law is above principled critique.

Indigenous constitutionalism reflects the sui generis (inherent, unique) laws in Indigenous communities and nations. These laws reflect the diversity of Indigenous societies across vast geographic distances and spans of time (Borrows, 2016). They may be written and/or oral and are highly intertwined with the operation of Indigenous lodges, medicine societies, and matriarchal and Two Spirit traditions (Fiola, 2023; Kennedy, 2009; Makokis, 2021). They are put to life in working with questions of interpersonal conduct, politics, economics, treaties, and responsibilities to the human community and to the plant, animal, and inanimate worlds, and human life stages from birth to old age. In that understanding, perhaps disability movement organizations should formally seek out and establish formal agreements with Indigenous polity, including band councils, hereditary leaders, matriarchal structures, regional organizations such as the Manitoba Metis Federation, Indigenous law enforcement (e.g., Nuxalk Guardian Watchmen), and advocacy organizations such as the Native Women's Association of Canada (Brave Noisecat, 2018).

I think anti-colonial ways for the movement have at least two aspects. First, legal recognition by Indigenous polities toward disability organizations would enhance Indigenous regard for them. It could widen the scope of freedom the disability organizations themselves may enjoy, as they increasingly comply with Indigenous legal interpretations and dialogues (Borrows, 2016). Interpersonal trust may increase. Legal obligations can be honored and fulfilled in accordance with the physical geography of the relationship. For instance, Anishinaabe law might be appropriate for some organizations in Winnipeg, nêhiyaw law for other Winnipeg groups, Nakoda law for various organizations in southern Alberta, and so on, depending on the players involved and the specific issue (Borrows; Kovach, 2009). For example, an Indigenous polity can evaluate a disability peer support program, ascertaining how the program might serve individual, community, and land-based needs while relating to Indigenous law (Yellowhead Institute, 2019).

Also, an Indigenous polity can institute a formal permitting system for disability movement activities (Yellowhead Institute, 2019). For example, a polity works with a care attendant training program (within a disability rights organization) to bring Indigenous law and discourse to it. If the program meets the polity's criteria and accepted community protocol, a permit can be granted. Given that traditional matriarchal councils uphold many Indigenous legal and educational systems, it may be appropriate for Indigenous women's organizations to oversee these obligations if capacity and interests exist. One can see the intersectionality of disability organizations, wherein many Queer, intersex, Two Spirit, and questioning individuals find some sense of belonging (Pelka, 2012), and in Indigenous communities where a resurgence of Indigenous Queer and Two Spirit knowledges is apparent (Fiola, 2023; Makokis, 2021). Thus, there might be interest from Indigenous Queer and Two Spirit roles, lodges, and governance systems in providing dialogue and evaluation procedures for these nascent permit systems (Rowe & Kirkpatrick, 2018). 2SLGBTQQIA individuals (Two-Spirit, lesbian, gay, bisexual, transgender, queer, questioning, intersex, and asexual) may thus have better, perhaps more loving, conversations regarding shared struggles and unique challenges. It can be seen intersectionally within Indigenous constitutional framework(s). Funding and resource sharing agreements to support this work are certainly needed, given that many Indigenous organizations already have full agendas—I am thinking grants, targeted government expenditures, and perhaps university and academic supports.

Given the complex human relationships involved and Canada's diverse physical geography, with many Indigenous and settler ethnic groups inhabiting any specified region, a generous and tolerant space for negotiations and new understandings is needed for this work to work. I suggest, following Borrows (2016), such permits would also need to comply with international law standards. I think it would lead to a more realistic, satisfying way of life for all involved.

Second, a more difficult, thorny problem, is the land question. The disability movement, and the settler colonial culture it is embedded within, has been historically ignorant of the issue. Indigenous communities are typically not, as an Anishinaabe knowledge keeper explained: "There is a respect that we need to show the land and it's relatedness to us. We are the land. If the land is sick, then it isn't going to be very long before we're going to get sick" (cited in Richmond, 2015, p. 51). Reconciliation in the disability context means a reconciliation with the land, an uphill struggle given Canada's addiction to ecology-destroying resource extraction (Jaffee & John, 2018; Thomas-Muller, 2017, 2021; Stienstra, 2015; Thurton, 2018). If advancements toward better relations are to take place, I would suggest that disability activists materially aid Indigenous polity in reoccupying their traditional lands as well as help restore ecological balance in areas damaged by irresponsible resource extraction (Borrows, 2016; Yellowhead Institute, 2019). That is one way the disability movement can contribute to Land Back's rematriation of territories.

Lateral Violence?

"All peoples were given a language, all peoples were given a law, all peoples were given songs. All peoples were given gifts to live into the world, and those are gifts from spirit and they are necessary in the world and they are necessary in building good relationships with each other."

– Dawnis Kennedy (in National Inquiry into Missing and Murdered Indigenous Women and Girls, 2019, p. 133)

There is a need to address how internalized racism (hatred toward oneself and one's ethnicity) and other oppressions—false beliefs, rumor-mongering, sabotage, and bad faith agreements—can render inoperable the agreements between a disability organization and an Indigenous polity. Those oppressions and bad ideas, known as lateral violence, can emerge from anywhere, from the disability movement, the Indigenous organization, or among third parties who are interested observers. It is known, after centuries of colonial oppression, that Indigenous individuals who have experienced generations of dispossession and systemic racism may slide into the role of aggressor in their own communities (e.g., Indigenous individuals badmouthing others on the reserve, coming from a place of spite and sabotage) (Bearpaw Media, 2006). Lateral violence also afflicts disability rights organizations (Chan, 2019; Chan, 2024). It is well-known that people who feel powerless may unleash their anger and negativity toward their peers rather than fighting the oppressive institutions that are truly responsible for their situation.

To prevent or remedy lateral violence, I propose guidance from observing and living Anishinaabe and nêhiyaw-Ininiw law as individual spirit-beings (which we all are, I suggest) with inherent interdependencies with earth, air, and water; respectively, the Anishinaabe seven grandfather/grandmother teachings (wisdom, love, respect, bravery, honesty, humility, and truth) (Borrows, 2019) and the four principles of the nêhiyaw/Cree related to the sacred pipe (truth, love, sharing, and strength) (Don Cardinal, personal communication, Thunderbird House, May to June 2003). This proposal may be suitable for Manitoba and Northern Ontario, but it will be different for other Indigenous territories with different knowledge systems. For example, John Borrows suggested that "love" (Zaagi'idiwin in Ojibway) is a key principle in Anishinaabe treaties with Canada. It is Zaagi'idiwin, which would help to soften hardened hearts on an organizational level (Borrows, 2019). To deal with lateral violence or other disturbances and imbalances of the heart, I have been taught there are certain protocols, ceremonies, and healing practices referred to as the medicine wheel. Each community may have its own medicine wheel. There is a sequence by which these ceremonies of the seasons of life, from birth to adolescence to adulthood to old age, serve as a circle (Marlene Syrette, personal communication, Batchewana First Nation, March 13, 2024). This circle work brings positive energy and guidance in conjunction with animate and inanimate beings and the spirit world (Marlene Syrette, personal communication, Batchewana First Nation, March 13, 2024). The medicine wheel and other practices have been deployed to aid organizations and other formal relationships that have fallen into disrepair and imbalance.

John Borrows (2019) suggested one ought to avoid what he called "the dangers of a single story" (p. 28). For him, love is not universal nor is it absolutely necessary in law and public affairs. Love is highly contextual, he suggested, and ought to be fiercely critiqued if appeals to love are patriarchal, patronizing, or infantilizing (Borrows, p. 28). Further,

> Thus, while I claim that love is extraordinarily important in legal and political affairs, I do not make the claim that it should ever be regarded as universally determinative in these spheres. Appeals to love must always be contextual. They must be rigorously scrutinized and intensely critiqued. They must be precisely calibrated to situations under review to ensure their application is liberating and enhances agency. My point is that love must always be regarded as only being provisionally relevant to the law. (Borrows, 2019, pp. 28–29)

I am proposing love as only one of many possible guides. There are other equally important teachings in Anishinaabe and nêhiyaw-Ininiw constitutional traditions, as well as equally important Canadian and American constitutional concepts like peace, order, good government, liberty, security, equality, and the pursuit of happiness (Borrows, 2019). The latter are equally ambiguous, and their invocation can be dangerously tempting for manipulation into abuses of power (Borrows, 2019). What I propose is a boundary-crossing exercise in political practice. Zaagi'idiwin and other Indigenous concepts can serve as promising but not absolute ideological anchors when wading into the turbulent waters of organizations and politics to establish the beginning of Indigenous jurisdiction to an issue like disability, which may cut to the heart of both personal hardships and political oppression in Indigenous communities and settler communities.

The Seven Grandfather and Grandmother Teachings and the Four Principles seem to work well together with other concepts of community and individual development in effectively addressing lateral violence and other cycles of oppression (Aboriginal Healing Foundation, 2005). Oppressed peoples often fatalistically consider their lives to be powerless and meaningless. One might take guidance from educator Paulo Freire's (1970) emphasis on becoming the subjects of life rather than objects in life being manipulated by outside forces. It may also be seen as circle work, wherein all are included in the circle of life and Creator's love, for personal healing and connection with all our relations (D. de Gagne, personal communication, January 1, 2025; Guyot & Christianson, 2019). Moreover, community psychology approaches to individual and community empowerment—such as empowerment workshops, townhalls, and, from Indigenous healing perspectives, the community's holistic sacred ceremonies—can work to increase people's sense of control, belonging, and self-worth (Aboriginal Healing Foundation). They can diminish the temptations of malicious gossiping, undermining, sabotaging, and other forms of lateral violence. These positive processes may make it more realistic to strike the boundary-crossing agreements between disability organizations and Indigenous communities.

Acknowledgments I acknowledge and give thanks to my colleague and friend, Daly de Gagne, who helped in the formulation and revision of this chapter. His teachings about Indigeneity, chaplaincy, psychotherapy, and life have nurtured my spirit. May we have further adventures and stories together. Chi miigwech.

I acknowledge John Borrows, whose ideas and presence played a major role in making this chapter possible.

I also acknowledge the writing of Margaret Kovach, although I have not met her personally, in guiding this chapter.

References

Aboriginal Healing Foundation. (2005). *Warrior-caregivers: Understanding the challenges and healing of First Nations men*. Aboriginal Healing Foundation.

Adelson, N. (2000). *"Being alive well": Health and the politics of Cree well-being*. University of Toronto Press.

Alfred, T. (2005). *Wasáse: Indigenous pathways of action and freedom.* Peterborough, ON: Broadview Press.

Albers, G. (2017). Treaties with Indigenous peoples in Canada. *The Canadian Encyclopedia.* https://www.thecanadianencyclopedia.ca/en/article/aboriginal-treaties

Alexander, B. (2008). *The globalization of addiction: A study in poverty of the spirit.* Oxford University Press.

Assembly of First Nations. (2017a). *First Nations and First Nation persons with disabilities engagement on federal accessibility legislation.* Assembly of First Nations.

Assembly of First Nations. (2017b). *Appendix D: Literature review pertaining to First Nations persons with disabilities in anticipation of federal accessibility legislation.* Assembly of First Nations.

Assembly of First Nations. (2022). *A distinct First Nations accessibility law discussion guide: Draft for discussion.* Assembly of First Nations.

Atherton, C. (2009). *Accessible movements: Developing a vision of social justice with Aboriginal disability and feminist organizations in Winnipeg Manitoba* (Unpublished Master's thesis). University of Manitoba.

Bearpaw Media. Miller, G. (Director). (2006). *Lateral violence.* https://www.youtube.com/watch?v=neWtt3sAqMM

Bell, C. (2010). Is disability studies actually white disability studies? In L. Davis (Ed.), *The disability studies reader* (3rd ed., pp. 374–382). Routledge.

Blackstock, C. (2009). The occasional evil of angels: Learning from the experiences of Aboriginal peoples and social work. *First Peoples Child and Family Review, 4*(1), 28–37.

Block, P., Kasnitz, D., Nishida, A., & Pollard, N. (2016). Occupying disability: An introduction. In P. Block, D. Kasnitz, A. Nishida, & N. Pollard (Eds.), *Occupying disability: Critical approaches to community, justice, and decolonizing disability* (pp. 3–14). Springer. https://doi.org/10.1007/978-94-017-9984-3_1

Borrows, J. (2016). *Freedom and Indigenous constitutionalism.* University of Toronto Press.

Borrows, J. (2019). *Law's Indigenous ethics.* University of Toronto Press.

Bradburn, J. (2023). Citizens plus (The red paper). *The Canadian Encyclopedia.* https://www.thecanadianencyclopedia.ca/en/article/citizens-plus-the-red-paper

Brave Noisecat, J. (2018). The resurgence of the Nuxalk. *Canadian Geographic.* Retrieved from https://www.canadiangeographic.ca/article/resurgence-nuxalk

Brian Sinclair Working Group. (2017). *Out of sight.* Retrieved from http://ignoredtodeathmanitoba.ca/index.php/2017/09/15/out-of-sight-interim-report-of-the-sinclair-working-group/

British Columbia Aboriginal Network on Disability. (2017). *National Indigenous federal accessibility legislation consultation.* Retrieved from http://www.bcands.bc.ca/wp-content/uploads/BCANDS-January-March-2017-Accessibility-Consultation-Report.pdf

Canadian Broadcasting Corporation. (2014, October 9). First Nations: Second-class care. *CBC.* https://www.cbc.ca/radio/whitecoat/first-nations-second-class-care-1.2794277

Carter, S. (1990). *Lost harvests: Prairie Indian reserve farmers and government policy.* McGill-Queen's University Press.

Chabasinski, T. (2012). Ted Chabasinski: "I would roam the hall looking for something…anything that would make the time pass.". In F. Pelka (Ed.), *What we have done: An oral history of the disability rights movement* (pp. 58–60). University of Massachusetts Press. (Original work n.d.).

Chan, W. (2019). *Leadership in the consumer and survivor movement in western Canada: A constructivist grounded theory study* [Doctoral dissertation]. University of Manitoba. https://mspace.lib.umanitoba.ca/bitstreams/e34efc79-82ed-499b-8364-f1712ec692d2/download

Chan, W. (2024). Mental health crises, advance directives, and the psychiatric survivor, consumer, and Mad workplace. *Journal of Social Work and Welfare Policy, 2*(2), 127. https://doi.org/10.33790/jswwp1100127

Chan, W. (2025). Indigenous leadership and the Canadian disability movement. *Disability Studies Quarterly, 44*(3) https://dsq-sds.org/index.php/dsq/article/view/7336/8378

Chandler, M., & Dunlop, W. (2018). Cultural wounds demand cultural medicines. In M. Greenwood, S. de Leeuw, & N. Lindsay (Eds.), *Determinants of Indigenous peoples' health* (2nd ed., pp. 147–160). Canadian Scholars.

Coulthard, G. (2014). *Red skin, white masks: Rejecting the colonial politics of recognition.* University of Minnesota Press.

Cowie, C. (2021). A vote for Canada or Indigenous nationhood? The complexities of First Nations, Metis, and Inuit participation in Canadian politics. *The Conversation.* https://theconversation.com/a-vote-for-canada-or-indigenous-nationhood-the-complexitics-of-first-nations-metis-and-inuit-participation-in-canadian-politics-169312

Crawford, C. (2010). *Disabling poverty & enabling citizenship: Understanding the poverty and exclusion of Canadians with disabilities.* Council of Canadians with Disabilities. http://www.ccdonline.ca/en/socialpolicy/poverty-citizenship/demographic-profile/understanding-poverty-exclusion

Daschuk, J. (2013). *Clearing the plains: Disease, politics of starvation, and the loss of aboriginal life.* University of Regina Press.

Davis, L. (2002/2010). The end of identity politics: On disability as an unstable category. In L. Davis (Ed.), *The disability studies reader* (3rd ed., pp. 301–315). Routledge.

De Leeuw, S., Lindsay, N., & Greenwood, M. (2018). Introduction to the second edition: Rethinking (once again) determinants of Indigenous peoples' health. In M. Greenwood, S. de Leeuw, & N. Lindsay (Eds.), *Determinants of Indigenous peoples' health* (2nd ed., pp. xvii–xlv). Canadian Scholars.

Deleuze, G., & Guattari, F. (1980). *A thousand plateaus: Capitalism and schizophrenia.* Les Editions de Minuit.

Demas, D. (2010). Triple jeopardy: Native women with disabilities. In D. Driedger (Ed.), *Living the edges: A disabled women's reader* (pp. 80–86). Inanna Publications.

Disabled Women's Network Canada. (2020). *Indigenous disability awareness month* [Video]. https://dawncanada.net/issues/idam2020/

Edwards, J. (2014). Canada's oil sands residents complain of health effects. *The Lancet, 383*, 1450–1451. https://doi.org/10.1016/s0140-6736(14)60703-0
Enns, H., & Neufeldt, A. (Eds.). (2003). *In pursuit of equal participation: Canada and disability at home and abroad.* Captus Press.
Fiola, C. (2023). Researching Métis spirituality: Insights and the work ahead. *Pawaatamihk Journal of Métis Thinkers, 1*(1).
Freire, P. (1970). *Pedagogy of the oppressed.* Continuum.
Galer, D. (2015). Disability rights movement in Canada. *The Canadian encyclopedia.* https://www.thecanadianencyclopedia.ca/en/article/disability-rights-movement#:~:text=The%20Canadian%20disability%20rights%20movement,cent%20of%20the%20Canadian%20population
Galloway, D. (2012). Donald Galloway: "We would draw from the civil rights movement…but we were not actively involved in the black movement." In F. Pelka (Ed.), *What we have done: An oral history of the disability rights movement* (pp. 218-222). : University of Massachusetts Press. (Original interview in 2001)
Gehl, L. (2020). *Indigenous women and girls with disabilities are targets of sexual violence.* https://dawncanada.net/news/idam-lynn-25-11-2020/
Guyot, B. (Investigative Reporter), & Christianson, D. (Director). (May 24, 2019). Justice resurging as Hollow Water community deals with controversial resource project. In P. Barnsley (Executive Producer), *APTN Investigates.* https://www.aptnnews.ca/national-news/justice-resurging-as-hollow-water-community-deals-with-controversial-resource-project/
Hockman, L. (2010). A longer journey of reflexivity. In D. Driedger (Ed.), *Living the edges: A disabled women's reader* (pp. 16–28). Inanna Publications.
Hooks, B. (1981). *Ain't I a woman? Black women and feminism.* South End Press.
Howlround Theater Commons. (2017). *The cultural apartheid of disability.* Retrieved from https://howlround.com/cultural-apartheid-disability
Independent Living Canada. (2015). *Independent Living Canada annual general report 2014-2015.* Retrieved from http://www.ilcanada.org/wp-content/uploads/2016/01/Annual_Report_2014-2015.pdf
Jaffee, L., & John, K. (2018). Disabling bodies of/and land: Reframing disability justice in conversation with Indigenous theory and activism. *Disability and the Global South, 5*, 1407–1429.
Kennedy, D. (Minawaanigogiizhigok). (2009). *Aboriginal rights, reconciliation, and respectful relations* [Master's thesis]. University of Victoria. https://dspace.library.uvic.ca/server/api/core/bitstreams/08440ea1-868f-4bcd-82ef-afb907fd87e2/content
Kirmayer, L. (2007). *Suicide among aboriginal people in Canada.* Aboriginal Healing Foundation.
Kovach, M. (2009). *Indigenous methodologies.* University of Toronto Press.
Krasowski, S. (2019). No surrender: *The land remains Indigenous. Regina*, SK: The University of Regina Press. https://doi.org/10.1515/9780889775978
LeFrancois, B. (2013). The psychiatrization of our children, or, an autoethnographic narrative of perpetuating First Nations genocide through "benevolent" institutions. *Decolonization: Indigeneity Education, & Society, 2*, 108–123.
Lord, J. (2010). *Impact: Changing the way we view disability. The history, perspective, and vision of the Independent Living movement in Canada.* Canadian Association of Independent Living Centers.
Lyon, D. (2005). Postmodernity: The history of an idea. In S. Hier (Ed.), *Contemporary sociological thought: Themes and theories* (pp. 255–263). Canadian Scholars' Press.
MacDowell, L. (2012). *An environmental history of Canada.* University of British Columbia Press.
Makokis, J. (wahpimaskwasis) (2008). *nehiyaw iskwew kiskinowâtasinahikewina – paminisowin namôya tipeyimisowin: Cree Women Learning Self Determination Through Sacred Teachings of the Creator* (Unpublished Master's thesis). University of Victoria.
Makokis, J. (2021, August 31). Gender from a Nehiyo maskihkiwiyiniw perspective within Treaty Number Six territory. *The Messenger.* https://cpsa.ca/news/understanding-sexuality-

and-gender-from-a-nehiyo-maskihkiwiyiniw-plains-cree-physician-perspective-within-treaty-number-six-territory/
Martin, C., & Walia, H. (2019). *Red women rising: Indigenous women survivors in Vancouver's downtown eastside*. Downtown Eastside Women's Center.
McAdam, S. (Saysewahum) (2015). *Nationhood interrupted: Revitalizing Nehiyaw legal systems*. University of British Columbia Press.
McCallum, M. J., & Perry, A. (2018). *Structures of indifference: An Indigenous life and death in a Canadian city*. University of Manitoba Press.
McNamara, J., & DuBrul, S. (Eds.). (2006). *Navigating the space between brilliance and madness: A reader and roadmap of bipolar worlds* (2nd ed.). AK Press.
McNeil-Seymour, J. (2018). Two-spirit resistance. In P. McFarlane & N. Schabus (Eds.), *Who's land is it anyways? A manual for decolonization* (pp. 52–56). Federation of Post-Secondary Educators of BC.
Miller, G. (2018). Madness decolonized? Madness as transnational identity in Gail Hornstein's *Agnes's Jacket*. *Journal of Medical Humanities, 39*, 303–323. https://doi.org/10.1007/s10912-017-9434-8
Mirza, M., Magasi, S., & Hammel, J. (2016). Soul searching occupations: Critical reflections on occupational therapy's commitment to social justice, disabilityrights, and participation. In P. Block, D. Kasnitz, A. Nishida, & N. Pollard (Eds.), *Occupying disability: Critical approaches to community, justice, and decolonizing disability* (pp. 159-174). : Springer. https://doi.org/10.1007/978-94-017-9984-3_11
Mosby, I. (2013). Administering colonial science: Nutrition research and human biomedical experimentation in Aboriginal communities and residential schools, 1942–1952. *Histoire Sociale/Social history, 46*, 145–172.
National Inquiry into Missing and Murdered Indigenous Women and Girls. (2019). *Reclaiming power and place: The final report of the national inquiry into missing and murdered Indigenous women and girls*. https://www.mmiwg-ffada.ca/final-report/
Neufeldt, A. (2003). Disability in Canada: An historical perspective. In H. Enns & A. Neufeldt (Eds.), *In pursuit of equal participation: Canada and disability at home and abroad* (pp. 22–80). Captus Press.
Olsen, T. (2018). This word is (not?) very exciting: Considering intersectionality in Indigenous studies. *NORA - Nordic Journal of Feminist and Gender Research, 26*(3), 182–196.
Ontario Human Rights Commission. (2020, November 1). *Why it's dangerous to be disabled and Indigenous in Canada*. https://www3.ohrc.on.ca/en/news-center/opinion-editorial-nationalnewswatchcom-why-its-dangerous-be-disabled-and-indigenous
Pelka, F. (Ed.). (2012). *What we have done: An oral history of the disability rights movement*. University of Massachusetts Press.
Prince, M. (2008). Inclusive city life: Persons with disabilities and the politics of difference. *Disability Studies Quarterly, 28*(1) https://dsq-sds.org/index.php/dsq/article/view/65/65
Prince, M. (2009). *Absent citizens: Disability politics and policy in Canada*. University of Toronto Press.
Prince, M. (2012). Canadian disability activism and political ideas: In and between neo-liberalism and social liberalism. *Canadian Journal of Disability Studies, 1*, 1–34. https://doi.org/10.15353/cjds.v1i1.16
Quinlan, L. (2018). *Accessibility and disability for Indigenous women, girls, and gender diverse people: Informing the new federal accessibility legislation*. Native Women's Association of Canada.
Ray, A. (2011). *An illustrated history of Canada's native people: I have lived here since the world began*. McGill-Queen's University Press.
Ray, S. J., & Sibara, J. (2018). Introduction. In S. J. Ray & J. Sibara (Eds.), *Disability studies and the environmental humanities: Toward an eco-crip theory* (pp. 1–25). University of Nebraska Press. https://doi.org/10.2307/j.ctt1p6jht5.4

Razack, S. (2015). *Dying from improvement: Inquests and inquiries into Indigenous deaths in custody*. University of Toronto Press.
Redikopp, S. (2021). Out of place, out of mind: Min(d)ing race in mad studies through a metaphor of spatiality. *Canadian Journal of Disability Studies, 10*(3), 96–118. https://doi.org/10.15353/cjds.v10i3.817
Richmond, C. (2015). The relatedness of people, land, and health: Stories from Anishinaabe elders. In M. Greenwood, S. de Leeuw, N. Lindsay, & C. Reading (Eds.), *Determinants of Indigenous peoples' health in Canada* (pp. 47–63). Canadian Scholars' Press.
Ross, L. (2012). *My personal reflections on the last 30 years of Manitobans with disabilities*. Retrieved May 17, 2015 from http://www.mlpd.mb.ca/download/making-a-difference-in-manitoba-2012.pdf
Rowe, G. (2020). *Resurgence of Indigenous nationhood: Centering the stories of Indigenous full spectrum doulas* [Doctoral dissertation, University of Manitoba]. https://mspace.lib.umanitoba.ca/items/1242a13b-6fec-4ec0-a6e6-80a9d07c6cf7
Rowe, G. (Host). (2022, October 31). Season 1 Episode 1: Making introductions: Gladys Rowe [Audio podcast episode]. In *Indigenous insights: An evaluation podcast*. https://gladysrowe.com/wp-content/uploads/2023/06/S1E1_-Gladys-Rowe.pdf
Rowe, G., & Kirkpatrick, C. (2018). *Na-gah mo waabishkizi ojijaak bimise keetwaatino: Singing white crane Flying North. Gathering a Bundle for Indigenous Evaluation*. Canadian Center for Policy Alternatives, Manitoba. https://policyalternatives.ca/sites/default/files/uploads/publications/Manitoba%20Office/2018/03/Gathering_A_Bundle_for_Indigenous_Evaluation.pdf
Schweik, S. (2011). Lomax's matrix: Disability, solidarity, and the Black Power of 504. *Disability Studies Quarterly, 31* (1). Retrieved from http://dsq-sds.org/article/view/1371/1539#endnote10. https://doi.org/10.18061/dsq.v31i1.1371
Senier, S. (2013). "Traditionally, disability was not seen as such": Writing and healing in the work of Mohegan medicine people. *Journal of Literary & Cultural Disability Studies, 7*, 213–229. https://doi.org/10.3828/jlcds.2013.15
Senier, S. (2017). Blind Indians: Kateri Tekakwitha and Joseph Amos's visions of Indigenous resurgence. In S. J. Ray & J. Sibara (Eds.), *Disability studies and the environmental humanities: Toward an eco-map theory* (pp. 269–289). University of Nebraska Press. https://doi.org/10.2307/j.ctt1p6jht5.12
Senier, S., & Barker, C. (2013). Introduction. *Journal of Literary & Cultural Disability Studies, 7*, 123–140. https://doi.org/10.3828/jlcds.2013.10
Shakespeare, T. (2010). The social model of disability. In L. Davis (Ed.), *The disability studies reader* (3rd ed., pp. 266–273). Routledge.
Sherry, M. (2010). (Post) colonizing disability. In L. Davis (Ed.), *The disability studies reader* (3rd ed., pp. 94–106). Routledge.
Siebers, T. (2008). *Disability theory*. University of Michigan Press.
Staggenborg, S. (2012). *Social movements* (2nd ed.). Oxford University Press.
Sterling-Collins, R. (2009). A holistic approach to supporting children with special needs. In R. Sinclair, M. Hart, & G. Bruyere (Eds.), *Wicihitowin* (pp. 65–87). Fernwood Publishing.
Stienstra, D. (2015). Northern crises: Women's relationships and resistances to resource extractions. *International Feminist Journal of Politics, 17*, 630–651. https://doi.org/10.1080/14616742.2015.1060695
Stienstra, D., Baikie, G., & Manning, S. (2018). "My granddaughter doesn't know she has disabilities and we are not going to tell her": Navigating intersections of Indigenousness, disability, and gender in Labrador. *Disability and the Global South, 5*, 1385–1406.
Tallbear, K. (2000). Shepard Krech's The Ecological Indian: One Indian's perspective. https://www.academia.edu/11421145/Shepard_Krech_s_The_Ecological_Indian_One_Indian_s_Perspective
Tam, L. (2013). Whither indigenizing the mad movement? Theorizing the social relations of race and madness through conviviality. In B. LeFrancois, R. Menzies, & G. Reaume (Eds.), *Mad matters: A critical reader in Canadian mad studies* (pp. 281–297). Canadian Scholars' Press.

Thomas-Muller, C. (2011). The seventh generation. In N. Sinclair & W. Cariou (Eds.), *Manitowapow: Aboriginal writings from the land of water* (pp. 367–369). Highwater Press.
Thomas-Muller, C. (2017). We need to start calling out corporate "redwashing": Redwashing is when corporations paint themselves as good neighbors by sponsoring Indigenous initiatives. *CBC News*. Retrieved from https://www.cbc.ca/news/opinion/corporate-redwashing-1.4030443
Thomas-Muller, C. (2021). *Life in the city of dirty water: A memoir of healing*. Penguin Random House Canada.
Thurton, D. (2018). Indigenous communities grapple with new relationship with oil sands industry: Leaders who once partnered with environmentalists and hosted Hollywood stars are now changing course. *CBC News*. Retrieved from https://www.cbc.ca/news/canada/edmonton/indigenous-communities-grapple-oilsands-development-1.4888470
Tremain, S. (2015). Foucault, governmentality, and critical disability theory today: A genealogy of the archive. In S. Tremain (Ed.), *Foucault and the government of disability* (pp. 9–23). University of Michigan Press.
University of Winnipeg. (2017). *Indigenization in the time of pipelines*. Retrieved from https://www.uwinnipeg.ca/indigenous/weweni/past-wewenis/indigenization-in-the-time-of-pipelines.html
Whyte, J. (2019). *The morals of the market: Human rights and the rise of neoliberalism*. Verso.
Withers, A. (2012). *Disability politics and theory*. Fernwood.
Yellowhead Institute. (2019). *Land back: A Yellowhead Institute red paper*. Retrieved from https://redpaper.yellowheadinstitute.org/wp-content/uploads/2019/10/red-paper-report-final.pdf
Zola, I. (1972). Medicine as an institution of social control. *The Sociological Review, 20*, 487–504.

Index

D. Nyaga, M. Zangeneh (eds.), *Critical Ethics on Mental Health and Madness*, Advances in Mental Health and Addiction,
https://doi.org/10.1007/978-3-032-10166-2

GPSR Compliance
The European Union's (EU) General Product Safety Regulation (GPSR) is a set of rules that requires consumer products to be safe and our obligations to ensure this.

If you have any concerns about our products, you can contact us on

ProductSafety@springernature.com

In case Publisher is established outside the EU, the EU authorized representative is:

Springer Nature Customer Service Center GmbH
Europaplatz 3
69115 Heidelberg, Germany

www.ingramcontent.com/pod-product-compliance
Ingram Content Group UK Ltd.
Pitfield, Milton Keynes, MK11 3LW, UK
UKHW020911180926
475648UK00002B/13

* 9 7 8 3 0 3 2 1 0 1 6 5 5 *